Constructing Justice and Security after War

Charles T. Call

UNITED STATES INSTITUTE OF PEACE PRESS
Washington, D.C.

The views expressed in this book are those of the author alone. They do not necessarily reflect views of the United States Institute of Peace.

United States Institute of Peace
1200 17th Street NW, Suite 200
Washington, DC 20036-3011

First published 2007

Printed in the United States of America

Cover photographs courtesy of the National Civilian Police of El Salvador and Georges Gobet/AFP/Getty.

The paper used in this publication meets the minimum requirements of American National Standards for Information Science—Permanence of Paper for Printed Library Materials, ANSI Z39.48-1984.

Library of Congress Cataloging-in-Publication Data

Constructing justice and security after war/ [edited by] Charles T. Call. p. cm

Includes bibliographical references and index.
    ISBN-13: 978-1-929223-89-3 (softcover : alk. paper)
    ISBN-10: 1-929223-89-7 (softcover : alk. paper)
    ISBN-13: 978-1-929223-90-9 (hardcover : alk paper)
    ISBN-10: 1-929223-90-0 (hardcover : alk paper)
    1. Postwar reconstruction. 2. Postwar reconstruction—Case studies.
I. Call, Charles
    HV639.C67 2006
    363.34'988—dc22

2006015924

Contents

Foreword v
Richard H. Solomon

Acknowledgements xi

Contributors xv

1. Introduction: What We Know and Don't Know
   about Postconflict Justice and Security Reform 3
   Charles T. Call

PART I LATIN AMERICA AND THE CARIBBEAN

2. The Mugging of a Success Story: Justice and Security
   Reform in El Salvador 29
   Charles T. Call

3. Justice and Security Reform after Intervention: Haiti 69
   Sandra Beidas, Colin Granderson, and Rachel Neild

4. Business as Usual? Justice and Policing Reform
   in Postwar Guatemala 113
   William D. Stanley

PART II AFRICA

5. Criminal Justice after Apartheid: Police and Justice
   Reform in South Africa 159
   Janine Rauch

6. Postgenocide Justice and Security Reform: Rwanda 193
   Charles Mironko and Ephrem Rurangwa

PART III THE BALKANS AND BEYOND

7. Too Little, Too Late? Justice and Security Reform in
   Bosnia and Herzegovina 231
   Michael H. Doyle

8. From Elation to Disappointment: Justice and Security
   Reform in Kosovo 271
   Colette Rausch

9. Lawyers, Guns, and Money: Justice and Security Reform
   in East Timor 313
   Ronald A. West

10. Engendering Justice and Security after War 351
    Tracy Fitzsimmons

PART IV CONCLUSION

11. Conclusion: Constructing Justice and Security after War...........375
   Charles T. Call

INDEX..411

Foreword

PRESIDENT GEORGE W. BUSH QUOTED PALESTINIAN Authority President Mahmoud Abbas in a speech at the National Defense University on March 8, 2005, saying that "we cannot build the foundations of a state without the rule of law and public order." Although the importance of rule of law may seem self-evident, many groups—from policymakers to scholars—have only recently recognized that building effective and legitimate state institutions on a legal foundation is one of the best ways to heal the effects of past wars and to prevent future wars. In fact, countries emerging from war comprise more than one-third of all new conflicts, and millions of people annually suffer the consequences of these wars: displacement, fear, insecurity, disease, injury, and death. It is all the more tragic when—as in twenty-first century Haiti, Liberia, Georgia, and Lebanon—the same populace experiences war only a few years after it welcomed peace.

Constructing Justice and Security after War, edited by Charles T. Call, addresses what both scholars and practitioners now recognize as a foundation of effective peace: effective, legitimate, and rights-respecting systems of justice and physical security. This volume provides nine case studies by distinguished contributors, including scholars, criminal justice practitioners, and former senior officials of international missions, most of whom have closely followed or been intimately involved in these processes. The wide-ranging case studies address whether and how societies emerging from armed conflict create systems of justice and security that ensure basic rights, apply the law effectively and impartially, and enjoy popular support. The authors provide detailed evidence of the overwhelming challenges involved, the efforts—and sometimes surprising ineptitude—of international actors who seem to learn little from previous experiences, and the resistance to and complexity of change. The studies examine the importance of social, economic, and cultural factors as well as institutional choices regarding the form, substance, and sequence of reforms.

v

This important volume provides useful information about a range of cases that are not often considered together. While many of the lessons learned are not new, the wealth of comparative data and informed analysis also brings some key issues into stark relief, some of which seem so obvious that one is taken aback by the degree to which the same problems emerge in different contexts. A driving hypothesis of the volume is that the transition itself creates a window of opportunity to push for reforms that would otherwise be very difficult to achieve. While there are many ways to achieve policy change, it is reasonable to expect that the shock of war and external intervention could be a catalyst to force a state to accept significant reforms to police and justice laws and institutions. The opportunity for change soon after a conflict ends should be seized, because the moment will not last.

A new and important insight that this volume makes clear is the role of any peace agreement in subsequent reform. Although it is sometimes difficult to reach detailed agreements, the clearer and more specific they are on reform, the greater the chances of success. The vagueness of Guatemala's accords impeded reform, for example, while El Salvador's peace agreement was easier to implement because security reforms were clearly delineated. The Dayton Peace Accords barely mentioned judicial and police reforms, leaving an array of international agencies to gradually develop the necessary strategies to establish the rule of law. In part because of the gradual development of judicial and police procedures, those who worked in police and judicial institutions were tempted by corruption and fearful of retribution, thus allowing rampant corruption and organized crime to seize the country. The cases of Kosovo, Haiti, and Rwanda sadly show that the absence of a peace agreement, and the victory by one side in an armed conflict, does not necessarily pave the way for successful security or judicial reforms.

The cases in this volume remind us that postconflict reform efforts are intensely political and not just technical exercises of tinkering with constitutions, laws, or practices. Resistance to reform will inevitably emerge from those who stand to lose from the demise of the old system.

Another essential theme the authors present is the importance of public awareness and intense citizen involvement in the reform process if there is to be any chance of success. The question of how to build public trust is discussed throughout the book, as is the need for awareness and education campaigns that are locally driven but supported by international actors. While reform processes will never be without difficulties, citizen participation must be established to ensure sustainability.

The involvement of civil society is crucial to the success of reform, but it is very hard to manage. Community participation was attempted in reforming the police force of South Africa, for instance, but community–police forums collapsed, and public rhetoric became increasingly reactionary in response to rising crime rates. Participation has been attempted in locations such as Haiti, Kosovo, Rwanda, Sierra Leone, and Afghanistan, but no matter the country, it is not easy to implement. Involvement requires many consultations, meetings, and related discussions. Indeed, countless hours may be spent in attempts to increase participation, but in the end many often still feel forgotten. This is when the drive for "efficiency" and the need to feel the country is making progress take over and participation is no longer deemed essential. Steps must be taken to ensure that participation is not discounted or discarded in postconflict societies.

Also of significant importance are composition and vetting— who are the police and judicial personnel? This concept is tightly linked to popular support. For instance, South Africa opted not to vet, or "screen," serving officials to see if they were suitable to continue working in the police, courts, and prisons, a decision that may have deepened the problems related to community involvement and crime that South Africa experienced. Vetting of both police and judicial institutions remains a major transitional justice issue, and community support for reformed state agencies will suffer if citizens are compelled to work with those who have committed transgressions against them.

Police reform is especially important because it affects many other areas of reform. Police and judicial reform must be linked in a manner that is real, pragmatic, and organic, not merely rhetorical. This volume also makes clear that both police and judicial reforms must take gender issues into account, going well beyond simply incorporating women into police forces and judicial institutions. With well-crafted programs, international support can have an especially significant long-term impact on women's security and their access to justice, contributing to greater equality.

While it is important that police forces be vetted and corrupt or inappropriate officers be removed, it must noted that corruption is common in states that are in disarray, and organized crime is often a new challenge requiring a creative response from a neophyte police force. Several cases in the volume show that international organizations must take greater account of the power, wealth, and violence of transnational organized crime in every phase of postconflict processes.

Finally, the volume shows that international actors can either facilitate or hinder the implementation of reforms, depending on who is involved and whether they can successfully extricate themselves from the country when—and often if—peace is established. The cases of Kosovo and East Timor indicate that the decision of international actors to be (temporarily) the judges and the street police of a foreign society should only be made as a last resort. And when such international transitional administration of justice and internal security occurs, the degree of attention paid to getting the right personnel, preparing them well, monitoring them carefully, and, above all, building local capacities to replace these international actors will all contribute to the eventual success of a peace operation.

Past Institute volumes that have addressed issues related to postconflict planning include *Engineering Peace: The Military Role in Postconflict Reconstruction*, by Colonel Garland H. Williams, which offers a framework for addressing postconflict reconstruction, and *Council Unbound: The Growth of UN Decision Making on Conflict and Postconflict Issues after the Cold War*, by Michael J. Matheson, which examines the UN Security Council's new, expansive exercise of legal authority in the post–Cold War period and its devising of bold and innovative methods to stop nascent wars and "threats to the peace." *Constructing Justice and Security after War* adds another level to the study of one of the most important issues of our time. As these case studies demonstrate, expectations for rapid change are high, and disappointment and frustration are all but certain, sometimes making it difficult for the citizens of a country recovering from war to appreciate any positive changes. I hope that those involved in planning and implementing postconflict international involvement will read this volume and take some of its lessons to heart as they pursue their own work.

RICHARD H. SOLOMON, PRESIDENT
UNITED STATES INSTITUTE OF PEACE

Acknowledgements

ANY EDITED VOLUME IS A DAUNTING AND collective undertaking, and I am grateful to an array of people who supported them and this endeavor. First, I thank the circle of scholars and policymakers who expressed support for a serious, comparative effort to analyze policing and justice reform efforts jointly, rooted not only in the planning documents of international agencies, but in the results on the ground across regions and countries. I am also grateful to the contributors, who showed patience and diligence in the repeated drafts in a lengthy process. The interaction among us helped the final product.

Over a period of years, a number of individuals and officials kindly provided interviews that contributed to my ability to conclude this project and to the ideas in my contributions here. These people include numerous unnamed officials and individuals in Haiti, Guatemala, South Africa, and Afghanistan. My thanks also to the following list of individuals, which is not comprehensive:

In El Salvador: Public Security Commissioner Salvador Samayoa; Directors-General of the PNC Rodrigo Avila and Mauricio Sandoval; numerous PNC deputy commanders; Supreme Court Magistrate and former Ombudsperson Victoria de Aviles; Ruben Zamora; Hector Dada; Francisco Altchul; Jose Miguel de la Cruz; and Loly de Zuniga.

UN officials based in the United States: Mark Kroeker, former deputy commissioner of the Civilian Police in the UN Mission in Bosnia and current police adviser to the UN Secretary General; his predecessors as chief of the UN Civilian Police Unit in New York, Om Prakash Rathor and Halvor Hartz, as well as Harry Broer and Gerry Beekman, both officers in that unit; Chris Coleman, then of the Peacekeeping Department's Best Practices unit; and Jamal Benomar, Eva Buzsa, and Francis James of UN Development Programme.

In Bosnia and Herzegovina: Jacques Paul Klein, special representative of the secretary general; Dennis Laducer, deputy commissioner of the International Police Task Force; Civil Affairs chief

David Harland; and Robert Gravelle, Civil Affairs officer in Sarajevo and later helpful in Liberia; Donald S. Hayes, principal deputy high representative; Michael G. Karnavas, chairman of the Brčko Law Revision Commission; and Bisera Turkovic, director of the Center for Security Studies.

In Kosovo: President Ibrahim Rugova; Ramush Haradinaj, then-deputy commander of the Kosovo Protection Corps; Christopher Albiston, UNMIK police commissioner; his human rights adviser Elizabeth Griffin; Thomas Hacker, deputy UN police commissioner; Kosovo Police School Director Steve Bennett; and William Irvine, chief of UN Penal Management Division.

The advice of colleagues and friends—including Bill Stanley, Sue Cook, David Holiday, Sanjeev Khagram, Antonio Donini, Madalene O'Donnell, Eric Scheye, Rama Mani, Peter Andreas, Nina Tannenwald, Keith Brown, Graham Day, John Walsh, Otwin Marenin, Bob Perito, Gordon Peake, Jim Ron, and the late Maggi Popkin—was especially helpful.

A stint as visiting fellow at the United States Institute of Peace in 2002–2003 offered a pleasant environment, for which I thank Joe Klaits, John Crist, and their excellent administrative staff. My thanks to Nigel Quinney and Amy Benavides, who worked on behalf of the United States Institute of Peace Press to get the volume to print quickly. Thanks are also due to a number of people who made administrative aspects smoother, including Professor Melissa Labonte, Judy Barsalou, Sheila Fournier, and April Hall.

Research and writing were supported by a solicited grant (#SG-89-01) from the Institute, which also assisted in the organization of a conference of the participants cosponsored by the Institute and Brown University's Watson Institute for International Studies. In addition, a Research and Writing Grant from the John D. and Catherine T. MacArthur Foundation supported the editor's research for the volume. I am grateful for these financial expressions of support, which were indispensable, as well as to the feedback from the conference participants.

Two contributions appeared previously elsewhere and are reprinted with permission. My case study of El Salvador first appeared as "Democratization, War, and State-Building: Constructing the

Rule of Law in El Salvador," *Journal of Latin American Studies* 35:4 (November 2003). The chapter by Tracy Fitzsimmons appeared in a largely similar form as "The Postconflict Postscript: Gender and Policing in Peace Operations," in Dyan Mazurana, Angela Raven-Roberts, and Jane Parpart (eds.), *Gender, Conflict and Peacekeeping* (Boulder: Rowman Littlefield, 2005, pp. 185–201).

One contributor in particular, Tracy Fitzsimmons, was indispensable to my completing this volume, and her participation, support, and patience are deeply appreciated. Finally, I thank my parents, David and JoAnn Call, for their abiding support, and dedicate this volume to them.

Contributors

Charles T. Call IS ASSISTANT PROFESSOR OF INTERNATIONAL Peace and Conflict Resolution at American University and senior adviser on peacebuilding to the International Peace Academy. In 2004 he worked as peacebuilding consultant to the UN Department of Political Affairs. Before that, he coordinated the Governance in War-Torn Societies Project at Brown University, where he published articles in *Global Governance, Comparative Politics,* and the *Journal on Latin American Studies.* His field research on police reforms includes work in Central America, Haiti, Afghanistan, Bosnia, Kosovo, South Africa, and the West Bank. He has served as consultant on police and justice reform issues to the U.S. Justice Department, the UN Development Programme, the Ford Foundation, the European Commission, and the U.S. Agency for International Development (USAID). He holds a Ph.D. in political science from Stanford University and a B.A. with honors from Princeton University.

*   *   *

Sandra Beidas served for several years in the Organisation of American States (OAS)/UN International Civilian Mission in Haiti, principally in coordinating monitoring, analysis, and reporting. She then became chief of the Human Rights Section of the UN International Civilian Support Mission in Haiti. She has subsequently worked with the Child Protection Section in the UN peacekeeping mission in the Democratic Republic of the Congo and as chief of protection with Office of the High Commissioner for Human Rights–Nepal.

Michael H. Doyle has been working in the Balkans since 1997. During his tenure as senior political analyst for the International Crisis Group from 2000 to 2003, he produced policy papers on a range of issues, including Bosnian constitutional change, justice for war crimes, and ethnic reconciliation in southern Serbia. Since 2004, he has been with the Office of the High Representative in Sarajevo, advising on rule of law reforms and specifically the restructuring of Bosnia's police forces.

Tracy Fitzsimmons is vice president for academic affairs and professor of political science at Shenandoah University. With regional expertise in Latin America, she has taught courses on world politics, Latin American politics, global democratization, political economy of development, and international perspectives on women and justice. Her research has taken her to Chile, Costa Rica, El Salvador, Haiti, Mexico, Guatemala, Dominican Republic, Croatia, and Bosnia. She has published a book and numerous reviewed articles and book chapters with a research focus on democratization, civil society, and global higher education. She is a graduate of Princeton University (B.A. in politics) and Stanford University (M.A. in Latin American studies; Ph.D. in political science).

Colin Granderson is the assistant secretary-general, Foreign and Community Relations, at the Caribbean Community (CARICOM) Secretariat. He was named ambassador at large of Trinidad and Tobago in 1993, where he was the executive director of the OAS/UN International Civilian Mission in Haiti. He earlier served as the coordinator of the OAS civilian presence in Haiti and was designated head of mission of the OAS election observation mission for the December 1995 presidential elections and also for the partial legislative and local government elections of April 1997 in Haiti. He has headed election observation missions for the OAS for general elections in Suriname and Guyana, and since joining the CARICOM Secretariat he has participated in election observation missions in Jamaica and The Turks and Caicos Islands. Additionally, he was a member of the advisory panel known as the Brahimi Commission that was convened by the UN secretary-general in March 2000 to review UN peace operations and make recommendations.

Charles Mironko is a social anthropologist specializing in comparative genocide, in particular the Rwandan genocide of 1994. He was a visiting fellow at the Watson Institute for International Studies from 2001 to 2003 and received his Ph.D. from Yale in 2004. He also has served as associate director, Genocide Studies Program, Yale University, and chief, Culture Section, Organization of African Unity, Addis Ababa, Ethiopia. He is currently the humanitarian affairs officer for the African Union Mission in the Sudan (AMIS), Darfur.

Rachel Neild is senior advisor with the National Criminal Justice Reform Program of the Open Society Justice Initiative. Justice Initiative's projects address ethnic profiling by police in Europe and support police accountability and transparency in Africa, Latin America, and Eastern Europe. She was formerly the director of the Public Security Reform Program at the Washington Office on Latin America, monitoring international police assistance and promoting democratic policing reforms in Central America, Haiti, and Mexico. She previously worked with the Inter-American Institute for Human Rights, Costa Rica, and the Andean Commission of Jurists, Peru, and has been a consultant on human rights and policing reforms for the Inter-American Development Bank, the Organisation for Economic Co-operation and Development, USAID, and the Canadian nongovernmental organization Rights and Democracy, among others. She has published numerous papers and reports on these issues and has served on a number of advisory boards.

Janine Rauch has degrees in criminology from the University of Cape Town, South Africa, and from Cambridge University, England. She has researched and published extensively on police reform and crime prevention in South Africa. After South Africa's first democratic election in 1994, she was appointed as an adviser to the Minister of Safety and Security. Since 2003, she has worked as an independent consultant, advising various government and donor agencies in Africa on crime reduction and security sector reform strategies.

Colette Rausch is deputy director of the United States Institute of Peace Rule of Law Program. She served with the Organization for Security and Co-Operation in Europe (OSCE) Mission in Kosovo, first as head of the Rule of Law Division and then as director of the Department of Human Rights and Rule of Law. She also served as the U.S. Justice Department's resident legal adviser in Bosnia and later as a program manager establishing criminal justice programs in post-conflict countries, including Kosovo. She also held positions as a federal prosecutor in Las Vegas, Nevada, and as head of the Nevada State Attorney General's Office Telemarketing and Consumer Fraud Unit. Her publications include "The Assumption of Authority in Kosovo and East Timor: Legal and Practical Implications," in *Executive Policing: Enforcing the Law in Peace Operations*, Renata Dawn, ed. (Stockholm International Peace Research Institute, 2003).

Ephrem Rurangwa is the joint general staff in charge of administration and personnel at Rwanda Defence Force Headquarters. From 2000 to 2003, he was the deputy commissioner general for operations of the Rwanda National Police, where he was responsible for implementing a major reform of the institution and later became the deputy commissioner for administration and personnel from 2004 to 2005. He previously served as a doctor in the Rwanda Patriotic Front in the armed struggle. He worked as head of medical services in the National Gendarmerie and later served as acting chief of military intelligence. He holds an M.D. from the Medical School of the University of Burundi.

William D. Stanley is associate professor of political science at the University of New Mexico. His research focuses on political violence, conflict resolution, and institutional reforms, with an emphasis on Central America. His articles have appeared in *International Organization, International Peacekeeping, Global Governance, Studies in Comparative International Development,* and other journals. He has published a book, *The Protection Racket State: Elite Politics, Military Extortion, and Civil War in El Salvador* (Temple University Press, 1996), as well as numerous chapters in edited volumes.

Ronald A. West is an independent consultant who has been working in the field since 1998. With an emphasis on community security and development, as well as institutional development of police forces, West has consulted on projects for the United Nations, USAID, and the World Bank in Haiti, East Timor, the Philippines, Jamaica, Sri Lanka, and Honduras. His work has covered various aspects of program design, management, and technical assistance, including service as chief of party on USAID-funded initiatives in East Timor and Jamaica. Prior to serving as a civilian police advisor to the United Nations International Police Assistance Mission in Haiti, West was a police officer in San Francisco. He received his M.A. from New York University in January 2000 and was awarded a fellowship by the Social Science Research Council in 2002. During the fellowship, West was based at Columbia University's Salzman Institute for War and Peace Studies. While there, he authored two works: a chapter on post-conflict reconstruction of the justice system in East Timor (forthcoming from the United States Institute of Peace Press) and a policy guide on police accountability and community policing funded by USAID and published by the National Democratic Institute for International Affairs.

Constructing Justice and Security after War

1

Introduction

What We Know and Don't Know about Postconflict Justice and Security Reform

CHARLES T. CALL

IN 2003, THE IRAQI REGIME OF SADDAM HUSSEIN FELL to U.S.-led forces. The widely publicized situation that unfolded immediately afterward—rampant looting, widespread citizen insecurity, and impunity for all sorts of crimes—surprised most observers and U.S. officials. It also enraged many Iraqis who had been receptive to the U.S. invasion.

Yet Iraq's unfortunate weeks-long dearth of security and law did not surprise those familiar with other postwar societies. Before Baghdad fell, insecurity plagued Afghanistan for more than a year after the demise of the Taliban regime. Indeed, as the United States and its allies demonstrated a growing and unprecedented military capacity to topple regimes from Haiti and Kosovo to Kabul and Baghdad, all of these postintervention societies displayed serious and persistent problems of citizen insecurity and an absence of the rule of law.

Interestingly, negotiated settlements of civil wars exhibited equally vexing, though qualitatively distinct, problems of insecurity.

3

El Salvador, South Africa, and Guatemala—three of the most successful peace processes of the 1990s—experienced worse violent crime *after* their wars concluded, leaping to the top of the world's homicide rankings. Organized crime in Bosnia deepened after the 1995 Dayton peace agreement. These and other cases underscore one of the central challenges of international security in the twenty-first century: How can external actors not only establish security in the immediate aftermath of war but also create self-sustaining systems of justice and security in postwar societies?

THE NEW RULE-OF-LAW CONSENSUS

This question has been neglected by scholars but is now recognized as a top priority by various international constituencies: the development industry, peacebuilding agencies, Western military forces, democracy promoters, and human rights organizations. Thomas Carothers refers to the "rule-of-law revival" during the 1990s, when Western governments and international organizations invested billions of dollars in programs to redraft constitutions and laws, strengthen judicial institutions, professionalize and reform police forces, curb corruption, and improve correctional systems throughout the former Soviet Union, Latin America, Africa, Asia, Eastern Europe, and the Balkans.[1] Among a plethora of development and security agencies, a new "rule-of-law consensus" has emerged.[2] This consensus consists of two elements: (1) the belief that the rule of law is essential to virtually every Western liberal foreign policy goal—human rights, democracy, economic and political stability, international security from terrorist and other transnational threats, and transnational free trade and investment; and (2) the belief that international interventions, be they through money, people, or ideas, must include a rule-of-law component.

These beliefs took root only in the 1990s. After having virtually eliminated foreign police aid and justice reform initiatives in the 1960s and 1970s, the United States was devoting a growing portion of its development assistance to promoting the rule of law by 2001. Two years later, the head of the UN Development Programme reported that 60 percent of its core funding went to "democratic governance," including justice and security sector reform programs, rather than to traditional programs like health care and education.[3] European donors, who did not offer significant support for policing and justice systems upon withdrawal from their colonies in the 1960s and 1970s, began to do so in the 1990s.

International financial institutions for forty years shunned involvement with security or justice institutions as "political" and outside the scope of their work. Yet by 2000 the World Bank and regional development banks had made the rule of law a centerpiece of their policy discourse, encouraging governments to rationalize their military expenditures and funding programs to disarm combatants and reconstruct judicial systems. These changes reflect a combination of factors: growing efforts to institutionalize human rights; broadened concepts of "development" and its links to governance; recognition that globalizing commerce requires institutions to protect capital; and frustration with the costs and risks to international military peacekeepers forced to police postwar societies.

Events of the twenty-first century have only strengthened the rule-of-law consensus. The attacks of September 11, 2001, helped convince conservatives that unstable peripheral states without a rule of law pose a threat to the West's security. Well-publicized looting and the security void that followed the fall of Baghdad starkly demonstrated the need for better international appreciation of and tools for this challenge. In mid-2004 UN secretary-general Kofi Annan released a UN report on the rule of law and transitional justice in postconflict societies.[4] Annan's annual address to the General Assembly that year focused on the rule of law, and he urged member states to "restore and extend the rule of law throughout the world," pledging to make strengthening the rule of law a priority for the rest of his term.[5]

What does this newfound attention to the rule of law mean for the peoples of war-torn societies? A growing number of analysts have recently concluded that international actors have enjoyed limited success in postwar peacebuilding. In particular, the difficulties of fostering self-sustaining justice and security systems have become apparent.[6]

Drawing on in-depth case studies of some of the most prominent (and successful) peacekeeping operations since the fall of the

Berlin Wall, this volume addresses the following central question: *Can societies emerging from armed conflict create systems of justice and security that ensure basic rights, apply the law effectively and impartially, and enjoy popular support?* If so, how? What is the appropriate role for international actors in these processes? Are there patterns indicating what sorts of conditions and choices enhance justice and security, and which ones have negligible or perverse effects?

FROM THE "RULE OF LAW" TO "JUSTICE AND SECURITY SECTOR REFORM"

Before examining what we know and don't know about these questions, a word about terminology is necessary. Obviously, the term "rule of law" is appealing to a number of constituencies, connoting legal frameworks, lawful conduct, and an orderly society.[7] Nevertheless, the rule of law is an imperfect concept for analysis of the bundle of national-level and local-level issues of external military defense, internal citizen security, and the perceptions and institutions of justice. The concept tends to focus on constitutions and laws (and lawyers) and less on military defense roles or citizen security systems and strategies.

Most scholars and practitioners embrace a minimalist and procedural definition of the rule of law, emphasizing legal rules for social, political, and commercial interaction. Carothers, for example, defines the rule of law as "a system in which the laws are public knowledge, are clear in meaning, and apply equally to everyone."[8] In this prevalent view, the rule of law represents a predictable means of resolving disputes and, crucially, a curb on the arbitrary exercise of state power—the "rule of law" over the "rule of man," as Aristotle put it.[9] Such a definition has the advantage of simplicity and allows for the analysis of relationships between the rule of law and goods like justice, security, participation, and economic growth.[10]

Yet this procedural definition fails to include just outcomes or conformity with human rights standards. In contrast to maximalist substantive definitions of the rule of law (which include fairness and human rights in the very content of the law), minimalist concepts can coexist with legalistic authoritarian regimes and with laws that discriminate or wholly exclude certain social groups.[11] As long as these unjust laws are applied consistently, minimalist definitions of the rule of law are met. Thus, apartheid South Africa and slave-holding U.S. states of the nineteenth century might all be character-ized as enjoying the "rule of law." Maximalist definitions, such as those used by the Organization for Security and Cooperation in Europe (OSCE), usefully embrace not only adherence to the law but also individual dignity and rights, effective institutions, and justice itself.[12] However, maximalist definitions defy commonly held notions of the rule of law and are virtually impossible to empirically assess. Perhaps the most salient disadvantage of the rule-of-law concept is its connotation of public order. The term conveys legality, or enforce-ment of and adherence to the law, rather than citizen security, legiti-macy of police and judicial institutions, or perceptions of justice.

In recent years some donor agencies have adopted an attractive alternative to the rule of law: the concept of "security sector reform" (SSR).[13] As defined by the British Department for International Development (DFID), one of its main champions, the "security sec-tor" refers to

> military, police, paramilitary, gendarmerie, machinery associated with ensuring accessible justice (police, judiciary, penal system), intelligence, customs enforcement and the civilian management and oversight authorities, including the Ministries of Defence and Finance.[14]

Although encompassing justice institutions, the concept of security sector reform has in practice heavily emphasized the military and security issues, especially demobilization and reintegration, to the detriment of both citizen security and justice issues. European donors placed more nominal emphasis on civilian components and control after 2000, yet the centrality of military forces and issues remained through 2005. Another term, "administration of justice," carries the converse liability, stressing justice with less focus on external or internal security.[15]

Consequently, this volume adopts the lexicon of "justice and security sector reform" (JSSR). In this sense, we seek to respond to valid criticism of the predominant literature by analyzing neither security nor justice institutions in isolation from one another and by uniting justice for past abuses on the one hand with justice in the present and in the future on the other hand. The UN Development Programme's adoption of a policy paper on justice and security sector reform in 2002 reflects the recognition of the value of uniting these two concepts.[16]

"Security" here refers principally to the safety of individual citizens, social groups, and the state from physical violence. However, the focus is narrower than "human security," concentrating on the citizen security elements of that broader concept that would require a full analysis of state capacities and strategies, which lay beyond the initial scope of the enterprise.[17] This volume addresses the range of direct threats to physical security of the population, with special attention given to citizens' perceived and actual security (i.e., citizen security) as well as public security.

We have deliberately sought to redress the imbalance of policy and scholarly discourse favoring *international* security over *internal* security. Much of the peacekeeping literature is implicitly concerned with advancing Western (especially U.S.) interests in combating instability, terrorism, drug trafficking, and other illicit transnational crime. Justice and security reforms are vital for addressing these important threats to international security. However, we emphasize the well-being of the inhabitants of postconflict societies, which is vital to the sustainable security and justice generally held to be valuable for international peace and security. Many case studies in this volume refer to the armed forces as a tool of external defense and security, but only to the extent that their role affects internal security, including their own role in aggravating insecurity through an inability or unwillingness to prevent human rights abuses or through their own commission of the same.

"Justice" refers to the ability of a society to resolve social disputes in a manner both nonviolent and accepted by disputing parties, even when they disagree with specific outcomes. Justice in the broadest sense is "fairness," though this equation permits multiple concrete concepts of justice.[18] The study of social justice is the study of specific social institutions, yet these institutions are not themselves equivalent to the presence or administration of justice. Justice reflects not only a complex package of formal state organizations but also civil society's interactions with the state and the mores, perceptions, and expectations of society. The chapters in this book seek to capture, even measure, the ability of formal justice systems to administer justice. Justice systems include constitutional and legal frameworks; formal courts and state offices of prosecution, defense, and monitoring of justice and rights abuses; and state and nonstate law enforcement capabilities, as well as informal and traditional institutions of conflict resolution.

Justice and security "reform" here refers to significant reconstitution of the structure, controlling organizations, and missions of the justice and security systems. Justice reform, for example, refers to attempts to reorient or redefine the overall character of the justice system, not attempts to modify specific institutions or behaviors in isolation from the other components of the justice system. Security reforms are defined in parallel fashion.[19] How do we actually measure security and justice? Before we answer this question, it is helpful to examine what we know and don't know about these issues in postwar societies.

WHAT WE KNOW AND DON'T KNOW ABOUT CONSTRUCTING SECURITY AND JUSTICE

This book tries to do three novel things. First, it seeks to examine some of the most prominent recent instances of a specific category—postwar societies—to shed light on the process of constructing the systems of justice and security. We hope not only to derive policy implications for international actors but also to add to the emerging study of the rule of law and justice and security sector reform.

That does not mean throwing out what we already know. Existing literature holds important knowledge to test and compare in analyzing these cases. Constructing justice and security involves state institutions: courts, police forces, prosecutorial offices, human rights ombudsperson offices, investigatory commissions, and so on. We know that state-building in industrialized democracies required long historical periods—decades, even centuries—to develop institutional legitimacy and to supplant loyalties to individual princes and lords. In addition, Europe's wars of the 1600s and 1800s institutionalized tax collection practices so as to mobilize the resources needed to wage wars, and the formation of large standing armies created the backbone of state power and replaced local power relations.[20]

Yet in today's postconflict societies, international actors are attempting to take shortcuts through those historical processes, creating public police forces and revamped judicial systems in a few months, while external resources are supplanting internal tax revenues and globalized communications are transmitting new ideas and expectations. It is not clear whether such efforts can succeed. State-building scholarship is skeptical, but policymakers remain sanguine about the achievements of postwar state-building throughout the past decade.[21]

Much of the scholarship on the rule of law, like the state-building literature, is similarly skeptical of postwar societies' ability to quickly forge systems of justice and security. Modernization theory and its more palatable successors assume that the rule of law and democracy are a function of the existence of certain cultural values peculiar to the Western middle class.[22] Alternative historical perspectives critique these assumptions, noting that the rule of law preceded democratic entitlements in many European industrialized democracies. Both of these views assume that the emergence of the rule of law is a lengthy historical process linked to cultural or economic transformations. In this view, hasty efforts to foster the rule of law in only a few years are futile, especially in poor, ethnically divided societies with low degrees of institutionalization.

Yet we know little about how the rule of law emerges. Serious empirical studies are rare, and the multifaceted nature of the rule of law means that multiple factors impinge on its emergence and character. Some scholars emphasize economic or cultural factors, implying structural constraints. Others emphasize institutional engineering, implying agency. This volume, situated largely within the latter category, seeks to look beyond short-term engineering, identifying patterns that may confirm or contradict structural accounts.

We aspire to a second novel contribution with this volume: the equal, integrated treatment of security and justice issues in empirical research. Perhaps the highest-profile recent literature focuses on *international* efforts to construct the rule of law, especially in developing societies and in postconflict settings. This literature focuses explicitly either on policing issues or on justice issues. It contains important insights and debates for postwar societies.

On the policing side, Otwin Marenin, David Bayley, and others stress the constraints to reform, arguing that changing police organizations is difficult and confronts inertia-plagued, day-to-day routines embedded in resistant organizational cultures.[23] More recent research has sought to define ways that reform is possible.[24] Others argue that moments of transition provide windows of opportunity for institutional reforms, including reforms of security doctrines and organizations.[25] Consonant with process-oriented approaches to democratization, these studies of postwar policing stress institutional agency, especially international factors—what these international organizations or foreign governments did, what they should have done differently, how they should have collaborated differently, how they accomplished their objectives—rather than the overall outcomes of rule of law.

Such research often emphasizes the viewpoints of international actors more than those of the populace experiencing justice and security reforms. For instance, Tor Tanke Holm and Espen Barth Eide's *Peacebuilding and Police Reform* and Robert Oakley, Michael Dziedzic, and Eliot Goldberg's *Policing the New World Disorder: Peace Operations and Public Security* illustrate the shortcomings of international actors in filling postconflict "public security gaps," the difficulties in finding the right international personnel for the right jobs, and the advantages of quality selection and training for new police recruits.[26] In contrast to soldiers, who generally have no fixed peacetime role, police professionals in every country usually carry out vital tasks on a daily basis to achieve their organizational aims. Therefore, police are seldom available in large quantities (say, hundreds or thousands) for dangerous jobs overseas. UN reports also have recognized these deficiencies.[27]

The latter two volumes emphasize order-maintenance tasks of postwar policing and focus heavily on international actors such as the UN Civilian Police, international military troops and gendarmes, and bilateral police advisers. Missing is systematic, focused comparative research from which reliable or robust generalizations about the success or failure of institutional development and sustainable security (as opposed to short-term order maintenance) can be drawn.[28] Marenin's *Policing Change, Changing Police* provides excellent, though disparate, case studies but analyzes only two postwar cases where international actors were heavily involved. Indeed, a number of excellent single case studies of police and justice reforms, especially of El Salvador and South Africa, provide valuable observations and conclusions.[29] This volume seeks to provide a more systematic, comparative examination of local security outcomes of, rather than international inputs to and outputs from, postconflict rule-of-law reform efforts. We hope to provide a rigorous analysis of a broad, important set of cases of postconflict security and justice institutional reforms and empirically grounded conclusions relevant for policymakers and scholars.

This is not to deny that some generalizations have achieved acceptance among most analysts of postconflict policing. Police reform decision makers, both national officials of new postwar regimes and international officials, increasingly adhere to a bundle of principles, including public policing, professionalism, basic respect for rights, an internal security doctrine that emphasizes protection of citizen rights rather than state interests, and some concept of democratic accountability. Scholars agree that police reform is deeply political, rather than simply a technical process. Thus, technical approaches to police assistance can be wasteful, even harmful, if used to advance repression or antidemocratic partisan agendas. Therefore, many analysts recognize that international police aid undermines reform goals if diplomatic and other leverage is not used when needed or if the overall political environment is antidemocratic.[30] In addition, scholarship on policing in transitional societies acknowledges that police reform takes years rather than months, that civilian models of policing are more appropriate than military models, that internal and external mechanisms of oversight have received too little attention, and that classroom instruction is no substitute for practical training and field supervision. All bemoan the inadequacy of international actors—be they bilateral powers that deploy insufficient or inappropriate resources, police advisers who blindly export their own models, international organizations that repeatedly fail to field sufficiently competent (or even qualified) staff, or all of the above when they refuse to permit local participation in security reform efforts. The deficiencies of justice and security reform are the same deficiencies that afflict state-building more broadly, as new research emphasized in 2003 and 2004.[31]

Furthermore, the police reform literature now routinely emphasizes the importance of integrating policing with judicial and penal systems. At a basic level, efficient, rights-respecting police serve no purpose if the courts regularly release suspected perpetrators because of corruption or incompetence. On a deeper level, the rule of law requires fair and clear laws, competent and legitimate judicial authorities (civil and criminal courts, prosecution, and defense counsel), competent and rights-respecting rehabilitation systems, and desirable internal security systems. The conceptual link between security and justice in postconflict reform agendas had achieved widespread rhetorical acceptance among policymakers by 2004 but was reflected neither in research nor, as seen in this volume, in practice.

Just as scholars of policing began to turn their attention to post-conflict and transitional societies in the 1990s, so too did some analysts of justice systems and judicial reforms. Studies by international financial institutions found that legal revision is insufficient to create a climate favorable for international investment and economic stability; institutional reforms are necessary as well. In Latin America, the region where international donors have long supported judicial reforms, donors modified programs to emphasize partnership with reform-minded officials, strengthening judicial independence rather than just efficiency, and the need for greater access to justice.[32] One of the most comprehensive studies, commissioned by the U.S. Agency for International Development (USAID), concluded that local initiative and ownership are often neglected but are fundamental to the success of international judicial reform efforts.[33]

Much comparative work on judicial reform reflects the same overemphasis on international actors and their interests as do most studies of policing. Recent writing on justice also reflects a separate bifurcation. Analysis of postconflict judicial reform has failed to engage efforts to address the role of those responsible for past human rights abuses. Similarly, edited volumes on accountability and judicial reform actors have focused more on accountability for past atrocities than on (re)building postwar judicial systems for present and future abuses. Neil Kritz's *Transitional Justice* series is among the most prominent, along with books by Priscilla Hayner and Martha Minow.[34] These works examine various means of dealing with past abusers, questioning whether a posttransition regime can credibly establish the rule of law if its very birth rests in granting impunity or amnesty for morally heinous acts.

However, those who seek redress for past atrocities rarely analyze the process of institutional reform of the justice system in a comprehensive manner.[35] Recently, we have seen some recognition of the need to integrate these two perspectives—past accountability and present judicial development—but written analysis has lagged.[36] Presenting studies that bridge the divide between dealing with past injustices and creating systems to address future injustices is the third novel endeavor of this volume.

One critique of these issues warrants attention. Some have questioned the motives behind the "rule-of-law revival," alleging that these revived efforts seek to suppress challenges—be they by organized workers, antiglobalization activists, or ethnic and religious groups seeking greater political power—to free-market capitalism and U.S. hegemony. David Rieff, for instance, refers to international human rights as the new "religion" of the global order, providing ideological justification to self-interested, usually harmful, interventions in developing (and developed) countries.[37] Advancing the rule of law, in this view, is window dressing for the exercise of power by Western capitals and capital.

This book assumes that the populations of the societies involved can, under some circumstances, benefit from internationally supported justice and security reforms. Clearly, the United States and other powerful countries pursue their own interests, and the Bush administration made no secret of its desire for order in postconflict Afghanistan and Iraq. Fostering the rule of law in war-torn countries serves the interests of those seeking a stable investment climate and those not wanting to expend human and financial resources on violent conflicts in far-flung countries, even when violence may be morally justified. Yet the world's torture victims, the bereaved relatives of those "disappeared," and millions of persecuted ethnic groups increasingly give voice to their demand for justice and for prevention of future atrocities. Iraqi and Afghan voices were insistent on the need for more order after U.S. intervention. The cases in this book demonstrate that international programs have, in some war-torn societies, helped improve security and justice, preventing at least some carnage, even as they advanced other not-so-humanitarian Western agendas.

MEASURING JUSTICE AND SECURITY

How should we assess, or measure, security and justice, or the rule of law? The contributors to this volume employ no single yardstick. Indeed, no single indicator is appropriate for every society, as the sources of insecurity vary in their nature and change over time. As suggested earlier, we believe that much prior literature focused on measuring the outputs of international programs rather than their impact on the societies where they were carried out, a tendency we seek to avoid.

In this volume we emphasize internal security over international security. In particular, we analyze both individual security (most relevant for common crimes like robbery and assault) and the security of the main social, political, and ethnic groups in society. Group security, often sidelined by liberal notions of individual security, is especially relevant after internal armed conflicts, especially conflicts over identity, and for marginalized groups like women. We seek to analyze the security, both subjectively perceived and objectively measured, of these groups. Analysis includes postwar patterns of human rights violations directed at certain ethnic groups and at members of formerly warring parties. We also examine patterns of violence against women and children, as Tracy Fitzsimmons does in her chapter devoted exclusively to postconflict issues of violence and gender.

Yet it is individual security, or rather *in*security, that seems to play an unexpectedly prominent role in the most successful cases of peace consolidation. We drew on official statistics of common crimes, especially violent crimes, and on independent crime data from international organizations where available. We sought out polling data measuring popular perceptions of citizen insecurity, justice systems, policing, courts, prosecutors, and human rights protections. We also relied on interviews with elites such as national-level security and justice officials, judges, police leadership, military officers, international peacekeeping officials, representatives of nongovernmental organizations working on human rights and justice issues, academic experts, and other social analysts. With these indicators, we seek to draw conclusions about outcomes in the areas of justice and security as understood within postconflict societies, rather than just strict conformity with the law or performance of international organizations.

THE CASES EXAMINED

This book examines the experience of countries that have recently undergone transitions from conflict with heavy international involvement. Specifically, it offers generalizations based on careful comparisons of justice and security reforms in postwar countries across Central America and the Caribbean, Africa, the Balkans, and East Timor. We have deliberately chosen cases that exhibit variation: some were civil wars and others interventions; some ended in negotiations and others in defeat; some enjoyed a past experience with relatively coherent formal institutions and others did not; some were provided with extensive security by international combat forces and others were not.

Studying countries emerging from warfare, be it civil war or intervention, offers two particular advantages. Much of what we know about the emergence of the rule of law is rooted in European or North American societies and emphasizes long historical patterns and slow-moving factors. In contrast to those experiences, postwar societies have almost all experienced wrenching disruptions of population, political regime, and economy. Some portion of their population was subjected to state violence, including mass murder and torture. All faced the challenge of redesigning new political regimes that would include leaders who had previously been pursued or persecuted. Consequently, reconstituting new systems of justice and security in short order became a necessity. Scholars have not sufficiently examined the experience of these postconflict countries in constructing security and justice, especially as such experience contrasts with the mainstream literature in this area.

Second, along with postauthoritarian regimes, postconflict societies may well signify the future trend of international involvement in fostering the rule of law and indeed of international development assistance. Since 1989 these countries have represented the highest-profile efforts in the world to bolster the rule of law. Of the many regime transitions between 1988 and 2002, constitutions were revised in most cases, including South Africa, Nicaragua, Georgia, and Afghanistan. In El Salvador, Haiti, Kosovo, and East Timor, the United Nations oversaw the selection, training, and organization of new civilian police forces with new doctrines and new training academies. UN international war crimes tribunals were erected for the former Yugoslavia and for Rwanda, the first since the Nuremberg trials fifty years earlier, leading to a new International Criminal Court. Guatemala, Afghanistan, Bosnia, and Kosovo experienced significant changes to their justice systems. In Kosovo and East Timor, UN cops gathered from dozens of nations became the police force for the entire territory, issuing parking tickets, investigating organized crime, and arresting murder and theft suspects. In all postwar cases, discrete projects unfolded with goals such as controlling corruption, training judges, revising laws, and enhancing human rights protections.

Postconflict societies became the locus of the most expensive and ambitious rule-of-law projects and prominent laboratories for international thinking about justice reform and security reform around the world. We have focused especially on the few years in the immediate aftermath of war termination, largely because the causal effect of peace processes or intervention can be expected to diminish after several years. In some cases, this focus may seem strange since important political events subsequently occurred (e.g., the reelection of President Jean-Bertrand Aristide and his resignation amid a generally recognized failure of state-building). However, we believe the lessons of these immediate postwar periods remain highly pertinent for other cases of transitions from war. The chapters that follow examine what these cases tell us about several questions: (1) the extent to which constructing justice and security is even possible in war-torn societies, (2) what role international actors played in the transitions, and (3) what relation different aspects of justice, policing, and law reform have to one another.

In considering these questions, the chapters address a number of additional questions:

- How does war transform or degrade security and justice systems?
- When wars end, what patterns of violence and crime emerge? What factors contribute to these patterns?
- What is the outcome of police reforms and justice reforms? In what areas were they more effective than others?
- How legitimate are new security and justice systems? That is, how do citizens perceive new justice and security systems? How do victims, past and present, perceive those systems?
- What informal or nonconventional (e.g., tribal, local, or religious) systems of justice, conflict resolution, and policing seem to have worked?
- Is there a trade-off between effectively combating postwar crime and enhancing respect for citizen rights? Are there ways to achieve both simultaneously?
- What repercussions do actions (or inaction) against past abusers have on new judicial systems? Do trials foster legitimacy for postwar justice systems, or can such systems flourish without addressing past atrocities?
- Who are the losers in security and justice reforms, and can their position be improved?

Most of the contributors to this book are analysts or practitioners who have been involved in security or justice policy positions. Even the academics here have worked as consultants to the U.S. government, the United Nations, or nongovernmental organizations addressing police or justice programs in the regions about which they write. All contributors personally know many of the pertinent decision makers on justice and security sector reform during the postconflict period.

We have deliberately chosen cases from diverse regions of the world to bolster the reach and robustness of the findings. Latin

America, as the source of many existing donor programs in supporting police reform and judicial reform, is the first region to appear in the volume. Case studies by Professors Charles Call on El Salvador and William Stanley on Guatemala show surprisingly different justice system outcomes from two apparently similar negotiated settlements to civil wars.

Haiti, the only nonwar transition in the volume, is included because judicial and police reforms were so central to the international reconstruction effort after U.S. intervention in 1994 to restore elected president Aristide to power. The chapter's authors are Rachel Neild, who monitored police reforms on behalf of the nongovernmental Washington Office on Latin America; Ambassador Colin Granderson, who headed the joint United Nations/Organization of American States Civilian Mission in Haiti (MICIVIH) from 1993 to 1999; and Sandra Beidas, who served as head of the human rights office for MICIVIH.

Chapters on two African cases present very different experiences of police and justice reform. Rwanda, unusual for the horrific genocide that was separate but related to an internal armed conflict that brought the victorious Tutsi-led Rwandan Patriotic Front (RPF) to power in 1994, shows the challenges of postgenocide justice reform, as more than 120,000 suspects were imprisoned in 2000 for having killed up to a million victims. Charles Mironko, an anthropologist and former diplomat of the Organization of African Unity, and Dr. Ephrem Rurangwa, who fought with the RPF and served at this writing as deputy commissioner for operations of the Rwanda National Police, coauthored this chapter.

Postapartheid South Africa, which also emerged from its own unique experience combining repression, oppression, and sporadic armed conflict, is known for its Truth and Reconciliation Commission. However, its efforts to build multiethnic justice and security systems and to confront one of the world's highest homicide rates have been less examined. Janine Rauch, a criminologist who helped write the Mandela government's crime prevention plan, sheds light on that process.

Two prominent instances of international efforts to support security and justice reforms during the 1990s are Bosnia and Kosovo.

Michael Doyle, an analyst with the nongovernmental International Crisis Group in Sarajevo, discusses Bosnia and Herzegovina's difficulty establishing multiethnic police and justice institutions in a bifurcated state under quasi-protectorate status. Colette Rausch, a former U.S. federal prosecutor who headed the Department of Human Rights and Rule of Law of the OSCE in Kosovo, examines efforts to build a new police force and new judiciary in that Yugoslav territory, an official international protectorate after the NATO-led war defeated Slobodan Milošević's forces in 1999.

East Timor's experience in erecting security and justice systems after its independence from Indonesia in 2002 shares a number of similarities with Kosovo's situation. Ronald West, who managed two USAID-funded projects that emphasized citizen access to justice, analyzes that country's experience, which along with Kosovo's is too recent to yield definitive conclusions about long-term effects but throws light on salient international efforts to construct security and justice in new political entities. Finally, Professor Tracy Fitzsimmons' chapter on gender issues in police and justice reforms in postconflict settings, based on fieldwork in the Balkans, Haiti, and Central America, adds an important and understudied dimension to the analysis. Arguing that peace may be harmful for women, she shows how justice and security reforms have enhanced women's security in some areas but failed in others.

Taken together, the case studies in these chapters represent perhaps the most optimal conditions for efforts to (re)constitute security and justice systems. In all cases, entrenched elite interests that generally resist changes to state institutions and practices have been weakened or ousted by force. We would expect posttransition settings, and especially postwar societies, to present an opportunity for institutional transformation.[38] New nominally democratic governments took power in every case. Such regimes should favor the processes and substance of justice. In addition, international diplomacy and development aid have deliberately sought to foster the rule of law in every case. Of course, war-torn societies present unique challenges, such as demobilized combatants and residual hatred. Poverty may have been exacerbated by war in places like Rwanda and Haiti. Nevertheless, we have selected cases that purportedly offer some tremendous advantages for postwar institution building. Some cases—El Salvador, South Africa, Guatemala, and Bosnia—represent the most successful instances of war termination and/or peacekeeping operations in the past decade. In other cases, such as Kosovo, East Timor, and Haiti, the slate was wiped as clean as possible by international forces that ousted old regimes and installed new ones.

What can these experiences tell us about going beyond immediate postwar security to the establishment of sustainable justice and security systems? In the end we hope both to improve the abilities of international and national actors to advance democratic institution building in postconflict settings and to refine emerging theorizing of state-building and peacebuilding. Although we have selected some of the most prominent efforts at postconflict state-building since 1989, we hope that the conclusions will hold relevance for the full pool of postconflict cases, including cases from the former Soviet Union, Northern Ireland, Central and West Africa, Afghanistan, and Iraq.

NOTES

1. Thomas Carothers, "The Rule of Law Revival," *Foreign Affairs* 77, no. 2 (1998): 95–106.

2. Others allude to this phenomenon. Rama Mani states that the "rule of law is a buzzword in policy discussions today, buoyed by newfound enthusiasm and support from donors and international organizations" in her draft "Exploring the Rule of Law in Theory and Practice," in *Rule-of-Law Programming in Conflict Management*, ed. Agnes Hurwitz (Boulder, Colo.: Lynne Rienner, forthcoming). Eric Scheye and Gordon Peake refer to the "exponential growth in the attention and resources devoted to SSR [security sector reform]" in their draft introduction to *Arresting Insecurity* (working title) (Boulder, Colo.: Lynne Rienner, forthcoming), 1.

3. Mark Malloch Brown, "Democratic Governance: Toward a Framework for Sustainable Peace," *Global Governance* 9, no. 2 (April–June 2003): 141–146.

4. Kofi Annan, *Report of the Secretary-General on the Rule of Law and Transitional Justice in Conflict and Post-conflict and Societies*, S/2004/616 (New York: United Nations, August 3, 2004).

5. Kofi Annan, secretary-general's address to the General Assembly, September 21, 2004, http://www.un.org/apps/sg/sgstats.asp?nid=1088.

6. See Scheye and Peake, introduction to *Arresting Insecurity;* David Bayley, *Democratizing the Police Abroad: What to Do and How to Do It* (Washington, D.C.: National Institute of Justice, 2001); and Bayley, "Policing Hate: What Can Be Done?" *Policing and Society* 12, no. 2 (2002).

7. See Allan Hutchinson and Patrick Monahan, *The Rule of Law: Ideal or Ideology?* (Toronto: Carswell Legal Publications, 1987); A. James McAdams, *Transitional Justice and the Rule of Law in New Democracies* (Notre Dame, Ind.: University of Notre Dame Press, 1997); Juan Mendez, Guillermo O'Donnell, and Paulo Sergio Pinheiro, eds., *The (Un)rule of Law and the Underprivileged in Latin America* (Notre Dame, Ind.: University of Notre Dame Press, 1999); Thomas Carothers, "The Rule of Law Revival"; Rama Mani, *Beyond Retribution: Seeking Justice in the Shadows of War* (New York: Polity Press, 2002); and Hurwitz, *Rule-of-Law Programming in Conflict Management.*

8. Carothers, "The Rule of Law Revival."

9. Aristotle *Politics*, 3.15–16.

10. In this sense, and others described later in this chapter, the conceptual difficulties of the rule of law parallel those concerning the definitions of democracy.

11. Mani, *Beyond Retribution*, 25–31.

12. In its definition of the rule of law, the OSCE, for instance, includes "not merely" formal legality but also "justice based on the recognition and full acceptance of the supreme value of the human personality and guaranteed by institutions providing a framework for its fullest expression." Organization for Security and Cooperation in Europe, quoted in ibid., 28.

13. On SSR, see Chris Smith, "Security Sector Reform: Development Breakthrough or Institutional Engineering?" *Journal of Conflict, Security, and Development* 1, no. 1 (2001); Organization for Economic Cooperation and Development/Development Assistance Committee (DAC), *Security System Reform and Governance: Policy and Good Practice* (Paris: Organization for Economic Cooperation and Development/DAC, 2004); Heiner Hanggi and Alan Bryden, *Reform and Reconstruction of the Security Sector* (Piscataway, N.J.: Transaction Books, 2003); Jane Chanaa, *Security Sector Reform: Issues, Challenges and Prospects* (Oxford: Oxford University Press, 2002); Scheye and Peake, *Arresting Insecurity;* and Michael Brzoska, "Development Donors and the Concept of Security Sector Reform" (Geneva: Geneva Center for the Democratic Control of Armed Forces, 2003).

14. UK Department for International Development, "Discussion Paper No. 1. Security Sector Reform and the Management of Defence Expenditure: A Conceptual Framework," Annex 3 in *Security Sector Reform and the Management of Military Expenditure: High Risks for Donors, High Returns for Devel-*

opment (report on an international symposium sponsored by the UK Department for International Development, London, February 15–17, 2000, par. 1).

15. "Administration of justice" was the dominant term in the judicial aid area of the U.S. Agency for International Development during the 1980s. See Thomas Carothers, *Aiding Democracy Abroad: The Learning Curve* (Washington, D.C.: Carnegie Endowment for Peace, 1999).

16. UN Development Programme, *Justice and Security Sector Reform: BCPR's Programmatic Approach* (New York: Bureau of Crisis Prevention and Recovery, November 11, 2002).

17. The innovative and useful concept of human security is defined by the Commission on Human Security as the protection of "the vital core of all human lives in ways that enhance human freedoms and human fulfillment." See Commission on Human Security, *Human Security Now* (New York: Commission on Human Security, 2003).

18. John Rawls, *A Theory of Justice* (Cambridge, Mass.: Belknap Press of Harvard University, 1971), 3–17.

19. Charles T. Call, "War Transitions and the New Civilian Security in Latin America," *Comparative Politics* 35, no. 1 (October 2002): 1–20.

20. Charles Tilly, *Coercion, Capital, and European States, AD 990–1990* (Oxford: Blackwell, 1990); and Tilly, *The Formation of National States in Western Europe* (Princeton, N.J.: Princeton University Press, 1975).

21. Roland Paris, *At War's End: Building Peace after Civil Conflict* (Cambridge: Cambridge University Press, 2004); Kimberly Zisk Marten, *Enforcing the Peace: Learning from the Imperial Past* (New York: Columbia University Press, 2004); and Charles T. Call and Susan E. Cook, "Democratization and Peacebuilding," *Global Governance* 9, no. 2 (April–June 2003). For more optimistic views, see Michael Doyle and Nicholas Sambanis, "International Peacebuilding: A Theoretical and Quantitative Analysis," *American Political Science Review* 94, no. 4 (2000): 779–801; Sambanis and Doyle, "Alternative Measures and Estimates of Peacebuilding Success" (unpublished paper, 2005); Francis Fukuyama, *State-Building: Governance and World Order in the 21st Century* (Ithaca, N.Y.: Cornell University Press, 2004); and Timothy Sisk, "Democratization and Peacebuilding," in *Turbulent Peace: The Challenges of Managing International Conflict*, ed. Chester A. Crocker, Fen Osler Hampson, and Pamela Aall (Washington, D.C.: United States Institute of Peace Press, 2001), 785–800.

22. See Seymour Martin Lipset, "Social Conflict, Legitimacy, and Democracy," in *Political Man: The Social Bases of Politics* (Garden City, N.Y.: Anchor Books, 1960); Adam Przeworski, *Democracy and the Market: Political and Economic Reforms in Eastern Europe and Latin America* (Cambridge: Cambridge University Press, 1991); and Larry Diamond, Juan J. Linz, and Seymour

Lipset, *Democracy in Developing Countries* (Boulder, Colo.: Lynne Reinner, 1989). Dietrich Rueschemeyer, Evelyne Huber Stephens, and John D. Stephens reflect a similar approach, rooted in the emergence of a working class, rather than the middle class, in *Capitalist Democracy and Development* (Chicago: University of Chicago Press, 1992).

23. Otwin Marenin, *Policing Change, Changing Police: International Perspectives* (New York: Garland, 1996), 313; David Bayley, "Who Are We Kidding?, or Developing Democracy through Police Reform," in *Policing in Emerging Democracies: Workshop Papers and Highlights* (Washington, D.C.: National Institute of Justice, October 1997), 59–64; Bayley, *Patterns of Policing: A Comparative International Analysis* (New Brunswick, N.J.: Rutgers University Press, 1985); Bayley, "The Limits of Police Reform," in *Police and Society*, ed. David Bayley (Beverly Hills, Calif.: Sage Publications, 1977); and Bayley, "The Police and Political Development in Europe," in *The Formation of National States in Western Europe*, ed. Charles Tilly (Princeton, N.J.: Princeton University Press, 1975).

24. Bayley, "Policing Hate: What Can Be Done?" and *Democratizing the Police Abroad.*

25. See Charles T. Call, "War Transitions and the New Civilian Security in Latin America," *Comparative Politics* 35, no. 1 (October 2002); William D. Stanley, "International Tutelage and Domestic Political Will: Building a New Civilian Police Force in El Salvador," *Studies in Comparative International Development* (May 1995); Mani, *Beyond Retribution;* Bayley, "Who Are We Kidding?, or Developing Democracy through Police Reform"; and Charles T. Call and Michael Barnett, "Looking for a Few Good Cops," *International Peacekeeping* 6, no. 4 (Winter 1999).

26. Tor Tanke Holm and Espen Barth Eide, *Peacebuilding and Police Reform* (London: Frank Cass, 2000); and Robert B. Oakley, Michael J. Dziedzic, and Eliot M. Goldberg, eds., *Policing the New World Disorder: Peace Operations and Public Security* (Washington, D.C.: National Defense University, 1998). See also Robert Perito, *Where Is the Lone Ranger When We Need Him?* (Washington, D.C.: United States Institute of Peace Press, 2004); and Graham Day and Christopher Freeman, "Operationalizing the Responsibility to Protect—the Policekeeping Approach," *Global Governance* 11 (April–June 2005): 139–146.

27. See the Brahimi Panel, *Report of the Panel on United Nations Peace Operations*, A/55/305 (New York: United Nations, 2000); and Kofi Annan, *In Larger Freedom: Towards Development, Security and Human Rights for All* (New York: United Nations, March 2005).

28. In *Policing the New World Disorder*, Oakley, Dziedzic, and Goldberg focus less on outcomes of police reform efforts and more on immediate post-conflict public security gaps and on alternatives to policing roles for international military forces. Holm and Eide's *Peacebuilding and Police Reform* (also published as the winter 1999 issue of *International Peacekeeping*) contains valuable thematic chapters and five case studies but fails to address identical questions and also focuses heavily on the role of international efforts rather than the results obtained. Nor did we the contributors to those volumes satisfactorily integrate judicial institutional development into our analyses of public security. A 1995 UNITAR conference report focused exclusively on the role of the UN Civilian Police rather than local police institutions. See Nassrine Azimi, ed., *The Role and Functions of Civilian Police in United Nations Peacekeeping Operations: Debriefing and Lessons*, report of a 1995 international conference in Singapore (Cambridge, Mass.: Kluwer Law International and UN Institute for Training and Research [UNITAR], 1996).

29. The best of these analyze police and judicial reforms in El Salvador and South Africa. For studies on El Salvador, see Gino Costa, *La Policía Nacional Civil de El Salvador (1990–1997)* (San Salvador: UCA Editores, 1999); Margaret Popkin, *Peace without Justice: Obstacles to Building the Rule of Law in El Salvador* (University Park, Pa.: Pennsylvania State University Press, 2000); Charles T. Call, "From Soldiers to Cops: 'War Transitions' and the Demilitarization of Policing in Latin America and the Caribbean" (Ph.D. diss., Stanford University, 1999); William Stanley and Charles T. Call, "Building a New Civilian Police Force in El Salvador," in *Rebuilding Societies after Civil War*, ed. Krishna Kumar (Boulder, Colo.: Lynne Rienner, 1996); Margaret Popkin et al., *Justice Delayed: The Slow Pace of Judicial Reform in El Salvador* (Boston: Hemisphere Initiatives and WOLA, 1996); and William Stanley, *The Protection Racket State: Elite Politics, Military Extortion and Civil War in El Salvador* (Philadelphia: Temple University Press, 1996). For studies on South Africa, see Mark Malan, "Peacebuilding in Southern Africa: Police Reform in Mozambique and South Africa," in *Peacebuilding and Police Reform*, ed. Holm and Eide; Jeffrey Lever and Elrena van der Spuy, "Challenges Facing Democratic Policing in South Africa" (unpublished paper, 2000); Wilfried Scharf, "Community Justice and Community Policing in Post-Apartheid South Africa: How Appropriate Are the Justice Systems of Africa?" (working paper, Institute of Criminology, University of Cape Town, 2000); Janine Rauch, "Police Reform and South Africa's Transition" (working paper, Institute of Criminology, University of Cape Town, 1998); Graeme Simpson and Janine Rauch, "Reflections on the National Crime Prevention Strategy" (working paper, Centre for the Study of Violence and Reconciliation, Johannesburg, 1996); Mark Shaw, *Point of Order: Negotiating South Africa's New Police Service* (Washington, D.C.: Center for Policy Studies, 2000); and Clifford Shearing, "Reinventing Police: Policing as Governance," in *Policing Change, Changing Police: International Perspectives*, ed. Otwin Marenin (New York: Garland, 1996). See also other case studies in Holm and Eide, *Peacebuilding and Police Reform*; and Oakley, Dziedzic, and Goldberg, *Policing the New World Disorder*.

30. Bayley, "Who Are We Kidding?, or Developing Democracy through Police Reform," 59, 63; Philip B. Heymann, "Principles of Democratic Policing," in *Policing in Emerging Democracies: Workshop Papers and Highlights* (Washington, D.C.: National Institute of Justice, October 1997), 18; and Otwin Marenin, "United States Police Assistance to Emerging Democracies," *Policing and Society* 8 (1998): 153–167.

31. Paris, *At War's End*; Fukuyama, *State-Building*; Zisk Marten, *Enforcing the Peace*; and Stephen John Stedman, Elizabeth Cousens, and Donald Rothchild, eds., *Ending Civil Wars* (Boulder, Colo.: Lynne Rienner, 2003).

32. See Rachel Sieder, "Rethinking Democratization and Citizenship: Legal Pluralism and Institutional Reform in Guatemala," *Citizen Studies* 3 (1999): 1; Mendez, O'Donnell, and Pinheiro, *The (Un)rule of Law and the Underprivileged in Latin America*; Margaret J. Sarles, "USAID's Support for Justice Reform in the Americas," in *Rule of Law in Latin America: The International Promotion of Judicial Reform*, ed. Pilar Domingo and Rachel Sieder (London: University of London Institute of Latin American Studies, 2001), 47–79; and McAdams, *Transitional Justice and the Rule of Law in New Democracies*.

33. Linn Hammergren, *Code Reform and Law Revision* (Washington, D.C.: U.S. Agency for International Development, 1998).

34. Neil Kritz, ed., *Transitional Justice* (Washington, D.C.: United States Institute of Peace Press, 1995); Priscilla Hayner, *Unspeakable Truths: Confronting State Terror and Atrocity* (New York: Routledge, 2000); and Martha Minow, *Between Vengeance and Forgiveness: Facing History after Genocide and Mass Violence* (Boston: Beacon Press, 1998).

35. One exception is Popkin, *Peace Without Justice*.

36. See, for example, the conference "Rebuilding War-Torn Societies: The Squaring of Truth Commission, Police Reform, Economic Development and Justice," Academic Council for the UN System (ACUNS), Yale University, March 2000; and the "Seminar on Peacekeeping and Peace Support Operations," International Peace Academy and Jane's Information Group, New York, November 2000.

37. David Rieff (presentation at "Justice and Local Governance after War: Afghanistan and Beyond," conference cosponsored by Watson Institute for International Studies, Brown University; Human Security Institute, Tufts University; and UN Development Programme, Boston, May 3, 2003).

38. Call, "War Transitions and the New Civilian Security in Latin America."

Part I
Latin America and the Caribbean

2

The Mugging
of a Success Story

Justice and Security Reform in El Salvador

CHARLES T. CALL

After long neglecting issues of citizen security and justice, democratization theorists have recently begun to recognize the importance of the rule of law. Some scholars have also called for more attention to state-building in the developing world.[1] Yet theorizing the construction of state institutions of security and justice has been piecemeal to date. Organization theory, the state-building literature, and cultural theories generally predict that reform is unlikely—difficult, resisted, and slow. Other theories, including those favored by scholars of transitions and postconflict reconstruction, are more optimistic that state-building and constructing the rule of law are possible, often in conjunction with political transitions.[2] Which of these schools of thought is right?

El Salvador's security and justice reforms, undertaken after its 1979–91 civil war, offer an opportunity to explore these competing claims. On conventional criteria, wartime El Salvador represents something between a "hard" and an "easy" case. Although agreement existed about its borders and ethnic tensions were absent, it was a poor country whose armed conflict affected most of its territory and whose political culture was deemed inimical to democracy and institutional reform.

My main argument is threefold. First, the case of El Salvador shows that justice and security are tremendously important for the survivability of democracy and its relevance for everyday life. Citizens' top sustained concern after the country's transition from authoritarian rule was crime; in 1999, 55 percent of Salvadorans cited crime as a justification for the toppling of democracy, twice as many people as cited any other reason.[3] Crime, rather than the military or economic crisis, represents the biggest threat to democracy in some countries.

Second, the Salvadoran experience indicates that, yes, statebuilding is possible in poor, postconflict societies but with certain patterns and limits. The case broadly confirms path-dependent "mode-of-transition" approaches that postulate heightened agency to adopt new rules and reform institutions during the uncertainty of transition periods. However, security reforms operate differently than judicial reforms. Military and police reforms conform more closely to the mode-of-transition approach than judicial reforms, occurring mainly during the window of opportunity provided by transitions and less likely before that window opens and after it has closed.[4] Even so, cultural and institutional skeptics are right to point to constraints, as the *formal* removal of authoritarian structures and personnel is easier than the *informal* transformation of state institutions and of society's attitudes about and demands from state services. Successful civilianization of internal security in El Salvador did not produce representative and accountable "democratic policing."[5] As in most industrialized democracies, police reforms occurred only in response to scandals once El Salvador's peace process was concluded.[6]

Third, judicial reforms were also tied to the opening provided by political transition but proved more feasible both before and after the country's peace process. The negotiations enhanced judicial independence from the executive and professional standards, but the justice system continued to be politicized, slow, and held in low regard. Institutional, economic, and cultural factors partly explain this pattern. Interestingly, the sharp postwar wave of violent crime also explains the pattern of judicial reform. Although the crime wave was the biggest obstacle to security and justice reforms, it also generated constituencies for new reforms outside the context of the peace process and sparked creative new strategies for reducing violence and improving justice. The crime wave underlies the most interesting paradox of El Salvador's police and justice reforms: international observers consider them a success story, but Salvadorans do not. This contradiction, reflecting divergent interests between international actors and citizens of postconflict societies, also points to the lack of conceptual agreement on what aspects of judicial and security reforms are important.

CIVIL WAR AND PEACE IN EL SALVADOR

In a ceremony in January 1992, the leftist Farabundo Martí National Liberation Front (FMLN) and the right-wing Salvadoran government, led by President Alfredo Cristiani, signed a global peace accord ending twelve years of civil war in a tiny Central American country that had become a Cold War battleground. Ten years later, El Salvador was widely considered one of the most successful negotiated settlements to a civil war in the world. The cease-fire between the two sides was never broken. By 1994 guerrilla forces were demobilized and reconstituted as a political party; significant demilitarization of society and the state had taken place; and elections had transformed the former guerrillas into the second most powerful party in the country. The peace accords were the catalyst for the incipient institutionalization of political democracy in El Salvador.[7]

The character of the Salvadoran war shaped the peace. Civil war was rooted in class and ideological, rather than religious or ethnic, divisions. A small number of landed elites controlled the state in alliance with a powerful military that guaranteed order in exchange for resources and autonomy.[8] The trappings of democracy coexisted with authoritarianism. Periodic, flawed elections occurred under a constitution between 1948 and 1979, in which military officers usually won the presidency.

Three features of the war influenced security and justice reforms. First, the peace emerged from a "strategic stalemate," in which each side eventually recognized its inability to defeat the other.[9] Second, international actors played an important role. The United States provided $3.2 billion in economic aid and $1.1 billion in military aid between 1980 and 1991, which was indispensable in preventing an FMLN victory.[10] After the fall of the Berlin Wall in 1989, the main international support for both parties declined, and both the Soviet Union and the new Bush administration backed a negotiated settlement. The United Nations played an important role in mediating the negotiations held between 1990 and 1992. Finally, human rights occupied a central place in the war, at home and abroad. An estimated 75,000 persons died during the war, the majority of whom were civilians killed at the hands of the government security forces and their affiliated death squads. Atrocities committed in El Salvador's civil war received tremendous international attention and sparked intense U.S. policy debate and scrutiny.[11]

THE PEACE AGREEMENT AND SECURITY AND JUSTICE REFORMS

Before and during the war, internal security was wholly militarized, and no police reforms occurred except to enhance the security forces' capacity to carry out counterinsurgency.[12] The Defense Ministry had constitutional responsibility for internal security and controlled the three main police forces: the urban National Police, the rural National Guard, and the Treasury Police. Death squads operated especially out of the police forces and military intelligence, although mainline army units committed massacres and torture during the war.

Impunity for human rights abuses, a central weakness of the security forces, reflected broader problems of the judiciary. El Salvador's three constitutional branches of government had existed for decades, but the courts and the formal judiciary remained highly politicized, corrupt, and unprofessional. Judges routinely retained part-time private practices to supplement low salaries. During the war, judges often took bribes, including from those representing accused guerrillas, and were often threatened or killed. Before 1991 not a single army officer was convicted of a serious human rights violation.

The Peace Agreement

El Salvador's peace agreement contained sweeping military and police reforms, with less ambitious, though still important, judicial reforms. Remarkable for their level of detail, the final accords provided the framework for security and justice policy for several years. Although radical change of the economic structure of the country was a central FMLN objective throughout the war, only about 10 percent of the final accords were dedicated to social and economic issues.

Cease-fire Provisions and Security Reforms

The cease-fire included concentration of the two military forces in specified sites in early 1992, followed by downsizing of the government army and the graduated demobilization and disarmament of guerrillas over a nine-month period. In addition, the military would abdicate all internal security functions except in unusual circumstances. Its three police forces would be dissolved, to be replaced by a single new National Civilian Police known by its Spanish acronym, PNC, outside military control, comprising at least 60 percent civilians who had had no combat role in the conflict. Paramilitary civil defense groups were disbanded. The military-controlled National Intelligence Directorate was replaced by a State Intelligence Organization (OIE) run by a civilian reporting directly to the president and supervised by the legislature.

Human Rights and Justice Reforms

The agreement created an Ad Hoc Commission to review the files of military officers and to recommend names to be purged; a UN-supervised Commission on the Truth for El Salvador (Truth Commission) to prepare a report assigning responsibility for the most egregious human rights violations of the war; and a Human Rights Ombudsperson's Office, headed by a mediator chosen by the legislature and independent of the executive, to receive complaints about, investigate, and report on human rights violations. Judicial reforms, less extensive than the reforms to coercive forces, included increasing the autonomy of the National Judicial Council from the powerful and politicized Supreme Court and restricting judges' ability to act as notaries public and thereby enter into conflicts of interest.

Mechanisms for Implementation

The accords stipulated that a National Commission for the Consolidation of Peace (COPAZ), comprising two representatives each from the government and the FMLN, plus one representative from each of several political parties, would be "responsible for overseeing the implementation of all the political agreements reached by the Parties."[13] With the signing of the final accord, a UN Mission in El Salvador (ONUSAL) was expanded to include the "verification and monitoring of the implementation of all the agreements" (Security Council Resolution 729), and the UN mission, supported by key countries (the "Four Friends plus One": Colombia, Venezuela, Mexico, Spain, and the United States), played an indispensable role in implementation.

THE EVOLUTION OF SECURITY REFORMS

Relative to that of other peace processes, implementation of El Salvador's peace accords enjoyed remarkable success. After foot-dragging, the government dismantled the National Guard and the Treasury Police and quartered its troops. The FMLN demobilized its 12,362 troops by December 1992, transforming itself into an active but divided political party.[14] The governing party, the Nationalist Republican Alliance (ARENA), won the presidency and a majority of both legislative seats and municipal governments in March 1994, a result recognized by all parties. The FMLN became the second most powerful party in the country, losing the presidential elections to ARENA in 1999 and 2004 but gaining a plurality of seats in the legislature in 2000 and control of the country's main city governments. In the security area—military, intelligence, and policing—civilianization was largely achieved.

Purging and Reforming the Military and Intelligence Units

Many provisions of the peace agreement aimed to transform the repressive and powerful armed forces. Unlike the FMLN, the government did not agree to dismantle its military forces; therefore, guerrillas and other groups considered institutional reforms to the military extremely important, not only as a guarantee for the FMLN's return to civilian life but also for the possibility of full democratization.

Most military leaders, not having been defeated on the battlefield, continued to view the FMLN as an illegitimate force and to reject any intrusion by civilians into military affairs. Because most of the commitments lay on the government's shoulders rather than the guerrillas', and because the military was probably the sector most resistant to the accords, much of the implementation phase focused on overcoming military opposition.

After resistance and delays, the military accepted most institutional changes: the dissolution of the three police forces under its control, the circumscribing of its internal security functions, the dismantling of paramilitary civil defense forces, the suspension of forced recruitment, and the modification of its doctrine and training under an Academic Council that included civilians of diverse political backgrounds. It also reduced its ranks ahead of schedule, dropping from 63,170 troops as of 1992 to some 30,500 by 1994, although this dramatic reduction was probably overstated owing to thousands of "ghost soldiers" on the original rosters, whose salaries were pocketed by corrupt officers.[15]

The new State Intelligence Organization was created under civilian presidential supervision, but the intelligence system remained highly military in character. It drew on old military intelligence personnel. In addition, the military continued to oversee the country's National Intelligence School, effectively expanding its coverage to civilians, and the Defense Ministry's intelligence units continued to focus on internal intelligence activities.[16]

Although the Ad Hoc Commission and the UN Truth Commission failed to bring the worst perpetrators of human rights abuses to justice in court, they helped to gain official acknowledgment of the government's atrocities and to shame some of the perpetrators. The Ad Hoc Commission, composed of three Salvadorans, was tasked with reviewing 2,293 officer files in four months, and few expected it would have much effect. In September 1992, however, the Ad Hoc Commission recommended the removal or transfer of 103 officers, including the minister and vice minister of defense, most of the generals, and many colonels.[17] Although military officers denounced the recommendations and President Cristiani refused to cashier all those named, in June 1994 the last of the officers were retired.

The purge of these senior commanders, the most thorough housecleaning ever of a Latin American army not defeated in war,[18] was made possible only by the report of the UN Truth Commission, a panel of three international notables. Published in March 1993, the Truth Commission report named the individual military officers and other persons responsible for the worst human rights violations during the war. Most damaging was the description of the role that Defense Minister Rene Emilio Ponce played during a meeting with his top commanders when he ordered the widely publicized 1989 massacre of six Jesuit priests and two female assistants.

The peace accord and the international pressure to comply with its provisions constituted indispensable conditions (absent an FMLN victory) for ousting these senior officers. The government's eventual compliance was influenced largely by pressure from the United Nations and donor countries. The newly elected Clinton administration threatened to withhold $11 million in U.S. military aid unless the government abided by the Ad Hoc Commission's report.

All in all, remarkable progress was achieved in military reform. For the first time in history, a Latin American military submitted its officer corps to external review and vetting. Its worst human rights violators were purged; its budget was reduced; and new levels of accountability and civilian input were reached. As of 2004, the army was roughly the same size as the PNC, and its missions and doctrine reflected significant emphasis on classic external defense functions and respect for human rights and for civilian control. The military generally did not challenge its postwar place in society.

At the same time, informal attitudes showed continuity and prior practices persisted. Much of the population viewed the military positively ten years after the war.[19] The armed forces continued to carry out internal security functions and retained a strong sense of institutional autonomy. In July 1993 President Cristiani called out the armed forces to patrol the highways as a means of curbing rising violent crime, including highway robberies, without seeking the requisite congressional approval. Additional internal security roles followed, including patrols of the annual coffee harvest as well as joint patrols with the new police force in which military personnel greatly outnumbered police officers.[20] Many officers bristled at the notion of civilian oversight or input, and the defense minister remained an active-duty general in 2004. Free from fear of prosecution, former military officers were active in business and held elected office.

Public Security and Police Reforms

Ten years after the war, perhaps the most acclaimed aspect of reconstruction in El Salvador remained the public security reforms set forth in the peace accords. The creation of the PNC was crucial for peace and democracy in El Salvador for several reasons. First, the agreement to integrate ex-combatants into the police unraveled what UN mediator Álvaro de Soto called the "Gordian knot" of the negotiations, namely, the army's refusal to accept the FMLN demand to incorporate its troops into the army. Instead, the FMLN settled for incorporation of its combatants into a new police force dominated by noncombatants and with a new civilian doctrine oriented toward protecting citizens rather than the state. Government negotiator David Escobar Galindo called the PNC the most significant *("más transcendental")* institution to come out of the reforms,[21] and UN secretary-general Boutros Boutros-Ghali hailed the new police force in 1995 as "one of the fundamental elements of the peace accords and perhaps the single component with greatest hopes."[22]

Those high hopes were initially met. In March 1993 the population of Chalatenango, a guerrilla stronghold, lined the roads to welcome the first deployments of the PNC, commanded by Subcommissioner Carlos López, a former urban FMLN commander. His second in command, Subcommissioner Luís Tobar Prieto, had been a National Police investigator. Tobar Prieto's reflections two years later illustrate the impressive degree of political integration and transformed attitudes during the early days of the PNC:

> Perhaps for those of us who lived that experience [the war] for ten or twelve years, the experience of Chalatenango was good for us, and for me personally it was excellent. We arrived there, a new police force with 19 posts, 400 people, to cover the department of Chalatenango. . . . I've always said the enthusiasm for work of those first classes of the PNC is incredible—people who came from

different backgrounds having lived through the war, but people
with the new doctrine, a new philosophy, convinced that there
had to be a change.[23]

The PNC quickly dismantled a criminal gang, and deployments to
other areas of strong guerrilla sympathy followed. In a December
1993 survey in those areas, 71 percent of respondents approved of the
work of the PNC and only 2 percent saw it as "bad" or "very bad."[24]

By 1994 the PNC had deployed to the remainder of the country, amid public demands for even quicker deployment. The decision
to mix ex-guerrillas, ex–National Police officers, and civilian commanders inside each territorial delegation helped prevent the force
from reproducing partisan divisions while providing sufficient security guarantees to the FMLN and its supporters.

The process of political integration and civilianization within
the police encountered obstacles and resistance, commanding significant UN attention.[25] Initially, the government and the military
resisted demobilizing the old security forces, withheld promised
resources, and successfully "smuggled" into the police academy military personnel who failed to meet the agreed-on conditions. Although
the existence of the PNC was never in question, uncertainty prevailed throughout the transition about whether the new police would,
as prescribed under the new constitutional provisions, supplant the
military, intelligence agencies, and prior police forces as the sole
source of internal security. In the hardest-fought struggle, the prior
Anti-narcotics Unit and a Special Investigations Unit were initially
transferred wholesale into the new police, in an apparent violation of
the accords and despite the reported presence of dirty cops in both.[26]
After significant UN pressure, members of the units were subjected
to individual scrutiny. Several resigned en masse, while others entered
the PNC, but two years were lost in the detailed negotiations. The
FMLN, especially after the discovery of an illegal arms cache in late
1993, acquiesced to government noncompliance on several issues
related to the PNC in exchange for immediate benefits, complicating
the United Nations' role.

Problems among former enemies inside the police were surprisingly few. Some academy cadets were hazed due to their political

past, and ex-guerrillas and ex–army officers sometimes expressed distrust of one another and disdain for civilians' lack of operational experience. Nevertheless, in only a few years, former FMLN commanders worked alongside ex-lieutenants of the old security forces with relatively few problems. Former guerrillas ceased to be active in partisan activities.[27] By 2002 some PNC officers and analysts believed that ex-guerrillas and civilians felt a sense of marginalization in the hierarchy, and the numbers showed that promotions had favored former military officers.[28] In the end, the incorporation of former enemies provided important security guarantees for the peace process and internal checks on police partisanship.

The Postwar Crime Wave

But ineffectiveness proved to be the Achilles' heel of the new police and justice system. The first signs of rising crime were documented in 1992 polling data, where crime almost tripled in frequency as a perceived problem facing the country.[29] Between 1993 and 1999, crime would consistently be ranked as the most important problem facing the country in surveys conducted by the Central American University's Public Opinion Institute (IUDOP).[30] In the 1993 survey, 88.6 percent believed crime to have increased and more than two-thirds were afraid of being assaulted in their own homes.[31] According to the same poll, 76 percent of respondents routinely failed to notify the authorities when victimized by a crime and 34 percent stated that they or an immediate family member had been robbed during the previous four months. Although ONUSAL initially downplayed the crime wave as a product of media hype, the mission's own crime statistics showed a 300 percent increase in crime between January and September 1993. Survey data show how crime supplanted war and politics as the "main problem" facing the country between 1991 and 1994, right as the war terminated (see figure 2-1). In mid-1993 crime became the "main problem facing the country" in people's eyes, and it topped the charts consistently until 2002.

National-level crime statistics confirmed people's perceptions. From 1992 to 1994, reported homicides rose from 3,229 annually to 7,673.[32] Kidnappings for ransom increased dramatically, and armed robberies of banks, armored cars, and automobiles became daily fare.

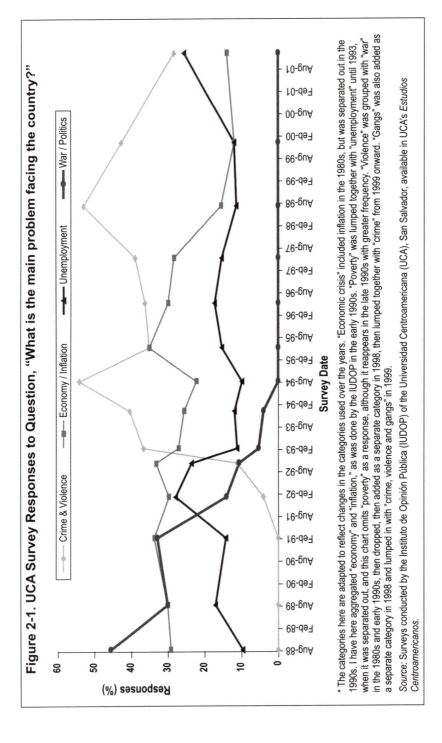

Figure 2-1. UCA Survey Responses to Question, "What is the main problem facing the country?"

* The categories here are adapted to reflect changes in the categories used over the years. "Economic crisis" included inflation in the 1980s, but was separated out in the 1990s. I have here aggregated "economy" and "inflation," as was done by the IUDOP in the early 1990s. "Poverty" was lumped together with "unemployment" until 1993, when it was separated out, and this chart omits "poverty" as a response, although it reappears in the late 1990s with greater frequency. "Violence" was grouped with "war" in the 1980s and early 1990s, then dropped, then added as a separate category in 1998, then lumped together with "crime" from 1999 onward. "Gangs" was also added as a separate category in 1998 and lumped in with "crime, violence and gangs" in 1999.

Source: Surveys conducted by the Instituto de Opinión Pública (IUDOP) of the Universidad Centroamericana (UCA), San Salvador, available in UCA's *Estudios Centroamericanos.*

By 1995 deaths by homicide exceeded the average annual number of deaths *during the twelve-year war,* and in 1996 El Salvador's homicide rate reached 139 per 100,000, the second highest in the world.[33] Political commentators noted how the country's major newspapers had become virtual crime reports, as the first few pages routinely were dedicated to the previous day's worst crimes and most significant arrests. The country's homicide rate rose immediately after the war (earlier statistics are not reliably available) and stayed extremely high throughout the 1990s.

Significant discrepancies exist among different government agencies' statistics for that decade. More careful analysis reveals that the attorney general's data probably exaggerated homicide rates, and problems with all data sources are evident.[34] Nevertheless, adjusted homicide rates still show El Salvador among the most violent countries in the world.

The crime wave appeared to crest in 1996, dropped in 1998, and then rose again when kidnappings and armed robberies peaked in 2000. The reasons for this pattern are unclear. Knowledgeable Salvadorans do not agree on these causes or on the veracity of the data. Victimization surveys—generally considered the best indicator of crime trends—show that crime declined after 1994 and diminished at an even higher rate in the late 1990s (see figure 2-2).

Given the perceived inability of the government to deliver justice and security, a surprisingly high portion of the population—46 percent—believed in 1996 that people had a right to take justice into their own hands. In some cases, people bypassed the judicial system. Between December 1994 and March 1995, a clandestine group calling itself the Black Shadow claimed responsibility for assassinating sixteen known criminals who had avoided prosecution in the eastern city of San Miguel. Five PNC officers, including the departmental commander, and several prominent citizens were arrested and charged in 1995, and the killings stopped. Alarmingly, public opinion was evenly divided between support for and repudiation of this "death squad" for common criminals.

In the face of the sustained crime wave in the late 1990s, the private sector, the media, nongovernmental organizations (NGOs), and new government bodies became involved in public security

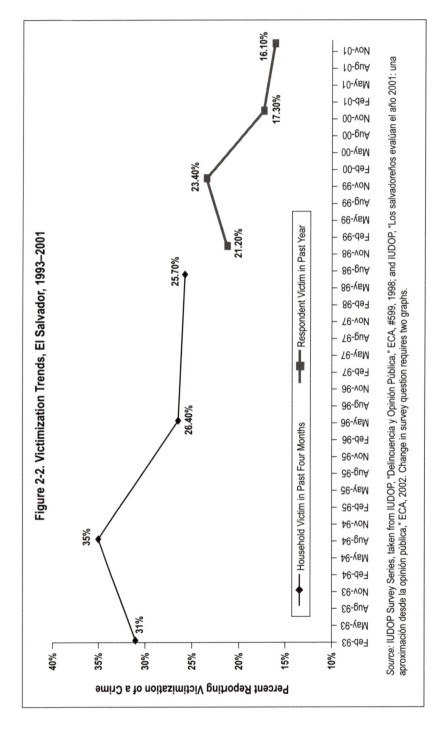

Figure 2-2. Victimization Trends, El Salvador, 1993–2001

Source: IUDOP Survey Series, taken from IUDOP, "Delincuencia y Opinión Pública," ECA, #599, 1998; and IUDOP, "Los salvadoreños evalúan el año 2001: una aproximación desde la opinión pública," ECA, 2002. Change in survey question requires two graphs.

policy. A blue-ribbon National Public Security Commission, formed in 1994 to keep police reforms on track, received policymaking authority under President Francisco Flores in 1999 and sought to develop comprehensive, long-range plans for crime prevention and reduction. In addition, active private security firms, regulated only loosely, skyrocketed from fewer than 10 in 1992 to more than 80 in 1995, and 265 in 2001.[35] Private security agents grew in number from 6,000 in 1996 to 18,943 by 2001, fostering concerns about unequal access to security and inadequate oversight of firms composed mainly of ex-soldiers. Legislation aiming to strengthen oversight and transparency of private agencies took effect in 2001.

Ironically, the very same conditions that made security reforms possible—that is, the transition from war cum democratization—also created obstacles to reform. The end of civil war and the political transition fueled a dramatic rise in crime for several reasons. First, the vast majority of combatants were demobilized over an extremely brief period when the war ended. Within one year, 12,362 guerrillas, some 20,000 soldiers, and about 30,000 civil defense guards were left unemployed. The number of persons circulating under arms decreased from 60,000 (including combatants on both sides) to only about 6,000 National Police officers, as all armed forces personnel were confined to quarters during the demobilization process in early 1992, leaving a public security gap.[36] The peace processes in both El Salvador and Nicaragua left thousands of weapons in civilian hands. In 2000, the Defense Ministry reported 165,186 firearms registered for personal or commercial use and an estimated 200,000 additional unregistered.[37]

Transaction costs of security reform also abetted growing crime. Disruption of the internal security system took its toll, and the eventual turnover of almost all the investigative units meant that networks of informants had to be reconstructed. A large number of former combatants were also implicated in criminal activity, sometimes working together in gangs. A 1999 survey sample of the country's prison inmates found that 22 percent of them had been members of the armed forces or the old security forces and 6 percent were ex-guerrillas.[38] Of prisoners between twenty-six and forty years of age, 44 percent were ex-combatants, even though only 6 percent of the general population had served in the war. Furthermore, while the retention of relatively few former police helped vacate a prior institutional culture of impunity and military-style policing, it also left fewer experienced police on the force. Even the former officers of the old security forces were fairly junior—none above the rank of lieutenant—with few years on the job when the war ended. Of course, the policing experience obtained during the war was not desirable preparation for civilian policing.

Shortcomings of Security Reforms

If more pessimistic advocates of cultural and state-building approaches cannot account for the rapid demilitarization of El Salvador's security system, they seem to accurately portray the difficulties of transforming day-to-day practices of security forces. The successful formal reform of policing did not lead to fully accountable, responsive citizen-oriented public security. Difficulties are visible in three areas.

First, corruption appeared to abate in the first years of the PNC's existence, but to worsen subsequently. As the number of high-profile kidnappings and other violent crimes grew in 1999, the involvement of PNC officers in these crimes also visibly increased. In 2000 the main quick-response unit was dismantled in its entirety because many of its members had formed a crime racket. One reason for escalating corruption as the force grew was ineffective internal discipline and control, preserving some of the authoritarian ways of dealing with the public. Following press reports of police involvement in several serious crimes in early 2000, the legislature granted the PNC director new interim powers to purge the police force. The *"depuración,"* probably the highest-profile experience of the PNC between 1998 and 2002, resulted in the dismissal of 1,215 officers and administrative personnel between August 2000 and December 2001, not counting another 1,485 persons dismissed through normal channels in 2000–2001.[39] This limited purge and reform, occurring well after the peace process concluded, seems to confirm the idea that scandal is most likely to spark police reform once a transition period is over.[40]

A second arena of continuity with prior policing was social expectations and relations with the coercive apparatus of the state. Changing institutions proved easier than changing state-society relations, and civilianization brought only a partial redefinition of police-society relations. Although many citizens reported less fear of approaching members of the police, the PNC's relations with society did not exhibit the trust and integration common in many industrialized democracies. As one man described to me after his car was stolen, "I wouldn't just go into a police station. I call my friends who are in the PNC when I need help."[41] The establishment of emergency services (911) for city and town dwellers with access to a telephone hastened police response, but also frustration in light of new expectations of practically immediate response. In a 1996 poll, 56 percent of respondents expressed "little" or "no" confidence in the PNC, 28 percent said they had "some" confidence in the PNC, and only 15 percent expressed "much" confidence in the new police force.[42] By 2001 the numbers had improved, as 25 percent expressed having "much" confidence in the police force and 45 percent expressed little or no confidence.

The difficulties of community policing experiments illustrate the problems of police-society relations. Early efforts by Security Minister Hugo Barrera to create a "neighborhood watch" program met with legislative objections and were widely viewed as a way for police to gather more intelligence on community members, possibly for partisan advantage. A pilot project ended after one of its leaders was found dead under mysterious circumstances. A second community policing initiative died with the change of government in 1999. The PNC maintained "Community-Oriented Policing" offices that acted mainly as public relations offices.

A final U.S.-funded program initiative called Community Police Intervention Patrols (PIP-COM) was linked to community policing but was widely recognized instead as targeted and active patrolling of regular routes.[43] The PIP-COM program illustrates the challenges of transforming the mentality of police officers. Encouraged to fill out "citizen contact cards" to gather information on suspects in neighborhoods, some PNC agents instead used the cards to gather data on all citizens with whom they had contact, including victims.[44] Although regular meetings with communities were held, agents sought to share and gather information more than to respond to community input.

A third arena illustrating the limits of reform is human rights. With the end of the war, political violence declined markedly. The United Nations reported a significant improvement in human rights between 1991 and 1995, including the complete cessation of "disappearances."[45] Detainees were routinely tortured before and during the war, but only nine cases of torture were reported to ONUSAL in the first nine months of 1993.[46] The Human Rights Institute of the University of Central America (IDHUCA) reported only twelve killings attributed to police or military forces in 1995, in contrast to an annual average of thousands during the war.[47] These dozen alleged killings were many times fewer than the 488 deaths attributed to common criminals during the same period. A "Joint Group," formed jointly of the United Nations and the Salvadoran government, helped deter political violence in the period leading up to the March 1994 "elections of the century."

As is typical of successful peace processes, state human rights violations increasingly took the form of excessive or otherwise illegal use of force by police officers against suspected common criminals. In 1997–98, for example, the Human Rights Ombudsperson reported 72 allegations of arbitrary killings (many involving police use of force), 15 allegations of forced disappearances, 12 complaints of torture, 799 cases of mistreatment, 447 complaints of arbitrary detention, and 931 complaints of lack of due process (e.g., slow justice, insufficient defense counsel, etc.).[48] These allegations do not represent verified violations of human rights—on investigation, for example, none of the cases of forced disappearances proved valid. By far, the most common perpetrators of violations of civil and political rights were not the military or the judiciary but the National Civilian Police.[49] These deficiencies tainted the reputation of the PNC, which, while viewed as the single institution that most defended human rights in communities, also was perceived as the organization that most *violated* human rights.[50]

Summing Up Security Reforms

The shape of police and military reforms was dictated largely by a highly detailed blueprint laid out in the peace agreements. Future-looking institutional reforms were rooted in the past, concerned especially with curbing the power of the armed forces in internal security and intelligence. As of 2004, El Salvador's touted police reform showed significant achievements. The public security system remained firmly under civilian control, significantly more accountable to elected authorities than any prior security force. The PNC was perceived by the population as the principal source of public order, citizen security, and criminal investigations in the country, and a principal defender of human rights. A poll conducted in 1995 showed that 49 percent of respondents believed that the PNC's conduct was better than that of the old National Police, whereas only 18 percent thought it worse.[51] Donors drew on El Salvador's police reforms as a model, and international police aid experts generally regarded the country's police reforms as the most successful postconflict internal security reforms of the decade.[52]

Political integration and civilianization of policing proceeded more successfully than the development of crime control capabilities. Despite positive sentiments about the young police officers and their work, many doubted their abilities. The PNC received high marks for its first deployments, but public confidence fell as the new force assumed security for the entire country and seemed unable to stem the crime wave. Improved civilian control and accountability failed to eliminate problems of ineffectiveness, abuse, and corruption. Nor did successful civilianization of the organizational hierarchies of police and intelligence ensure the civilianization of police interaction with citizens. International actors were pleased that security reforms unfolded roughly as agreed on in the peace process, especially given the poor record of security reform projects elsewhere. Yet the attitude of Salvadorans was decidedly more mixed. I turn now to issues of justice, where expectations were lower and obstacles higher.

THE EVOLUTION OF JUSTICE REFORMS

The Salvadoran conflict helped bring human rights to the fore of international discourse and activity during the 1980s. It is unsurprising that much of the peace agreement focused on ways to prevent human rights abuses in the future. These provisions, however, focused more on the security arena and on redressing past abuses than on constructing a reformed judiciary. El Salvador's justice reforms had their origins during the war, were advanced by a few provisions of the agreement, deepened through the Truth Commission's report, and subsequently evolved due to international funding and pressure, the crime wave's impact, and civil society's activism. Although international analysts did not consider the country's justice reforms a model, they viewed the experience as a moderate success.

Wartime Judicial Reform Efforts

Unlike in many other armed conflicts, El Salvador's criminal justice reforms were initiated, though without much success, during the war itself. Corruption, cronyism, and subordination of the criminal justice system to the executive all increased under the pressures of the armed conflict. Fear played an important role in judicial inaction on human rights violations.

During this period, U.S. assistance provided the engine for judicial reform efforts.[53] Expenditures for the United States Agency for International Development's (USAID) bilateral Administration of Justice (AOJ) project for El Salvador, its first in Latin America, totaled $9.2 million between 1984 and 1989. The U.S. project concentrated on gaining convictions in high-profile cases, especially when the victims were U.S. citizens.[54] It also supported judicial training and the creation of a Salvadoran Legal Reform Commission (CORELESAL) to draft new laws.

Faced with an evident lack of political will among Salvadoran elites to support comprehensive reform, wartime judicial reform efforts focused instead on improving technical capabilities such as caseloads, case management, judicial administration, police investigative skills, and forensics capabilities.[55] Strikingly absent from these efforts were plans to address the questions of power over the justice system, the independence of the judiciary, and the integrity of the process (even FMLN-affiliated groups bribed judges to free people from jail).[56] Despite their shortcomings, USAID-funded efforts to redress human rights violations assuaged congressional reservations and ensured continued flow of U.S. military and other assistance through the 1980s, responding to overriding U.S. counterinsurgency aims.

Unsurprisingly, these efforts did virtually nothing to spark prosecution for political murders, enhance judicial independence from the executive, or alleviate fear of violence among lawyers, prosecutors, and judges.[57] Military, political, and economic elites—including the entrenched right-wing Supreme Court—stymied reform. From the start of the war to this writing, no intellectual author of a war-related killing has ever been convicted.

At the same time, El Salvador's experience illustrates that some wartime judicial reform efforts may be worthwhile. Judicial reforms undertaken during El Salvador's war lay the groundwork for new attitudes about judicial independence and accountability and advanced modernization of certain codes. CORELESAL drafted new criminal procedure codes, new criminal codes, and new family and juvenile justice codes that all became the core of new laws after the conflict. Furthermore, the U.S.-funded efforts helped develop greater support within the legal community for increasing judicial independence and for reducing the tremendous power of the Supreme Court over the entire judiciary. In contrast to these judicial reforms, police reform efforts undertaken during the heat of El Salvador's war yielded few benefits and implicated donors in the security forces' human rights violations.

The Truth Commission

El Salvador's war crimes were addressed through a combination of purges, truth telling, and institutional reforms to government security and judicial institutions. The Ad Hoc Commission and the UN Truth Commission became the main vehicles for both purging the armed forces and exposing their involvement in egregious human rights violations. Unlike with more recent processes, no prosecutions for atrocities occurred after the war because of the amnesty law passed in 1993.[58] Instead, days after the Truth Commission released its report, the legislature quickly heeded President Cristiani's call to pass a sweeping amnesty law. Understood to bar criminal prosecutions, civil suits, and judicial investigations into the fate of victims, the law also extended immunity from prosecution to the FMLN's members for political crimes. Victims received no reparations.[59]

The first step to securing judicial integrity during the peace process was the establishment of the Truth Commission, which remains the most visible mechanism addressing past atrocities in El Salvador. The Truth Commission was charged with investigating "grave acts of violence" after 1980. It investigated thirty-two prominent cases and described the nature of death squad organizations during the war. The commission's report named sixty-two military officers, six FMLN leaders, and several civilians as having committed or covered up the country's most serious wartime human rights violations.[60] It estimated that the military and paramilitary death squads were responsible for 95 percent of all human rights abuses committed between 1980 and 1992 and that the FMLN was responsible for the remainder. As described earlier, the report effectively ended the military careers of those named in it. The Truth Commission's report had a tremendous impact, affecting the military institution, the reputations and electoral possibilities of leaders from both sides of the war, and the pace and depth of reforms to the institutions of human rights and justice.

The Truth Commission also made a series of recommendations for reforms to the judicial system. The commission surprised the government by calling for the resignation of the entire sitting Supreme Court and for further decentralization and depoliticization of the court system. Explicitly doubting that El Salvador's weak judicial system would be capable of prosecuting those named in its report, the Truth Commission recommended instead that they be barred from holding public office for at least ten years, with a permanent ban on holding defense or internal security posts.

Although both sides had agreed to abide by the Truth Commission's findings, the government quickly made clear that it would not do so. Members of the government negotiating team criticized the commission's work as biased and exceeding its original mandate.[61] The chief justice of the Supreme Court, ARENA-appointed Mauricio Gutiérrez Castro, defiantly announced that the peace accords were an agreement of the executive branch and did not touch the judiciary, and that "only God" could remove him from his post.[62] The government and the FMLN eventually ignored the suggested ban on holding public office, and some alleged perpetrators sought and won seats in the Assembly.

Several weaknesses undermined the power of the Truth Commission's recommendations. It operated under a short, six-month life span and omitted hundreds of extrajudicial executions and kidnappings, selecting only exemplary cases. In addition, the Truth Commission's methods discouraged confessions by perpetrators, perversely punishing those who came forward and acknowledged their role. Finally, victims received little attention. Only a handful of the 75,000 victims' families received information about the fate of their loved ones, and none received psychological services or compensation, although the Truth Commission called for reparations and other steps toward reconciliation.[63] Nevertheless, the Truth Commission represented perhaps the most important public instrument of truth, accountability, and an end to impunity ever to emerge in El Salvador. Its recommendations lay the foundation for subsequent enhancement of judicial independence and professionalism.

Judicial Independence and Accountability

The Salvadoran case illustrates the difficulty and resistance that judicial reforms, even more than police reforms, are likely to confront unless the judicial branch has already been completely disarticulated. Given the adamant resistance by the Supreme Court to reforming the judicial system, few changes occurred until after the new government and Assembly took office in mid-1994. After lengthy partisan debate, a new Supreme Court was elected in conformity with the process contained in the constitutional amendments passed as part of the peace process. The National Judiciary Council and civil society, through the bar association, submitted ranked nominations for Supreme Court magistrates to the Legislative Assembly, which approved its choices by a two-thirds majority to staggered terms of nine years, rather than the previous terms, which coincided with the electoral cycle.

The resulting Supreme Court was decidedly more professional, more politically plural, and less partisan, although political party ties continued to be important in the selection process. As justices supported by the left, center, and right parties were named to the bench, the justice reforms could be said to have *pluralized* the courts more than *depoliticized* them, but with improved merit standards. Indeed, some believe that partisan wrangling and political criteria became more important in the 1997 and 2000 selection processes of Supreme Court magistrates. El Salvador's short experience thus far casts doubt on the proposition that pluralization will lead to depoliticization of the judiciary.

Despite some important steps toward devolving the power of the Supreme Court to lower courts and to the National Judiciary Council, the judicial system remained highly centralized. In particular, the Supreme Court retained a determinant voice in the selection and removal of lower-court judges. In 1994 the National Judiciary Council was able to commence a process of reviewing judges. Investigations launched into judges' records by a Department of Investigations created by the Supreme Court resulted in a high number of suspensions and other sanctions against lower-court judges. However, when the term (1994–97) of the first postwar chief justice ended, only 31 judges out of 520 had been removed, only one officially for corruption.[64] Five years later, the Supreme Court still seemed reluctant to discipline lower judges. Despite recommendations by the National Judiciary Council to sanction 230 judges based on its 2000–2001 evaluations, the court disciplined only 19 judges in 1999, 15 in 2000, and 48 in 2001.[65]

The Attorney General's Office and Criminal Procedure

Beyond the courts and police, among the most important areas of judicial reform in El Salvador was the legal system, whose transformation involved changes in the role of the attorney general's office, in criminal law, and in procedures for administering justice. Under the Continental inquisitive system of justice historically prevalent in Latin America, the instructing judge was charged with directing investigations, supervising the work of police and prosecutors. Unlike with the Anglo-American accusatory system's reliance on oral trials and competing cases presented by the defense and the prosecution, instructing judges primarily sift through written evidence to determine guilt or innocence. The peace process, international trends, and U.S. aid contributed to a transformation of the judicial system in

El Salvador toward the accusatory model, with generally positive results in efficiency and transparency. Yet, again, these reforms carried costs.

Compared with the police reforms, the transformation of the role of the attorney general's office was gradual, but it encountered similar problems. Since 1950 the attorney general (*fiscal general*) and prosecutors (*fiscales*) have always formed part of the Public Ministry, charged with representing the interests of the state and society and with defending the juridical interests of the poor. The 1991 constitutional reforms passed as part of the peace process granted the attorney general's office the power to "direct" investigations rather than just "safeguard" (*"vigilar"*) them.[66] Subsequent reforms and the adoption of new criminal laws endowed the prosecutor with greater responsibilities still, reducing both judicial power and police discretion in criminal investigations. The 1991 reforms also enhanced political plurality and merit in the selection of the attorney general, requiring a two-thirds legislative majority.

Among the most significant changes in criminal justice were new codes adopted in the 1990s. The more modern codes had their foundations in wartime design, postwar international aid, and recognition of the need to improve justice in the face of crime and low prestige for the judiciary. In April 1998, after significant international input and domestic debate and delay, a new criminal procedure code (CPC), a new penal code, and a new sentencing law went into effect. The new CPC significantly modernized the criminal justice process, moving it toward a more adversarial system while retaining some inquisitorial elements. Jury trials and oral testimony became more prevalent, and prosecutorial discretion (including the introduction of plea bargaining) was widened. Important limits on police and judicial abuses were adopted, as well as procedural guarantees, including eliminating the admissibility of confessions outside a lawyer's presence, limiting the time for phases of the judicial process, capping the length of pretrial detention, and requiring immediate appointment of defense counsel.[67]

Yet the enhanced role of the prosecution in the judicial system was not matched by corresponding resources or institutional development. The 1991 constitutional reforms stipulated that 6 percent of the national budget would go to the judiciary, but the Public Ministry was excluded. Consequently, the courts were over-resourced, while the remainder of the justice system suffered from poor funding. As with the police, the attorney general's office needed to grow quickly, improve personnel, and retain some expertise despite a large number of underqualified personnel. The peace accords provided for none of these exigencies. One-third of prosecutors in 1997 were not attorneys. The budget of the Public Ministry and its size were inadequate for assuming many tasks formerly carried out by police and judges. The UN Development Programme and bilateral donors supported projects to train prosecutors and bolster their ability (and confidence) to take control of investigations from the police. Like the PNC, the attorney general's office grew at such a high rate that quality control was sacrificed. At the end of 2000, more than half the prosecutors had fewer than three years on the job.[68] With the enhanced role of the prosecutor, the corresponding role of defense attorneys also gained importance, but training and funding for these offices remained low, putting poor defendants at greater jeopardy.

The justice sector experienced many of the same limits to reform as the security sector. The government began to remedy these problems only several years after the war, when special legislation provided for a process of *depuración* similar to that of the PNC was adopted and additional funding provided.[69] Corruption among prosecutors had by then become apparent. The peace process failed to address deficient legal education and curriculum or problems in the process of approval of lawyers to the bar, which began to receive attention only several years later.[70]

A year after the new codes went into effect, evidence suggested improvements in efficiency in case management, coordination within the justice sector, conviction rates, and citizen access to justice.[71] The new codes, especially the CPC, directly addressed the legal pitfalls that had permitted state torture and terror and brought the country largely into conformity with international human rights standards. Yet they also contributed to a serious backlash in public opinion. Notorious convicts were released under a provision of the new Penal Code that gave double or triple credit for pretrial days served as a deterrent to the practice of lengthy illegal detentions and as a means to reduce the prison population.[72] More than half the respondents in a 2001 survey thought that the new codes had not helped reduce crime.[73] Critics used the new laws as a scapegoat to distract from inadequacies of the criminal justice system and from socioeconomic and postwar factors in the crime wave.

At the same time, the crime wave and dissatisfaction with high levels of violence generated creativity in criminal justice reform. Civil society played a relatively minor role in the negotiation and implementation of El Salvador's police reforms, but its role grew in both security and justice reform in the 1990s. Research organizations became more sophisticated in their analysis, providing data and analysis of public safety issues used by policymakers and advocates. In response to the inability of tougher law enforcement and legal measures to stem crime, several projects focused on violence prevention, seeking to address broader factors associated with violent behavior. These programs included working with youth, child abuse programs, drug rehabilitation, neighborhood watch programs, and domestic violence education and prevention. One project involving the police, scholars, and NGOs gave university researchers access to data on small arms in exchange for help in improving the PNC's database management and capacity.[74] Donors like the Inter-American Development Bank and the United Nations shifted attention to violence prevention and reduction in innovative programs. By the late 1990s, NGOs and think tanks played an increasingly important role in improving police operations and planning and in judicial reform and code revision.

Justice, Gender, and Youth

The evolution of security and justice for women and children followed a pattern similar to that of overall reforms. Security reforms improved the formal place of women in the police but informally exhibited considerable continuity with the past, as cultural patterns were slow to change. The new PNC included women in the country's security forces for the first time. By March 2002 women composed 7.1 percent of the PNC's sworn officers, an important gain, but still below the majority proportion of the population they represented.

The proportion of women officers increased with each career grade, reaching 15 percent of senior officers.[75]

At the same time, enhanced protections did not ensure security or justice for women. Peace exposed women to increased domestic violence as combatants returned home accustomed to violence and with dim employment prospects.[76] Reported domestic violence and rapes increased in the first several postwar years, owing partly to new laws criminalizing domestic violence and marital rape and partly to greater reporting.[77] In addition, senior policewomen tended to be channeled to nonoperational posts, and many police and judicial personnel failed to enforce the new laws.

The peace process had less impact on women's representation in the courts than in the PNC, as women already occupied many judgeships. By 2002 women made up 40 percent of judgeships in the country, but with reduced rates (only 16 percent) at the higher magistrate level.[78] While the peace process helped provide an opening for human rights generally, several advances in the status and treatment of women and minors were not directly attributable to the peace process. A new juvenile justice code, drafted during the war and enacted in 1994, provided that minors under eighteen would be tried in separate courts, limited minors' sentences to seven years, and included alternatives to incarceration. Many Salvadorans blamed the new protections for minors for a perceived increase in crime by juveniles, especially skyrocketing numbers of youth gangs, and a backlash ensued.[79] Both the new youth and family codes reflected international trends and activism as much as domestic factors. Between 1994 and 1998, all five Central American republics passed youth criminal codes in conformity with the UN Convention on the Rights of Children.[80]

Judicial Efficacy and Legitimacy

By 2002 judicial reforms had achieved some improvements in technical areas but not in public opinion. Perhaps reflecting the deleterious effects of the crime wave, the image of the judiciary did not improve in the years immediately following the war. In a 1994 poll, only one-fifth of respondents reported increased confidence in the judicial system over the previous five years.[81] In 1996 more than half of the populace expressed little or no satisfaction with the work of the

Supreme Court and only 7 percent was "very satisfied" with its work. Also in 1996, four times as many people thought the country's justice system was "corrupt" as thought it "honest."[82]

Those figures did not improve over time. A World Bank project stated in 2002 that justice reform efforts "have had mixed results in effectiveness and gaining citizen confidence."[83] Gains in case management and sentencing rates were not matched by greater legitimacy. In a 1998 poll, respondents ranked the Supreme Court at the bottom of the list of institutions that "best defend human rights" in the country, after the army, the church, the police, and human rights groups.[84] Similarly, twice as many people blamed judges for the high crime rates in 1998 as blamed the police.[85] In one poll in 2001, 48 percent expressed a lack of confidence in the judiciary, a higher percentage than found ten years earlier, when the war ended.[86] As of fall 2001, 57 percent of the country's prison population had not been tried.[87]

Ten years after the peace accords, the judicial system remained weak, inefficient, antiquated, overly partisan, and subject to corruption. The vagueness of the accords' provision regarding the judiciary played a role, as did political horse trading and a virtual stalemate within the legislature over constitutional and legal reforms and judicial procedures. More serious for political stability, within four years of the peace accords, polling data revealed support for the return of a hard-liner to confront growing crime.[88]

CONCLUSION

El Salvador's postwar security and justice reforms suggest several important conclusions for understanding the rule of law and state reform. First, skeptics about the possibilities for rapid state transformation are wrong, at least under certain circumstances. Postwar settings where the prior state is not victorious provide windows for some success in state reform. The weakening or dislocation of state power that occurs when a state is forced to negotiate an end to war opens the door to institutional reform, especially the demilitarization of internal state institutions.[89] El Salvador experienced important transformation of decades-old military and police doctrines, training, and deployments, as well as important modernization, pluralization, and greater independence of the judicial system. These changes were relatively rapid and significant, accomplished with an important international role in design and implementation. While one can question the choices made by international actors, they undeniably helped create and sustain security and justice reforms. These reforms included more than simple professionalization of selection and promotion; they affected doctrines, structures, and conduct. Agency by national and international actors can pay off in the face of structural obstacles posed by culture, economic structure, and warfare.

Yet some caveats are required. State reforms in El Salvador removed the most visible and notorious vestiges of prior institutions more successfully than they inaugurated new concepts and practices. Getting rid of old practices is easier than institutionalizing new ones. Despite resistance, the peace process effectively displaced the military as the protagonist in policing and intelligence gathering, removing the highly militarized character of internal security doctrine, personnel, and training. It proved more difficult to instill a commitment to public service, community input and participation, and accountability. Civilianization did not produce full accountability, transparency, or conformity to standards of "democratic policing."

Nor did it produce effectiveness. Indeed, the transaction costs of demilitarization heightened the postwar crime wave. The success of El Salvador's police reform was mugged by a dramatic rise in violent crimes and perceived insecurity. Statistics, although overstated, reveal high levels of violent crime as the main weakness of postwar security in El Salvador and the biggest threat to the survival of electoral democracy. Of course, the case also illustrates the importance of improving statistics-gathering capacity in efforts to establish the rule of law. El Salvador, ironically, also served as a laboratory for innovative experiments in preventing and reducing violence, involving NGOs, think tanks, and government agencies.

If El Salvador shows what types of state-building *can* occur in postwar settings, it also indicates that the circumstances of the armed conflict and of its termination created state reform possibilities. First, the circumstances of this society and its war compare favorably to many other situations. The small size, relative ethnic and religious homogeneity, and history of formal electoralism made negotiated settlement easier and more likely to hold than in larger and more divided societies with no experience of elections. Although the salience of patron-client networks remained strong in El Salvador, formal organizations (be they parties, state ministries, or nongovernmental organizations) generally transcended individuals and survived leadership changes, making for a higher degree of institutionalization. The stalemated armed conflict also created propitious conditions for democratization and state-building, as some theorists have argued.[90] Finally, the great powers concurred on a strong UN role and relatively generous reconstruction funds compared with those allocated for some subsequent missions.

On the other hand, some conditions limited the possibilities for state reform. A history of elections and separation of powers—even under authoritarianism—can also undermine reform efforts. Opposition parties can veto new proposals; judiciaries can proclaim their independence from the executive and reject reforms; and new governments can abandon or reverse achievements. Political culture and informal clientelism played a role in the difficulty of defining new relations between police and society and in persistent corruption. Although El Salvador's economy grew in the years immediately following the war, a recession and continued inequity prevailed, rooted in neoliberal economic policies and the structure of the economy. These economic structures and choices contributed to common crime and to limits on state resources to confront it.

El Salvador illustrates how international image of a reform process can diverge from local perceptions. The police reform, held up as a model, enjoyed some notable successes, but its inability to adequately combat rising criminal violence, to weed out corrupt or criminal personnel, and to inspire confidence among the population also merit analytic attention. Other postconflict societies have encountered problems of rising crime, backsliding on reforms, penetration by corruption, and disillusionment among the populace. Without clearly understanding the complex relationships among different elements of the security and justice systems, the sources of resistance to postwar reform, the impact on future justice of measures to deal with the past, and the divergence of local and international perspectives, our understanding of postconflict peacebuilding and international policies will suffer.

NOTES

This chapter draws from the author's "Democratization, War, and State-Building: Constructing the Rule of Law in El Salvador," *Journal of Latin American Studies* 35, no. 1 (November 2003): 827–862. Reprinted with permission.

The author is grateful for helpful comments from David Holiday, William Stanley, Maggi Popkin, Don Chilsolm, Commissioner Jaime Vigil, Miguel Cruz, Tracy Fitzsimmons, and three anonymous reviewers, who bear no responsibility for any errors.

1. Dietrich Rueschemeyer, "After State Failure" (paper presented at the conference "Democratization after War," Brown University, Providence, R.I., April 2002); and Peter B. Evans, Dietrich Rueschemeyer, and Theda Skocpol, *Bringing the State Back In* (Cambridge: Cambridge University Press, 1985).

2. Juan Linz and Alfred Stepan, *Problems of Democratic Transition and Consolidation* (Baltimore: Johns Hopkins University Press, 1996); Guillermo O'Donnell, "On the State, Democratization and Some Conceptual Problems," *World Development* 21 (October 1993): 1355–1369; Larry Diamond, *Developing Democracy: Toward Consolidation* (Baltimore: Johns Hopkins University Press, 1999); Marina Ottaway, "Think Again: Nation-Building," *Foreign Policy* (2002); United Kingdom, Department for International Development (DFID), *Understanding and Supporting Security Sector Reform* (London: DFID, 2002); William C. Prillaman, *The Judiciary and Democratic Decay in Latin America* (New York: Praeger, 2000); and Pilar Domingo and Rachel Sieder, *Rule of Law in Latin America* (London: University of London, 2001).

3. Mitchell A. Seligson, José Miguel Cruz, and Ricardo Córdova, *Auditoría de la democracia, El Salvador 1999* (San Salvador: Public Opinion Institute [IUDOP], 2000), 156.

4. See Charles T. Call, "War Transitions and the New Civilian Security in Latin America," *Comparative Politics* (October 2002): 1–20.

5. On "democratic policing," see David Bayley, *Democratizing the Police Abroad: What to Do and How to Do It* (Washington, D.C.: U.S. National Institute of Justice, July 2001); and Charles T. Call, "Pinball and Punctuated Equilibrium: The Birth of a 'Democratic Policing' Norm?" (paper presented at the International Studies Association conference, Los Angeles, March 2000).

6. Lawrence W. Sherman, *Scandal and Reform: Controlling Police Corruption* (Berkeley: University of California Press, 1978).

7. Elisabeth J. Wood, *Forging Democracy from Below* (New York: Cambridge University Press, 2001); Terry Lynn Karl, "El Salvador's Negotiated Revolution," *Foreign Affairs* (Spring 1992); George Vickers, "A Negotiated Revolution," *NACLA Report on the Americas* 25, no. 5 (May 1992): 4–8; and Tommie Sue Montgomery, *Revolution in El Salvador: From Civil Strife to Civil Peace*, 2nd ed. (Boulder, Colo.: Westview Press, 1995).

8. William D. Stanley, *The Protection Racket State: Elite Politics, Military Extortion and Civil War in El Salvador* (Philadelphia: Temple University Press, 1996); Philip J. Williams and Knut Walker, *Militarization and Demilitarization in El Salvador's Transition to Democracy* (Pittsburgh: University of Pittsburgh Press, 1997); Mariano Castro Morán, *Función política del ejército salvadoreño en el presente siglo* (San Salvador: UCA Editores, 1989); and James Dunkerley, *The Long War: Dictatorship and Revolution in El Salvador* (London: Verso, 1985).

9. Karl, "El Salvador's Negotiated Revolution."

10. James Dunkerley, *The Pacification of Central America* (London: Verso, 1994), appendix 7.

11. Cynthia J. Arnson, *Crossroads: Congress, the President and Central America, 1976–1993* (University Park, Pa.: Pennsylvania State University Press, 1993).

12. In 1989 the Cristiani government reversed the only purported attempt to "civilianize" the National Police. Charles T. Call, "From Soldiers to Cops: War Transitions and the Demilitarization of Policing in Latin America and the Caribbean" (Ph.D. diss., Stanford University, 1999).

13. This mandate is from Section I.1 of the New York accords, signed on September 25, 1991, the contents of which were explicitly reaffirmed in the Chapultepec Accord.

14. Montgomery, *Revolution in El Salvador*, 227.

15. Williams and Walter, *Militarization and Demilitarization in El Salvador's Transition to Democracy*, 162.

16. United Nations, ONUSAL Human Rights Division, *9th Report of the Human Rights Division* (New York: United Nations, August–October 1993), 25.

17. Letter from United Nations secretary-general Boutros Boutros-Ghali to the Security Council, S/25078, January 1993.

18. Williams and Walter, *Militarization and Demilitarization in El Salvador's Transition to Democracy*.

19. Public Opinion Institute (IUDOP), "Encuesta de evaluación del año 2001," Informe #91 (San Salvador: IUDOP, 2001).

20. Call, "From Soldiers to Cops"; and William Stanley, *Protectors or Perpetrators: The Institutional Crisis of the Salvadoran Civilian Police* (Washington, D.C.: Washington Office on Latin America and Hemisphere Initiatives, January 1996).

21. David Escobar Galindo, interview with author, San Salvador, January 1995.

22. Boutros Boutros-Ghali, *Secretary-General's Report to the General Assembly*, A/50/517 (New York: United Nations, October 6, 1995), par. 7.

23. Subcommissioner Luís Tobar Prieto, interview with author, San Salvador, November 23, 1995.

24. Poll by Public Opinion Institute (IUDOP), University of Central America (UCA), conducted in Chalatenango and Cabanas. Results published in IUDOP, *Estudios centroamericanos* (*ECA*), November–December 1993, 1154.

25. Gino Costa, *La Policía Nacional Civil de El Salvador (1990–1997)* (San Salvador: UCA Editores, 1999).

26. The head of the Anti-narcotics Unit, who had been appointed deputy chief of the new PNC, was forced to resign under suspicion of involvement in illicit activities. According to UN investigators, thirteen of the roughly one hundred prior SIU investigators were implicated in political murders or their cover-up *after* the cease-fire. UN document in author files; Call, "From Soldiers to Cops," 1999; and Costa, *La Policía Nacional Civil de El Salvador,*1999.

27. Ex-FMLN PNC officers and FMLN party officials, interviews with author, San Salvador, 1996.

28. Of the eighteen serving commissioners (the highest career rank) in March 2002, eight were former military officers, four were civilians, and five were former guerrillas (one unknown). The initial quotas would have yielded no more than four ex-combatants from each side (20 percent of total), and at least nine civilians. Author's data.

29. Polls conducted in January, May, and October 1992, cited in IUDOP, *ECA*, November–December 1992, 1072, table 2.

30. See poll results in IUDOP, *ECA*, September 1993, August 1994, May–June 1995, May–June 1996, and June 1997.

31. IUDOP, "La delincuencia urbana," *ECA*, April–May 1993, 471–479. In contrast to all other IUDOP polls cited herein, this poll was limited to urban respondents, whose perceptions of crime are likely more severe than those of rural residents.

32. Reliable statistics are hard to come by. The 1992 figures are from the director of statistics, state prosecutor's office (*fiscalía*). The 1996 figures exclude nonintentional homicides; from José Miguel Cruz, Álvaro Trigueros, and

Francisco González, *El crimen violento en El Salvador* (San Salvador: IUDOP, 2000).

33. El Salvador's rate passed even Colombia's and was matched only by South Africa's. See World Bank study cited in Juanita Darling, "In New Book, Slain Poet Again Speaks to His Countrymen," *Los Angeles Times*, September 6, 1997, 2.

34. Cruz, Trigueros, and González, *El crimen violento en El Salvador.*

35. Call, "From Soldiers to Cops." On private security, see Lidice Michelle Melara Minero, "Los servicios de seguridad privada en El Salvador," *ECA*, no. 636 (October 2001): 907–932.

36. The concept received systematic treatment in Robert B. Oakley, Michael J. Dziedzic, Eliot M. Goldberg, eds., *Policing the New World Disorder: Peace Operations and Public Security* (Washington, D.C.: National Defense University, 1998).

37. Ministerio de Defensa, "Cuadro de armas registradas a nivel nacional por departamento y tipo, 1994–2000" (San Salvador: Ministerio de Defensa). Author files.

38. Cruz, Trigueros, and González, *El crimen violento en El Salvador*, 101.

39. PNC director M. Sandoval provided the author with "Decree 101" *depuración* figures in March 2002. Normal disciplinary figures are from the El Salvador section of the U.S. Department of State's *Country Reports on Human Rights Practices, 2001.*

40. Sherman, *Scandal and Reform.*

41. Anonymous interviewee, interview with author, San Salvador, September 1995.

42. See IUDOP poll of July–August 1996, Informe #57 (San Salvador: IUDOP, 1996), 103.

43. Louis Cobarruvias, ICITAP El Salvador project manager, interview with author, San Salvador, March 2002. Crime rates dropped in the neighborhoods where the PIP-COM program was implemented.

44. Two PNC agents, interview with author, San Salvador Centro Station, March 2002.

45. Boutros Boutros-Ghali, *Report of the Secretary-General on the United Nations Observer Mission in El Salvador*, S/1995/220, March 24, 1995 (New York: United Nations, 1995), par. 29.

46. *Ninth Report of the Director of the Human Rights Division of ONUSAL*, August–October 1993, table 4.

47. "Los derechos humanos en 1995," *Proceso*, no. 691, 29.

48. See Procuraduria para la Defensa de los Derechos Humanos, "Informe de labores, junio 1997–mayo 1998" (San Salvador, 1998), 230–238. Figures reflect complaints from June 1, 1997, to May 31, 1998.

49. *Informe de la Procuraduria para la Defensa de los Derechos Humanos: Julio–diciembre 2001* (San Salvador: Procuraduria de los Derechos Humanos, 2002).

50. IUDOP poll of February 1998, *ECA,* April 1998, 364–365. Responses of "nobody" outranked all other answers.

51. IUDOP, "Encuesta de evaluación del año 1995," Informe #52, Cuadro 32, 39. Some 27 percent responded that the conduct of the PNC was the same as that of the old police.

52. Luis Salas and Laura Chinchilla proclaim it "the most far-reaching and important" public security reform in Latin America in their "UNDP Security Sector Reform Assistance in Post-conflict Situations: Lessons Learned in El Salvador, Guatemala, Haiti, Mozambique, Somalia and Rwanda" (draft report prepared for UN Development Programme, June 20, 2001). El Salvador was the only country to be named by all six experts and former U.S. and UN officials asked in personal interviews in January–February 2002 to name the most successful police reforms of the past decade.

53. In addition to these internationally inspired initiatives, some Salvadoran-led efforts slightly enhanced judicial independence in the new constitution of 1983. Margaret Popkin, "The Challenge of Building the Rule of Law in Post-war El Salvador" (paper presented at the conference "Building the Rule of Law in the Context of a Peace Process," Institute for Latin American Studies, University of London, 2000), 73–76.

54. Lawyers Committee for Human Rights, *Underwriting Injustice: AID and El Salvador's Judicial Reform Program* (New York: Lawyers Committee for Human Rights, 1989); and Popkin, "The Challenge of Building the Rule of Law in Post-war El Salvador."

55. See Popkin, "The Challenge of Building the Rule of Law in Post-war El Salvador," 57–73; General Accounting Office (GAO), *Foreign Assistance: Promoting Judicial Reform to Strengthen Democracies,* GAO/NSIAD-93-149 (Washington, D.C.: U.S Government Printing Office, September 1993); and Thomas Carothers, *Aiding Democracy Abroad: The Learning Curve* (Washington, D.C.: Carnegie Endowment for International Peace, 1999).

56. Carothers, *Aiding Democracy Abroad;* and Michael Dodson, "Assessing Judicial Reform in Latin America," *Latin American Research Review* 37, no. 2 (2002): 200–220.

57. See Lawyers Committee for Human Rights, *El Salvador: Human Rights Dismissed* (New York: Lawyers Committee for Human Rights, 1986).

58. Previous amnesty laws were passed in 1983, 1987, and 1992 to free political prisoners on both sides. Popkin, "The Challenge of Building the Rule of Law in Post-war El Salvador," 40.

59. Ibid., 6, 150–151. In 2002 a U.S. jury awarded three Salvadoran torture victims $54 million in a civil suit brought against two Salvadoran generals living in the United States.

60. See UN Commission on the Truth, *From Madness to Hope: The 12-Year War in El Salvador*, S/25500 (New York: United Nations, 1993).

61. Jack Spence and George Vickers with Margaret Popkin et al., *A Negotiated Revolution? A Two-Year Progress Report on the Salvadoran Peace Accords*, report of Hemisphere Initiatives and Washington Office on Latin America (Boston, Mass.: Hemisphere Initiatives, 1994), 6.

62. The widely reported quote can be found in Amnesty International, "El Salvador: Paz sin justicia," editorial, Amnesty International Index: AMR 29/12/93/2 (London: Amnesty International, June 1993).

63. Popkin, "The Challenge of Building the Rule of Law in Post-war El Salvador," 5.

64. Ibid., 212. By 2002 the total number of judges had grown to 640, with 322 justices of the peace, 251 first-instance judges, 52 second-instance magistrates, and 13 Supreme Court magistrates. Figures provided to author by the Supreme Court, Sala de lo Civil, March 7, 2002.

65. U.S. Department of State, "El Salvador" in *Country Reports on Human Rights Practices for 2001*, (Washington, D.C.: U.S. Government Printing Office, 2002), Section 1(e).

66. My translation. On the attorney general's office, see Comisión Especial para una Evaluación Integral de la Fiscalía General de la República, *Diagnóstico Integral y Recomendaciones para el Fortalecimiento de la Fiscalía General de la República* (San Salvador: Fiscalía, 2001), 1–13.

67. Popkin, "The Challenge of Building the Rule of Law in Post-war El Salvador," 219, 235–241.

68. Comisión Especial para una Evaluación Integral de la Fiscalía General de la República, *Diagnóstico Integral y Recomendaciones para el Fortalecimiento de la Fiscalía General de la República*, 37.

69. The attorney general's budget more than doubled from 1997 to 1999 but still remained one-fifth of the budget of the courts. Ibid., 73.

70. Popkin, "The Challenge of Building the Rule of Law in Post-War El Salvador."

71. Ibid., 240.

72. Ibid., 239.

73. "Jueces los peor evaluados," *Prensa Gráfica*, May 31, 2001, 5.

74. Marcela Smutt, UNDP, interview with author, San Salvador, March 2002.

75. The regional average in 1999 was 8 percent. In June 2001 the percent of females at each rank was 15.8 percent of *comisionados*; 14.5 percent of *sub-comisionados*; 11.1 percent of *inspectors*; 10.4 percent of *sub-inspectores*; 5.8 percent of *sargentos*; 5.3 percent of *cabos*; and 6.9 percent of *agentes*. El Salvador figures provided by the director-general of the PNC in March 2002. In 1996 women composed only 6.1 percent of the PNC.

76. Tracy Fitzsimmons, "Engendering a New Police Identity?" *Peace Review* 10, no. 2 (1998): 269–274.

77. Reported rapes climbed steadily from 382 in 1996 to 818 in 2001. Annual data given to author by the PNC.

78. In 2002 females accounted for 256 of the country's 640 judges, that is, 44.7 percent of justices of the peace; 40.2 percent of first-instance judges; 17.3 percent of second- instance magistrates; and 13.3 percent of Supreme Court magistrates. Figures provided by *Sala de lo Civil, Corte Suprema de Justicia*, current as of March 7, 2002.

79. Some 236 youth gangs existed in 1993, and estimated gang membership had grown to 30,000–35,000 by 2001. Maria L. Santacruz Giralt and Alberto Concha-Eastman, *Barrios adentro: La solidaridad violenta de las pandillas* (San Salvador: UCA Editores, 2001), 13.

80. UN Development Programme, *Estado de la region en desarrollo humano sostenible* (New York: UNDP, 2000).

81. U.S. Information Agency, *Benchmarks in Democracy Building: Public Opinion and Global Democratization*, special report, interviews conducted in El Salvador in September 1994 (Washington, D.C.: U.S. Information Agency, 1994), 55.

82. IUDOP, "Encuesta sobre derechos humanos y el sistema judicial" (San Salvador: IUDOP, July–August 1996), 80, 83.

83. World Bank, "El Salvador—Judicial Modernization Project," Project # SVPA64919, prepared May 2002, 1.

84. IUDOP, "Encuesta de evaluación de derechos humanos y la PDDH" (San Salvador: IUDOP, 1998), 35.

85. IUDOP, "Encuesta de opinion sobre delincuencia" (San Salvador: IUDOP, July 1998), 20.

86. CID-Gallup poll in "Jueces en la mira," *Diario de Hoy*, February 14, 2002.

87. Figures provided to author by Corte Suprema de Justicia, March 2002.

88. "Piden mano dura contra el crimen," *El Diario de Hoy,* January 30, 1996, 2.

89. Call, "War Transitions and the New Civilian Security in Latin America."

90. Terry Lynn Karl, "Dilemmas of Democratization in Latin America," *Comparative Politics* 23, no. 1 (October 1990); and I. William Zartman, *Ripe for Resolution* (Oxford: Oxford University Press, 1989).

3

Justice and Security Reform after Intervention

Haiti

Sandra Beidas, Colin Granderson, and Rachel Neild

A DECADE AFTER THE 1994 INTERNATIONAL INTERVENTION to restore democracy, Haiti was again in crisis. A sixth United Nations mission (the United Nations Stabilization Mission in Haiti, MINUSTAH) was in the country attempting to establish sufficient security to hold elections in early 2006 to restore constitutional order after Jean-Bertrand Aristide's forced 2004 resignation following armed uprisings across the country. The tale of efforts to build security and justice in Haiti after the 1994 intervention to restore Aristide to power following his ouster in a 1991 military coup during his first term as president is a story of resounding failure. Today, analysts observe that Haiti meets "nearly every definition of a failing state."[1]

The reasons for failure in Haiti are multiple and overwhelming: a long and inauspicious history of weak institutions and predatory politics, social exclusion and grinding poverty; the economic and political devastation wrought by the 1991–94 military regime and the international economic embargo against it; the inexperience of and overwhelming demands on the Haitian governments; the demands of a grueling electoral timetable and the emergence of new political competition and political violence; the mutual suspicions and contrasting cultures of Haitians and donors; the limitations of reform initiatives; and on and on. Even as, in explanatory terms, the failure of reforms to Haitian security and justice institutions was overdetermined, it remains important to reflect on the experience and derive lessons that may serve in other settings and in ongoing efforts to stabilize the situation in Haiti itself.

Several salient points reappear throughout this chapter and shape the analysis. First, like prior international experience in Kosovo but unlike those in El Salvador and Guatemala, the international intervention in Haiti followed the collapse of a negotiated settlement. No broad road map for democratization and reform was laid out in accords or any other political agreements. Discussions of institutional reforms were held piecemeal, and some were far more advanced than others—particularly concerning policing, because this issue directly implicated international desires to avoid putting peacekeeping troops into constabulary roles.

In implementing reform programs, donors struggled with the "lack of absorptive capacity" of the Haitian government, often riding roughshod over Haitian concerns in their need to meet highly pressured military and political timetables set in Washington, D.C., or New York rather than in Port-au-Prince. The level of coordination between donors varied, and donor competition also hindered the implementation of programs. Coordination with the Haitian government was even more troubled and declined progressively as political competition and dominance became the overriding preoccupation of the key Haitian actors.

In addition to the challenges created by limited political will, deeper obstacles reflected profound structural issues that were neither adequately understood nor anticipated by donors or Haitians in the planning and goals set for reforms. Haiti has suffered a history of military rule and political exclusion and remains abysmally poor, with a literacy rate of maybe 30 percent at most.[2] Prior institutions were little more than job creation programs for the politically connected (the military was the only organization with nationwide reach), and social, economic, and political interactions were rooted in personal patronage networks.

The emergence of the popularly based Lavalas movement and the election of Jean-Bertrand Aristide as president in 1990 offered hope for change in Haiti.[3] This was rapidly dashed by the military coup of 1991 and reawoken by the 1994 intervention and promise of international assistance. The collapse of reform efforts and ongoing, persistent political crisis reflect a fundamental failure of accountability. New Haitian political actors have consistently reverted to the traditional politics of exclusion, and the international community's strategies have proved incapable of overcoming the lack of accountability of Haitian politics to the Haitian people. The failure of security and justice reforms is one part, but a core part, of this story.

HAITI AND THE "PREDATORY STATE"

Haitian history is marked by military rule and paramilitary social control mechanisms. After winning independence in 1804 in the world's only successful slave uprising, Haiti was ruled almost constantly by military generals, a trend that was unchanged by the United States' 1915–34 occupation. When Haiti's infamous civilian dictator François "Papa Doc" Duvalier came to power in 1957, he built a paramilitary bulwark against the Forces Armées d'Haiti (FAdH)—the notorious *tontons macoutes*. Over time, the repressive system was strengthened by "section chiefs" (*chefs de section*) and local "attachés," deputized civilians through whom the military controlled and extorted local communities.[4] The police were simply a fourth branch of the armed forces, and personnel rotated in and out of different services with no more than a change of uniform. Attempts to challenge military prerogatives led to military coups.[5]

Haiti's legal system reflects this history of rule by force rather than by law. The civil law system in 1825 adopted the French Napoleonic Code. Legal proceedings are to this day conducted almost entirely in French (a language spoken by no more than 20 percent of the population), creating a "legal apartheid."[6] The court system has always lacked resources and power[7] and was subordinated to the military of the regime in power and used to repress rather than to protect rights.[8] The exclusion of much of society from formal justice contributed to the development of informal justice, including lynching and dependence on rough justice at the hands of local leaders and communities.[9]

Years of authoritarian rule meant that Haitian civil society had no tradition of participation. Traditional relations of patronage reinforced social fragmentation and exclusion, thriving in the face of extreme poverty. Nonetheless, small student groups and a popular radio station played key roles in articulating public opposition to Jean-Claude Duvalier, Papa Doc's son.[10]

Following Jean-Claude Duvalier's flight into exile in 1986, Haiti saw renewed efforts to promote democratic reforms. A new constitution, approved by a plebiscite in 1987, finally ended the legal distinction between "citizens" and "peasants"; gave Haitian Creole (*Kreyol*) equal legal status with French; created a police force separate from the military; and sought to strengthen judicial guarantees of human rights, including by granting the full force of domestic law to international rights treaties that Haiti has ratified. These measures were not implemented immediately. Haiti experienced ten years of instability, although with somewhat lessened political repression creating just sufficient political space for the growth of an embryonic civil society. Popular organizations and other civil society groups emerged, and many Haitians joined the Lavalas movement, which coalesced behind the leadership of then priest and liberation theologian Jean-Bertrand Aristide and swept him to victory with 76 percent of the vote in the 1990 presidential elections. Aristide lasted seven months in office until he was overthrown in a September 1991 military coup and left for exile.

The military regime used the "section chiefs" and "attachés" to repress political opponents. In addition, a new paramilitary force called the Revolutionary Front for Advancement and Progress in Haiti (FRAPH)[11] emerged in August 1993. The civil society segment that formed the backbone of the Lavalas movement was targeted for repression. A subsequent National Commission on Truth and Justice found that 8,000 individuals were victims of abuse, including torture and execution, and an estimated 300,000 were internally displaced. Tens of thousands of Haitians also tried to flee the country in rickety boats.[12] By the time of the 1994 intervention, many civil society organizations had been decimated.[13] No internal armed resistance ever materialized.

Return and Reform in an Evolving Political Environment

In the late 1980s the vast majority of Haitians viewed Aristide as the bright new hope for their country, but in the United States, the Republican administration of President George H. W. Bush viewed the progressive priest with suspicion. Although initially taking a strong stance against the coup, U.S. officials viewed the Haitian military and the country's virulently anti-Aristide economic elite as important counterbalances to Aristide.[14] Despite a renewed commitment to restore democracy under President Bill Clinton, U.S. support for Aristide continued to reflect a desire for "balance" in Haiti. This encouraged military intransigence and led to the collapse of a first attempt to return Aristide in 1993.[15] Spurred by further domestic political pressures, the Clinton administration resolved to intervene militarily in Haiti, with UN Security Council authorization. A last-minute negotiation led by former president Jimmy Carter brokered an agreement to permit U.S. forces to enter the country—and promised amnesty for FAdH members, exile for key coup leaders, and assistance in professionalizing the military. On September 20, 1994, 21,000 U.S. troops entered Haiti, and on October 15 Aristide returned to a ransacked presidential palace to make another effort—with promises of massive international assistance—to build democracy in his country.

At this point, a number of enabling factors appeared to favor social and economic development as well as the institutional revamping that an eviscerated Haiti so desperately required: endemic political instability had come to an end; the long-standing stranglehold of the army on the body politic and key institutions had been broken; the political commitment and the resources of the international community were in plentiful supply; on the ground, a conducive environment existed amid a genuine yearning at both the government and societal levels for change for the better; and among the many priorities facing the new government, the establishment of a new civilian and professional police force and reform of the judicial system were seen as critical to the enjoyment of the rule of law and to the restoration of democracy.

The calm and stability of those early months were progressively eroded by two developments whose repercussions continue to be felt. First, the dismantling of the army in December 1994, the ineffectiveness of the demoralized interim security force, and the gradual fielding of a leaderless and hastily trained "rookie" police force led to a security void in which armed crime and banditry prospered. This situation would be worsened by the emergence of Haiti as an important transit point for drug trafficking, with its attendant security and corruption problems. The inability of the new police to contain rising crime and their increasing recourse to traditional brutality would eventually alienate the initial public support.

Second, the unity of the wider democratic sector and, subsequently, that of its most important component, the Lavalas movement of President Aristide, would be shattered by the series of flawed elections that commenced in June 1995 and continued through 2000. In many respects this development reaffirmed the old political ways whereby those in power ensure at all costs their own entrenchment and the exclusion of their opponents. Intra-Lavalas disagreement over crucial policy issues such as privatization and public sector reform also contributed to the infighting.

The consequences of the political crisis for institution building and governance were devastating. Infighting within the governing majority led to the resignation of the prime minister in June 1997 following the flawed partial elections of April 1997, to government paralysis, and ultimately to political stalemate, which resulted in the suspension of parliament by the president in January 1999. As the political crisis persisted, relations between the government and the international community started to fray. A range of international technical and financial aid commitments would eventually be put on hold because of the protracted political standoff. Political instability, the curtailment of assistance, and the diversion of government attention and commitment rapidly started to unravel the progress that had been achieved in reforming the police and justice system.

Increasing political polarization also led to a heightening of political intimidation and violence. This was especially striking as the parties jockeyed for power in the run-up to the May 2000 parliamentary and local government elections and unfortunately coincided with the February end of the UN field presence. More ominously, the new Haitian National Police (HNP) was not allowed to stay above the fray. Certain elements of the police were subverted or hounded out of the institution, and the partisan conduct of some police during the electoral period further blemished an institution already diminished by low morale, criminal and corrupt activities within its ranks, and, later, allegations of coup plotting.

The degradation of the situation following the disputed general elections of May 2000 and the opposition boycott of the November 2000 presidential elections increased the international isolation of the Haitian government. Despite the February 2001 inauguration of Aristide to his second presidential term, direct international assistance to the government was suspended by the largest foreign donors pending clarification of the electoral controversy. Internal tensions rose and violence escalated with the partisan participation of popular organizations and groups of thugs (*chimères*), many apparently linked to the government.

Instability increased through 2003, culminating in an internecine struggle between Aristide and the increasingly prominent pro-Aristide gang leader Amiot Metayer and his "Cannibal Army." In response to Metayer's killing—generally assumed to have been on government orders—his gang seized the city of Gonaives on February 5. Former military members in exile in the neighboring Dominican Republic were quick to profit from the situation and returned to Haiti to take leadership of the Cannibal Army, now renamed the Artibonite Resistance Front for the Overthrow of Jean-Bertrand Aristide. On February 22, 2004, they took control of Cap Haitien, Haiti's second-largest city, and threatened to march on Port-au-Prince. On February 29, faced by evident lack of support from either the United States or France, Aristide resigned and fled the country.[16] Since that time, a weak interim government and a slow-off-the-mark and limited international mission have failed to control rising insecurity. Haiti's economy is a shambles, with drug trafficking being one of the major sources of revenue. Elections scheduled for fall 2005 were repeatedly postponed due to political infighting, major organizational and resource challenges, and violence carried out by a murky array of armed actors, the latest manifestation of a familiar set of "spoilers" in Haiti—military, paramilitary, political and criminal gangs, business elites, and organized crime.

PLANNING AND IMPLEMENTATION OF INSTITUTIONAL REFORMS

Total Demilitarization, Partial Disarmament, and Reintegration

Despite U.S. commitments to the Haitian military during negotiations, after his return Aristide quickly took steps to demobilize the Haitian army. The section chief system was again dismantled and FRAPH melted away, although their informal networks persisted for a time. A U.S.-funded demobilization and reintegration program proved controversial as it provided job training and assistance to the very people who had terrorized the nation for three years.[17] Meanwhile, victims of human rights abuses received no compensation, nor did Haiti's desperately poor population see much economic improvement—particularly as basic food prices failed to drop significantly despite the end of the economic embargo.

Haitian calls for a major disarmament campaign met with a limited response from U.S. authorities in the form of a gun buy-back program that ultimately recuperated some thirty thousand weapons. After their experience in Somalia, U.S. authorities were reluctant to engage in aggressive house-to-house searches. Officials also questioned whether many more weapons would be found beyond those collected through the buy-back program.[18] To Lavalas sectors, this looked like another indication of U.S. reluctance to weaken anti-Aristide forces. In hindsight, it is not clear whether more aggressive disarmament would have improved the security situation. Weapons possession boomed after 1994, as large numbers of guns were imported in connection with drug trafficking and as individuals sought to protect themselves against rising crime rates that the formal criminal justice system was unable to control.

It is remarkable that Aristide made the decision to dissolve the military despite some international objections. Yet over time, Aristide came to incorporate more and more former military into the police and shadier paramilitary/criminal gangs. Other former military groups remained staunchly anti-Aristide and were suspected of committing armed attacks on police stations and the National Palace in Port-au-Prince in 2001. The Dominican Republic provided a convenient retreat from which it proved easy for former military to return to Haiti and take a leading role in the 2004 armed uprising. In the face of demands for the reinstatement of the military, the interim government has been ambivalent, and it has become clear that an important number of leaders support this proposal, as do many communities, which see the military as the only institution capable of restoring order. Few opposition and civil society figures have spoken out against the armed groups, and there is alarmingly little debate on this important question. International actors have raised concerns about reinstating the military, on the grounds of their past political intervention and poor human rights record and because Haiti does not have the financial wherewithal to fund both a professional police force and a military. The interim government established a National Commission for Disarmament in February 2005 to work with the UN peacekeeping mission, but its commitment and authority were unclear. A more robust approach with strong international support is clearly necessary if the estimated three hundred thousand weapons in the hands of armed groups are to be dealt with.[19]

Transitional Justice: An Unfulfilled Promise

The almost immediate dismantling of the FAdH and the disappearance of FRAPH and the *chefs de section* system indirectly addressed the issue of institutional accountability, but they did not address the widespread Haitian aspiration for *Jistis pou tout moun* (justice for all)—punishment of perpetrators of past abuses and an end to impunity.

In March 1995 the Haitian government set up the National Commission on Truth and Justice (CNVJ), whose Haitian and international staff were mandated to establish the truth about serious human rights violations between September 29, 1991, and October

15, 1994, identify perpetrators, and investigate the existence of para-military groups acting under the protection of the state.[20] But the CNVJ suffered setbacks from the start, particularly in its limited resources and disagreements about methodology. In the end, it collected some 5,400 testimonies representing more than 8,000 vic-tims, but time and resource constraints meant that only a few cases were investigated. The CNJV offered no incentives for perpe-trators to come forward with information. Limited publicity for the information-gathering process—explained by the CNVJ as a way of reducing victims' fears of coming forward—was also criticized by local NGOs as a serious constraint.

Aside from the UN and Canadian government funding for the CNVJ, international community support for efforts to end impunity was mixed. The Clinton administration, which had negotiated the departure of military leaders from Haiti shortly after the promulga-tion of an amnesty law in early October 1994, refused to return thou-sands of documents seized by U.S. soldiers that belonged to FRAPH and the FAdH that could have provided valuable inputs for the CNVJ and for prosecutions. The United States also refused to extra-dite FRAPH leader Emmanuel Constant (who gave an interview to the TV show 60 *Minutes* describing his relationship with the CIA). The passivity of the multinational forces in the face of suspected perpetrators, and their at-times friendly relationship with former FRAPH members, did not induce in the population much confidence in their willingness to contribute to ending impunity.[21] The United Nations/OAS Civilian Mission in Haiti (MICIVIH) was also criti-cized early on for not taking a more aggressive role in assisting judi-cial personnel in pursuing cases.[22]

The official CNVJ report—*Si M Pa Rele*—was handed to Presi-dent Aristide in February 1996, shortly before the end of his term of office. In addition to analyzing patterns of violations, it included spe-cial investigations with forensic findings and named victims and alleged perpetrators. The government's response to the report was widely criticized.[23] It failed to distribute the report immediately or to pursue its recommendations, including one of the most important: establishing national committees to follow up on the recommenda-tions and to provide rehabilitation and compensation. Important new information on certain cases that could have been used to relaunch judicial cases was ignored. Key recommendations for judicial reform, though they later fed into judicial reform discussions, were also not immediately acted on. The report received remarkably little circulation.

Other initiatives that were taken to address the issue of past abuses included the creation of an office of international lawyers to help prosecute such cases and a special criminal investigations brigade in the police, which continued to work on a select group of cases. But the judicial system did not have the capacity or the willingness to systematically pursue cases of abuses committed by the military or by others subsequently.

The issue of reparations was not adequately addressed, in spite of recommendations by the CNVJ, MICIVIH, and Haitian NGOs.[24] A three-person Bureau de Poursuites et Suivi with a budget of 60 million gourdes was set up by the Ministry of Justice in 1997 to provide rehabilitation and compensation for abuses during the coup years.[25] While the office did complete some projects successfully, particularly community projects, it was widely criticized for its lack of transparency, criteria, and regulations.[26] The office was closed in 1999. For many, past abuses are now part of a much broader problem of impunity, the extent of which has emerged as attempts to establish a new, more accountable police force and reform the justice sector have seriously foundered. As will be seen, the scarcity of political will to deal with impunity and accountability except on a highly selective basis raises serious questions regarding the extent to which reforms can be carried out, given that challenging impunity threatens powerful interests.

Starting from Scratch—Haiti's Police Reform, Planning Reform, and Interim Policing

The creation of the Haitian National Police was, for a time, the success story of institution building in Haiti. Discussions of security sector reforms, begun under the Clinton administration in 1993, took on increased urgency and pace as the scenario turned to intervention. The need for legitimate domestic security capabilities took on paramount importance for U.S. political and military authorities, who, in the wake of U.S. casualties in Somalia, would not permit a constabulary role for U.S. peacekeeping forces in Haiti.

The July 1993 Governors Island Agreement called for a reform that would create separate police and military forces, as specified in the 1987 constitution. The document did not elaborate further but served as the basis for an intense strategic planning process primarily between U.S. officials and the Aristide government in exile. U.S. officials refused to accept Aristide's initial proposal for a totally decentralized police force, in which local authorities select the police, on the grounds that it risked a new patronage-based and highly politicized structure.[27] For Haitian authorities, the civilian control and character of the police were paramount. Despite mutual political suspicions, discussions between the United States and the Haitian government reached agreement about three broad areas of police reform: the creation of a new police force from the ground up, rather than from a transition of existing military police units; a new police law defining the mission, role, and function of the new force; and the establishment of salaries at living-wage level to prevent corruption.[28]

The human rights situation deteriorated rapidly after the Governors Island Agreement, yet Haitian and international officials continued to follow the agreement's blueprint, and a new police law was drafted by Minister of Justice Guy Malary and officials from ICITAP (United States Department of Justice International Criminal Investigation Training Assistance Program). On October 14, 1993, Malary—the figure at the center of discussions of the most sensitive human rights and institutional reform issues for the military—was assassinated. Amid a wave of political violence carried out largely by FRAPH with military complicity throughout October, the entire peace process ground to a halt. The police law was finally approved by a new parliament in 1995.

When Aristide returned in October 1994, the Interim Public Security Force (IPSF) was created to police the country until the new HNP was set up. The IPSF was composed of about 3,000 former FAdH members "vetted" to exclude human rights violators, given six days of "retraining," and deployed under the watch of 800 international police monitors (IPMs). At Haitian government insistence, the IPSF also included some 900 "police trainees" selected from the

Haitian refugees in the camp at the U.S. base in Guantanamo, Cuba, and given rapid training. Popular hatred of the FAdH and inadequate vetting processes meant that Haitians had no confidence in these forces, and IPSF members were typically afraid to leave their barracks without international accompaniment.[29] They were permitted to apply to serve in the HNP, and a 9 percent ceiling was set for the total number of former military members who could enter. Far fewer than this managed to pass the entrance exams, however, and military participation in the ranks of the HNP was minimal.

From the Haitian perspective, the IPSF was deeply problematic as its poor performance allowed crime to flourish. It is not clear what alternative security arrangements could have been found given international reluctance to undertake constabulary functions and Haitian reluctance to accept formal accords that ceded sovereignty. The IPSF can be considered a qualified success in that it provided a transitional arrangement while the new HNP was created. Despite the increase in crime, the process of returning Aristide to Haiti was not seriously threatened or impeded (although this probably had more to do with the deterrent effect of 21,000 U.S. troops and international police monitors, despite a legal mandate that did not endow them with policing functions or powers). The "safe and secure" environment called for in UN Security Council Resolution 940 was considered to be established, and in March 1995 the United Nations Mission in Haiti (UNMIH) took over from the U.S.-led multinational force.

Following the intervention, the structure of police assistance took shape, with the United States, through ICITAP, playing the lead role in refurbishing an old military barracks in Port-au-Prince as the new police academy. While the United States dominated the design and running of police recruitment and training, other countries also provided support, with police trainers from Canada and France working alongside the Americans. Training in Haitian law was conducted by Haitian lawyers, while international trainers focused on police practices and operations. MICIVIH also participated from 1995 onward, providing human rights training in the academy and in the field.[30] Once the initial intensive training period was completed, the focus shifted to training Haitians to take control of all academy training.[31]

Nearly 900 UN Civilian Police (CIVPOL) officers monitored the newly deployed HNP and provided field training throughout the country. At the outset, CIVPOL was under Canadian leadership, whose approach to field training included an effort to promote community policing practices such as school visits, provision of regular reports on police activities to the local authorities, sports activities, and other forms of community outreach such as market day visits and participation on radio programs. In 1996 leadership of CIVPOL passed to French gendarmerie officers, who reassessed CIVPOL's activities and changed their emphasis, provoking considerable friction with ICITAP.

Beyond the training and monitoring activities, the United States, Canada, France, and the UN Development Programme (UNDP) also provided senior advisers to the director general of the police and to the heads of other units, supporting their planning and decision making. While personal skills and relationships play a strong role in the success of such consultants, overall, most Haitian police leaders found these international advisers useful and provided donors with a high degree of access to top decision makers and processes. These positions were maintained after bilateral and CIVPOL training assistance and monitoring declined. The final UN mission in Haiti, MICAH (International Civilian Support Mission in Haiti), focused on strengthening management through advisers to senior regional and national HNP commanders.

Overall, U.S. police assistance to the HNP between 1995 and July 2000, when the program was suspended, totaled $65,294,000; in the same period Canada provided some $30 million in aid, and the UNDP $6 million.[32] These figures do not include the costs of deploying the UN CIVPOL mission, which totaled many additional millions of dollars. Haiti received massive assistance for police reform, and despite problems in coordinating the provision of assistance and some donor competition, donor coordination and cooperation were markedly better in Haiti than in El Salvador or Guatemala, where donors at times pursued radically different strategies and even political goals at odds with each other.

Implementing Police Reform

The original planning—before the USS *Harlan County* incident (see note 15 above), when a negotiated transition without intervention was assumed—had envisioned training 5,000 police in five years. Following the intervention and the dismantling of the FAdH, the new Haitian police force became an integral element of the exit strategy for international forces in Haiti. Training and deployment of the HNP were compressed into a period of a little more than a year. Starting in late 1995, international donors (led by the United States and Canada) embarked on a grueling timetable that involved setting up the first police academy in Haiti's history and recruiting and training 4,000 civilian police by February 1996.[33] In May 1995 concerns about increasing crime and insecurity led to a U.S. decision to increase to 7,000 the number of National Police to be trained by March 1996. This decision overwhelmed the capacity of the Haitian academy and, despite objections from the Haitian government, the United States decided to conduct half the training at Fort Leonard Wood, a U.S. military base in Missouri.

At the outset, Haitian government engagement was limited. Aristide had just returned to the country and was getting his government up and running; furthermore, the basic agreements reached in Washington had satisfied some of the most urgent Haitian concerns. However, the pressure to "stand up" the HNP as quickly as possible to fill the security void and reluctance to engage in often-difficult discussions with the Haitian government fostered a tendency toward unilateral decision making by U.S. policymakers that failed to improve relations with the Haitian government or actively support their engagement with police reform.

In the early days, donors made no attempt to reach out to civil society sectors, either to provide more information about the reform and the principles of democratic policing or to solicit their insights and inputs, or to try to mitigate the natural perception that the HNP was fundamentally an international project.[34] Nonetheless, when academy authorities, following critiques from international rights groups, set up a "Wednesday night forum" and invited civil society groups to talk with trainees, they had trouble filling the slots. Civil society groups were reluctant to engage with institutional reforms of a state apparatus they continued to mistrust profoundly, and they also remained suspicious of the intentions of the donor community.

The first contingents of HNP were deployed in July 1995. By the end of 1996, nearly 6,000 HNP had been deployed. There were immediate problems. Police infrastructure and logistical support barely existed. The physical infrastructure was in an appalling state, with basic equipment lacking. Most serious was the absence of a command-and-control structure. In the rush to "stand up the force" and in the absence of agreement between the Haitians and donors on how best to proceed with leadership development, recruitment and training of HNP commanders had taken a backseat. The first HNP agents in the field were leaderless, and although CIVPOL provided key support, they were not present in every town or village where the HNP were deployed, leaving many HNP officers largely to their own devices.

Unsurprisingly, operational and disciplinary problems emerged rapidly, and there was a resurgence of human rights violations. Incidents of abuse included a handful of killings and excessive use of force, particularly in crowd-control situations, when the inexperienced HNP panicked and shot into crowds.[35] Importantly, however, the abuse was not politically motivated, and other aspects of police behavior showed improvement; for example, police made attempts to avoid arbitrary detention by transferring detainees more regularly before judges and introducing uniform detention registers. Donors responded by developing additional training to address these shortcomings and by initiating a program to create specialized crowd-control units.

Public attitudes toward the police reflected deeply ingrained expectations of authority. In early 1996 a local priest described the evolution in local relations with the HNP:

> At first, the people welcomed the police enthusiastically. However, they soon came to see the new police as weak because they were not tough enough and some people became aggressive toward the police, jeering and throwing rocks at them. Then, the police arrested some delinquents and beat them severely in the lock-up.

After this, the people felt that things were better and calmer relations have been established.[36]

For their part, many HNP quickly developed a "chief mentality"
manifested in displays of superiority, disdain for work on the street,
and arrogant attitudes toward the populations they were meant to
serve.[37] Nonetheless, the contrast to former security forces was striking, and in 1997 the HNP reportedly enjoyed a public support rate of
70 percent—more than that enjoyed by any other Haitian institution.[38] Over time, however, the accumulation of incidents of abuse of
authority, corruption, and crime within the ranks and the belief that
they were not accountable would eventually erode public support for
the HNP.

In February 1996 President René Préval succeeded Aristide and
appointed new police leadership. Haitian government engagement
with the police reform flourished under Secretary of State for Public
Security Robert Manuel and HNP director general Pierre Denizé,
who brought back the HNP's first inspector general, Eucher Luc
Joseph, who had proven aggressive in punishing infractions. Manuel
and Denizé worked with donors and CIVPOL to develop a five-year
strategic police development plan and launched a recruitment and
training program to address the leadership vacuum.[39] The next eighteen months saw rapid progress in the institutional development of
the HNP, not only with the installation of police leadership and
ongoing training, but also with the creation of command-and-
control structures, development of operational procedures, and
improvement of police resources and internal oversight mechanisms
with the reinforcement of the Office of the Inspector General.

This was the period of the best relations and cooperation
between the international agents and the Haitian police and authorities. Close and effective coordination was achieved through monthly
and weekly meetings between Haitian officials and donors, chaired
respectively by President Préval and Director General Denizé, at
which progress on the strategic plan was reviewed, donor assistance
was coordinated, and common priorities were set. However, these
meetings ended in August 1997. Haitian government–UN cooperation
deteriorated sharply after Special Representative of the Secretary-

General Enrique Ter Horst publicly criticized serious irregularities in the electoral process and the inadequate official Haitian response and announced that in consequence UN technical electoral assistance would be cut off.

Despite the important progress made in police reform, crime continued to loom large among public concerns. The lack of data is such that it is impossible to know actual crime rates in Haiti, but media coverage increased and there was a clear public perception of a significant rise in crime. Crime rates probably fluctuated, but with a clear trend of increasing over time. Periodic waves of political insecurity also continued.

The HNP performed poorly as they faced mounting crime owing to their inexperience, weak command, and small numbers and the lack of a functional judiciary. In addition to a boom in private guards and security companies, other responses to rising crime included vigilante killings and the development by some local elected authorities of their own security forces—without any legal basis, regulation, or oversight. In some instances, police supported the creation of neighborhood *brigades de vigilance* that were responsible for abuses and even involved in lynchings. Clashes often resulted from occasional HNP efforts to disarm these parallel security forces. The HNP were confronted now and then with angry mobs demanding the release of prisoners or protesting against police abuse. A number of police stations were ransacked, and several police were lynched, including a local police chief in Limbé.[40] Despite the troubled path of police-community relations, in the face of increasing crime, many communities continued to demand a greater police presence and call for improved police response to their security needs. Rural areas, in particular, were and still are seriously underpoliced, a reality that has led to ongoing, unrealized proposals to create a separate rural police corps.[41]

Despite the weakness of the HNP, the new police were operating in a way none of their predecessors ever had. One result was a rapid increase in the number of detainees and consequent overcrowding in prisons and increasing rates of extended pretrial detention. Increased arrest rates did not translate into improved investigations, however. The HNP did not work properly under investigating judges as prescribed under Haitian law, accusing judges of corruption and incompetence and sometimes taking the law into their own hands and preemptively "punishing" alleged criminals. For their part, judges pointed to extensive technical deficiencies in police investigative procedures as one of the reasons underlying ongoing problems with criminal proceedings.

Police Abuse and Accountability

The HNP's human rights record also remained troublesome, despite the important advances in institutional development. As the police force became consolidated, certain patterns of abuse became more systematic, particularly beatings of criminal suspects and holding detainees in police custody well beyond the prescribed forty-eight hours. At the rank of the HNP station commander ("commissariat"), levels of abuse clearly varied depending on the rotation of specific police commanders. Overall, Port-au-Prince has always had both the highest concentration of crime and the most serious cases of police abuse. Although it would seem that most abuses were not part of official government policy (at least initially), the absence of disciplinary measures for certain types or cases of abuse gave the impression that they were at a minimum tolerated by authorities, in some cases at the highest level. Killings of police—sixty-six were recorded by MICIVIH—contributed to the problem as they provoked revenge attacks by the HNP, resulting in some of the worst incidents of police abuse. While many of the killings occurred during personal fights or were gang related and not political, few were cleared up or brought to the courts, and HNP morale suffered as a result.[42]

One of the important successes of this period was the building up of the HNP internal disciplinary system—the Office of the Inspector General—which received significant assistance from ICITAP, CIVPOL, and MICIVIH. Between November 20, 1995, and September 30, 1997, the inspector general fired 163 police and suspended 381, referring 46 additional cases to the courts (by late 1999, the total number of police fired had risen to 407).[43] This level of accountability was unprecedented in any Haitian institution. However, one of the major problems in trying to stem human rights abuse by the HNP, in addition to the weakness of the police command structure, was the lack of judicial action in most cases of police abuse. Police soon realized that they were highly unlikely to face any further consequence for human rights abuses than the loss of their job.[44] While the police recognized the relative lack of punishment for their abuses, they nevertheless became deeply resentful of the inspector general and felt singled out because of the lack of discipline and accountability for all other state employees.

As of January 1998 there had been not a single successful prosecution for a police killing and only some five or six criminal cases for nondeadly police abuse. In September 2000 four officers, including a police commissioner, were convicted, fined, and sentenced to three years' imprisonment for the May 1999 extrajudicial execution of eleven people in the Carrefour Feuilles neighborhood of Port-au-Prince. While the trial demonstrated what could be achieved, it was unfortunately the exception in a pattern of police impunity.

Reform Undermined

In the following years, the institutional decline of the HNP became increasingly obvious. First, drug trafficking through Haiti boomed in the last years of the 1990s. The annual report of the U.S. Office of Drug Control Policy estimated that in 1999 as much as 13 percent of the cocaine entering the United States was passing through the Dominican Republic and Haiti.[45] The report also stated that in many areas police, including senior officers, were involved in the drug trade. This involvement appears to have been primarily opportunistic and localized rather than structural and endemic to the force.

Second, a political onslaught against the HNP began. In 1999 Aristide partisans initiated a series of political attacks (graffiti, flyers, and demonstrations) against top police authorities—notably Denizé and Joseph, but particularly Manuel—ostensibly for their failure to control crime. In October 1999 Manuel resigned suddenly before leaving the country.[46] The following day a former army commander who had been advising the HNP and was rumored to be Manuel's successor was assassinated.

In May 2000 Inspector General Eucher Luc Joseph suddenly left his post, reportedly removed because he would not halt an investigation of drug trafficking in northern Haiti that allegedly implicated a number of police commanders. Subsequently, the inspector general's office faced serious difficulties in remaining operational, with a number of constraints, including lack of resources and threats to investigators at times. The office offered little public account of its work other than occasional announcements of investigations it had been undertaking, which undermined its credibility.

While the HNP initially received praise for their efforts to develop an electoral security plan for the May 2000 congressional and local elections, their record during the campaign period was marred by incidents when "police failed to intervene and on a few occasions appeared to collude in the violence." However, on other occasions "police were attacked when they intervened to stop violent demonstrators."[47] Following the elections, the HNP arrested 146 people, roughly one-third of them members of the opposition, including several candidates.

While at a technical level advisers continued to make some progress in systems development (e.g., recruitment standards and processes and the antinarcotics unit), at the institutional level the HNP was floundering and serious morale problems had led to a significant rate of attrition.[48] In July 2000 the United States cut off its assistance for police reform, indicating that the Haitian government was not demonstrably committed to reform and that continued U.S. assistance could not be justified for an increasingly corrupt and politicized HNP.

Aristide's return to the presidency in February 2001 did little to change this picture, and the situation deteriorated further after his departure in February 2004. New police authorities appear to have been selected for their political loyalty rather than their leadership capacity, and anecdotal evidence suggests that a significant number of former FAdH members were given mid- and senior-level leadership positions. In response to public concerns about crime, Aristide announced a campaign of "zero tolerance," which was denounced by Haitian human rights groups as likely to promote police abuse, vigilantism, and lynching. In December 2001 a strange attack against the presidential palace was described by the government as a coup attempt implicating former police officers. The political opposition claimed that it was orchestrated by government sectors to justify a government clampdown.

During the 2004 armed takeovers of Gonaives and Cap Haitien, police stations and courthouses were ransacked and destroyed. In the aftermath of the uprisings, the transitional government and the international community did nothing to disarm the various groups, leaving parts of the country in the effective control of former military elements. The interim government also furthered the militarization of the HNP, incorporating about two hundred former soldiers into the police with no vetting in January 2005.[49]

The security situation continued to deteriorate, with a wave of violence in September 2004 in which eighty people are known to have been killed, among them eleven police officers, in gun battles between the HNP and Aristide supporters in Port-au-Prince's volatile slums. Between March 2004 and June 2005 more than fifty officers were killed.[50] The police response was marked by increasing brutality in their actions in the slums and human rights abuses, including execution-style killings. Police enjoyed total impunity for all of these acts. The Office of the Inspector General was nonfunctioning and CIVPOL, while acknowledging HNP responsibility for these acts, did nothing to investigate or prosecute them.[51] Many police have also been deeply implicated in criminal activities, including armed robbery, kidnappings, and drug trafficking. In 2005 the UN mission (MINUSTAH) embarked on a program to vet the police to remove violators and criminals, and to recruit and train new officers to improve the security situation and create an environment in which democratic process could stand a chance of success. A decade after the 1994 intervention, it seemed that everything had come full circle: police reform in Haiti was back where it had started.

Justice Reform

On President Aristide's return to Haiti in 1994, the Haitian justice system was in a deplorable state. Judicial reform was to be the cornerstone for the establishment of the rule of law following the return to constitutional government. In 2002 a vision and strategy for reform still had not been agreed on and implemented and international aid had been suspended. Subsequent political upheaval completely undermined what little progress had been made, including reversing the few court judgments that were reached in key human rights cases.

Planning for reform had begun briefly in 1991 but was interrupted by the coup d'état. Preparations that began in 1993 following the Governors Island Agreement included a planned national conference on judicial reform,[52] a MICIVIH report on administration of justice throughout the country requested by the justice minister, and the planning of an $18 million USAID project.[53] All of these initiatives were interrupted by the collapse of the Governors Island process in October 1993. Between then and the return of Aristide in October 1994, little discussion and planning occurred, although there was much focus on police reforms.

Attempts to relaunch the judicial reform process after the September 1994 intervention were riddled with problems from the start. The government lacked human and material resources and experience in planning. This limited absorptive capacity contributed to Haitian difficulties in establishing leadership over the process. There was little coordination between donors, who for the most part failed to help the Government of Haiti (GOH) develop the necessary leadership capacities and pursued their own agendas instead. Rather than being a forum from which to launch a process of consultation leading to an agreed-on reform framework, early meetings of the GOH and the international community were essentially little more than cursory information-giving sessions about projects, most of which were funded by the United States. Attempts to bring on board the national bar association in early reform efforts were met with resistance. Local human rights groups, accustomed to an adversarial relationship with government, were reluctant to participate in discussions with the authorities.

Reports, recommendations, seminars, working groups, and other initiatives regarding judicial reform have not been lacking over the years. The problem has been implementation, particularly sustainable implementation. Many of the reports suggested a consensus on some of the key issues for reform: establishing an independent judiciary, professionalizing the judiciary through training, strengthening the Ministry of Justice and court management, reforming outdated codes and procedures, improving access to justice so that it served more than a privileged few, strengthening accountability, and ending impunity.[54]

Stopgap Responses by Donors

In the absence of a comprehensive long-term reform framework from the outset, some emergency steps were taken beginning in 1995. The Ministry of Justice replaced many allegedly corrupt judges and those who supported the previous regime; however, the transparency and the legality of the process were called into question since criteria for the selection and dismissal of judges had not been established.[55] Donors conducted some basic emergency training for most judicial personnel that year—before the process of removing judges had been established. Within two years, two-thirds of the justices of the peace (many of whom had received the training) had been replaced.

Bilateral donors initiated a range of projects in 1995. USAID embarked on a five-year project encompassing support for the Ministry of Justice, case management systems, legal assistance, supply of materials, emergency training, and the development of the École de la Magistrature (EMA).[56] Canada funded court reconstruction and a law library at the EMA and assisted the Ministry of Justice. The French also supported the EMA and gave assistance to the Ministry of Justice, legal aid, and grants for judicial personnel to study in France. A third legal aid project was funded by the European Union. MICIVIH provided technical assistance and training and monitored the administration of justice throughout the country.

The EMA was one of the few projects with some tangible success though it had a difficult trajectory. With time, the Haitian authorities gradually assumed many of the responsibilities, including some of the budget, and French assistance to the project continued. Though there were protracted delays owing to political and funding problems, the EMA recruited, trained, and deployed a number of judges, recruited through an unprecedented, rigorous selection procedure.[57] However, human and material resources remained scarce, and the school's statutes, drafted in 1999–2000, were never approved by parliament. The "success" of the EMA was perhaps best reflected in private comments by some lawyers who blamed it for a new breed of judges who insisted on correct procedures, thereby obstructing the lawyers' work. Such comments are also an indication of the costs implied by judicial reform for one powerful sector.

In addition to the EMA, extensive on-the-job training/advice (particularly by MICIVIH, OPDAT [the U.S. Justice Department's Office of Overseas Prosecutorial Development, Assistance, and Training], and USAID contractor Checchi) and other types of assistance, such as ad hoc seminars and conferences on legal issues, sought to help professionalize judicial work. It is clear from certain trials and proceedings that progress has been made on an individual basis, but the broader impact of professionally trained individuals remains severely limited by ongoing structural weaknesses of the judicial system and continued external pressures.

Many early decisions on priorities and project funding were made by external actors with little initial local input, raising the questions of suitability to local realities and ownership of the reform process by the host country. Donor impatience to see results—the quick-fix approach—also dictated choices that would not necessarily bring about long-term changes or local ownership. Some priorities identified early on by the Ministry of Justice have never been addressed in any systematic way, for example, the rehabilitation and strengthening of the justice of the peace courts and the offices of the Civil Registry (the latter are responsible for issuing birth certificates among other things; many Haitians still do not have this key document). These courts and offices had the most interface with the population and were viewed as a means for improving access to justice.

Rates of pretrial detention have frequently been used as a barometer to measure progress in judicial performance, though sporadic releases and speedier case processing did not necessarily improve the quality of justice or address structural weaknesses. Technical assistance focused on solving the problem of prolonged pretrial detention to strengthen respect for due process and eliminate arbitrary arrests and detention. Statistics from the national prison administration suggest that in a number of regions, cases were indeed being dealt with more quickly by 1999. With collaboration among MICIVIH, OPDAT, and several first-instance tribunals, Haitian authorities were holding more regular criminal hearings (assizes) by then. But the bulk of the problem of prolonged pretrial detention remained in Port-au-Prince, where judicial resources were particularly strained and where little support had been given to improving court management.[58]

Piecemeal short-term initiatives with quick visible results (a number of releases) predominated over longer-term approaches, possibly to respond to international pressure for prompt results and an exit strategy, and sustainability was lacking.[59] The government set up the Commission pour palier les lenteurs de la justice, later called the Bureau de Contrôle de Détention Préventive (BUCODEP), and appointed a group of legal assistants to the National Penitentiary, but the problems persisted.

Haitian Government Justice Reform Planning

In 1997, with assistance and funding from the European Union, the Préval government established the Commission préparatoire à la réforme du droit et de la justice (Preparatory Justice and Law Reform Commission, hereafter Preparatory Commission), made up of donors and Haitian and international experts. The Preparatory Commission's July 1998 report offered broad policy recommendations and a five-year strategic plan to strengthen the Ministry of Justice, establish judicial independence, improve due process and access to justice, reform outdated laws, and work with both judicial actors and civil society to appropriate the changes and develop new judicial practices. To this end, the report recommended the establishment of a National Justice Reform Commission including extensive representation from civil society. A core focus was to "guarantee the respect and defence of human rights," and another significant stipulation was that the reform *must be Haitian, in spite of the necessary external support.*[60] President Préval agreed to a series of steps to launch the reforms, but as political crisis deepened and relations with the international community deteriorated, implementation stalled and donors suspended aid to the Preparatory Commission.

Further problems for all judicial reform initiatives were the lack of continuity and internal disputes in the Ministry of Justice. A new minister of justice, appointed in March 1999, revived hopes of reform when he set up working groups of Haitian and international experts to draft texts of a series of laws,[61] even though the initiative did not pursue the overall strategic plan of the Preparatory Commission. While considerable headway was made in drafting new legal codes, a new minister of justice took office following Aristide's inauguration in February 2001. By this time, most foreign aid to the justice sector had been suspended owing to the ongoing political crisis and a perceived lack of political will to carry out judicial reform.[62] The process stalled again as another minister—the sixth in seven years—took office in March 2002.[63]

Insufficient human and material resources, lack of continuity, the priority placed on police reform, and suspension of international aid are real but inadequate explanations for the lack of progress in judicial reform. Judicial reform threatens the control of the system enjoyed by the executive and powerful conservative sectors such as bar associations. The executive still controlled all aspects of the judicial system, including the selection and dismissal of judges.[64] A revamped Conseil Supérieur de la Magistrature was finally set up in 2006 by the interim government. Justices of the peace enjoy no security of tenure. The executive (especially through prosecutors, or *commissaires du gouvernement*) and the police had often overridden or ignored judicial orders, particularly in political or other sensitive cases. Judicial impartiality was also frequently called into question; the system processed cases against opposition activists suspected of acts of violence and persistently failed to prosecute associates of the regime in power accused of violence. The government's interest in maintaining ongoing guarantees of impunity has increased with the protracted and often-violent political crisis.

Assessing Ongoing Impunity

Haitian courts were unable or unwilling to try human rights abuses committed before or after 1994, or drug trafficking and violence by popular organizations. There have been a handful of unprecedented trials, such as the Carrefour Feuilles trial, which was mentioned earlier, and the 2000 trial of former military and FRAPH members accused of killings in Raboteau in 1994. The Raboteau case took five years to come to trial and showed the feasibility of holding proceedings that met most of the requirements for a fair trial. At the same time, this trial benefited from political will, better-trained judicial personnel, and appropriate resources, as well as international support in the form of international lawyers for the prosecution and MICIVIH/MICAH technical advice. It demonstrated greater judicial professionalization than the earlier major trials in 1995 and 1996 for the 1993 assassinations of prominent Aristide supporter Antoine Izmery and Justice Minister Guy Malary. Yet such effective, politically supported trials remained the exception rather than the rule. Several hundred complaints of pre-1994 abuses monitored by MICIVIH made little headway through the courts. Only a few resulted in the conviction of former soldiers or their associates and, following the resurgence of the former military in 2004, several key convictions have been overturned (discussed later).

Likewise, few post-1994 abuses have been prosecuted by the courts, though there were some timid efforts by judges, particularly in the provinces, to prosecute members of the new police force. But police officers frequently failed to obey judicial summons, believing themselves to be above the law. Even police officials complained at times that cases of police abuse that they handed over to the courts in Port-au-Prince were not actively pursued, though there were a number of cases of police detained at times in connection with armed gangs and drug trafficking.

Judicial personnel enjoy little oversight. The CNVJ, MICIVIH, and the 1998 Judicial Reform Law all recommended the establishment of a commission of judges to investigate serious abuses, no such entity was ever created. Such a mechanism, with international support as in the Raboteau case, could have helped to overcome the problem of investigative and other weaknesses of the court system and restored confidence in the system.[65]

The 2002 investigation into the murder of journalist Jean Dominique epitomizes the struggle to establish a professional, independent judiciary. Death threats to and intimidation of judges, prosecutors, and journalists; the killing of a key witness; a four-month delay in renewing the mandate of the main judge, who had carried out an extensive investigation; parliament's refusal to lift a senator's immunity; and the failure of police to execute arrest warrants issued by the judiciary are just some of the obstacles documented in this case by Haitian and international human rights organizations.

While much attention was focused on high-profile political cases, impunity also continued for much common crime and violence, and the public perception was that the justice system remained profoundly corrupt—particularly in drug trafficking cases. The prevailing impunity for criminal activities also created a problem of distinguishing between violent crime and political violence. Violent crime had the effect of "masking" political crimes, and in some cases, attacks or killings portrayed in the media as politically motivated may well have been profit-motivated common crime. The absence or weakness of police and judicial investigations permitted both criminal impunity and ongoing political impunity.

Internal accountability mechanisms within the judiciary, such as the Judicial Inspection Unit, procedural rules, and definitions of roles and statutes, essential for ensuring professional judicial practices and developing new ones, were never implemented. The Judicial Inspection Unit, though it exists, lacked a mandate and resources and had no clear definition of role or functions, even though texts and proposals had been drafted. Unfortunately, the Ombudsman's Office, set up in 1997, did not develop into a credible independent institution to protect human rights and act as a moral authority and oversight mechanism.

The pace of judicial reform programs was undeniably limited by the lack of financial resources and by the precedence of police reform. For 1996 and 1997, the HNP received roughly five times the domestic budget resources as the Ministry of Justice proper and the judicial system combined.[66] The international community spent a total of $43 million from 1993 to 2001 on the justice sector, and slightly more than $100 million on the HNP during five years.[67] However, more than anything else, as with the police reforms, judicial reform was overshadowed by the deepening political crisis and rising tensions between the international community and the GOH.

As noted, courthouses were ransacked and judges fled during the 2004 uprisings. Subsequently, the judiciary again became a tool of government, holding Aristide supporters in extended pretrial detention without charge. The reversal of several of the few convictions for past human rights abuses is a striking symbol of ongoing impunity and the former military's new influence. In August 2004 Louis Jodel Chamblain, a FRAPH leader who had been convicted in absentia for the 1993 murder of Antoine Izmery (an early Aristide backer), was absolved in a farcical one-day retrial following his return to Haiti as a leader of the 2004 uprisings. On March 21, 2005, the Supreme Court reversed on technical grounds the convictions of the fourteen military and FRAPH leaders for their roles in the Raboteau massacre—generally viewed as a landmark case in the fight against impunity. International condemnation of these judicial actions and of police abuse has made little headway with the interim government, which claims that it cannot be held responsible for human rights violations.[68]

Creating Demand for Justice

Given Haitian history and experience, it is unsurprising that there is no broadly held concept of state institutions serving the public interest. The challenge is how to start the process of building up regulatory mechanisms to end impunity where there is little political will to do so and where civil society still has only limited capacity to demand accountability in any structured way.

Justice sector reforms pursued by donors failed to confront these issues, focusing overwhelmingly on the technical supply side of justice while paying little attention to the demand side, or to the social, economic, and cultural context.[69] Some small alternative dispute resolution and mediation programs were undertaken,[70] but educational initiatives and the broad civil society engagement necessary to generate increased demand for justice and show that a functioning justice system can protect the rights of all, not just the select few, were lacking. Efforts to establish the rule of law had very little impact on most Haitians' lives. Indeed, it is the failures of the system that are all too evident, beyond the impunity in past and present human rights cases to the inability of the system to deal with increasing common crime and violence.

The lack of economic development, persistent extreme poverty, and delays in setting up a national legal aid system have continued to severely limit access to justice. Several separate legal aid projects were initiated in different parts of the country through local NGOs,[71] but these projects (which were of varying effectiveness) constituted a drop in the ocean. A cohesive national policy has yet to be implemented, in spite of proposals made during reform discussions. Bringing the bar associations on board has represented one of the obstacles.

At times donors and Haitians had clearly divergent views of justice, including about the right not to be arbitrarily detained and the right to be presumed innocent, as well as issues relating to minors. Haitian authorities—and the population more broadly—often viewed prolonged detention and illegal arrests of former military members as a necessity justified by the poor state of the justice system. If these individuals were "known criminals," greater justice was done through locking them up, even if this violated international norms, than through leaving them on the streets because of difficulties in processing their cases. These deep-rooted assumptions underscore the need for a long-term approach to changing attitudes and building respect for fundamental human rights.

Prison Reform

At the time of Aristide's return in October 1994, the prison system was in a deplorable state and still controlled by the military, even though the 1987 constitution required the setting up of a prison administration within a civilian police force. Prison conditions were appalling; cruel, inhuman, and degrading treatment was commonplace.

In spite of the gravity of prison conditions at the time, there was little interest initially in embarking on prison reform in 1994. The multinational force began paying systematic attention to the prisons only in January 1995.[72] Following two UN assessments requested by MICIVIH,[73] a reform project was drafted. USAID and UNDP agreed to provide initial funding for a two-phase project: setting up a civilian prison administration, training, and measures to tackle immediate problems, such as introducing prison registers and prisoner dossiers (phase one); and training, rehabilitating buildings, and technical assistance for setting up and consolidating the prison administration (phase two).

By mid-1995, the Haitian government had created a new autonomous civilian prison administration—the Administration Pénitentiaire Nationale (APENA)—and trained 429 prison guards (280 former IPSF and 140 civilians). The program put in place a system of food distribution by the NGO Bureau de Nutrition et de Développement (BND) and carried out urgent repairs to prison buildings. The creation of a unified system of prison registers was an unprecedented improvement in the monitoring of the legality of detention, helping end the formerly commonplace phenomenon of the "forgotten prisoner." A new, separate facility was opened in Port-au-Prince to house women and minors. Some disciplinary measures were taken against staff involved in cases of ill-treatment, and a three-person commission was eventually set up within the Office of the Inspector General. A system of medical care was in place by the end of 1995. A permanent training center had also been established.

The success of these early efforts reflects the active participation of the Haitian authorities and good coordination with and between the donors involved (the UNDP, the International Committee of the Red Cross [ICRC], MICIVIH, the BND, MNF, and subsequently the UN peacekeeping missions). The improvements in the prison system were notable. Unfortunately, these achievements proved hard to consolidate and experienced setbacks and delays, particularly after APENA was brought under the Haitian National Police in 1997 in accordance with constitutional requirements. At that time and later, inadequate access to food and poor sanitary conditions were reported, at times jeopardizing the health and even the lives of detainees. While MICIVIH judged that physical ill-treatment of detainees was not systematic, there were incidents of beatings as punishment for attempted escapes and riots. In November 2001 journalists were invited to photograph hundreds of detainees lying naked on the ground, many with marks from beatings, at the National Penitentiary following a prison riot after the reported beating to death of a detainee by prison guards. In addition, the lack of improvements to the judicial system in terms of processing cases of prolonged detention strained already stretched prison resources, particularly in Port-au-Prince.

Prison reform is one area where international support continued as of 2002, under the auspices of the UNDP, and where the impact of reforms was still visible despite setbacks. Consolidation of this progress was hampered by delays in recruiting APENA personnel and implementing regulations, lack of resources, weak management capacity, lack of medium- and long-term commitment on the part of the international community, and a lack of political will on the part of the Haitian authorities. As with the police and courts, as the political situation collapsed, prison reform faltered. Prisons are again used for the prolonged pretrial detention of opponents, and several spectacular jailbreaks—apparently facilitated by, or at least certainly not impeded by, guards—proved the system's inability to challenge the impunity of those in power.

CONCLUSION

The case of Haiti is important for understanding international police and justice assistance. Despite a significant international investment of aid, financial assistance, and political energy to build democracy and the rule of law, very few sustainable gains were visible eight years after the United States launched a military intervention in the name of restoring democracy. Ten years later, the country was mired in a crisis of political intolerance and violence; familiar patterns of "winner-take-all politics" were supported by increasing political and criminal violence perpetrated by the police, former soldiers, and a panoply of armed gangs supported by political parties, business sectors, and drug trafficking.

Efforts to forge institutional reforms across all levels of state activity—from the efforts to build the rule of law discussed here to other ambitious public sector reforms—completely failed to transform Haiti's centralized, impoverished state apparatus. Even the most striking institutional transformation—the dissolution of the army—may be reversed.

Countries do not emerge from conflict with rebuilding plans in hand, nor with the capacity to hit the ground running. The absence of early local planning and vision in this crucial area as well as a balance of power unfavorable to the Haitian authorities left the way open for those elements of the international community, in particular U.S. authorities, who had done extensive groundwork, particularly for policing reforms, to take charge of reforms. U.S. predominance further impeded the buy-in by Lavalas authorities, many of whom, despite Clinton's pivotal role in returning Aristide to Haiti, tended to view the United States as an ideological opponent, not an ally. Consequently, early reform priorities and project funding decisions were made by external actors with little initial local input. This raised the question of suitability to local realities and of ownership of the reform process by the host country.

It is not surprising that the pace of change within the components of the wider judicial sector was uneven. Justice reform is a complex endeavor, and policing issues took precedence, largely because of international military priorities to protect forces and exit promptly. These circumstances created a range of problems. Increased police efficiency in arresting lawbreakers allied with judicial delays led to prison overcrowding. The progress in prison administration and the treatment of prisoners always ran the risk of being overwhelmed by chronic overcrowding, a consequence of these continuing judicial inefficiencies. Judicial and prosecutorial inability to process arrested criminals led police to take the law into their own hands; a properly functioning justice system is key to the successful professional growth of the police. Gains made in the domain of policing were rapidly reversed because of weak leadership, political interference, and corruption.

The investment in time, energy, goodwill, and resources in post-conflict judicial system construction in Haiti has not paid the expected dividends. Despite some advances, most notably in judicial training and the prison system, the justice system continues to be plagued by long-standing structural problems. Coordination of disparate reform efforts remained a nightmare until the Ministry of Justice began to assume leadership responsibility in mid-1995. The first institutional efforts to put in place a reform plan that would give the Ministry of Justice a stronger voice in determining Haitian reform orientations and priorities began in April 1996, but the plan was not completed until July 1998 with the presentation of a white paper on judicial reform outlining a policy and strategy framework. This document obtained the support of the donors but was never implemented.

The lack of continuity at the highest policymaking level militated against proper planning and building on initial accomplishments. Furthermore, clashing personalities, prickly sensitivities, and internal policy differences, as well as unhappiness about the priorities advanced insistently by certain partners within the international community, resulted at times in recourse to the Haitian evasive tactic called *marronage*, involving silent, foot-dragging resistance. This, in turn, led to protracted paralysis at the decision-making level and, consequently, to the stagnation of the reform process.

Donor sensitivity and understanding of local context were often lacking and were sometimes worsened by donor impatience with the unwillingness or lack of country capacity to lead and coordinate reform efforts, the lack of local financial and human resources, and the country's very limited ability to absorb large amounts of assistance. But donors did not step back and develop slower and more participative processes that might have facilitated joint appropriation of program objectives and implementation. Nor did donors undertake strategies to promote broader public understanding of and support for the reforms. Donors tended to go it alone even when this meant conflicts with the government and erosion of Haitian ownership and investment in the reform. Given the weak condition of Haitian civil society, it is perhaps understandable that donors did not see important partners or an easy area in which to expend energy and resources. Yet transforming social attitudes is necessary to foster respect for individual rights and the rule of law. There was a clear need, for example, for Haitians and donors to figure out how to erase the prevailing view among judicial officials and the wider society that an arrested individual was by definition guilty and deserved whatever fate he or she received. Few results of the short-term, stopgap initiatives in the justice sector have been sustainable, and police reform, while relatively successful in the short run, also foundered. A slower process, with greater emphasis on the social environment of the reforms, might not have produced much more in the short term, but it might have helped create more basis for a longer-term, more incremental reform process and avoided the frustration and dashed expectations produced by the real or perceived failure of the strategy.

Despite the limitations or failures of "top-down" efforts to reform state institutions, very few "bottom-up" strategies have been undertaken. One of the few bright spots of the past few years has been the reemergence of civil society groups, some of which have begun to take a more active role in demanding and facilitating change, most notably in political negotiations, and the growth of an independent and lively press. Without arguing that larger civil society engagement would have turned the tide in Haiti, there was room for involving civil society in discussions, and systematic training for different civil society sectors would probably have been well received, particularly in the early days of reforms. Such activities should probably be considered and structured in the context of a long-term civil society–building strategy. Otherwise, civil society groups that understand their relation to the state in adversarial terms are likely to play a role in critiquing the failures of reform but unlikely to be engaged in protecting what progress is achieved. Unfortunately, since the failed elections of 2000, government critics (especially among the press, human rights groups, and other NGOs) came increasingly under attack, often at the hands of armed thugs rather than state agents. None of these cases was ever investigated or prosecuted.

Ultimately, security and justice reform in Haiti foundered for political reasons. Ironically, the electoral cycles of democracy may have undermined the establishment of the rule of law. It is clear that the political timetable for the return of electoral democracy, with constant elections at local, regional, and national levels from 1995 on, created significant difficulties for the reform process. The electoral jousting aggravated divisions among former political allies as they sought to distinguish themselves from one another, consolidate or build political parties, and obtain resources for their participation in the elections. Elections focused attention on attaining control of the state and its meager resources rather than on defining the shape that a new, democratic Haitian state should have. The reemergence and growing brutality of the winner-take-all style of politics generated a powerful demand for continued impunity for those in government and their allies. That said, the failure of the National Commission on Truth and Justice also points to a deeper failure of accountability that, despite the limited international support and U.S. obstruction of the process, is ultimately attributable to Haitian authorities' inability to use the transition to start to challenge deep-rooted social and political structures of impunity and marginalization. Instead, old elites persist, with some erosion of their prerogatives, while new political elites continue the repressive and predatory style of traditional Haitian politics.

One of the costs of the slow progress or failure of reforms in Haiti may be the deep cynicism that today prevails among most Haitians and donors who have worked there. At the political level, this is most visible in voter apathy and low turnout in repeated elections. Given the favorable combination of international intervention, tremendous international attention and goodwill, and pledges of some US$3 billion in aid, the meager results have dashed high hopes for change. While one would hope that lessons might have been learned from the failures of international intervention, the current demobilization program is marked by a deeply flawed approaches, police and judicial reforms appear to be back where they started in 1994, and, again, elections are viewed as the only hope for attaining sufficient government legitimacy on which to start to build long-term development programs. Whatever lessons donors and Haitians have drawn from the past twelve years, they were unable to escape Haiti's vicious cycle of winner-take-all politics.

Postconflict societies are plagued by formidable structural, social, and political constraints. It must, however, be borne in mind that the roots of conflict and institutional collapse do not disappear with the signing of a peace accord or the imposition of a political solution. Rebuilding institutions in such a context is a complex and daunting task. It requires considerable ingenuity, sensitivity, patience, and determination from both local and external actors. Their respective inputs need to be carefully meshed to prevent the former from being relegated to a secondary role. However, slippage is a constant threat. Short-term gains are often marginal compared with the resources invested. This seeming inability to deliver results places intense pressure on the local actors. It also creates problems of political and financial sustainability for external partners who already have difficulty maintaining commitment for the long haul that postconflict reconstruction inevitably requires.

NOTES

1. International Crisis Group, *A New Chance for Haiti?* ICG Latin America/Caribbean Report No. 10 (Port-au-Prince and Brussels: International Crisis Group, November 18, 2004).

2. Haiti ranked 146th of the 173 countries rated by the United Nations Development Programme in the *Human Development Report 2002* (New York: United Nations, 2002).

3. The Lavalas movement emerged from popular (peasant) organizations and the base church movement in Haiti. Lavalas means "landslide" in Haitian Creole and signified the goal of sweeping away the old political order.

4. Each of Haiti's nine departments was divided into military districts, subdistricts, and sections. The section chief was appointed by the commander of the subdistrict. In practice, section chiefs purchased their appointments and then sold positions of assistant or attaché to others. In some sections, hundreds of assistants were reported to exist. Section chiefs dominated the life of rural Haiti for decades, imposing arbitrary taxes, making illegal arrests, and demanding payments to conduct offices or desist from beating prisoners and committing other brutalities. See Lawyers Committee for Human Rights, *Paper Laws, Steel Bayonets: Breakdown of the Rule of Law in Haiti* (New York: Lawyers Committee for Human Rights, November 1990); and Washington Office on Latin America (WOLA), *Policing Haiti: Preliminary Assessment of the New Civilian Security Force* (Washington, D.C.: WOLA, September 1995).

5. Michel S. Laguerre, *The Military and Society in Haiti* (Knoxville: University of Tennessee Press, 1993), 6.

6. U.S. Agency for International Development, 1993 Administration of Justice project document.

7. Courts frequently lacked—and still do—legal texts, paper, desks, office space, and so on. Judicial personnel, many without even a law degree, were often picked for their political or social allegiances rather than for competence. Salaries were abysmal, and no training was available.

8. The long-neglected and poorly functioning Civil Registry (État Civil) also meant that a substantial proportion of Haitians did not have birth certificates or other civil documents.

9. "Social groups—knowing only the brutal and predatory manifestations of the State—have developed informal justice practices outside the official administration to regulate the majority of lives," according to the Ministry of Justice in its *CPRDJ Report, 1997.* See also Gerard Barthelemy, *Dans la splendeur d'un après-midi d'histoire* (Port-au-Prince: Éditions Henri Deschamps, 1996).

10. Amy Wilentz, *The Rainy Season: Haiti since Duvalier* (New York: Simon and Schuster, 1989).

11. The French acronym FRAPH sounds the same as the French word for "strike" or "hit."

12. Human Rights Watch, *Silencing a People: The Destruction of Civil Society in Haiti* (New York: Human Rights Watch and the National Coalition for Haitian Refugees, February 1993).

13. Ibid.

14. The United States unilaterally created a set of exemptions to the trade embargo imposed by the Organization of American States following the coup.

15. During negotiations, U.S. officials offered the Haitian military incentives such as a blanket amnesty and military assistance. These encouraged the FAdH to test the limits of U.S. commitment to Aristide and led to the breakdown of the Governors Island Agreement permitting Aristide's return to Haiti. On October 30, 1993, a gang of lightly armed but rowdy and aggressive FRAPH members gathered on the dock in Port-au-Prince to oppose the landing of the first contingent of U.S. peacekeepers, aboard the USS *Harlan County*, anchored in the bay. Scarred by recent combat casualties in Somalia, the administration ordered the *Harlan County* to pull out, and the process collapsed.

16. See International Crisis Group, *A New Chance for Haiti?* ICG Latin America/Caribbean Report No. 10 (Port-au-Prince and Brussels: International Crisis Group, November 18, 2004), 9–11.

17. Johanna Mendelson, "Beyond the Mountains, More Mountains: Demobilizing the Haitian Army," in *Peacemaking and Democratization in the Western Hemisphere*, ed. Tommie Sue Montgomery (Coral Gables, Fla.: North-South Center Press at the University of Miami, 2000).

18. D. Williams, "Perry Indicates U.S. Disarmament of Aristide Opponents Is Unlikely," *Washington Post*, November 28, 1994.

19. International Crisis Group, *Spoiling Security in Haiti*, Latin America/Caribbean Report No. 13 (Port-au-Prince and Brussels: International Crisis Group, May 31, 2005), 6, 9.

20. See Colin Granderson, "Institutionalising Peace: The Haiti Experience," in *Honoring Human Rights: From Peace to Justice* (Washington, D.C.: Aspen Institute, 1998).

21. For an account of the United States' ambivalent policy toward FRAPH, see Bob Schacochis, *The Immaculate Invasion* (New York: Viking Press, 1999).

22. Granderson, "Institutionalising Peace."

23. In the face of government passivity, local NGOs ended up distributing extracts or the full report, and in 1998 the Plateforme des Organisations Haitiennes des Droits de l'Homme (POHDH) published a critical summary. It was also in 1998 that MICIVIH was asked by the authorities to facilitate copying and distribution in any significant quantities, in spite of its readiness to do so earlier.

24. In 1999 the human rights organization MAP VIV published *Jalons pour une politique de réparation* based on a nationwide survey of victims of abuses and their needs. It highlighted the challenges of developing reparations policies when the majority of the population has suffered the economic devastation of an embargo.

25. About US$4 million—at an exchange rate of 15 gourdes to US$1.

26. The head of the office, with the minister of justice, made discretionary choices about which projects to fund. For a comprehensive assessment of approaches to impunity in Haiti after 1994, see MICIVIH's report *La Lutte contre l'impunité et pour la réparation,* published in 1999.

27. Jan Stromsem and Joseph Trincellito, "Peacebuilding in Haiti: Lessons Learned in Building the Haitian National Police" (paper presented at the International Peace Academy meeting "Lessons Learned Seminar: Peace-Building in Haiti," Security Sector Reform: The Haitian National Police, New York, January 23–24, 2002), 14.

28. Ibid., 2. The police salaries were set at a level some three times higher than those of local judicial authorities, causing serious parity problems. There were also concerns about the fiscal sustainability of police pay. Then U.S. ambassador William Swing commented, "[W]e have given the Haitian fewer police than they need, and more than they can afford."

29. The problem was somewhat alleviated in Port-au-Prince when Dany Toussaint was made head of the IPSF. He confronted and had some successes against rapidly emerging gangs and armed criminals who were starting to plague the densely populated slum neighborhoods. This won him considerable popularity, although he has long been a very controversial figure with U.S. authorities, who accuse him of covering up alleged political murders and drug trafficking. He later became a prominent member of the Haitian Senate.

30. MICIVIH training was also broadened to support a pilot project in community policing in the north of Haiti. While the project was quite successful at the local level, when an attempt was made to initiate a similar project in Les Cayes and integrate it more centrally into HNP policing, Haitian authorities who never saw community policing as a priority rejected it.

31. The academy experienced serious problems later on because of prolonged delays in the selection of new recruits. Thus, instructors had no recruits to train, in addition to a lack of resources. By 2001 all foreign advisers had been withdrawn from the academy owing to the suspension of aid.

32. General Accounting Office (GAO), *Foreign Assistance: Any Further Aid to Haitian Justice System Should Be Linked to Performance-Related Conditions* (Washington, D.C.: GAO-01-24, October 2000).

33. Despite the general stricture on military rollovers, the IPSF and Guatanamo police did enter certain units of the HNP, primarily a ministerial guard unit, the traffic unit, and the prison guard.

34. WOLA and Human Rights Watch made these recommendations to donors. See WOLA, *Policing Haiti*; and Human Rights Watch/Americas, National Coalition for Haitian Rights, and Washington Office on Latin America, *The Human Rights Record of the Haitian National Police* (New York and Washington, D.C.: Human Rights Watch, National Coalition for Haitian Rights, and Washington Office on Latin America, 1997). See also Stromsem and Trincellito, "Peacebuilding in Haiti." Engaging civil society would not have been easy. The capacity of Haitian civil society, and of the popular organizations that provided the underpinning of the Lavalas movement in particular, was limited to start with, and the latter, having been the primary targets of military repression, were in considerable disarray.

35. MICIVIH, *La Police Nationale d'Haiti et les Droits de l'Homme*; and Human Rights Watch/Americas, National Coalition for Haitian Rights, and the Washington Office on Latin America, *The Human Rights Record of the Haitian National Police*.

36. Local priest, interview with Rachel Neild, Gonaives, February 1996.

37. See Human Rights Watch/Americas, National Coalition for Haitian Rights, and Washington Office on Latin America, *The Human Rights Record of the Haitian National Police*.

38. USAID official, conversation with Rachel Neild about an unpublished opinion poll conducted by USAID in Haiti. The reliability of the figure cannot be ascertained given lack of information on the methodology of representativity of the sample.

39. The recruitment and training plan sought to exploit three candidate pools—university graduates, former military members, and the brightest elements within the HNP—to rapidly improve the police leadership. To an important degree this was achieved. For further discussion, see WOLA and NCHR, *Can Haiti's Police Reform Be Sustained?* (New York and Washington, D.C.: Washington Office on Latin America and National Coalition for Haitian Rights, January 1998). See also the UN reports of the secretary-general, available at www.un.org.

40. MICIVIH, *Human Rights Review*, October–December 1999, http://www.un.org/rights/micivih/rapports/hrr99q4.html.

41. The idea of *agents rurales* who would have less education and training and lower pay than the regular HNP officers was resisted by various sectors within the Lavalas movement and by human rights groups, who feared that it risked creating "second class police for second class citizens." However, the Haitian government clearly cannot afford to significantly increase the size and therefore budget of the HNP, which already consumes more than 75 percent of the Ministry of Justice's budget.

42. MICIVIH, *Human Rights Review*.

43. See WOLA and NCHR, *Can Haiti's Police Reforms Be Sustained?* See also early October 1999 figures provided by the inspector general in MICIVIH, *Human Rights Review.*

44. Judicial impunity for police abuse was aggravated in June 1997, when a judge released six HNP officers accused of summary executions. In April 1997 MICIVIH submitted proposals to improve judicial action against police abuse, including draft terms of reference for a special prosecutor for police abuse.

45. International Narcotics Control Strategy Report 2000 and 2004, cited in International Crisis Group, *Spoiling Security in Haiti*, 4–5.

46. Robert Manuel states that top government officials informed him that his security could not be guaranteed. Robert Manuel, conversation with Rachel Neild, Guatemala, November 2000.

47. Amnesty International, *World Report 2001* (London: Amnesty International, 2001).

48. While no reliable figures exist, most donors were estimating anecdotally that at least 1,000 HNP officers were no longer turning up for work. In addition, large numbers of police were fired for corruption, desertion, and abuse. Most donors estimated that the force had no more than 3,500 personnel in 2001.

49. International Crisis Group, *Spoiling Security in Haiti*, 13.

50. Ibid., 10.

51. Ibid., 11.

52. Document produced by Kurzban Kurzban and P. A. Weinger on behalf of President Aristide, September 13, 1993.

53. The report, *Analysis of the Haitian Justice System with Recommendations to Improve the Administration of Justice in Haiti*, was completed in 1994 and made available to actors in the justice sector following the return to constitutional rule. An updated version, *Le Système judiciaire en Haiti*, was published in May 1996.

54. Identifying reform as a key step toward ending impunity and preventing atrocities like those that characterized previous regimes, the National Truth and Justice Commission made a series of recommendations for strengthening the judiciary in its 1996 report. A retreat organized by the Ministry of Justice at the Hotel Xaragua in April 1996 produced *Éléments d'orientation pour une réforme de la justice en Haiti* (Elements to Orient Judicial Reform in Haiti).

55. A 1995 Decree on the Organisation of the Judiciary partially outlined the structure and functions of the judiciary and created judicial inspection agents, but some provisions need bringing into line with the constitution.

56. These programs were mainly conducted through the contractor Checchi Consulting Company and the U.S. Justice Department's Office of Overseas Prosecutorial Development, Assistance, and Training (OPDAT). There was no coordination between selection of judges for training and the removal of judges, and USAID officials often expressed frustration that the Ministry of Justice was firing trained judges.

57. In 1997 the EMA took in its first group of sixty trainee judges, who graduated the following year. The selection of those students and of the subsequent group of forty was carried out according to an unprecedented, rigorous examination monitored and supported by the international community. The EMA has also focused on periodic training sessions for justices of the peace and a series of seminars for police and judges. Seminars on forensic medicine (supported by Médecins du Monde) have led to the setting up of a small, much-needed team of forensic experts.

58. A Checchi project was withdrawn, agreement was not reached on a replacement project, and MICAH advisers assigned to Port-au-Prince courts were withdrawn shortly after deployment when the mission ended.

59. Case-tracking systems set up by OPDAT and Checchi may have helped expedite proceedings in certain provinces but were never implemented in Port-au-Prince, and some registration systems were reportedly not maintained after the advisers left. The government never officially adopted the systems, and both projects were closed by 2000, when funding ended and USAID failed to reach an agreement with the GOH on subsequent projects.

60. Shortly before the report was finalized, a curious Judicial Reform Law was passed that did little more than list the areas to be reformed, included three clauses related to past human rights abuses and reparation that have only partially been implemented, and ended with a singular clause requiring that the state ensure the departure of all foreign armed personnel from Haiti as their presence hindered the establishment of the rule of law.

61. The draft laws related to, inter alia, the Judicial Inspection Unit, legal aid, statutes for the judiciary and the EMA, a law on the independence of the judiciary, and an organic law on the Ministry of Justice.

62. By this time MICIVIH and its successor mission, MICAH, both of which provided or were intended to provide extensive support for strengthening the judiciary, had also been withdrawn.

63. A small UNDP team continues to work with the Ministry of Justice on strengthening the ministry's office and on other reform-related issues.

64. For an account of the work conditions given by Port-au-Prince justices of the peace, see Haiti Solidarité Internationale, *Haiti: Les Tribunaux de Paix* (Port-au-Prince: Haiti Solidarité).

65. In November 1996 a group of judges was appointed to make up such a commission, named the Unité Pénale Nationale, and given training by MICIVIH with French government support, but the initiative was suspended sometime afterward by the authorities. The idea resurfaced in the 1998 Judicial Reform Law but has never been implemented. See MICIVIH, *La Lutte contre l'impunité et pour la réparation en Haiti.*

66. UN Development Programme, *Justices en Haiti* (New York: United Nations, 1999).

67. U.S. Government Accounting Office, "Any Further Aid to Haitian Justice System Should Be Linked to Performance Related Conditions" (Washington, D.C.: GAO, October 2000).

68. International Crisis Group, *Spoiling Security in Haiti,* 16.

69. See UNDP, *Justices en Haiti,* 1999.

70. Mediation/conciliation techniques for justices of the peace developed in a pilot project by MICIVIH in an area dominated by land conflict have now been incorporated into training programs at the École de la Magistrature. Other initiatives include a five-year program organized by Peace Brigades International. See Peace Brigades International, Haiti, *Bulletin #13,* July 1999.

71. The largest, funded by Checchi through several local NGOs, was severely criticized, and its claims that thousands had received legal aid and were released were publicly called into question during a U.S. documentary on CBS TV. Funding to another, the Belgian NGO Réseau des Citoyens network, was eventually withdrawn owing to the European Union's suspension of aid to Haiti. A third project, legal assistance in justice of the peace courts, was organized by Haiti Solidarité Internationale with French funding. Amicale des Juristes also provided limited legal assistance with foreign assistance.

72. This came after a change of command of the MNF, and several months after a U.S. officer carried out a visit to the National Penitentiary without permission because of concerns about conditions there. Lieutenant Lawrence Rockwood was threatened with court-martial for this act and eventually received a dishonorable discharge.

73. The UN Human Rights Centre and the UN Crime Prevention and Criminal Justice Division conducted the assessments in January 1995.

4

Business as Usual?

Justice and Policing Reform in Postwar Guatemala

WILLIAM D. STANLEY

I N 1997 THE GUATEMALAN GOVERNMENT AND REBELS FROM the Guatemalan National Revolutionary Unity (URNG) signed the last
in a series of peace accords, most of which had been brokered by
the United Nations. The accords appeared, on the surface, to provide an opportunity and framework for addressing a series of problems that had plagued Guatemala and contributed to the outbreak of
civil war, including massive state violence, political exclusion, institutionalized racism, and a near-complete failure of the justice system
to hold abusive military leaders accountable. The accords covered an
unusually comprehensive set of issues, including such things as government support for agriculture, the use of indigenous languages in
education and administration, and other cultural and collective
rights. With respect to violence and justice, the accords called for a
United Nations–sponsored truth commission to investigate past
abuses, creation of a new civilian police force, reduction in the institutional power and prerogatives of the military, intelligence reform,
and reforms of the judicial system. International donors pumped millions of dollars into the police, judiciary, prosecutors, and public

113

defenders. The United Nations Verification Mission in Guatemala (MINUGUA) verified implementation and worked to develop state institutions. UN officials portrayed the Guatemala process as a major success, on the strength of the very comprehensive accords as well as the very participatory process for implementation.

Unfortunately, the record of actual accomplishments is very limited. Many provisions of the accords were never implemented. With respect to security and justice, only a few military officers were convicted and sentenced for human rights crimes, and these few successes resulted largely from legal interventions by Guatemalan non-governmental organizations (NGOs), backed by international political support. The routine functioning of the judicial system remained extremely deficient; the Public Ministry (MP), responsible for prosecution, showed signs of systemic incompetence; the police were reformed more in name than in practice; intelligence reform lagged; and international resources were wasted through a lack of coordination and failure to hold Guatemalan agencies responsible for effective use of the resources provided. While average Guatemalans had somewhat better access to the justice system, victims of crimes had little chance of seeing the arrest and successful prosecution of their victimizers. Politically motivated threats and violence persisted and even increased in 2003–04, particularly against accountability advocates. During the presidential administration of Alfonso Portillo (2000–2004), criminal networks appeared to enjoy increased freedom and influence.[1]

The fundamental problem appears to be the circumstances under which Guatemala's war ended. The most intense period of the conflict ended more than a decade before the final peace, and the government prevailed. Internationalized peace negotiations provided an orderly and peaceful context for reincorporating former rebels into a more open political system. However, the weak rebels could not demand significant, specific, verifiable concessions by the government. The accords were thus a vague list of desiderata, with few solid commitments for change. Within Guatemala, the war had, if anything, strengthened the armed forces vis-à-vis civilian authorities. Liberalizers and modernizers within both military and civilian circles embraced the peace process as a means to gain international support for reforms that they otherwise lacked the power to advance.[2] But the basic distribution of military, economic, and political power remained unchanged. Moreover, the international community proved a weak ally: stung by conspicuous failures in Somalia and Rwanda, as well as setbacks in Bosnia, the United Nations was in desperate need of a success. It tended to whitewash difficulties in Guatemala and shied away from confrontation when the government failed to implement agreed-to reforms.

Thus, as a context for efforts to promote justice and public security reforms, Guatemala was like many other societies undergoing highly controlled transitions from authoritarian rule. Unlike the "war transitions" that Charles Call describes as providing unique opportunities for major democratizing reforms in Latin America, neither Guatemala's war nor its peace process altered the many forms of de facto, financial, social, and coercive power available to privileged sectors of society under the old order.[3] Those who benefited from the old order retained substantial capacity to resist change, and important sectors of Guatemala's political and economic elite opposed effective rule of law.

Under these circumstances, international actors hoping to realign Guatemala's security and justice institutions could expect resistance. To succeed, donors needed a highly coherent, strategic, and politically conditional assistance program. In practice, lack of unity and coordination among the international missions doomed whatever limited prospects existed for profound justice and security reforms in the near term.

CHARACTERISTICS OF THE OLD ORDER

Guatemala's civil war (1961–96) left the country severely in need of justice, both in the form of accountability for past crimes and in reforms of state institutions to prevent recurrence of wartime atrocities. The war produced some of the most intense violence against civilians of any contemporary conflict in the Western Hemisphere. An estimated 150,000 people were murdered, some 50,000 were "disappeared," tens of thousands fled abroad, and some one million were internally displaced.[4] Government forces committed the vast majority of violent acts against noncombatant civilians, which included targeted killings of regime critics and opponents, forced disappearance, and genocide directed at native peoples, who collectively make up roughly half of the Guatemalan population. Torture was common, murder victims were frequently mutilated, and the government established concentration camps that eroded and disrupted indigenous cultures.[5] While the army committed most of the violence, police were also involved, particularly in urban areas. Military intelligence organizations in particular played a leading role in the most notorious killings of high-profile victims. All government forces enjoyed near-complete impunity for repressive violence.

Deficiencies of the justice system were an integral feature of wartime counterinsurgency and political repression. With very rare exceptions, officials of the state were not held accountable for crimes they committed during and immediately after the conflict. This impunity extended beyond presumably politically motivated crimes to overtly pecuniary crimes such as smuggling, extortion, narcotics trafficking, car theft, illegal logging, and kidnapping for ransom, involving current and former military officers and extensive criminal networks.[6]

Militarism and injustice can be traced directly to the late nineteenth century, when Guatemalan Liberals built up the military and used it to enforce massive changes in land tenure and to ensure labor availability for commercial coffee production.[7] The result was a large standing military force whose primary mission was domestic social control, and an economic elite that was dependent on, and ideologically committed to, military repression. From the 1930s onward, the military adopted an ideology that combined racism against Guatemala's indigenous majority with anticommunism.[8]

A brief political opening from 1944 to 1954 brought social welfare reforms, union activism, and a major land reform that redistributed fallow lands to individual families. This opening ended with an intervention by the United States Central Intelligence Agency, which ousted the elected president and installed a military dictatorship.[9] A coup attempt by moderate elements of the armed forces was suppressed in 1960, resulting in the consolidation of a hard-line, anticommunist military regime. This exclusionary regime soon engendered armed opposition by communist activists and disgruntled former military personnel. In the 1960s a guerrilla movement based in the eastern provinces was defeated and about 15,000 civilian lives were lost. Guerrillas reemerged in the 1970s with a new strategy of building political support among indigenous peoples in the western highlands and northern regions of the country. Intense conflict ensued between 1978 and 1983, during which the military carried out a massive, indiscriminate campaign that eliminated some 440 villages, killing and "disappearing" more than 150,000 people. Tighter systems of social control, including concentration camps and mandatory "civilian self-defense patrols" (PACs), limited the rebels' ability to recruit, obtain support, and move around the countryside. By 1983 the rebels had been strategically defeated, though they managed to continue sporadic operations until the war's end in 1996. As the intensity of the conflict ebbed, government forces continued to carry out human rights crimes, including periodic massacres, disappearances and murders of regime opponents, torture, and illegal detentions.

The military could carry out violence on this scale because it enjoyed complete impunity. Military personnel fell under military legal jurisdiction (*fuero militar*), and even where civilian courts had jurisdiction, they did not dare to investigate and bring charges against military officers. Military repression was deeply institutionalized. The army maintained fortified bases across the countryside and specialized intelligence units such as "The Archive" (later known as the Presidential General Staff). It trained extremely violent special counterinsurgency units such as the "Kaibil" commandos, maintained the PACs, and controlled the police.

Subordination of the police to the military resulted in weak, incompetent, repressive, and corrupt institutions that rarely met the needs of the public.[10] The National Police (PN) had some 12,500 agents in the final stages of the conflict, but more than half were actually administrative and support personnel. The understaffed PN could count on only about 5,000 police on duty on any given day, serving twelve million inhabitants.[11] Some 90 percent of the police force had "no formal professional training, either because they lacked the minimum educational level for it or because they received police jobs through political connections."[12] The PN lacked the capacity for planning, internal controls, and systematic promotion and advancement of police personnel. It had undergone a gradual process of reform and reorganization during the 1980s and early 1990s, with an increased capacity to train its own officers, and a Professional Responsibility Office (ORP) provided for some internal oversight and modestly improved investigative capacity, but the military cut these reform efforts short. Procedures for training and commissioning more senior officers and commanders were highly irregular.[13] While some police detectives distinguished themselves by their willingness to investigate human rights crimes, overall the PN participated actively in political repression and supported military impunity. The indigenous majority was barely represented in the PN, which drew most of its personnel from Ladino-dominated provinces in the eastern part of the country.[14]

The justice system was little better. Also highly corrupt, the judiciary functioned, until the early 1990s, on the basis of inquisitorial, written procedures typical of unreformed civil law systems. Judges directed investigations, prosecutions, judgment, and sentencing. Cases typically languished for extended periods before resulting in verdicts. A 1997 survey found that nearly 70 percent of Guatemalans characterized the justice system as "inadequate" and only 30 percent of the public saw the courts as consistently defending the rights of people.[15]

Following a general trend in the Americas, and responding to U.S. technical assistance and political pressure, Guatemala adopted a reformed Criminal Procedure Code (Código Procesal Penal [CPP]) in 1994. The new CPP moved the country toward an adversarial, oral system under which a new Public Ministry carried out prosecutions. Neither the MP nor the courts proved capable of actually following the procedures laid out in the CPP. An important innovation introduced by the 1994 code, though, was a provision for private accusers (*querellantes adhesivos*), who could independently seek information and petition the courts. This provision proved crucial to the few postwar successes in prosecuting human rights criminals, as it provided Guatemalan NGOs with the opportunity to push cases along and appeal unjust rulings.

A Counsel for Human Rights (Procurador de Derechos Humanos [PDH]) was responsible for investigating alleged human rights crimes. The PDH had been largely ineffective since its creation in the 1980s, then briefly achieved some reputation for effective advocacy in the early 1990s under an assertive *procurador* with political ambitions, Ramiro de León Carpio.

Reforms Embodied in the Peace Accords

Direct talks between the government and the URNG rebels began in 1991, with Guatemalan bishop (now cardinal) Rodolfo Quezada Toruño as mediator and both the United Nations and the Organization of American States as observers. Beginning in 1993, the United Nations assumed the role of mediator, and talks continued under two consecutive presidential administrations, resulting in final accords and a definitive cease-fire in late 1996. The United Nations deployed a human rights monitoring mission, MINUGUA, which was later expanded to verify all aspects of the accords.

Justice for Past Human Rights Crimes

In June 1994 the government and the URNG agreed to a Commission for Historical Clarification (CEH) that would begin work once a cease-fire was in place. The CEH's mandate was to investigate and report impartially on acts of violence and human rights violations associated with the armed struggle and to make "specific recommendations to encourage peace and national harmony," with particular attention to preserving the memory of victims and fostering a culture of mutual respect. The three commissioners, who would work for six to twelve months, were to include the UN "moderator" for the negotiations as well as two prominent Guatemalans.[16] The commission was not allowed to attribute responsibility to any individual, nor was its work to have "any judicial aim or effect." Neither party was obligated to implement the commission's recommendations. On the face of it, this agreement was much weaker than the Salvadoran accord that provided for a truth commission whose recommendations would be binding and that had the authority to name individual perpetrators. These limitations were widely rejected by civil society groups in Guatemala, to the point that further negotiations by the URNG halted for about a year, as it mended its relations with various constituencies.[17]

A subsequent agreement required the government to designate a state agency to handle compensation and assistance to victims of human rights abuses under a National Reconciliation Act. This same act was to establish a procedure for adjudicating which specific crimes associated with the armed conflict should benefit from amnesty. Crimes such as genocide, as well as political murders not clearly associated with the armed conflict, were not eligible for amnesty.[18]

Justice Reforms

Several different accords proposed elements of reform for the judicial system. For example, the Agreement on the Identity and Rights of Indigenous Peoples called for the government to create "legal offices for the defense of indigenous rights," install "popular law offices to provide free legal assistance for persons of limited economic means in municipalities in which indigenous communities are prevalent," establish an Office for the Defense of Indigenous Women's Rights, and promote laws prohibiting discrimination against indigenous people, especially women.[19]

This accord also sought to address indigenous communities' lack of access to the justice system and required the government to draft legislation that would "recognize the right of the indigenous communities to manage their own internal affairs in accordance with their customary norms, provided that the latter are not incompatible with the fundamental rights defined by the national legal system or with internationally recognized human rights." Since indigenous customary law and national legal norms could not always be reconciled, the accord also required the government to improve indigenous peoples' access to the national justice system by providing free legal advisory services and court interpreters.[20]

The Comprehensive Agreement on Human Rights did not call for specific reforms but rather reaffirmed the government's commitment to uphold the human rights instruments it had already signed. The government agreed to support initiatives to improve the capabilities of the office of the Counsel for Human Rights[21] and, in an agreement on socioeconomic issues, to create a new framework to govern and track ownership, provide for restitution and conflict resolution in cases of land usurpation, and defend rural labor rights.

The core reforms related to the justice sector were embodied in the Agreement for the Strengthening of Civilian Authority and the Role of the Armed Forces in a Democratic Society (AFPC). The AFPC flagged as key problems "antiquated legal practices, slow proceedings, absence of modern office management systems and lack of supervision of officials and employees."[22] Proposed remedies included constitutional reforms that would provide for "reasonable and prompt resolution of social conflicts and provision of alternative conflict-resolution mechanisms" and various measures to professionalize the system, by raising salaries, training standards, and disciplinary accountability. The agreement called for the creation of an independent Public Defender's Office to deliver free criminal defense services to the poor and proposed that the government increase spending on the judiciary and the MP by 50 percent more than 1995 levels. A Commission on the Strengthening of the Justice System was charged with specifying further reforms.[23]

Police Reforms

The AFPC called for disbanding existing police forces and proposed constitutional language regarding the creation of a new civilian police force:

> The National Civil Police shall be a professional and hierarchical institution. It shall be the only armed police force competent at the national level, whose function is to protect and guarantee the exercise of the rights and freedoms of the individual; prevent, investigate and combat crime; and maintain public order and internal security. It shall be under the direction of the civil authorities and shall maintain absolute respect for human rights in carrying out its functions.[24]

The new National Civil Police (PNC) was to be governed by the Ministry of the Interior, and the multiethnic and multicultural character of Guatemala was to be "taken into account in the recruitment, training and deployment of police personnel." Extensive training was to be provided at a new police academy, and basic police training was to last a minimum of six months. The AFPC also called on the government to deploy 20,000 new police by late 1999. For a process beginning in early 1997, this was obviously a very ambitious schedule. The government agreed to emphasize the criminal investigation capacity of the police, promoting strong coordination with the MP (prosecutors) and the judiciary. Communities were to participate in proposing police candidates. The 1996 Agreement on the Implementation, Compliance and Verification Timetable for the Peace Agreements committed the government to take steps within a year to "strengthen the Police Academy so that it can train new police personnel as officers, inspectors, commanders and superintendents and retrain existing personnel." This last provision implied a mechanism by which new police personnel could gain direct access to the upper ranks (commanders and superintendents) of the police force. As will be discussed later, this was not the case in practice.

No explicit provisions were made for transitional security, other than keeping the old National Police in place while the new police were trained and deployed. No UN civilian police observers were requested; UN police presence during implementation was confined to a few individuals in verification and "institutional strengthening" roles.

Intelligence Reform

The AFPC called for the establishment of a Civilian Intelligence and Information Analysis Department under the Ministry of the Interior, with a mission to fight organized and common crime. A new civilian Strategic Analysis Secretariat would provide information and analysis to the president. All intelligence units were to respect the "separation between intelligence and information-gathering functions, and the operations to which they give rise," in obvious reference to the previous involvement of military intelligence units in death squad activity. The president was to close down the Presidential General Staff and establish a new civilian entity to provide security for the executive.[25]

Limitations of the Accords

The accords present a number of weaknesses, some more obvious than others. As already noted, the agreement on the CEH provided a weak mandate. The judicial reforms were vague, exhorting more efficient and professional performance without offering a substantive diagnosis of the flaws in the system. The proposed police reforms also lacked concrete measures, failing to specify, for example, police doctrine; mechanisms for accountability and discipline; educational requirements for access to different levels of the police hierarchy; procedures for recruitment, selection, training, and specialization; mechanisms for incorporating civilians into the senior ranks; and standards for reflecting the "multiethnic and pluricultural" nature of Guatemalan society.

A careful reading of the accords reveals that the government seldom committed to actually *do* anything. Mostly, it promised to introduce legislation or propose constitutional reform language. The government did unequivocally commit to raising taxes and spending in some categories, but since the executive lacked fiscal authority, these commitments were not enforceable. The three governments that negotiated and signed elements of the accords could seldom obtain legislative cooperation from Congress. Legislative weakness has persisted with the two most recent administrations. The Jorge Serrano government (1991–93) attempted an auto-coup in 1993 in an ill-conceived attempt to overcome legislative obstacles. Interim president Ramiro de León Carpio (1993–96) lacked a party base and had little legislative support. The party of Álvaro Arzú (1996–2000), whose government signed the final accords, held a slim majority in the legislature, but his party lacked discipline, and the president could seldom sustain a majority on controversial issues such as tax increases. Arzú's successor, Alfonso Portillo (2000–04), began his term with a legislative majority for the Guatemalan Republican Front (FRG). Notwithstanding his pro–peace accords rhetoric, it became clear after about a year that he was either uncommitted to the accords or unable to deliver the votes of his divided party. Current president Oscar Berger (2004–08) lacks a legislative majority for his own party and thus depends on forming a center-right coalition in the legislature in support of any peace accord–related measures.

Many of the most substantive elements of the peace accords depended on the passage of constitutional reforms, which had to first be ratified by popular referendum. Legislators wrangled for months about the specific terms of the extensive and complex reforms. Then a legal challenge questioned the proposal to present all the accords in a single package, and the court ruled that the reforms must be disaggregated into four issue areas. After significant delay, a package of reforms was put before confused voters in May 1999. Despite active support for passage of the reforms from all of the major political parties, as well as voter turnout and education efforts by international missions, the reforms were voted down. Urban voters were particularly negative about the reforms, reflecting in part a highly effective media campaign that depicted the reforms in sometimes overtly racist terms as a threat to the existing social order.

IMPLEMENTATION

Justice for Past Human Rights Crimes

The CEH, despite its weak mandate, produced a report that had significant political impact and potentially set the stage for future prosecutions. The CEH began work in August 1997 and then asked for two six-month extensions to permit thorough collection of testimony and other evidence.[26] The commission identified 42,275 victims, including 23,671 victims of arbitrary execution and 6,159 victims of forced disappearance for the period 1961–96. The commission's overall estimate, based on evidence from previous studies and extrapolations from the numbers of orphans, was 200,000 civilian deaths and disappearances.[27]

The commission presented its conclusions in an emotional public ceremony on February 25, 1999.[28] Its basic findings—that the military was responsible for 93 percent of the total human rights violations and other acts of violence—were expected. But the forceful charges of genocide and racism on the part of the armed forces came as a surprise and revived expectations for future prosecutions related to these crimes.

The CEH issued recommendations on reparations for war victims and reforms to the judicial system and security apparatus and proposed that Congress create a foundation, with government and civil society participation, to monitor implementation. The government neither implemented the commission's recommendations nor meaningfully refuted the CEH's basic findings. Despite its limitations, the CEH effectively served its primary function of establishing a credible public record of past atrocities and making these public facts politically salient.[29] The CEH also documented the damaging subordination of the country's judicial institutions to the objectives of the counterinsurgency state. This position reinforced the accords' call for institutional reforms and increased financial resources for courts, prosecutors, and public defenders.

The CEH report was shaped, in part, by the earlier Recovery of Historical Memory (REMHI) project of the Human Rights Office of the Catholic Archdiocese of Guatemala.[30] The idea of a church-led truth commission predated the CEH accord but gained greater momentum and institutional commitment from the church because of the CEH's limitations. Despite working with limited resources, the REMHI project compiled case testimony involving 25,123 murders, 3,893 forced disappearances, and 4,219 cases of torture.[31] REMHI provided transcripts of all its depositions to the CEH, supplementing the CEH's own work. REMHI's finding that government forces and paramilitaries committed 89.7 percent of serious violations was closely comparable to the CEH's estimate. It is somewhat difficult to assess the separate impact of the REMHI report. Because it was issued by the Catholic Church, which was widely perceived in government circles as sympathetic to the URNG, the report was somewhat easier for the political right to dismiss. However, its powerful presentation of facts and analysis was difficult to refute, and it likely reinforced the internal position of CEH staff members who wanted the commission to take a strong position with respect to genocide. The head of the REMHI project, Bishop Juan Gerardi Conadera, was murdered two days after presenting the report to the public. This murder was at once a signal of how threatening the report was to certain sectors within the armed forces and a credible threat of further violence against other human rights advocates and opposition leaders.

The prosecution of suspects in the murder of Gerardi became one of two landmark efforts (the other being the trial of men accused of killing anthropologist Myrna Mack) that demonstrated both the potential and the severe limitations characterizing the Guatemalan justice system. The Gerardi investigation was hamstrung from the outset by an incompetent performance by the MP in the protection and collection of physical evidence at the scene. A series of different prosecutors handled the case, and nine witnesses or potential witnesses were murdered.[32]

Despite these overwhelming obstacles, justice was eventually done in this case. Civil society organizations and international donors applied significant political pressures. The Human Rights Office of the Archdiocese (ODHA) participated in the case as a private accuser, maintaining pressure on the judiciary to act, increasing transparency of the proceedings, and keeping the international community informed of the status of the evidence and investigation. In 2000 incoming president Alfonso Portillo declared in his inaugural address that his government would successfully prosecute the Gerardi case. Ultimately, four men were convicted and sentenced to lengthy prison terms: a retired army colonel who formerly headed military intelligence; his son, an active duty captain associated with the Presidential General Staff (EMP); an enlisted specialist from the EMP; and a priest who was an accessory to the crime. This was the first conviction of military officers for a politically motivated murder. Death threats forced the lead prosecutor to leave the country one month after the verdicts.[33] Notwithstanding the many missteps along the way, the Gerardi convictions demonstrated that successful prosecution of powerfully connected individuals for political violence was possible, but only when significant political and private legal resources were brought to bear.

Two conspirators were convicted for the 1990 murder of Guatemalan anthropologist Myrna Mack: the enlisted man who actually carried out the murder and a colonel who ordered the killing.[34] Two other high-ranking officers were acquitted. The Myrna Mack Foundation, led by Myrna Mack's sister Helen Mack, served as a private accuser in the case. The prosecution faced numerous obstacles, including death threats, frivolous petitions, and other delaying tactics by the defense. The courts generated bizarre procedural rulings and opaque explanations for verdicts. Following the initial convictions, an appeals court acquitted the colonel who ordered the crime. One investigator was murdered; others fled the country following threats. More than two dozen judges withdrew or were removed from the case, suggesting extensive threats and corrupt influence over the proceedings.[35] Ultimately, the Supreme Court reinstated the conviction of Colonel Juan Valencia Osorio in January 2004. Regrettably, Colonel Valencia escaped from custody three days later and remains at large.

Despite Valencia's escape, the conviction was a remarkable and important accomplishment. Many of the key legal briefs and petitions that kept the case alive were the work of Helen Mack and the Myrna Mack Foundation, which also simultaneously pursued, and won, a ruling against the Guatemalan state through the Inter-American Court for Human Rights.

Whether future human rights prosecutions will be successful in practice remains in doubt given the institutional weaknesses of the system and the unchecked coercive powers of the old order. Efforts at prosecution involving less internationally prominent victims have consistently failed. Defense attorneys filed abusive and frivolous motions with the Supreme Court and the Constitutional Court, and unknown parties murdered witnesses and threatened and bribed judges and (especially frequently) prosecutors.[36] Future prosecutions will depend on greater physical protection for prosecutors, judges, and their families; far better collection and use of physical evidence; better legal education of judges; stronger accountability mechanisms; and sanctions for frivolous legal motions. These, along with needed reforms to improve access and efficiency, have been addressed only to a limited degree by the postwar reforms. If the courts were strengthened, the potential number of amnesty-ineligible cases could be substantial: forensic anthropologists have carried out more than two hundred exhumations of "clandestine cemeteries" containing remains of victims of army/paramilitary massacres. This work has continued, despite increasing threats.[37]

Implementing Reform of the Justice System

Postwar implementation of justice sector reforms[38] built on the 1994 Criminal Procedure Code (CPP). A heightened awareness among Guatemalan jurists of the possibilities for a better system provided a foundation for postwar initiatives, but the shift to oral proceedings under the CPP has been gradual and incomplete. The Commission on Strengthening of the Judiciary (CFJ) included an appropriate range of highly qualified individuals and analyzed the institutional flaws of the courts, the MP, and public defense. Sometimes its recommendations diverged from diagnoses suggested in the accords; for example, the accords focused on the importance of separating judicial and administrative functions, whereas the CFJ found that the main obstacles to judicial efficiency had more to do with a lack of clarity regarding procedures for case assignment, as well as an unclear division of labor between judges and lower-level officials. These problems resulted in extremely heavy workloads for some judges, little work for others, handling of cases by lower-level functionaries who lacked authority to make decisions, and frequent sidelining of some cases owing to inappropriate assignment. The CFJ found that similar problems afflicted the MP and, like other observers, also stressed the poor quality of available legal education in Guatemala.[39]

A Commission for Follow-up and Support for Strengthening the Legal System (CSA) monitored implementation of the CFJ's recommendations, as well as of the preexisting Five-Year Plan for Modernization of the Judiciary. This commission provided authoritative, critical analysis of draft legislation.[40]

The reforms proposed and implemented were diverse and extensive. New laws established the Public Defender's Office (1998), professional standards and open, merit-based competitions for judgeships (1999), and civil service selection procedures and a judicial code of ethics (2000). Under review were a General Process Code that would extend adversarial, oral proceedings to noncriminal cases; a law criminalizing ethnic discrimination and sexual harassment; a Penitentiaries Law; a Judicial Career Law for the MP; and a variety of draft laws relating to further reform of the criminal procedure code, criminal investigations, and so on.[41]

Probably the greatest progress was made in the area of access to the justice system, largely through international donations (see table 4-1).[42] More than one hundred new courts were created in rural areas, and the total number of judges and magistrates has nearly doubled since the mid-1990s. Some courts hired interpreters to assist indigenous clients, and the court system built an additional eighty-three justice of the peace offices. As of late 2004, the U.S. Agency for

International Development (USAID) had developed some fifteen "Justice Centers" that combine courts, prosecutors, public defenders, and (in some locations) the PNC under one roof, in an attempt to more closely integrate services.

Table 4-1. International Donations to the Justice Sector, 1997–2002 (excluding USAID)

Branch	Project Goal	Grants	Loans
Judiciary			
	Judicial Functions	$2,851,915	$10,400,000
	Access	$1,203,555	$15,234,000
	Anticorruption		$2,300,000
	Institutional management	$2,150,000	$3,311,000
	Social communications		$3,200,000
Public Defense			
	Institutional strengthening	$1,930,000	$2,748,000
Public Ministry (Prosecutors)			
	Institutional strengthening	$1,406,959	$2,770,000
	Criminal investigation		
	Training		
	Construction and equipment		$909,000
Coordination Agency for Modernization of the Justice Sector			
	Legal area	$133,000	$3,037,000
	Institutional area	$1,388,850	$5,969,000
Ministry of the Interior			
	Planning Unit		$583,000
	PNC	$45,197,654	
	Penitentiaries		$478,216
	Integrated Case Management System		$702,000
Supreme Electoral Tribunal			
	Institutional strengthening	$700,000	$1,911,187
Ad-Hoc Commission for Follow-up and Support for Strengthening the Justice System			
	Technical support	$300,000	
Universities/Law Faculties			
	Institutional strengthening	$24,000	

Source: Unpublished tables provided by UNDP, Guatemala, author file.

Note: USAID does not report its activities in a way that facilitates enumeration of spending on specific projects; thus, its projects are mentioned, but not quantified, by the UNDP tables.

The judges selected through open competitions under the new Judicial Career Law have demonstrated greater commitment to their jobs, greater propensity to use legal reasoning in issuing decisions, and greater independence. An analysis by MINUGUA suggested that newer judges were also less likely to owe their appointments to powerful political cronies.[43] The new Public Defender's Office demonstrated a comparatively high commitment to effective service. However, the quality of legal work still left much to be desired, as reported by a MINUGUA assessment: "Faced with a new case, the majority of staff public defenders do not develop a strategy that coherently integrates the facts of the case, applicable legal norms, and the real circumstances facing the client."[44] Despite these shortcomings, full-time public defenders generally outperform private attorneys, who provide defense services under contract to the state, and USAID had a project under way to improve the performance of these contractors, who outnumbered public defenders.[45] Overall, the public defenders performed at least as well as the attorneys of the MP, and often better. "They are probably doing too well," remarked one USAID official: defenders obtained acquittals in some highly visible cases, leading to political backlash as some members of the public saw the reformed system as too lenient and protective of accused criminals.[46]

The MP remains a weak spot that undermines the system as a whole. A USAID study found that of 90,000 complaints received by the MP during 1998 in Guatemala City alone, clerical staff arbitrarily dismissed roughly one-third without any basis in official criteria. Of the remainder, only about 1,100 resulted in indictments, and these resulted in virtually no convictions.[47] Presumably, cases generated by the MP itself fared better than those generated by public complaints, but this performance is clearly disastrous.

The poor performance of the prosecutors appears attributable to three flaws: (1) inappropriate involvement of clerical staff in case screening, for which they are not qualified, (2) very weak legal work by prosecutors themselves, and (3) intimidation of victims and witnesses, resulting in nearly 100 percent recanting testimony or withdrawing cooperation. An analysis by MINUGUA of indictments written by prosecutors found that virtually none of them demonstrated the abilities to describe the relevant facts of a case and link those facts to relevant written and case law.[48] In high-profile cases such as the Gerardi murder, it has also been evident that prosecutors themselves are subject to intimidation, forcing them to withdraw from cases or flee the country. In this climate of coercion and corruption, professional dedication suffers. MINUGUA reported "an excess of professional zeal is at times interpreted as contrary to the interests of the institution."[49] According to the Guatemalan Institute for Comparative Studies and Penal Sciences, 87 percent of prosecutors (and 25 percent of judges) reported having been pressured by superiors or "other influential parties."[50] Weaknesses of the MP have been compounded by budgetary starvation. For FY 2003, for example, the ministry received only $44.7 million of the $96.2 million it had requested. This amounts to only $2.60 per capita, and only $185 per case processed.[51]

Similar shortcomings affect the courts themselves at all levels. The courts continue to be badly managed, in part because of poor delineation of clerical and judicial functions. Judges vary tremendously in their qualifications, but the average skill level is poor: like prosecutors, judges typically show little ability to identify the most salient facts, to identify and use relevant laws, and to render decisions that are explicitly based on a combination of fact and applicable law.[52] Decisions are often based on technical, bureaucratic criteria or are apparently arbitrary. Decisions rendered under the new CPP are not substantially different in quality, indicating that oral, adversarial proceedings do not necessarily produce changes in judges' legal habits of mind. These shortcomings are not particularly responsive to training (the most common form of international assistance) because they have their roots in the poor quality of legal education.

Also like prosecutors, judges are subject to intimidation, threats, and actual murder. At least thirteen judges were killed from March 2000 to March 2001, and the Myrna Mack Foundation reported 158 cases of "threats, intimidation, and attacks against judges, prosecutors, lawyers and others linked to the justice system" during 1999.[53] Security provisions for judges are obviously inadequate, and the poor overall performance of the justice system creates a vicious cycle: those who would intimidate or murder judges are not deterred because the likelihood of being held accountable is very low. The state's primary response to this problem has been to explore offering life insurance to judges.[54]

In Guatemala's penitentiaries, prisoners are held under conditions that violate basic human dignity and threaten prisoners' health and physical integrity. Frequent riots claim the lives of dozens of prisoners each year.[55] Based on a survey conducted by MINUGUA in 1999, 63 percent of the prison population had not been convicted or sentenced. In many cases, prisoners had been held for longer than they could have been sentenced for had they been tried and convicted of the crimes for which they were arrested. Approximately 3.5 percent of prisoners were being held for petty misdemeanors, which is unconstitutional.[56] Yet hundreds of prisoners—including violent criminals and convicts in highly visible cases—have escaped in recent years, pointing to extensive corruption among prison guards and other authorities.[57]

Little progress was made in implementing the agreement to recognize indigenous customary law under the existing legal system. This provision of the accords presented very real legal difficulties in recognizing group and community-based rights and procedures under a liberal constitutional framework based on individual rights and equal protection under the law. Indigenous communities typically viewed customary law as a dynamic and contextual oral tradition and therefore resisted the idea of written codification.[58] Moreover, some customary practices violate international human rights standards that Guatemala has agreed to uphold, so clear criteria were needed regarding the authority indigenous communities could exercise. The May 1999 defeat of proposed constitutional amendments addressing these issues left little avenue for further progress on recognition of customary law.

Implementing Police Reform

While implementation of judicial reforms predictably faced significant structural and long-term obstacles, such as the poor quality of legal education in Guatemala, police reform faced fewer intrinsic obstacles. Police require less training and formal education than judges. Effective models of civilian policing existed in El Salvador,

Honduras, Nicaragua, and Costa Rica,[59] and significant international assistance was available. Yet implementation of police reform was deeply flawed. Recruitment, selection, and training of police officers resulted in a large "new" police force that was too poorly educated and trained to provide effective policing and protect individual rights. Although new civilian recruits constituted a majority of the force, the entire senior officer ranks were drawn from the old police agencies. Civilians can enter directly to the "subaltern officer" ranks after a two-year training program but would require many years to rise through the ranks to the top levels of commissioner or commissioner general. Unless this situation changes, new civilians will not reach the top ranks for nearly a generation.[60] Internal disciplinary mechanisms are weaker than in peer police forces, and the criminal investigations section consists largely of personnel who lack the education and vocation to be effective investigators.

Planning for the new PNC began before the agreement on strengthening civilian authority was signed. The government negotiated an exclusive relationship with the Spanish Civil Guard (GCE) to be the primary source of advice, technical assistance, training, and material assistance to the new police. According to Interior Minister Rodolfo Mendoza, the Arzú government chose the GCE for two reasons. First, it wanted to avoid the contradictions that result from having multiple international donors trying to build one institution. Second, the GCE endorsed the government's priority to build up a force very rapidly, avoiding the transitional policing vacuum that developed in El Salvador.[61] Once the GCE project was established as a bilateral project, the European Union designated the GCE team to implement a subsequent grant of €31.7 million.

The GCE advisers were from a highly militarized rural police force whose organization and techniques are not particularly modern. The focus, from the start, was on rapid recruitment, training, and deployment. These goals were achieved. However, quality, diversity, and organizational rationality often suffered. The GCE supported the government's view that minimum physical stature requirements were appropriate to screen future police. When various groups criticized this as discriminatory against the Mayan population, the GCE asked for proof that Mayans were shorter on average than other Guatemalans.[62] Eventually, the stature requirements were adjusted to facilitate recruitment of qualified indigenous candidates.

GCE officials, while serious about producing a PNC that was significantly superior to the old system, nonetheless took a pragmatic and expedient approach. Observers of training at the academy uniformly remarked that course content was extremely theoretical, that is, lacking in concrete guidance on how police should deal with various circumstances. Although the peace accord called for six months of training for all PNC agents, members of the old force received only three months' worth, which was to be followed by supplementary training in the field.[63]

As with the judges and prosecutors, the weak educational background of many recruits limited the results that could be obtained through training. But for the PNC the problem was largely self-inflicted. The government made a very halfhearted effort to recruit civilians into the police, working largely through appointed provincial governors, which resulted in narrow recruitment through political patronage networks. The examination process required costly travel and overnight stays. These factors combined to produce small applicant pools. The Academy of the PNC (APNC) had to reduce educational and exam score standards to keep the numbers up. Inexplicably, simpler examinations were given to applicants with lower educational backgrounds, resulting in a selection bias in favor of less educated applicants.[64] The screening process initially lacked effective background checks. Once these were instituted, police officials discovered that many applicants had forged papers and criminal antecedents. This inevitably raised questions about how many criminals had already entered the police under false pretenses, but no systematic retroactive check and purge took place. Overall, selection was characterized by "errors, superficiality, and sloppy procedure."[65]

Recruitment for specialized units such as the Criminal Investigations Section (SIC) was similarly flawed, as police leadership assigned agents to investigative courses without regard to their education, analytical skills, or even criminal antecedents. According to one U.S. International Criminal Investigations Training and Assistance Program (ICITAP) official, personnel entering investigative training classes were "clearly substandard, even compared to Haiti."[66]

The average detective has a sixth-grade education, and brief training courses are not sufficient to offset educational weakness. The SIC has been chronically understrength, and its personnel are frequently misused for tasks more appropriate to uniformed police. Perhaps most crippling, personnel who have received investigative training are often rotated out of the SIC. Of all police investigators trained under international programs, fewer than fifteen worked as detectives by early 2005.[67] Higher-ranking SIC officials generally write reports and provide court testimony, even when they were not directly involved in the investigation. When lower-level personnel do testify, they are ineffective in explaining what they observed and the evidence collected.[68]

GCE advisers drafted the disciplinary code for the PNC, largely reproducing the GCE's own military-style code. This document gives primary authority to police commanders to discipline their troops. It also provides some protection to the accused, but the code provides no mechanisms by which subordinates can report misconduct by superiors.[69] This omission contributed to armed mutinies by lower-level police agents when superiors acted abusively. The code also lacks any provision for an independent internal investigative or disciplinary unit (except for a tribunal that reviews the most serious infractions). There is no explicit mechanism for processing and acting on complaints from the general public. The code is so complex that most PNC officers (and GCE advisers) could not apply it effectively when presented with real or hypothetical cases.[70] According to one UN official, "This breeds impunity, which leads to public distrust."[71]

The PNC's Office of Professional Responsibility (ORP) is a carry-over from the old PN days. It was created largely at the initiative of ICITAP, modeled on the Federal Bureau of Investigation's (FBI) own office of the same name. ORP ostensibly reports to the deputy director of the PNC, but in practice to the director. It initiates investigations when asked to by the director, police commanders, the Human Rights Counsel, MINUGUA (until its departure in 2004), or private individuals. Observers credit the ORP with effective and sometimes courageous investigations. Particularly noteworthy was the ORP's investigation of homicides and theft of massive quantities of drugs from evidence storerooms, allegedly committed by members of the Department of Anti-narcotics Operations (DOAN). The lack of an explicit role for the ORP under the disciplinary code and its lack of an independent authority base limit its impact. An Office of the Inspector General was finally created in early 2005, headed by a retired army colonel. Its effectiveness remains unknown.

Given the combined weaknesses of recruitment, screening, and internal controls, the PNC soon accumulated an unenviable record of criminal conduct. While its human rights record is somewhat better than that of the predecessor institutions, as of late 2002 there was a backlog of some 1,500 cases of very serious criminal conduct by PNC personnel. According to one UN official, "the police are over-whelmed by the number of internal criminal cases." About half of these crimes involved corruption, and the rest were "criminal cases including major crimes such as robbing armored cars, rapes, armed robberies, car theft. This puts the whole force at risk."[72] Moreover, the majority of those under indictment for serious crimes in 2002 were still on the job, as the disciplinary code prohibits removal of officers charged with crimes until a court reaches a verdict and issues a sentence. Fewer than 200 police agents had been dismissed from the PNC for cause, "a figure that does not conform to the reality of the situation," according to one UN official.[73]

The police were further undercut by policies of the Alfonso Portillo government, which by July 2003 had appointed four ministers and eight PNC chiefs, including some individuals whose reputations sparked widespread questions. One observer characterized this as "planned chaos," intended to undercut police effectiveness and enhance impunity.[74] Furthermore, Portillo repeatedly cut the PNC budget, transferring the equivalent of millions of dollars to the Ministry of Defense. The result was predictable: the APNC, which had just decided to extend basic training courses to a full year, cut them back to six months again. Student stipends went unpaid for a time, resulting in attrition from the academy class.[75] The police for a time had virtually no fuel for vehicles, crippling their operations, especially in rural areas.

Frequent turnover at top levels of the PNC and the Governance Ministry has continued under the Oscar Berger government. Perhaps even more threatening to the PNC's performance is frequent turn-over of precinct commissioners and other midlevel authorities. Informed observers suspect that these frequent rotations are intended to facilitate police corruption schemes.[76] Whatever the reasons for rapid command turnover, it has contributed to police management characterized by U.S. officials as "zero" or "near zero," and to ineffi-cient use of resources: around 80 percent of PNC arrests are for mis-demeanors such as public drunkenness, while violent criminals act without hindrance. Of 145 police instructors who completed an internationally funded "train the trainers" course, none are currently assigned to the police academy.[77]

Functional Integration of the Justice System

Not only do the components of the justice system perform poorly individually; they also do not work well together, performing neither as intended nor as required by law. The most egregious conflict is between the MP and the PNC over control of criminal investiga-tions. The Criminal Procedure Code requires the PNC to conduct investigations, under the direction of the MP. The prosecutors do not trust the quality of police investigators, with good reason. Yet rather than working with the police leadership to define what skills and performance prosecutors need from the PNC/SIC, the MP created its own detective corps, known as the Department of Criminal Inves-tigations (DICRI). The ministry is allowed under its organic law to have a group of specialists to conduct tests and analysis, but there is no basis in law for it to conduct its own investigations, nor for its investigators to testify. Little is known about the composition of the DICRI, but it appears to be made up largely of former military and police personnel. There does not appear to have been any externally verified screening of these investigators on their criminal anteced-ents, commitment to human rights, or other qualities. Moreover, the MP has maneuvered politically to obtain an interinstitutional agree-ment with the PNC that gives the former a monopoly over homicide investigations in the capital city. This exclusion of the PNC/SIC has created frustration on the part of the police and distrust on the part of many observers, who see any monopoly over investigations as increasing chances of impunity for violent criminals. Whatever the

weaknesses of PNC investigators, the police have nonetheless distinguished themselves by undertaking a number of dangerous and politically charged investigations, while MP investigators have embarrassed
themselves through gross mishandling of several high-profile cases,
particularly the Gerardi murder.

Numerous other violations of law are routine. The constitution
requires that prisoners be placed at the disposition of a competent
authority (widely interpreted as meaning a judge) within six hours.[78]
In practice, in rural areas where judges are available for only a limited
workday and where travel distances are a major obstacle, this requirement is widely violated. Even in urban areas, police customarily make
the majority of arrests at night (mainly for misdemeanors, as noted
earlier), and these prisoners see a judge, at best, the following day.
According to one attorney who has monitored the workings of the
system closely, "Courts *never* let someone go because the judge isn't
available."[79] Approximately 99 percent of arrests are in flagrante
delicto—that is, the police claim to have caught the accused red-
handed. The facts presented by the police themselves, such as descrip-
tions of how witnesses led them to the home of the accused, often
overtly contradict the claim of *flagrancia*. The SIC, which of all
police units should make arrests based on judicial warrants obtained
through investigations, in fact makes the majority of its arrests in flagrante delicto as well.[80]

Judges routinely accept arrest reports that are patently unlawful, pointing to the extent of political influences and incompetence
affecting the judiciary. This practice also suggests a de facto conniv-
ance of the police, prosecutors, and courts in allowing illegal procedures to persist. Judges admit in private and in conferences that they
are subject to political pressures and cannot throw out large numbers
of illegal arrests without risking disciplinary action (for being too soft
on criminals).[81] Notwithstanding the new criminal procedure code,
the postwar reforms, and the millions spent by outside agencies to
promote the rule of law, the Guatemalan justice system functions
much as it always has.

International donors have not contributed to unity of purpose
and action on the part of the security and justice systems. Interviews
with officials in UNDP, ICITAP, EU/GCE, USAID, MINUGUA,

and other international missions indicated that donors were divided on key issues, such as the appropriate role of the MP and the PNC/SIC, who should control the crime laboratory, and whether the role of justices of the peace should be expanded, as well as more mundane issues, such as how many SIC detectives should be deployed in the capital versus at other locations. These officials often expressed suspicion of one another's intentions, motives, and even competence. The disunity of international donors has amplified, rather than dampened, the parochialism of Guatemalan state institutions.

In response to an Inter-American Development Bank project, the Guatemalan government created a Coordinating Agency for Modernization of the Justice Sector. This entity has confined itself largely to technical questions and only began in 2002 to address the deeper legal, policy, and institutional problems that characterize the system.[82]

Implementing Intelligence Reform

Intelligence reforms have moved slowly, suggesting power struggles behind the scenes. As of mid-2005, civilian intelligence capacity remained incipient, while the military's capacity remained largely intact. Despite a clear mandate from the AFPC, the Arzú government failed to close down the notorious EMP. Under considerable pressure from civil society and from abroad, the Portillo government finally disbanded the EMP in October 2003. Its replacement, the Secretariat for Administrative and Security Affairs (SAAS), incorporated about 100 of the 564 former staff of the EMP, raising concerns that the EMP merely continued under a new name. A new intelligence unit was created within the Ministry of Defense at the same time, and the legislation for the EMP failed to require transfer of the EMP's files to the new entity. It appears the military maintains control over decades of domestic political intelligence, not to mention likely incriminating information about the EMP itself.[83] The new civilian Secretariat for Strategic Analysis (SAE) was formed in 2001. It has lacked adequate budget and independent intelligence-gathering capacity and has been the subject of intense power struggles within the executive.[84] As of mid-2005, the Directorate General for Civilian Intelligence under the Governance Ministry had yet to be created, pending completion of legislation. Assuming the legislation passes, a few years will be required to build up civilian intelligence capacity. In the meantime, the military maintains a de facto monopoly on domestic intelligence, even though this activity is outside its mandate as defined under the peace accords.

From 2000 onward, civil society activists and international observers grew increasingly worried about the apparent existence of criminal networks linking former military intelligence figures and various state officials. Following intensified death threats and violence, presumably coming from these shadowy networks, domestic human rights groups joined with international organizations and foreign states in calling for the creation of a Commission for the Investigation of Illegal Bodies and Clandestine Security Apparatuses (CICIACS). On March 13, 2003, the Portillo government agreed to establish CICIACS, combining national and foreign investigative personnel in an organization similar to the Joint Group that investigated illegal armed groups in El Salvador. Various legislative and constitutional problems blocked establishment of the CICIACS during the Portillo administration. The Berger government agreed with the United Nations in 2004 that CICIACS would be a strictly international commission. Issues still unresolved in mid-2005 included how to modify the national secrecy laws, as well as the criminal procedure code, to enable an international CICIACS access to government files and the authority to contribute to prosecutions as a private accuser.[85] If ultimately approved, CICIACS will be an unusual experiment in internationalizing the investigation of organized crime. It would be, in a sense, an admission that Guatemala's institutions cannot do the job. If effective, however, it might break the back of the criminal remnants of the wartime intelligence apparatus and enable the new institutions to function in a climate less fraught with organized violence and intimidation.

Public Safety and Justice Outcomes

The administration of Álvaro Arzú expedited transition to the PNC specifically to avoid the kind of postwar public security vacuum and crime wave it had observed in neighboring El Salvador.[86] This strategy appears to have been partially effective but only in the short run.

Table 4-2. Annual Crime Incidents Reported by PN/PNC

	1995	1996	1997	1998	1999	2000	2001	2002	2003	2004
Homicides (violent deaths)	3,260	3,619	3,988	3,310	2,655	2,905	3,210	3,630	4,237	4,507
Physical assaults	4,378	5,280	5,561	4,728	4,704	5,401	5,798	6,511	6,610	6,443
Kidnappings	5	233	148	61	37	28	32	45	37	51
Rapes	44	110	167	220	323	366	416	365	379	363
Property crimes	11,350	11,072	12,030	13,107	14,597	18,605	17,553	18,121	19,106	18,766
Arrests (all categories)		20,314	21,679	49,837	69,713	67,713	77,679	60,025	50,475	50,259

Sources: Statistical tables provided by MINUGUA, author files; data for 2002–04 provided by the Policía Nacional Civil de Guatemala, author files. Total arrests for 1995 unavailable.

Table 4-3. Homicides, Homicide Rate, and Homicides Using
Firearms, National Institute of Statistics (INE), 1986–2004

Year	Homicides	Rate per 100,000	Percent by Firearms
1986	1,572	19.8	57.4
1987	1,891	23.2	55.4
1988	1,968	23.6	57.4
1989	1,636	19.1	62.3
1990	1,663	18.9	63.0
1991	1,691	18.8	63.3
1992	1,690	18.3	61.4
1993	1,693	17.9	62.0
1994	2,041	21.0	63.1
1995	1,970	19.7	68.4
1996	2,166	21.1	72.8
1997	3,002	28.5	73.5
1998	2,806	25.6	76.7
1999	1,978	17.8	72.8
2000	2,167	19.3	76.0
2001	2,304	20.0	79.6
2002	2,794	23.7	78.8
2003	3,359	27.8	83.5
2004	2,647	21.4	86.2

Sources: Data for 1986–99 cited in Centro de Investigaciones Económicas Nacionales (CIEN), *Estudio sobre la magnitude y el costo de la violencia en Guatemala* (Guatemala: CIEN, 2002), 8; data for 2000–2004 from INE, author files.

There was a surge in homicides, physical assaults, kidnappings, and rape in 1996 (on the eve of settlement) and 1997 (the first year of implementation; see tables 4-2, 4-3, 4-4). In 1998 and 1999, as the PNC deployed throughout the country, homicides, physical assaults, and kidnappings fell back to presettlement levels. The incidence of rape and property crimes continued to climb, however. The drawbacks of the expedited and sloppy development of the PNC soon revealed themselves as the frequency of all major crimes climbed

Table 4-4. Divergent Annual Homicide Figures and Homicide Rates: Three Different Sources

	MP		INE		PNC	
Year	Number of Homicides (MP)	Homicide Rate per 100,000 (MP)	Number of Homicides (INE)	Homicide Rate per 100,000 (INE)	Number of Homicides (PNC)	Homicide Rate per 100,000 (PNC)
1996	7,795	76.1	2,166	21.1	3,594	35.1
1997	8,021	76.3	3,002	28.5	3,952	37.6
1998	8,343	77.3	2,806	25.6	3,282	30.4
1999	8,224	74.2	1,978	17.8	2,628	23.7
2000	8,069	70.9	2,167	19.3	2,867	25.2
2001	8,057	69.0	2,304	20.0	3,209	27.5
2002	7,673	65.1	2,794	23.7	3,630	30.8
2003	9,210	76.2	3,359	27.8	4,237	35.1
2004	11,237	90.7	2,647	21.4	4,507	36.4

Sources: Centro de Investigaciones Económicas Nacionales (CIEN), *Estudio sobre la magnitude y el costo de la violencia en Guatemala* (Guatemala: CIEN, 2002), 8–17, 137; Ministerio Público, *Memoria de Labores* (Guatemala: Ministerio Público, 2002, 2003, and 2004); population estimates for homicide rates from INE, author files.

inexorably from 1999 through 2003. Only when the corrupt and unstable administration of Alfonso Portillo was out of office in 2004 did some crime indicators appear to ease.[87] Throughout the period, firearms were involved in a growing share of homicides.

The impact of crime varies in complex ways according to social class, ethnic identity, gender, and rural/urban residence. Official crime statistics show that the mainly indigenous western departments had by far the lowest homicide rates, while the heavily Ladino eastern departments and southeastern coastal provinces had much higher rates. For example, Jutiapa, bordering El Salvador, had 52.4 homicides per 100,000 inhabitants, compared with 4.4 per 100,000 in the northwestern province of Huehuetenango.[88]

A 2001 victimization survey showed that a higher percentage of urban residents were victimized than rural residents. For rural people, victimization rates generally increased with higher social status.

Table 4-5. Comparative Perception of Security: Guatemala versus El Salvador

Perception of Security	Guatemala		El Salvador	
	Men	**Women**	**Men**	**Women**
Very secure	35%	33%	25%	21%
Fairly secure	39%	40%	34%	35%
Somewhat insecure	19%	18%	24%	24%
Very insecure	7%	9%	17%	20%

Source: Adapted from Dinorah Azpuru, *La cultura democrática de los Guatemaltecos en el nuevo siglo, V estudio* (Guatemala: Association for Research and Social Studies [ASIES], 2002), 149, table VI.3.

Table 4-6. Confidence in Justice Institutions: Guatemala versus El Salvador

	Guatemala	**El Salvador**
Public Ministry	43%[a, b]	55%
PNC	43%	59%
Courts	42%	52%
Human Rights Procurator	43%	63%

Source: Adapted from Dinorah Azpuru, *La cultura democrática de los Guatemaltecos en el nuevo siglo, V estudio* (Guatemala: Association for Research and Social Studies [ASIES], 2002), 140, table VI.6.
[a] Percentage of respondents reporting some or much confidence in the named institutions.
[b] Percentage of respondents reporting the indicated level of security or insecurity.

However, there were some exceptions: while wealthier residents of rural areas were hardest hit by crime, poorer urban respondents also reported high rates of victimization (probably a result of urban gang activity). Indigenous people in the Guatemala City area, as well as in the northeast of the country, were more frequently victimized than Ladinos.

Overall, 11 percent of urban respondents versus 5 percent of rural respondents reported being direct victims of thefts not involving physical aggression in the past year, while 5 percent of urban and 2 percent of rural respondents suffered armed robberies.[89] In repeated surveys conducted by the Guatemalan Association for Research and Social Studies (ASIES) in 1997, 1999, and 2001, victimization rates were remarkably constant, with only 1 to 2 percent variations during two-year periods, and no observable trend.[90] In comparative terms, Guatemala has the highest rates of armed robbery and property theft in Latin America. However, the homicide rate of 20 per 100,000 in 1995 was less than one-sixth that in El Salvador (138 per 100,000), and well below the Latin American average of 31 per 100,000.[91]

Some 26 percent of Guatemalans report that they feel somewhat or very insecure (see table 4-5). Urban people feel less secure than rural people, which is not surprising given the higher rates of armed robberies and property crimes.[92] But overall, Guatemalans report feeling safer than do Salvadorans, despite the higher rates of property crimes and armed robbery in Guatemala. This suggests that homicide rates may have a disproportionate effect on perceptions of insecurity—a logical supposition in any case.

Reformed security and justice institutions performed badly, in the view of most Guatemalans. Only 42 percent of respondents in a 2001 survey had some or much confidence in the courts and only 43 percent trusted the police (see table 4-6). Of respondents who reported having been directly victimized in a crime, 60 percent reported the authorities were attentive to their complaint, but 63 percent reported negative results from the complaints.[93] A constant media drumbeat about crime and the failings of state agencies likely contributed to public distrust and dissatisfaction.[94] Confidence levels in security and justice institutions were markedly lower than in El Salvador, despite the higher reported levels of insecurity in El Salvador. This suggests that despite facing a very violent and challenging environment, the more deeply reformed Salvadoran institutions perform better and earned a greater degree of public trust.[95]

CONCLUSION

Seven and a half years after Guatemala's war ended, the population was insecure and not guaranteed equal protection before the law. Only a handful of military officers had been held accountable for their wartime crimes, and the police and the justice system dealt ineffectually with violent crime. Reform of the police had been handled in a way that squandered opportunities to achieve deep changes in organizational culture, procedures, standards, and performance. Budget cuts and ill-considered appointments by the Portillo government caused further setbacks, while turf battles between agencies crippled the system. Throughout the security and justice sectors, educational deficits undercut the decision making and judgment necessary for effective and fair functioning of a system based on individual liberties and equal protection.

This outcome, however unsatisfactory for the general public, reflects at least to some extent the preferences of much of the Guatemalan political elite. While lack of leadership and management capacity clearly contributed to the numerous damaging decisions since 1996, the extent to which state policies have undermined the rule of law suggests deliberate intent (either on the part of policymakers themselves or on the part of powerful constituents that policymakers were unable to resist). Both the Arzú and Portillo governments sent early signals of a commitment to building a functioning state and rule of law. Arzú proved unable to deliver on promises, while Portillo seemed often to actively sabotage the justice system. The political weakness of the URNG, the resulting vagueness of the peace accords, and the lack of a coherent and effective business-oriented party conspired to prevent formation of a strong counterweight to the various reactionary forces both inside and outside the state. Members of the criminal, privatized remnants of the counterinsurgency state have been effective in perpetuating the Hobbesian climate and impunity that benefit them, at the expense of legitimate entrepreneurs and the general public.[96]

To counteract these powerful domestic opponents of the rule of law, the international community would have needed to use strong aid conditionality, explicitly linking overall aid levels and particularly aid to politically exploitable domestic programs, to progress on justice, public security, and intelligence reforms. With MINUGUA in place, and a high initial degree of consensus among donors on macroeconomic policy, the United Nations was institutionally positioned to lead. Regular Consultative Group meetings provided an additional mechanism for explicitly linking aid programs to progress on priority issues. As already discussed, however, the United Nations faced multiple disincentives to incur risks or act decisively in Guatemala. Moreover, the chief of mission's style privileged mediation over confrontation. No other international actors proved willing to incur substantial political costs to confront the Guatemalan state and insist on real changes. The six friends of the peace process—Norway, the United States, Mexico, Venezuela, Spain, and Colombia—had demonstrated some measure of commitment, but none of them saw institutional stagnation in Guatemala as sufficiently alarming to trigger stronger political interventions. Among other donors, the European Union in particular showed great reluctance to use aid conditionality. With no strong coordinating leadership, petty squabbles and turf wars emerged among international donors, amplifying the already deep divisions between Guatemalan agencies such as the PNC and the MP.[97] With MINUGUA closed down at the end of 2005, potential international leverage diminished. In the future, international donors will need to act very strategically, and with great unity, to reinforce the positive forces and counteract the ongoing influence of the hidden powers.

Despite the adverse political setting and the opportunities missed by the international community, there are some positive signs. The long-term efforts by various international donors to promote judicial reform have generated increased awareness among a core community of Guatemalan jurists of the need for sustained, deep reforms of the system. Much of the judicial analysis and legislation generated as part of the peace process was of high quality. Moreover, a sophisticated community of NGOs has demonstrated substantial capacity to monitor, criticize, and propose solutions to observed problems. The successes of NGOs in obtaining convictions against accused perpetrators of human rights crimes, so soon after the end of the war, compare favorably with many other postconflict and postauthoritarian cases. Independent investigations by NGOs banked substantial amounts of physical evidence of past war crimes, leaving open the possibility— perhaps many years away—of prosecutions for perpetrators of genocide. The possibility of successful prosecutions increased markedly in July 2005 when the Counsel for Human Rights (PDH) discovered (in a disused former police building) a cache of some thirty thousand police files documenting thousands of killings and disappearances carried out by government forces during the conflict. Included were such items as lists of disappeared children and to which families they had been given.[98] Assuming the PDH adequately protects these documents, and appropriate organizations step forward to serve as private accusers, significant prosecutions could well result.

It appears that members of the old order see the risks of prosecution as very real. The pattern of violence and intimidation against accountability activists—including the assassination of Bishop Gerardi—suggests real alarm on the part of the old guard.[99] So does the intensity of political opposition to and clandestine interference with judicial, prosecutorial, and police reforms.[100]

Guatemalan and international advocates of justice and citizen security do have important assets to work with in the future. While the opportunities of the immediate postwar context were missed, those opportunities were not as great as the trappings of an international peace process made them appear. Results of the 2004 elections—particularly the voters' rejection of the presidential candidacy of former dictator Efraín Ríos Montt (FRG)—suggest a decline in the political fortunes of the public allies of the old order. The Berger administration has incorporated into senior positions a number of individuals who have distinguished records of advocacy and effectiveness on justice and human rights issues. This political shift, combined with the ongoing support of international actors, may provide a basis for greater justice in the future.

NOTES

1. Susan Peacock and Adriana Beltrán, *Hidden Powers in Post-conflict Guatemala: Illegal Armed Groups and the Forces behind Them* (Washington, D.C.: Washington Office on Latin America, 2003).

2. William Stanley and David Holiday, "Broad Participation, Diffuse Responsibility: Peace Implementation in Guatemala," in *Ending Civil Wars: The Implementation of Peace Agreements*, ed. Stephen John Stedman, Donald Rothchild, and Elizabeth Cousens (Boulder, Colo.: Lynne Rienner, 2002).

3. Charles T. Call, "War Transitions and the New Civilian Security in Latin America," *Comparative Politics* 35, no. 1 (October 2002). Honduras replaced military-controlled police with a civilian force, creating a new civil-

ian investigations police from a clean slate and then shifting street cops to civilian control with tighter restraints.

4. Commission for Historical Clarification, *Guatemala Memory of Silence* (Guatemala: United Nations, 2000).

5. Commission for Historical Clarification, *Guatemala Memory of Silence*; George Black, *Garrison Guatemala* (New York: Monthly Review Press, 1984); Michael McClintock, *The American Connection: State Terror and Popular Resistance in Guatemala* (London: Zed Books, 1985); Ricardo Falla, *Massacres in the Jungle: Ixcán, Guatemala 1975–1982* (Boulder, Colo.: Westview Press, 1994); and Centro de Investigación y Documentación Centroamericana, *Violencia y contraviolencia: Desarrollo historico de la violencia institutional en Guatemala* (Guatemala: Editorial Universitaria de Guatemala, 1990).

6. Peacock and Beltrán, *Hidden Powers in Post-conflict Guatemala*, 11.

7. James Mahoney, *Legacies of Liberalism: Path Dependence and Political Regimes in Central America* (Baltimore: Johns Hopkins University Press, 2001).

8. McClintock, *The American Connection.*

9. Piero Gleijeses, *Shattered Hope: The Guatemalan Revolution and the United States, 1944–1954* (Princeton, N.J.: Princeton University Press, 1991).

10. MINUGUA prepared in 1995 a lengthy *Preliminary Analysis of the Organization and Problematic of the National Police,* which documented the capabilities and limitations of the existing police force. Many of the problems noted at that time, such as the weakness of internal disciplinary mechanisms, have merely been reproduced in the new PNC. Anonymous MINUGUA officials, interviews with author, Guatemala, May 1999.

11. Jack Spence et al., *Promise and Reality: Implementation of the Guatemalan Peace Accords* (Cambridge, Mass.: Hemisphere Initiatives, August 1998), 31.

12. Ibid.

13. Mario Rene Cifuentes, former PN chief, interview with author, Guatemala, June 17, 1998.

14. In Guatemala the term "Ladino" refers to communities and individuals who identify primarily with Hispanic culture, rather than with the indigenous cultures of Guatemala. The term is usually a cultural, rather than racial, label, although upper-class Ladinos often consider themselves white. PN officer responsible for human resources, interview with author, Guatemala. The PN was supplemented by the Treasury Guard (GH) and the Mobile Military Police (PMA). The GH was a small force that dealt with taxation, licensing, customs, and related matters. The PMA was a military unit that provided additional policing services but functioned largely as a state-owned security company that provided fee-based guard services to banks and other vulnerable institutions, using auxiliary personnel who were largely former soldiers.

15. Luis Pásara et al., *Funcionamiento del sistema de justicia en Guatemala: Un análisis de comportamientos institucionales* (Guatemala: MINUGUA, March 2000), 15; and Mitchell Seligson et al., *La cultura democratica de los Guatemaltecos, tercer estudio* (Guatemala: Association for Research and Social Studies [ASIES], 1998), 87.

16. In the event, UN moderator Jean Arnault became the chief of the verification mission MINUGUA. Christian Tomuschat, a German law professor and former UN independent expert on human rights for Guatemala, became head of the CEH. The other two members of the commission were Guatemalans, Otilia Lux Cotí, a Mayan educator, and Alfredo Balsells Tojo, a prominent lawyer.

17. Western diplomat, interview with author, Guatemala, May 19, 1999.

18. *The Guatemalan Peace Agreements* (New York: United Nations Department of Public Information, 1998), 192–193.

19. Ibid., 62–63.

20. Ibid., 76–77.

21. Ibid., 24–25.

22. Ibid., 133.

23. Ibid., 136.

24. Ibid., 140.

25. Ibid., 148–149.

26. Ibid., 55–56. The accord provided for only one extension.

27. Commission for Historical Clarification, *Guatemala Memory of Silence.* The full report can also be found on the website of the American Association for the Advancement of Science, http://shr.aaas.org/Guatemala/ceh/.

28. See Mireya Navarro, "Guatemalan Army Waged 'Genocide,' New Report Finds," *New York Times*, February 26, 1999.

29. In this regard, the CEH accomplished more than the UN Truth Commission in El Salvador, whose findings and recommendations were strongly and effectively contested by the government.

30. Human Rights Office, Recovery of Historical Memory (REMHI) project, Archdiocese of Guatemala, *Guatemala: Never Again!* (Maryknoll, N.Y.: Orbis, 1999). This citation is for the abridged, international version in English translation. The full four-volume report is available at http://www.odhag.org.gt/INFREMHI/Default.htm.

31. Ibid., 289. REMHI's methodology also invited deponents to give more information about the individuals who were killed, as well as the impact of the crime on themselves, their families, and the community. See Priscilla Hayner, *Unspeakable Truths: Confronting State Terror and Atrocity* (New York: Routledge, 2001), 45–49, 83–85.

32. Rachel Sieder, Megan Thomas, George Vickers, and Jack Spence, *Who Governs? Guatemala Five Years after the Peace Accords* (Cambridge, Mass.: Hemisphere Initiatives, 2002), 38.

33. Ibid., 37.

34. Myrna Mack had been conducting research into the destruction of indigenous communities as a result of the government's counterinsurgency campaign. These research activities presumably provided government agents with the motive for murdering her.

35. Sieder et al., *Who Governs?* 38.

36. Guatemalan law imposes no restrictions on defense attorneys' use of motions for abrogation (*casación*) or legal protection (*amparo*), and there are no sanctions for frivolous or abusive petitions. Thus defense attorneys can effectively block prosecution for years. Other cases that illustrate the difficulty of prosecution in human rights cases include the trial of twenty-five soldiers charged with killing eleven returned refugees in Chisec, Alta Verapaz, in October 1995 (they were convicted of manslaughter but allowed to buy out their sentences for US$0.67 per day); an April 2001 Constitutional Court decision annulling arrest warrants against nineteen military officers accused of a 1982 massacre of three hundred people at Dos Erres, Petén; the cases against "civil patrollers" for the 1982 massacres at Agua Fría, El Quiché, and Río Negro, Baja Verapaz (convicted on second attempt, now under appeal; implicated military personnel were never tried); and the April 1999 appeals court revocation of thirty-year prison sentences against two civil patrollers convicted of murdering presidential candidate Jorge Carpio Nicolle.

37. Carlos Loarca, interview with author, Guatemala, August 6, 2002. Loarca estimated that there would be four hundred to five hundred exhumations of multiple graves completed within the next four or five years.

38. I will group the judiciary, public ministry, public defenders, and corrections in this section, leaving the police for separate discussion in the subsequent section.

39. Comisión de Fortalecimiento de la Justicia, *Una nueva justicia para la paz* (Guatemala: Magna Terra Editores, 1998).

40. MINUGUA, Area Jurídica, "Informe Final," December 2001, 17.

41. Ibid., 25.

42. International programs included MINUGUA's "institutional strengthening" project for the police and justice system; the United Nations Development Programme (UNDP), which supported development of the new MP; the

European Union (EU), the primary donor to the police development project; the Inter-American Development Bank (IDB), which had a project to modernize and increase interagency cooperation within the justice system; USAID, which emphasized local-level cooperation among courts and prosecutors; ICITAP, which trained police investigators and sought to modernize information systems; and the government of Japan (facilities for police academy).

43. Pásara, "Los jueces provenientes de concurso, ¿son distintos?" in *Funcionamiento del sistema de justicia en Guatemala*.

44. Antonio Maldonado, "Calidad y eficacia en los defensores públicos de planta," in *Funcionamiento del sistema de justicia en Guatemala*.

45. USAID official, interview with author, Guatemala, August 7, 2002.

46. Deborah Kennedy, USAID, interview with author, Guatemala, August 9, 2002.

47. Steven E. Hendrix, "Guatemalan 'Justice Centers': The Centerpiece for Advancing Transparency, Efficiency, Due Process, and Access to Justice," *American University International Law Review* 15, no. 4 (2000): 813–868, cited in Sieder et al., *Who Governs?* 35.

48. Manuel Garrido, "Actuación y perfil de los fiscales," in *Funcionamiento del sistema de justicia en Guatemala*, 25–41.

49. MINUGUA, Area Jurídica, "Informe Final," 10.

50. As reported in *Central American Report*, August 17, 2001, quoted in Sieder et al., *Who Governs?* 35.

51. "Ministerio Público con la mitad de fondos solicitados en 2003," *Inforpress Centroamericana*, no. 1479, September 6, 2002.

52. Luis Pásara, *Las decisiones judiciales en Guatemala* (Guatemala: MINUGUA, 2001), 79–120.

53. Fundación Myrna Mack, *Hechos que afectan la independencia judicial y administración de justicia en Guatemala: Amenazas, intimidaciones y atentados contra jueces, fiscales y abogados* (Guatemala: Fundación Myrna Mack, August 1999), quoted in Sieder et al., *Who Governs?* 26.

54. MINUGUA, *Informe ante la reunión del Grupo Consultivo para Guatemala* (Guatemala: MINUGUA, May 7, 2003), 7.

55. "Grupos criminales se apoderan de sistema penitenciario," *Inforpress Centroamericana*, April 4, 2003.

56. MINUGUA, *La situación penitenciaria en Guatemala* (Guatemala: MINUGUA, April 2000).

57. Sieder et al., *Who Governs?* 36.

58. Anonymous MINUGUA attorney, interview with author, Guatemala, June 12, 1998.

59. While planning for transitional security in El Salvador was clearly inadequate, the performance of the Salvadoran PNC overall has been far better than that of the predecessor National Police. Compared with the Guatemalan force, the Salvadoran PNC is more transparent, reflects a much higher degree of civilian control, and has earned a higher degree of public trust, despite facing an extremely difficult postwar crime wave.

60. UN official, interview with author, Guatemala, June 8, 1998.

61. Rodolfo Mendoza, minister of the interior, presentation, Washington, D.C., November 10, 1997.

62. Anonymous UN official, interview with author, Guatemala, May 19, 1999.

63. Ibid.

64. MINUGUA official, interview with author, Guatemala, May 20, 1999; and APNC official, interview with author, Guatemala, May 21, 1999.

65. MINUGUA official, interview with author, May 20, 1999.

66. Anonymous ICITAP officials, interviews with author, Guatemala, June 12, 1998, and May 15, 1999.

67. Eric Scheye, "Reflections on Community-Based Policing Programming in Guatemala" (Washington, D.C.: U.S. Agency for International Development, April 2005).

68. Celvin Galindo, special prosecutor for organized crime, interview with author, Guatemala, May 26, 1999. Galindo was responsible for prosecuting the accused murderers of Bishop Gerardi and was subsequently forced to leave the country. He returned to serve as the anticorruption prosecutor under the Berger government, in which capacity he has again been threatened.

69. GCE colonel Agapito Arnaíz, interview with author, Guatemala, May 18, 1999.

70. ICITAP officials, interviews with author, Guatemala, May 15, 1999.

71. Anonymous UN official, interview with author, Guatemala, August 7, 2002.

72. Anonymous UN official, interview with author, Guatemala, August 8, 2002.

73. Ibid.

74. Quoted in Scheye, "Reflections on Community-Based Policing Programming in Guatemala," 3–4.

75. Verónica Godoy, Family Members and Friends against Crime and Kidnapping (FADS), interview with author, Guatemala, August 6, 2002.

76. Scheye, "Reflections on Community-Based Policing Programming in Guatemala," 7.

77. Ibid., 2.

78. *Constitución política de la Republica de Guatemala*, Article 6.

79. Famuel García, interview with author, Villa Nueva, Guatemala, August 5, 2002.

80. Ibid.

81. Ibid.

82. Deborah Kennedy, USAID, interview with author, Guatemala, August 9, 2002.

83. Mike Leffert, "Guatemala's EMP Is Gone, but Threat Remains," *NotiCen* (Latin America Data Base), November 6, 2003. The files were most likely retained by the Department of Strategic Intelligence of the Ministry of Defense, which was created simultaneously with the dissolution of the EMP. See Rebeca Botello, "Inteligencia civil a paso lento," *Inforpress Centroamericano*, October 8, 2004.

84. Edmundo Urrutia, former secretary of strategic analysis, personal communication, February 7, 2005. See also Botello, "Inteligencia civil a paso lento."

85. Peacock and Beltrán, *Hidden Powers in Post-conflict Guatemala*, 69–74.

86. Mendoza, presentation.

87. Both PNC and MP figures continue to show increased homicides in 2004, while the National Statistics Institute (INE) showed a decline. Of these the INE statistics are probably more reliable and valid, as they are based on coroners' reports. The PNC figures conflate homicides with violent deaths that may have been accidental, and the MP changed their data collection procedures partway through 2004, most likely resulting in their dramatic increase in reported homicides in 2004.

88. Centro de Investigaciones Económicas Nacionales, *Estudio sobre la magnitude y el costo de la violencia en Guatemala* (Guatemala: Centro de Investigaciones Económicas Nacionales, 2002), 11.

89. Dinorah Azpuru, *La cultura democrática de los Guatemaltecos en el nuevo siglo, Vestudio* (Guatemala: Association for Research and Social Studies [ASIES], 2002), 144.

90. Ibid., 141.

91. Centro de Investigaciones Económicas Nacionales, *Estudio sobre la magnitude y el costo de la violencia en Guatemala*, 32–36. The 1995 figures, of course, predate the end of the war. For the later 1990s, the Salvadoran rates were somewhat lower, and the Guatemalan rates somewhat higher, depending on the year (1998 was the peak year at 28.5 per 100,000).

92. Azpuru, *La cultura democrática de los Guatemaltecos en el nuevo siglo*, 149.

93. Ibid., 140, 145.

94. Jean Arnault, special representative of the UN secretary-general, interview with author, Guatemala, June 22, 1998.

95. William Stanley, "Building New Police Forces in Guatemala and El Salvador: Learning and Counter-Learning," *International Peacekeeping* 6, no. 4 (Winter 1999): 113–134; and Stanley, "International Tutelage and Domestic Political Will: Building a New Civilian Police Force in El Salvador," *Studies in Comparative International Development* 30, no. 1 (Spring 1995): 30–58.

96. Peacock and Beltrán, *Hidden Powers in Post-conflict Guatemala*.

97. For general principles on methods of coordination, see Bruce D. Jones, "The Challenges of Strategic Coordination," in *Ending Civil Wars*.

98. Mike Leffert, "Enormous Wartime Archive Discovered in Guatemala," *Noticen* 10, no. 27, Latin America Data Base, July 21, 2005.

99. Peacock and Beltrán, *Hidden Powers in Post-conflict Guatemala*, 9–12.

100. Carlos Loarca, Center for Legal Action on Human Rights (CALDH), interview with author, Guatemala, August 6, 2002.

Part II
Africa

5

Criminal Justice after Apartheid

Police and Justice Reform in South Africa

JANINE RAUCH

SECURING APARTHEID

THE SYSTEM OF APARTHEID WAS DESIGNED TO ENTRENCH white minority rule and racial segregation in South Africa. It was characterized by a highly racialized form of capitalism and by large-scale social engineering to ensure the subjugation of black South Africans, who make up 80 percent of the country's population. Although the apartheid system existed formally only from 1960 to 1990, it was built on a legacy of two hundred years of white colonial rule and rested on strong foundations of racial exclusion and economic exploitation, which had been established by successive generations of Dutch and British colonists. Popular resistance to colonialism and apartheid was led by the African National Congress (ANC), which was formed in 1912 and banned by the apartheid government in 1960. The United Nations declared apartheid a crime against humanity, and a large-scale international campaign developed to isolate the South African government and support the ANC and other liberation movements.

One of the key features of the apartheid system was the racial organization of the state. The security institutions were similarly organized—the South African Police and judiciary were dominated by white officers at the senior level. South Africa under apartheid was notorious for the brutality of the security forces and the widespread violation of human rights. During the thirty years of formal apartheid (1960–90), an estimated 78,000 people were detained without trial because of their political activities against the system, and seventy-three deaths in police detention were recorded. In the last years of the system, security forces engaged in high levels of torture, extrajudicial executions, and disappearances of pro-democracy activists.

The role of enforcing racist and unpopular laws, as assigned to the police, courts, and prisons during the apartheid years, created a profound crisis of legitimacy for the criminal justice system in South Africa. In many respects, the police played a military role, crushing popular protest and engaging in South Africa's civil war, as well as supporting white regimes in independence struggles in neighboring states.[1] Under successive apartheid governments, the police, the intelligence service, and the military vied for political dominance and greater slices of the national budget. By the late 1980s the apartheid state was in severe crisis, forcing the police, the military, and the bureaucracy to devise joint strategies and tactics to defeat the liberation movements, and an integrated National Security Management System (NSMS) was established to oversee the successive states of emergency that were declared after 1985.[2] By 1986 the government had expanded its counterinsurgency presence, had organized vigilante networks, and was engaging in widespread human rights abuses. As Gavin Cawthra describes:

> Police and troops poured into townships around South Africa, set-
> ting up joint bases and commandeering facilities. They patrolled
> the streets in armoured vehicles. Curfews and other restrictions
> were imposed, meetings were banned and, where resistance had
> been intense, townships were sealed off by troop cordons and razor-
> wire barricades, while the police went from door to door searching
> for dissidents. . . . Nearly 30,000 people were detained in 1986.[3]

This period of repression further cemented the alienation of the
police from the majority black population. Police officers were not
just unpopular; they were the targets of abuse and violence from pro-
democracy quarters. In some places, police officers and their families
were unable to live in ordinary residential areas for fear of attack, and
special barracks were provided alongside police stations.

By the late 1980s, international isolation of the apartheid
regime was intensifying as sanctions took effect. After the South
African military was defeated in battle in Angola in 1998—for the
first time—the influence of the security agencies began to wane
within the apartheid government, and a new breed of "enlightened"
Afrikaners began to emerge, advocating reform, accommodation,
and dialogue with black leaders. The repressive strategy had resulted
in virtual civil war in South Africa's cities and rural towns, high levels of militarization, fear and conflict between its citizens, and the
alienation of an entire generation of black children from schools and
most other institutions and symbols of authority, including their
families and traditional social structures.

In 1989 a more liberal wing of the ruling National Party took
control, and F. W. de Klerk was appointed state president. The following year he unbanned the ANC and the other liberation movements, releasing Nelson Mandela and other ANC leaders from
prison, which marked the commencement of a protracted period of
negotiations toward democracy. This period, culminating in open
elections in 1994, was characterized by brutal domestic conflict and
rising crime rates.

One of the features of the negotiated transition in South Africa
was the breakdown of racially exclusive and repressive apartheid
structures responsible for administering various material aspects of
life—notably systems of law enforcement, education, and welfare

provision—without immediate replacement by legitimate or effective alternatives. This "deregulation of social control"[4] facilitated increased levels of violence and raised difficult questions about the usefulness of notions of "democracy" and "reconciliation" in the process of reconstruction and development.[5] Writers on the South African transition argue that, because of the preceding decades of state repression and armed resistance, violence had gained social sanction as a means of maintaining or acquiring political power.

Criminal and communal violence escalated in the early 1990s, providing brutal context for the political negotiations over the new constitution and making the future of the security agencies a central issue.[6] When negotiations began, the South African government had eleven police agencies, five different militaries, and various intelligence organizations and branches of the judiciary. The ANC, on the other side of the table, had its "armed wing" and an "intelligence department," and there was a small "armed wing" in one of the other liberation movements—the Pan Africanist Congress (PAC). The government elected in April 1994, dominated by the ANC under President Nelson Mandela, faced an awesome task in reconstructing its inherited criminal justice and security agencies into the unified security agencies envisaged in the new constitution, acceptable to all South Africans and able to address the complex problems of crime facing the country.

THE REFORMS AND IMPLEMENTATION

Security reforms passed through four identifiable, at times overlapping, phases between 1994 and 2002.

Phase One: Designing Democratic Laws and Institutions

The first phase of criminal justice reform under the new postapartheid government was driven by the imperative to establish a more democratic security system, which would comply with the human rights requirements of the country's new constitution and move away from confession-based prosecutions toward evidence-based justice. The main emphasis was on institutional design,[7] specifically on creating a range of mechanisms to ensure greater accountability of the justice institutions. In the absence of a credible, professional police service, or expertise within its own ranks to take over the management of policing, the ANC at least wanted to secure compliance of the justice and security agencies with human rights standards, the law, and the directions of the elected government. Senior ANC politicians were appointed as cabinet ministers responsible for justice, police, intelligence, and defense. Parliamentary oversight committees were established to oversee each of these key portfolios, although with varied impact.

The government restructured the bureaucracies responsible for administering justice and security. A ministry-level Department for Safety and Security was created, made up of a single new, central South African Police Service (SAPS), itself an amalgam of the eleven apartheid police agencies, and the civilian Secretariat for Safety and Security, which was responsible for civilian oversight and policy guidance to the minister for safety and security.[8] On the military side, a national Department for Defence was created, made up of the South African National Defence Force (SANDF) and a civilian Secretariat for Defence.[9] A National Prosecuting Authority (NPA) was established, and the Department of Justice saw a separation between administrative functions and magistrates. In addition, various independent oversight or investigatory bodies were created by law, such as the Independent Complaints Directorate (to investigate complaints against the police), the independent inspecting judge (to monitor human rights standards and complaints in prisons), and the Human Rights and Gender commissions.

A key element of democratic restructuring in South Africa revolved around the appointment of new officials (i.e., those aligned with the ANC or with the struggle against apartheid) to senior positions in the new structures and what to do with the holdover officials. A clause in the negotiated agreement and the constitution guaranteed jobs to all existing civil servants, including security forces. In the military and intelligence forces, the ANC appointed its own stalwarts to most top command posts.

In contrast, most of the top operational positions of the criminal justice sector initially went to holdover bureaucrats. The director-general of justice, the national commissioner of police, and the commissioner of correctional services were all senior officials who had served during the apartheid era. However, the newly created structures geared toward human rights and accountability were all led by ANC or liberal-aligned individuals—the Constitutional Court, the Human Rights Commission, the Independent Complaints Directorate, and the Public Protector. This arrangement suited the proponents of the old order well: they were left with some control over daily operations, while the new government's people threw their energies into initiatives and institutions that were fairly marginal to the business of providing peace and security. In the first postelection period, little attention was paid to escalating levels of crime, which seemed to indicate merely that criminal victimization was no longer mainly experienced by the poor but was beginning to be felt across the entire population, a symptom of democratization.

Given the immense difficulties of transforming inherited state institutions and building formal mechanisms of democratic control, the emphasis of the ANC's policies in the early transition period lay on community-level accountability—unsurprising, given that it did not yet feel that it had full control over national-level executive agencies but could rely on its support base in the majority of South African communities.

Notions of "community policing," gleaned from contact with the international police fraternity, gained currency in police circles in the late 1980s, and similar discourses on "community justice" and "community prosecutions" resonated well with traditional and customary forms of justice. The first "community policing" structures were introduced in the early 1990s, and the 1994 interim constitution contained a detailed requirement that the new police service establish a Community Police Forum (CPF)[10] at every police station to enable consultation with the local community.

Policy guiding the implementation of community policing in South Africa shifted substantially after the democratic government was elected in 1994. Initially focused on providing structured oversight of the police, community policing shifted from enabling structured liaison and communication to emphasizing collaborative problem solving and subsequently to providing a framework for participatory and complementary local-level crime reduction. In

Table 5-1. Crime Trends for Murder, Rape, and Vehicle Theft

Crime	1994	1995	1996	1997	1998	1999	2000	2001
Murders reported	19,672	19,131	18,639	17,709	17,878	17,371	15,457	15,054
Murder rate per 100,000 population	50.9	48.5	46.2	43.0	42.4	40.3	35.0	33.3
Rape reported	29,399	33,139	36,137	37,905	35,105	36,022	37,556	37,711
Rape per 100,000 population	76.1	83.9	89.6	91.9	83.3	83.5	85.1	83.5
Vehicle thefts reported	77,429	76,617	71,713	74,476	80,130	77,709	74,657	74,281
Vehicle theft per 100,000 population	200.4	194.1	177.8	180.6	190.2	180.2	169.2	164.5

Sources: South African Police Service, Department of Safety and Security, http://www.saps.gov.za.

2002 the CPFs were virtually defunct in most parts of the country, although they had served a useful purpose in rebuilding relationships between the police and the black majority in the early postelection period.

The imperative toward "community participation" and "community accountability" in the administration of criminal justice was also evident in the courts and the prison system. A system of lay assessors was added to the magistrates' courts in order to introduce representatives of the community into the adjudication of cases, and community-based corrections were introduced, albeit on a small scale. Little of the rhetoric of community-based justice was actually turned into policy or implemented in practice; however, as Wilfried Scharf and Daniel Nina point out, "there is no country where civilian adjudication has been incorporated into the formal system without major problems."[11]

Phase Two: Prevention as a Response to the Crime Crisis

Table 5-1 provides a sample of reported crime trends for three categories of crime in South Africa since 1994. It is not possible to compare with pre-1994 data, as no national crime statistics were kept before 1994. Despite numerous problems with the recording systems used by the police, this table provides evidence that crime levels in South Africa were generally stable or declining. Even so, South Africa's murder rate remained among the highest in global rankings, and highly publicized armed robberies and carjackings contributed to a perception that crime was rapidly growing. Rates of reported rape, child abuse, and other forms of interpersonal violence showed increases, which may reflect greater reporting to the police.

In the early transition period, it became clear that increasing public concern about crime, and rising levels of reported crime, would require new responses. No matter how "transformed" the institutions of criminal justice became, they were unlikely to be able to deal with the volume of cases. The Department of Safety and Security was tasked with leading an interagency effort to find new solutions. In a split that has subsequently come to characterize the government's approach to crime, the SAPS developed a "high-density" policing strategy, which would focus on hotspot areas and involve a return to more repressive police tactics (like roadblocks and cordon-and-search operations), while the civilian Secretariat for Safety and Security led an interdepartmental team to consider *prevention* strategies that would ultimately reduce the number of criminal cases entering the justice system. This latter venture resulted, in 1996, in the production of South Africa's National Crime Prevention Strategy (NCPS). This strategy motivated a shift in emphasis from crime control to crime prevention, that is, a shift toward understanding crime as a social issue requiring a wide array of developmental and preventive measures, instead of only the traditional criminal justice responses.

The NCPS comprised four approaches: (1) an attempt to repair the criminal justice system, (2) promotion of "environmental design" opportunity-reduction strategies to reduce some forms of crime, (3) a program to strengthen community values and promote public participation in crime prevention, and (4) a focus on cross-border crime. It promoted a multidepartmental approach to the prevention of crime and aimed to provide a means by which the police, other government departments, the private sector, and the nongovernmental community could coordinate their activities and increase their preventive effect.

Following the NCPS, a 1998 white paper on safety and security advocated targeted, multiagency crime prevention strategies that would focus on offenders and victims and the environments in which they live, as well as on the "root causes" of specific types of crimes. This approach was characterized as "developmental" or "social" crime prevention. Neither the NCPS nor the white paper was ever fully implemented, as the public climate of increasing levels of fear and panic made long-term, developmental and preventive approaches unpalatable.

The only aspect of the original NCPS that the government seriously pursued was the reengineering of the criminal justice process. Even here, the emphasis was on coordination and reducing duplication, rather than fundamental system change. Business against Crime, a consortium of big business interests, led this effort, believing that its traditional advocacy tactics had failed to move the government. The initial attempts to integrate, rationalize, and streamline the administration of criminal justice under the auspices of the

NCPS provided the first significant entry point for management consultants, who later came to shape and drive the early system reform effort. At this stage, tensions emerged between the need for an efficient criminal justice system and the desire for protection of human rights. Problems involving the administration of bail, prison overcrowding, and the treatment of juvenile suspects threw these contradictory imperatives for criminal justice reform into sharp relief.

Phase Three: Managerialism as a Response to the Crime Crisis

The third phase of criminal justice reform in South Africa was dominated by management consultants and businesspeople, who argued that private sector "efficiency" approaches should be adopted to solve problems in the administration of criminal justice. The vehicle for this approach was an Integrated Justice System (IJS) initiative that grew out of the original work on reengineering criminal justice processes. This approach resonated with developments in criminal justice administration in the first world—the "value for money" drive and the emphasis on customer-oriented public services that had been under way in Europe and the United States for more than a decade. As such, it tended to appeal to donors and also fitted well with the ambitious tone concerning public sector reform that was set by the second ANC administration of President Thabo Mbeki after 1999.

The IJS initiative and the other managerial strategies adopted from 1997 onward focused solely on law enforcement and the administration of justice, leaned heavily toward information technology approaches, and made no attempt to engage with the social dimensions of crime and victimization. These strategies were underpinned by the naive belief that if the system were "fixed" and functioning well, it would be able to process and deter any volume of crime. Despite repeated attempts to sell this model as the panacea for South Africa's severe crime problem, the public remained skeptical of the ever-increasing numbers of "plans" and "strategies." President Mbeki's new cabinet took a more hands-on approach in an attempt to demonstrate more effective control of the situation.

Phase Four: Getting Tough

Despite new institutional design, improved compliance with the constitution, improved accountability, and better technology, by 2000 the information technology systems were producing data show-ing declining prosecution and conviction rates, high levels of recidi-vism, and large numbers of pretrial detainees. The criminal justice system was not getting any better at processing crime, and the per-ceived high levels of crime remained a top issue of public concern. Once again, the pressure to deal with the crisis of volume in the criminal justice system provoked a new set of reform initiatives. This fourth wave in criminal justice sector reform in South Africa was characterized by the imperative to simultaneously prioritize the most serious, most prevalent, or most politically damaging crime problems and to "crack down hard" on the factors that cause or facilitate those problems. The Police Service and its new minister, Steve Tshwete, led this approach, which came to be known as Operation Crack-down. The strategy had three main components: to focus on the highest-crime areas in the country ("hotspots"), to focus on crime syndicates, and to begin work on medium-term social crime preven-tion initiatives that were intended to ameliorate the socioeconomic and development deficits conducive to high rates of criminal activity in the high-crime areas.

Implemented since March 2000, this framework continued to shape government policy and the implementation of reforms within South Africa's criminal justice system as of 2003. Ironically, it resem-bled the best versions of the apartheid generals' Total Strategy,[12] with its combination of tough law enforcement methods and "softer" social strategies such as poverty alleviation and urban renewal.

Following the police's "hotspot" approach, the Department of Justice prioritized certain court sites for major improvement and cer-tain types of crime for "fast-tracking" through the courts. The National Prosecuting Authority also adopted the approach of priori-tizing certain cases for prosecution, and its Directorate of Special Operations[13] was seen to crack down on various organized-crime bosses and syndicates. The judiciary and magistrates were under enormous pressure to impose heavy sentences, and as a result, the crisis in the prison system deepened. By the end of 2004, there were more than 185,000 inmates in South African prisons, which had an approved bed capacity for 113,000 prisoners.[14]

Government discourse on "community participation" had been tainted with ambivalence and cynicism by the time the Crackdown approach emerged. In the policing arena, the SAPS in 2000 announced its intention to "rationalise existing government liaison structures with communities." On the one hand, the managerialists saw community consultation, participation, and accountability as onerous and obstructive of a more streamlined and effective criminal justice "machine." On the other hand, the Crackdown approach relied on populist political support. Significant urban police resources during the Crackdown period were devoted to policing illegal immigrants, traffic violations, and roadblocks. Search operations caused disruptions to residents' lives. Yet the popular response to the early operations was overwhelmingly positive.

ASSESSING THE IMPACT OF THE REFORMS

Change of Personnel

To build the legitimacy of the new South African police service and facilitate improved relationships with the black majority population, two aspects of the composition of the police service had to be addressed: the racial composition of the police organization, particularly at the top level, and the fate of police officials who had perpetrated gross human rights violations under apartheid.

The archetypal image of a police official in apartheid South Africa was of a rather brutish, uneducated, working-class, Afrikaans-speaking white man. Viewed together, however, the eleven apartheid police agencies were by 1994 roughly representative of the racial composition of the South African population—64 percent of the combined personnel of the police organizations were black. Even the prior South African Police (SAP) alone (which contributed 80 percent of the personnel to the total) was not as dramatically unrepresentative as many observers had believed—55 percent of its members (mainly in the lower ranks) were black.

Yet the old South African Police was characterized by the predominance of white Afrikaner males in its most senior ranks. By mid-2001, 46 percent of the officer corps of the new SAPS was made up of black South Africans, as was 73 percent of the total number of uniformed police officials.[15] Official statistics (see table 5-2) showed progress, especially at the most senior levels.

Table 5-2. Racial Composition of the South African Police Service

Year	Junior Ranks		Middle Ranks		Senior Ranks	
	Black	White	Black	White	Black	White
1995	66%	34%	11%	89%	25%	75%
1999	70%	30%	29%	71%	27%	73%
2002	73%	27%	44%	56%	53%	47%

Source: Steve Tshwete, minister of safety and security, budget speech delivered to parliament, Cape Town, 2002.

The police have been one of the most successful government departments in changing the racial composition of their top ranks, but this has not been without costs: "political displacement, social bewilderment, and rank-and-file demoralisation."[16] In the justice sector, the main battle over racial composition played out in the judiciary. According to Louise Stack, judicial appointments made by the Judicial Service Commission until 1997 led to some improvements in representivity—half the appointments made between 1994 and 1997 were of either black or female judges. In the lower courts, a system of "lay assessors" was introduced in an effort to broaden participation in the judicial system, and to make courts more comfortable for defendants unfamiliar with the environment.[17]

The second important personnel issue was the problem of dealing with officials—particularly in the police and intelligence services—who had been involved in apartheid atrocities. Throughout the negotiations period, the ANC had made clear its intentions to reform the police gradually, rather than radically. Although the ANC would not tolerate abuses of human rights, it would not victimize perpetrators of such abuses committed in the past, as long as the perpetrators abided by new government doctrine. A post-amble to the constitution required legislation that would provide mechanisms and criteria for the granting of amnesty. Before the finalization of negotiations, there was tension within the ANC about whether or not to pursue the idea of a truth commission to deal with past abuses.[18] The negotiations about the amnesty provision contained in the postscript to the constitution revolved around the vexing question of how to deal with perpetrators of past abuses, who, by virtue of the agreements reached in the transitional negotiations, would retain their jobs in the new South African security establishments. This agreement was one of the defining features of the South African transition and precluded immediate and sweeping personnel changes in the country's security and justice agencies.

Provision of some form of amnesty and indemnification of those responsible for past atrocities was a precondition to participation by some parties in the negotiation process that led to the formulation of South Africa's new constitution and the first election. In fact, some analysts argue that were it not for the political compromises on the question of amnesty, there may have been no negotiated settlement and no democratic election in South Africa. The final agreement was not to a general or unconditional amnesty, but an amnesty available to perpetrators only in exchange for full disclosure. This reflected the dominant logic of the South African transitional justice model, one of truth and reconciliation, rather than of justice and accountability. This model sought to combine the process of granting amnesty to perpetrators with the processes of officially establishing the truth about past human rights abuses, providing victims with some form of reparation, and making recommendations to prevent any recurrence of systematic human rights violations.

With the establishment in 1994 of the South African Truth and Reconciliation Commission (TRC), the ANC government had to clarify its position on previous abuses by police officials. Mandela insisted that his government was opposed to, and had no intention of conducting, a witch hunt against the police as a result of activities arising from orders given to the police by the apartheid regime.[19] He urged police officers not to dwell on possible investigations by the TRC but to get on with the job of law enforcement and community

policing. The appointment of George Fivaz as the first national commissioner of the SAPS was a crucial moment in the transformation
process. Although he had been a senior police officer under apartheid, he had never been involved in political policing or human
rights abuses, and he was Mandela's direct appointee. He called for
the SAPS to make a "clean and definite break with the past," which
remained one of the themes of his leadership.

Few police officials voluntarily came forward to seek amnesty
during the early period of the TRC's operations, but the TRC received
a number of amnesty applications—mainly from police officers—at
the end of 1996. This sudden slew of applications for amnesty was
the result of the successful prosecution of Eugene de Kock—a notorious apartheid police assassin who, during his trial, provided extensive
information about other senior state operatives who were involved
in gross human rights abuses—which signaled the possibility of other
police officers being convicted for crimes committed during apartheid duty.[20]

Of 1,674 correct amnesty applications made to the TRC, approximately 300 were made by security force personnel (police, army, and
intelligence) seeking amnesty for 827 incidents of human rights violations.[21] Amnesty was granted for 70 percent of these incidents.[22] For
the police officials (or former police officials) who applied, it appears
that the primary factor in generating amnesty applications was the
threat of prosecutions, rather than a change of heart or a desire to
reconcile with their victims. Such motivations may have existed,
especially among the very small number of black police officials who
applied for amnesty. However, from the side of the TRC, fairly limited resources were put into investigation and prosecution, and this
meant that the direct threat of prosecution against former police officials who had abused their powers was limited. Of those police officials
who had applied for amnesty, most were no longer in the SAPS by
late 2002. Their departure from police ranks may have been associated with the restructuring of the police service or offers of generous
retrenchment packages, rather than with the TRC process itself.

The TRC process therefore directly touched only a very small
minority of police officials in South Africa, mainly those who had
held senior positions in the old Security Branch. It helped rid the

new SAPS of some of the worst and most senior officers implicated in serious crimes. The TRC also underscored a new climate of official intolerance and public rejection of state abuses committed in the course of duty, laying the groundwork for improved citizen service and relations.

Yet two factors limited the potential impact of the TRC on police reform. First, the TRC's focus was on "gross violations of human rights," and second, only overtly party-related "political" motivations were considered in the granting of amnesty. This meant not only that the everyday police abuses against black people were not scrutinized by the TRC but also that even "gross human rights violations" that were not overtly *political* in nature were not regarded as material. The vast majority of police officers, not just the members of the specialized security police and riot units, were probably involved in perpetrating some type of human rights violations during the apartheid era. Virtually no "ordinary" incidents were scrutinized by the TRC, because they did not fall within the commission's legal definition of politically motivated violation of human rights.

Crime Trends in Postapartheid South Africa

The relationship between crime rates and the success of police reform is, at best, indirect, given that crime trends reflect a wide range of variables largely beyond the control of police organizations, even in stable democratic societies. In South Africa, as in most other post-conflict societies, this calculation is made even less meaningful because of fundamental problems with the nature of official crime data. The problems with crime data in South Africa were so severe that, as late as 2001, the government declared a "moratorium" on the production of official crime statistics and began a second major overhaul of the crime recording systems.

Data suggest that feelings of safety declined significantly after 1994, according to annual public opinion and victim surveys conducted by the Human Science Research Council (HSRC).[23] In 1994 the majority (73 percent) of respondents said that they felt safe or very safe, while 16 percent felt unsafe or very unsafe. By 2000 this had shifted significantly, with only 44 percent of respondents reporting that they felt safe or very safe, and 45 percent reporting that they

felt unsafe or very unsafe. If addressing fear of crime has been a serious objective of government efforts since it was first mentioned in
the NCPS in 1996, the HSRC data suggest spectacular failure in
this regard.

One victimization survey,[24] conducted by the Institute for Security Studies (ISS) of 20,000 respondents located in forty-five of the
country's highest-crime areas, contained some useful data. More than
one-third (37 percent) of the respondents indicated that they, or a
member of their households, had been victims of crime in the twenty
months preceding the survey.[25] The most common forms of criminal
victimization experienced by these victims were burglary in their
home (27 percent), robbery involving some form of violence or threat
of violence (20 percent), assault (18 percent), vehicle theft (10 percent), and sexual assault (6 percent).[26] Although recorded crime rates
appear to be stabilizing, the experience of victimization is remarkably
common in "free" South Africa, with gender violence one of the
most serious problems.

In international comparative terms, numerous scholars and
news reports have since 1996 listed South Africa as having one of
the highest homicide rates in the world. Its rate of 51 per 100,000 left
it third (behind Swaziland and Colombia) out of sixty-two reporting
countries in the 2000 rankings of the UN Office on Drugs and Crime
(UNODC). The soundness of these rankings, which omit more than
one hundred developing countries, is questionable.[27] Country-level
victimization surveys conducted by the UNODC between 1992 and
2001 found that nearly 23 percent of South African respondents
reported having been victimized by at least one crime. This placed
South Africa somewhere in the middle of the twenty-two countries
surveyed by the UNODC, although the country led the rankings for
reported robberies.[28]

The Caseload in the Criminal Justice System

The "tough-policing" approaches adopted in South Africa beginning
in 2000 increased the pressure on the rest of the criminal justice system and placed the police in a precarious position. The initially positive public response to this type of policing would be undermined if
the rest of the criminal justice system were unable to follow through

with speedy and similarly tough sanctions. The government's "tough-on-crime" policies posed the danger of lengthy delays in the criminal courts, massive overcrowding in South Africa's prisons, an ever-increasing number of pretrial detainees, increasing numbers of deaths as a result of police action and in police custody, rising xenophobia resulting from the notion that "foreigners" are responsible for South Africa's growing crime problem, and increasing numbers of arrests in certain crime categories, resulting in increases, rather than decreases, in recorded police statistics. By June 2000, Steve Tshwete, then minister of safety and security, admitted that the "successful implementation of the [SAPS] strategic and operational plan hinges, in the main, on a tighter consolidation of the criminal justice system."[29]

Despite low levels of prosecutions and convictions, new bail and minimum-sentencing policies led to substantial changes in the prison population. In April 1998, immediately before the implementation of minimum-sentence legislation, only 19 percent of the sentenced prisoners were serving a term of longer than ten years. The proportion of long-term prisoners had increased to 36 percent by late 2004.[30]

The initial imperative for criminal justice reform in South Africa was to build legitimacy and democratize the system.[31] However, by 1998 the overburdened justice administration was in danger of collapse. The failure of early efforts at systemwide coordination was evident. By 2001 the police were forced to contemplate the consequences of their strategic choices, as arrestees came out of the "revolving doors" of bail hearings and prison cells at ever more rapid rates.[32] The tension between the politicians' need to be seen as "tough" on crime and the need to reduce the volume in the criminal justice system became an underlying dynamic of criminal justice reform for several years. Some of the real "miracles" of South Africa's transition are the lack of prison riots in overcrowded prisons and the fact that courts can function at all under the weight of their caseload.

Human Rights

Police and prosecutors directed significant efforts and resources—including large amounts of international aid—at improving compliance with human rights standards during the early period of the transition to democracy. At the institutional level, numerous bodies were established to oversee and investigate allegations of abuse by justice and security institutions: the Human Rights Commission, the Commission on Gender Equality, the Public Protector, the Independent Complaints Directorate (which investigates police agencies only), the Independent Investigating Judge (prisons only), and the Magistrates Commission (magistrates only).

Table 5-3. Complaints Recorded by the Independent Complaints Directorate

Period	Deaths as a Result of Police Action	Criminal Assaults and Attempted Murders by Police	Assaults by Police Classified as "Misconduct"
April 1997– March 1998	518	157	67
April 1998– March 1999	558	311 (to January 1999)	69
April 1999– March 2000	472	500	143

Source: Independent Complaints Directorate, http://www.icd.gov.za.

Despite this elaborate institutional arrangement, government commitment to meaningful oversight began to be questioned in the late 1990s because of lack of support, both political and financial, to some of the key oversight institutions. The security and justice ministers under President Mbeki showed ambivalence, wishing to appear "hard on criminals" while supporting improved human rights performance.

Statistics provided by the Independent Complaints Directorate show continuing high levels of the use of lethal force by the police in the late 1990s (see table 5-3).[33] Despite a decline in the number of persons killed by police (both on-duty and off-duty), the problem of police brutality continued in South Africa. In a detailed analysis of police shootings, David Bruce and G. O'Malley made a "conservative" estimate that, between 1996 and 1998, members of the SAPS were involved in an average of 6,225 shooting incidents per annum.[34]

During this period, an average of 467 people were shot dead by the police each year, and an estimated 1,307 people were injured in police shootings per year. The official incident reports kept by the police showed that 15 percent of these police shootings were not legal.

The most striking change in policing in South Africa is the dramatic decline in the number of people killed in public demonstrations and gatherings. Exact numbers are not available, but deaths in demonstrations at the hands of public order units are now rare in South Africa. The decline in the numbers of persons killed in public order incidents also resulted from significant changes in the legal framework for the control and conduct of protests and other public gatherings.

Professionalizing Service Delivery

The SAPS's professional performance has improved only marginally in the years since its establishment in 1995, and its perceived effectiveness against crime has declined. In 1998 the majority of respondents in the country's first National Victimisation Survey thought that the police were performing as badly as, or worse than, they had under apartheid.[35] In line with a governmentwide emphasis on improving the delivery of services to the public after the second presidential election in 1999, most of the criminal justice agencies implemented Service Delivery Improvement Programmes, which fit comfortably with the efficiency approaches introduced after 1997.

A national sample survey was conducted in October 2000, five months after the Crackdown police strategy began to be implemented and five years after the establishment of the new South African Police Service. It found that members of the public who had visited one of the high-crime police stations were overwhelmingly satisfied with the attitude of the police officials and with the treatment they had received.[36] More than 70 percent of respondents who had reported a crime to the police were happy with the service they received from the police at the time of reporting the incident. The perceived ability of the police to deal effectively with complaints and reports deteriorated between the time the initial report was filed and when an arrest (if any) was made. Less than half the respondents had ever heard from the detectives about the progress on their case.

These findings reinforce the notion that improved police-community relations and access to justice will result in new problems for the other components of the justice system.

Corruption

The promotion of integrity in the criminal justice system was a key element of reform in the early post-1994 period. The new government was well aware of corruption in the system, as many officials had directly observed it as subjects of police detention and torture. Integrity efforts focused on apartheid abuses, and very little attention was paid to corruption in the early years. However, corruption soon became a major public concern in relation to criminal justice. In addition to bribery by the police and escapes from prison, a common subject for newspaper exposés was the sale of dockets by prosecutors.

The SAPS National Anti-corruption Unit (ACU) started operating in 1996, and its key objective was the "effective prevention and investigation of corruption within the SAPS."[37] Until the end of 2000 approximately 250 members of the ACU were tasked with investigating allegations of corruption committed by police members across the country. Apart from the sheer numbers of cases reported[38]— more than 40,000 cases in 1999 and more than 70,000 cases in 2000—a striking feature of the ACU data was the discrepancy between the number of cases reported and the number of police officials subsequently formally charged, and then finally convicted, in a court of law.

The Institute for Democracy in South Africa found that almost 50 percent of the population believed in 2000 that "almost all" or "most" public officials (not just police) were involved in corruption.[39] A 1996 Johannesburg Victimisation Survey revealed that of the bribery and corruption experiences reported, 53.6 percent involved members of the South African Police.[40] The Institute for Security Studies survey conducted at forty-five of the highest-crime police station areas found that 31 percent of the respondents believed that policing had worsened since 1994, and 29 percent of these listed corruption as the main reason for the decline in local policing.[41] The most common suggestion (23 percent) made by survey respondents to improve public confidence in the police was to deal with police corruption and integrity. Corruption became a serious problem for public confidence in the justice system during the 1990s, one that required more creative approaches than simply mobilizing more resources to confront it.

Vigilantism and Private Policing

Research by Bronwyn Harris and others[42] found that vigilante methods generally remained consistent throughout the period 1980–2000, but definitions and explanations of what constitutes vigilante violence have altered considerably. Owing to a range of methodological problems, it is impossible to assess whether there was any change in the volume of vigilante incidents under democracy.

Harris's study suggests that vigilante actions in pre-1994 South Africa were defined by recourse to politics and political intention. In general the "vigilante" label was applied to violent actions conducted in support of the apartheid state. After 1994, however, vigilantism was predominantly defined with reference to a "crime-fighting" motive—many vigilante incidents were depicted by participants as community-based crime fighting or as self-help policing in situations where the state police agencies were simply absent or unable to deal with a problem.

While vigilantism remained controversial and newsworthy, the parallel phenomenon of private security for rich communities and corporate citizens was not subjected to much regulation or policy critique in the early postapartheid period—perhaps because of the enormous size of the phenomenon.[43] The growth in South Africa's private security sector—particularly the protection of business premises—had begun during the latter days of apartheid, to ensure protection of goods and personnel from the popular antiapartheid uprisings of the late 1980s and the political violence that continued into the early 1990s. Thus the growth of private policing should not be interpreted only as the consequence of a failure of criminal justice in the postdemocracy period.

CONCLUSION: LESSONS FROM SOUTH AFRICA

Rebuilding Legitimate Justice Institutions in High-Crime Context

The main imperative for criminal justice reform in South Africa was the desire to reshape and reform the institutions of criminal justice—police, courts, and prisons. Although there was simultaneously a strong lobby for "transformation" rather than "reform," the most important postdemocracy imperative for the newly elected ANC government was to create state institutions (especially in the security sector) that reflected the new postapartheid political dispensation.[44] The emphasis on institutional reform and away from prevention was strongly supported by donors and local business, which lent resources to a managerialist approach. Perhaps as a result of this internal focus on institutional reform, the process of reform lost touch with its context—an environment of incredibly high levels of violent crime. The political and public pressure regarding crime eventually saw the early designs for reform abandoned in favor of a "war on crime," with quick fixes and "get-tough" measures the order of the day by 2002. Some improvements coincided with this new get-tough policy, but a causal link is unclear. Certainly, broader prevention measures lost ground or were abandoned.

Shifting strategies of reform left the South African criminal justice system half reformed and half unreconstructed, even less able to address common crime than when it was a blunt instrument of a more repressive state. Reform initiatives and the uncertainty they generate reduce the overall capacity of the criminal justice system, even if only in the short term. South Africa's new human rights framework created new challenges for the administration of justice and required new skills that were simply not present in formerly repressive institutions. "Tough-on-crime" policies created more pressures for detentions and culpatory evidence, especially at the pretrial phase, which may have fueled high levels of police abuse and low levels of prosecution and conviction.

The key lesson from South Africa is that processes of security or justice reform in transitional societies are not simply about rebuilding institutions. They are about enabling the institutions, from the outset of the transition process, to deal *in new ways* with *new forms of crime*. Transformation or reform processes need to simultaneously achieve these two—very complex and sometimes competing—goals.

Officials, reformers, and advocates of change need to stay in touch with the dynamics of crime and, perhaps more important, with public opinion about crime and fear. As Mark Shaw predicted in 1995, "any public debate around crime, now and in the future, will be influenced decisively by the ability—actual and perceived—of policing institutions to combat crime and influence personal safety."[45]

Transitions create opportunities for new forms and volumes of crime. This context needs to be explicitly anticipated and planned for at the outset of reform processes; otherwise, it may derail even the best-intentioned reform efforts. Much of the work on crime in transitions focuses on syndicated crime and the growth of transnational economic crime. Increased reporting and incidence of interpersonal violence in transitional societies tend to be ignored.

The strong emphasis in South Africa on accountability and human rights performance created its own problems. The process of reform was marked by extreme forms of "political correctness" about human rights, which, at times, hindered the police in their attempts to tackle the growing crime problem. Despite the great improvement in accountability of security and justice institutions, those institutions are widely perceived as unable to protect the citizenry. This raises the specter of failure in making justice reform an integrated and useful component of the broader democratic project of reconstruction and development.

Corruption (and crimes committed by officials inside the criminal justice agencies) are major delegitimizers of the "reformed" institutions. In the South African case, corruption was often underestimated and viewed merely as resistance to change. Corruption prevention (or the promotion of "integrity") was not sufficiently emphasized in the overall reform program.

Shattered Communities and Uncivil Societies

The development of crime reduction policies in the new South Africa failed to adequately engage social capital devastated by decades of apartheid. The original ANC view[46] that community-based structures and high levels of "community participation" in reform processes would be the ultimate guarantee of police accountability and transformation has been belied by the collapse of the community-police forums and the increasingly reactionary public discourses on crime in South Africa. Perhaps the conclusion to draw is that the original emphasis on community involvement was inappropriate—or overly ambitious—once elected, representative government was in place.

Communities are never homogeneous, simple, or benign, particularly in postconflict societies. In South Africa, this is illustrated by high levels of interpersonal violence, xenophobia, and ongoing local conflicts. Old patterns of division, intolerance, and conflict do not simply disappear when a democratic order comes into existence. Mamphela Ramphela puts it this way:

> Why [is there] such a gap between the values and rights enshrined in our Constitution, and the reality of the continuing violations of those rights. Why are the watchdog institutions not having the desired effect on our society? What are the impediments to the success of these institutions? . . . If you have had a society that criminalized normal behaviour, and normalized criminal behaviour, it will not be easy to change that society simply on the basis of an excellent Constitution, watchdog institutions, and people who affirm their commitment to a democracy. It will require the focused building of a *culture* that recognizes the very faulty foundations of our society.[47] (emphasis added)

Transitional societies are probably more criminogenic than most. The challenge of repairing the social fabric—creating peace and reconciliation, repairing families and communities shattered by apartheid—is closely related to new thinking about crime prevention. In his address to the opening of parliament in 2002, President Mbeki acknowledged that trends in crime require an improvement in the "moral fibre" of society, the strengthening of community bonds, and the improvement of basic socioeconomic conditions.[48]

Some elements of modern crime prevention theory advocate that "social" crime prevention is the most critical—interventions that address families, children, parenting, physical environments, joblessness, and education. In a postconflict, developing country like

South Africa, characterized by extremely high levels of inequality, marginalization, and exclusion, this aspect of crime prevention is hardest to implement and sustain. Although elements of this "social" approach to crime prevention are evident in various policies of the new South African government, they tend to be abandoned easily in the face of media, public, and political pressure for "tougher" action against crime.

The Impact of the TRC and Transitional Justice

The South African TRC demanded an unrealistically "neat" and clear-cut division between violence committed in the name of a known political organization on one hand and criminal violence on the other. Only those whose abusive behaviors were specifically targeted at political ends and whose behaviors were fairly extreme, by normal human rights standards, were required to consider applying for amnesty. This meant that the majority of justice and security sector personnel were able to avoid examination of the history of "ordinary" abuses of the rights of citizens—routine torture, secondary victimization, omissions of aspects of basic criminal procedure, and so on. Only those who faced a realistic chance of prosecution for their past abuses needed to actually apply for amnesty—the limited investigative resources of the TRC meant that it was unlikely that any evidence would be uncovered except that which was voluntarily disclosed by perpetrators.

In South Africa's transitional justice approach, a small number of criminal prosecutions were launched against high-profile security officials—such as Wouter Basson (former head of the military's chemical warfare program) and Magnus Malan (former minister of defense)—who had not applied for amnesty. While the failure of these (and other) prosecutions illustrated the limitations of criminal prosecutions as a mechanism for dealing with past abuses in South Africa, the threat of prosecution was acknowledged by the TRC to be the key motivator for security officials to apply for amnesty and make disclosures about their conduct under apartheid.

Although transitional justice tools such as amnesties or pardons may contribute to future cultures of lawbreaking and impunity, they have undeniably had some benefits for the processes of institutional reform in the South African police—in particular, the retention of some skilled personnel owing to the TRC's decision not to recommend lustration,[49] the development of a close political relationship between the government and the police leadership to secure stability within the police service, and an intangible contribution to a moral culture of reconciliation and coexistence.

However, transitional justice tools were far less successful in application to the South African military, which failed to participate meaningfully. This raises the question of how these and other tools could have better contributed to rebuilding popular respect for the rule of law and to the transformation of security and justice institutions in other postconflict settings. In South Africa, prosecutions and the TRC process failed to adequately provide for reparations, to engage the important institutional reforms discussed here, and to develop a sustained engagement with civil society that would strengthen its capacity.[50]

Many writers have argued that proper evaluation of the efficacy of various "transitional justice" mechanisms in South Africa (such as the Truth and Reconciliation Commission) must be situated within the context of political and criminal violence. That violent context poses key challenges to the transformation of inherited criminal justice institutions and to a liberal democratic discourse on human rights and security. Graeme Simpson argues that it is necessary to shift the conversations about transitional justice from an exclusively retrospective scrutiny of past injustices to a strategic and proactive engagement with the new challenges that face justice institutions in emerging democracies—an approach that demands simultaneous engagement with both the past and the future.[51] I (and the other contributors to this volume) have sought to address this challenge.

Adherence to human rights standards in criminal procedure is an area where the intersection between past and future is most stark. Ambitious legislation and human rights standards created the illusion of "overnight change" in the way the security and justice systems would approach human rights; however, these changes remained largely at the policy level. Public complaints against the police and the number of deaths in police custody increased steadily in the immediate posttransition period. Abuses occurred despite the existence of a Bill of Rights in the new constitution and of many "oversight" and "watchdog" agencies, and despite a range of human rights education programs for police officials. The failure of the TRC to make strategic and effective recommendations, and the failure of the security and justice agencies to take heed of TRC recommendations, led to a situation in which some forms of police abuse and brutality were worse in the "new" democratic South Africa than they were under apartheid. The situation was facilitated by a public opinion climate that favored "tough-on-crime" approaches and contained little sympathy for suspects or perpetrators of crime. The government's ambiguity about the entire TRC final report—the ruling party reacted negatively to some of the TRC's findings about its own conduct during the struggle against apartheid—may also be a reason why there has been no political pressure on the security and justice agencies to implement and report on progress with respect to the TRC's recommendations. Unless the outcome of the transitional justice process is strongly supported by the posttransition government (and by the leadership of the judiciary, the prosecution service, and the police service), it is unlikely to make significant impact on the transformation of those institutions.

The impact of the TRC on the security and justice sectors has been minimal, primarily because reform of these sectors was already under way, and the TRC process was somewhat marginal to the grander project of reforming the apartheid state. The TRC process did not add any original, strategic value to that process. Truth-telling and the threat of prosecution may have added some momentum to the process of security sector reform, perhaps by contributing to a changed moral climate in South Africa,

> from one where police abuse went primarily unsanctioned to one where the potential for that sanction is far greater. The TRC existed at a particular watershed moment, a moment where it was important to demarcate what had happened in the past, from what was to come. In so far as the new society is willing to, and has the means to, sanction police abuses, the TRC is an important part of what makes such sanction legitimate. The question now is whether South African society has the means and the will to impose such sanction for abuses by the police.[52]

Key features of the South African political transition—the nature of the negotiated transition that saw all state personnel retain their jobs through the transition, and the particular form of transitional justice that was selected—as well as specific features of the local context (factors contributing to high levels of violence and mortality) render the "lessons" from South Africa difficult to export to other contexts. Given the complexity of the posttransition situation, the level of institutional reform in the security and justice sectors is fairly remarkable, although the reforms may not have materialized in the forms envisaged by policymakers at the time of transition. Perhaps part of the reason for the ongoing international interest in the outcome of South Africa's transition process is that the questions of disorder, human rights, conflict, and reconciliation continue to be the key markers for success.

NOTES

1. The former South African Police were deployed in the "bush wars" in Namibia, Angola, Zimbabwe, and Mozambique; they also participated in cross-border raids on the bases of the exiled liberation movements.

2. According to Gavin Cawthra, "Military and police personnel were prominent at all levels in the NSMS, with the police taking command of the lower levels and playing the dominant role in operational command. The very fact that the primary threat was now seen as domestic and not external meant that the police began to reassert their role in strategic intelligence and hence in influencing state strategy. The emergency also required the substantial strengthening of the police, which began to draw away some of the state funds which would previously have flowed to the defense force." Gavin Cawthra, *Policing South Africa* (London: Zed Books, 1993), 32.

3. Ibid., 32–33. One-third of the people detained in 1986 were under the age of eighteen. Under apartheid, "township" denoted a residential area demarcated for black people.

4. Graeme Simpson and Janine Rauch, "Political Violence: 1991," in *Human Rights Yearbook 1992*, 1st ed., ed. N. Boister and K. Ferguson-Brown (Cape Town: Oxford University Press, 1993).

5. See Brandon Hamber, "Dr. Jekyll and Mr. Hyde: Problems of Violence Prevention and Reconciliation in South Africa's Transition to Democracy," in *Violence in South Africa: A Variety of Perspectives*, ed. E. Bornman, R. van Eeden, and M. Wentzel (Pretoria: Human Sciences Research Council,

1997); Hamber, "Living with the Legacy of Impunity: Lessons for South Africa about Truth, Justice and Crime in Brazil," *Latin American Report* 13, no. 2 (July–December 1997); and Graeme Simpson, "Rebuilding Fractured Societies: Reconstruction, Reconciliation and the Changing Nature of Violence—Some Self-Critical Insights from Post-apartheid South Africa" (unpublished paper commissioned by the UN Development Programme, 2000).

6. See Mark Shaw, *Partners in Crime? Crime, Political Transformation and Changing Forms of Police Control*, Research Report No. 39 (Johannesburg: Centre for Policy Studies, 1995).

7. This involved the adoption of several new laws: Criminal Procedure Amendment Acts of 1995 and 1996; Justice Laws Rationalisation Act, 1996; General Law Amendment Act, 1996; International Co-operation in Criminal Matters Act, 1996; Abolition of Corporal Punishment Act, 1997; Criminal Law Amendment Act, 1997; National Prosecuting Authority Act, 1998; Judicial Matters Amendment Act, 1998; Witness Protection Act, 1998; Firearms Control Act; Prevention of Organised Crime Act, 1998; Domestic Violence Act; and Special Investigating Units and Special Tribunals Act, 1996.

8. The Secretariat for Safety and Security was created with the express purpose of providing civilian input into policing policy and more specifically into the process of police reform. It thus had two critical mandates: (1) to design policy for the police agency and (2) to monitor the performance of the police against these policy goals.

9. For more on defense reform in South Africa, see Rocklyn Williams, "African Armed Forces and the Challenges of Security Sector" (paper presented at the African Security Dialogue and Research [ASDR] conference "Security Sector Reform and Democratisation in Africa: Comparative Perspectives," Accra, Ghana, February 2002).

10. The small change in the name was intended to signify a new approach—"communities" come first.

11. Wilfried Scharf and Daniel Nina, *The Other Law: Non-state Ordering in South Africa* (Cape Town: Juta, 2001), 70.

12. Eric Pelser and Janine Rauch, "South Africa's Criminal Justice System: Policies and Priorities" (unpublished paper presented at the 2001 South African Sociology Association conference, Pretoria, 2001), 6.

13. The Directorate of Special Operations was also known as the Scorpions.

14. Judicial Inspectorate of Prisons, 2004.

15. Gareth Newham, "Out of Step: Integrity and the South African Police Service" (draft chapter for book edited by Carl Klockars, 2001).

16. Elrena van der Spuy, "Crime and Its Discontent: Recent South African Responses and Policies," in *Crime and Policing in Transitional Societies,* Konrad Adenauer Stiftung Seminar Report No. 8 (Johannesburg: Konrad Adenauer Stiftung, 2001), 168.

17. See Louise Stack, *Courting Disaster? Justice and South Africa's New Democracy,* Research Report No. 55: Transition Series (Johannesburg: Centre for Policy Studies, 1997).

18. According to Frederick Van Zyl Slabbert in *After the TRC: Reflections on Truth and Reconciliation in South Africa,* ed. Wilmot James and Linda van de Vijver (Claremont, South Africa: David Philip Publishers, 2000).

19. Nelson Mandela, address to the opening of parliament, February 17, 1995.

20. See Martin Meredith, *Coming to Terms: South Africa's Search for Truth* (New York: Public Affairs, 1999); and Pumla Gobodo-Madikizela, *A Human Being Died That Night: A South African Story of Forgiveness* (Boston: Houghton Mifflin, 2003).

21. Janine Rauch, "The South African Police and the Truth Commission," *South African Review of Sociology* 36, no. 2 (2005): 208.

22. Carnita Ernest, "A Quest for Justice: An Analysis of the TRC Amnesty Hearings" (unpublished paper, Centre for the Study of Violence and Reconciliation, Johannesburg, 2003).

23. Cited in Martin Schonteich, "Sleeping Soundly—Feelings of Safety: Based on Perceptions of Reality?" in *Nedbank ISS Crime Index* 5, no. 2 (March–April 2001): 4.

24. Eric Pelser and Antoinette Louw, "Community Policing and Police Service Improvement Study: Project Report" (unpublished paper, Institute for Security Studies, Pretoria, 2001).

25. That is, from January 2000 to September 2001.

26. It is extremely difficult to accurately capture experiences of sexual and gender crimes in this type of survey. For a critique of South African victim surveys in this regard, see Lisa Vetten, "The Influence of Gender on Research: A Critique of Two Victim Surveys," *Development Update* 2, no. 4 (1999).

27. Antony Altbeker, "Puzzling Statistics: Is South Africa Really the World's Crime Capital?" *Crime Quarterly* 11 (Pretoria: Institute for Security Studies, 2005), http://www.iss.org/za/Pubs/CrimeQ/No.11/Altbeker.htm (accessed June 4, 2005).

28. Ibid.

29. Steve Tshwete, minister of safety and security, review debate on criminal justice cluster in National Council of Provinces, Cape Town, June 8, 2000.

30. Judicial Inspectorate of Prisons, 2004.

31. See Rauch et al., "Creating a New South African Police Service: Priorities in the Post-election Period," occasional paper (Johannesburg: Centre for the Study of Violence and Reconciliation, July 1994); Elrena van der Spuy, "Crime and Its Discontent: Recent South African Responses and Policies," in *Crime and Policing in Transitional Societies*, Konrad Adenauer Stiftung Seminar Report No. 8 (Johannesburg: Konrad Adenauer Stiftung, 2001).

32. Lukas Muntingh estimated that recidivism in South Africa is in the region of 85 percent to 94 percent. Lukas Muntingh, *After Prison: The Case for Offender Reintegration* (Pretoria: Institute for Security Studies, 2001).

33. There are a variety of problems with the recording and classification of these official ICD statistics; however, they illustrate general trends. See David Bruce, "New Wine from an Old Cask? The South African Police Service and the Process of Transformation" (draft paper presented at John Jay College for Criminal Justice, New York, May 2002).

34. David Bruce and G. O'Malley, *In the Line of Duty? Shooting Incident Reports and Other Indicators of the Use and Abuse of Force of Members of the SAPS Research* (Pretoria: Independent Complaints Directorate, October 2001).

35. The National Victimisation Survey (conducted in 1998, with a relatively small sample) revealed that only 26 percent of respondents thought that the effectiveness of the police had improved, while 32 percent of respondents thought that the police had stayed the same, and a majority of 42 percent thought they had become less effective since the 1994 democratic elections.

36. This may reflect initiatives to improve front-line service during the past few years but may result from relatively low expectations, and pleasant surprise, at the police service encountered.

37. SAPS, cited in Newham, "Out of Step" (draft chapter for book edited by Carl Klockars, 2001).

38. The ACU receives cases from all sources, including citizens' complaints, other police units, the Independent Complaints Directorate, and even members of criminal syndicates that experience a "fallout" with the police members they are working with.

39. Lala Camerer, "Just How Corrupt Is SA?" *Business Day*, August 2, 2000.

40. Beatty Naude, "To Catch a Cheat: Comparing Corruption and Fraud Victimisation Data," *Crime and Conflict*, no. 21 (Spring 2000).

41. One of the problems with using this source is that police corruption may be more prevalent in the high-crime areas than elsewhere. However, there is no other national data set that is as comprehensive.

42. Bronwyn Harris, *A Foreign Experience: Violence, Crime and Xenophobia during South Africa's Transition,* Violence and Transition Series, Vol. 5 (Johannesburg: Centre for the Study of Violence and Reconciliation, August 2001); Bill Dixon and Lisa Johns, *Gangs, Pagad and the State: Vigilantism and Revenge Violence in the Western Cape,* Violence and Transition Series, Vol. 2 (Johannesburg: Centre for the Study of Violence and Reconciliation, May 2001); and David Bruce and Joe Komane, "Taxis, Cops and Vigilantes: Police Attitudes towards Street Justice," *Crime and Conflict,* no. 17 (Spring 1999).

43. According to the Institute of Security Studies, the number of active private security officers registered with the Security Officers Interim Board at the end of 2000 was 184,328.

44. Mike Brogden and Clifford Shearing, *Policing for a New South Africa* (London: Routledge, 1993); and Rocklyn Williams, "African Armed Forces and the Challenges of Security Sector Reform."

45. Mark Shaw, *Partners in Crime?*

46. This was the view expressed in various documents produced by the ANC's Police Policy Group in the early 1990s. See, for example, Étienne Marais and Janine Rauch, "Policing South Africa: Reform and Prospects" (paper presented at the Institute for Democracy in South Africa conference, "Policing in South Africa in the 1990s," Van der Bijl Park, October 1992); and Janine Rauch et al., *Creating a New South African Police Service.*

47. Mamphela Ramphela, "Law, Corruption and Morality," in *After the TRC: Reflections on Truth and Reconciliation in South Africa,* ed. Wilmot James and Linda van de Vijver (Claremont, South Africa: David Philip Publishers, 2000).

48. Thabo Mbeki, address to the opening of parliament, Cape Town, February 2002, http://www.gov.za.

49. The TRC's inability to actually investigate and prosecute any perpetrators of apartheid violations was also a factor.

50. Graeme Simpson, "'Uncivil Society' Challenges for Reconciliation and Justice in South Africa after the Truth and Reconciliation Commission" (unpublished paper presented in Sweden, April 2002).

51. Ibid.

52. David Bruce, "New Wine from an Old Cask? The South African Police Service and the Process of Transformation" (draft paper presented at the John Jay College for Criminal Justice, New York, May 2002).

6

Postgenocide Justice and Security Reform

Rwanda

Charles Mironko and Ephrem Rurangwa

THE POSTGENOCIDAL SITUATION IN RWANDA PRESENTS overwhelming challenges to institutional attempts to ensure any measure of justice and security for the society as a whole. A devastated, traumatized population, a demolished physical infrastructure, the institutions of government looted and vandalized by their previous occupants, and the legacy of the most serious human rights abuses in humankind's recent history all confront one of the world's poorest countries in Rwanda. Nevertheless, a reform process has been initiated. In this chapter we outline its creation and effects, focusing on the transformations that have occurred in the Rwandan judiciary since the genocide and on efforts to deal creatively with the problem of trying large numbers of suspected genocide perpetrators in a situation of diminished capacity. We also review recent measures to rebuild a national police force to enforce the country's laws and protect its citizens. In both analyses, we argue that the only viable strategies for dealing with the extreme situation in Rwanda are to set clear priorities, keep expectations very modest, and rely on local authorities and institutions where possible.

THE RWANDAN JUDICIARY

Overview of the Rwandan Judiciary

This section describes some of the major features of the judicial system in pre- and postgenocide Rwanda, as well as the international and domestic justice initiatives (specifically, the traditional village courts known as *gacaca*) that have been implemented to resolve the practical difficulties associated with processing the thousands of Rwandan genocide cases still awaiting trial.

As in many other African countries, Rwanda's judicial system is closely linked to the state-building projects of the government of the time, and judicial reforms can often be best understood in terms of their political utility. Thus, while the first leader of postcolonial Rwanda, Gregoire Kayibanda, made few changes to the colonial judicial system after he came to power in 1962, President Juvénal Habyarimana between 1973 and 1993 abolished the Supreme Court as an institution and parceled out its various branches (Court of Appeal, Constitutional Court, and State Council) for separate administration. Such judicial reforms matched parallel initiatives elsewhere within the state infrastructure; Habyarimana's political reforms included not only the creation of a single-party system under the Mouvement Révolutionnaire National pour le Développement (MRND) but also ensuring widespread control of that system through the MRND National Committee, which took over the responsibilities of the offices of the prime minister, the Ministry of Defense, and various other institutions, all of which were then dissolved.

This system remained in operation until August 4, 1993, when the Rwandan government, as a signatory to a power-sharing arrangement under the Arusha Peace Agreement, was obliged to carry out judicial reforms. As a result, the 1991 constitution was restored, and many laws were amended or revised, including those that had disbanded the Supreme Court.[1] A Council of Magistrates was also appointed. Similar revisions to the judicial system continued after the Rwandan Patriotic Front's ascent to power following the 1994 civil war and genocide; these included

- The establishment of military courts (December 1995)

- The creation of the Rwanda National Police to replace the National Gendarmerie (June 2000)
- The establishment of the Rwandan Bar Association (Barreau du Rwanda) (April 1997, modified in September 1999 and March 2000)
- The Rights and Protection of the Child against Violence (January 2001)
- Organic Law No. 8/96, enacted by the parliament in 1996 to govern the prosecution of the offenses of genocide and crimes against humanity committed after October 1, 1990

Domestic System of Justice

The well-planned genocide that claimed the lives of up to one million Tutsi and antigovernment Hutu in 1994 also left the judiciary in a shambles. As the Tutsi-dominated Rwandan Patriotic Front (RPF) drove the Hutu *génocidaires* from the country, the latter sought to loot or damage government offices. The courts and all their equipment were destroyed; the new Ministry of Justice lacked even basic office supplies, let alone vehicles and communication technology to carry out investigations. A primary task of judicial reform, therefore, was the reconstruction of the physical infrastructure. More pressing, however, was the need to rebuild the judiciary's *human* infrastructure. Few legal professionals of any kind remained in the country; some had fled, some had been killed, and others were imprisoned on suspicion of participation in the genocide. In late 1994 Ministry of Justice reports indicated that there were only thirty-six judges and fourteen prosecutors and assistant prosecutors available in the entire country. In Kigali, the capital, only two prosecutors were at work, and the Ministry of Justice was operating from a hotel room.[2] A 1995 World Bank report says, "Of an estimated corps of 1,100 magistrates before the war, less than 200 magistrates have reported for duty."[3] Finally, according to government statistics, the number of judges fell from 750 before the genocide to 244 after, prosecutors from 87 to 14, and investigators from 193 to 39.[4]

The creation of programs to replace these critical elements was thus a pressing need. However, the devastated judiciary simultaneously faced a task of daunting size and complexity: the need to investigate and prosecute tens of thousands of alleged genocide perpetrators, over and above the country's normal criminal and civil caseload. As the backlog of cases grew, so did the prison population. The central prison in Kigali, which was built to hold 1,500 prisoners, housed more than 5,000 in November 1994. Among the 4,623 genocide suspects in Kigali prison, only 1,224 suspects had appeared before the magistrate in 1994. By 1996 a few formal courts were able to create files for about 80,000 detainees; but as late as 1999 conditions in the Rwandan prisons remained untenable and showed signs of even more pronounced deterioration. According to a chalkboard in the Kigali prison manager's office in March of that year, 7,822 genocide suspects were being held in Kigali prison; 7,251 had files, while 571 had none; 1,040 prisoners had pleaded guilty; 123 were being tried for the first time, whereas 103 prisoners were on appeal; and 28 prisoners had been sentenced to death, 8 to life imprisonment, and 63 to one to twenty years' imprisonment.[5]

The prison situation drew criticism from various local and foreign sources. According to Gérard Prunier, the government's actions indicated a "'go slow' policy" intended to "extract a maximum of political advantages from the situation."[6] However, subsequent attempts to decrease the prison population proved equally unpopular for the government, albeit with genocide survivors rather than NGOs and the international community (see later). It is clear that other pressing domestic and regional factors (the reconstruction of civilian infrastructure, provision of security and welfare, and the civil war in neighboring Zaire) were serving to divert government attention and resources.

Tensions arose between the Rwandan government and international actors who had previously failed to respond to the genocide and whose subsequent rush to assist refugees ironically seemed to favor the Hutu génocidaires. As Larry Minear and Randolph C. Kent point out:

> Rwandans were also puzzled by aid groups of conferences, workshops, and seminars on reconciliation only months after the genocide had ended. While to aid agencies it seems essential to move quickly to reconstruction, Rwandans believed that generous assis-

tance to refugees and dispassionate discussions of reconciliation
begged profound questions of justice.[7]

Disagreements of this type were also responsible for the Rwandan
parliament's refusal to allow foreign judges to preside over genocide
cases on the grounds that outsiders could not properly adjudicate the
matter.[8] This decision clashed with the desires of bilateral donors
such as France, who wanted to support the recruitment of judges
from francophone countries to speed up the process of genocide trials, instead of offering to pay for the construction of new prisons.[9]

In the face of growing detentions of genocide suspects—the
number reached some 120,000 in 1996, more than 1 percent of the
country's population—the Ministry of Justice began training new
magistrates and investigators in 1994. However, a year after the genocide began, there was still no single court in Rwanda with sufficient
equipment and staff to deal with genocide cases. As late as 1997, only
10 to 20 percent of magistrates' positions were filled—and not all of
these by professionally qualified people. The ministry thus still faced
the task of expanding its professional ranks, improving magistrates'
competence, providing them with adequate equipment, and building
the public prosecutor's office and courts. Out of necessity, the ministry organized a six-month training period for criminal investigators
and public prosecutors because without sufficient infrastructure and
human resources, it would be almost impossible to carry out trials of
the genocide suspects already in prison by 1995.

As a result, the Rwandan parliament passed Organic Law No.
08/96, Organization of Prosecutions for Offenses Constituting Genocide or Crimes against Humanity Committed since October 1, 1990,
which went into effect on August 30, 1996. This law classified genocide suspects according to four categories. Category One consists of
genocide planners, organizers, supervisors, and rape offenders (including those who sexually tortured their victims). Category Two includes
instigators and perpetrators of serious attacks with intention to kill.
Category Three consists of accomplices in serious crimes (short of
rape and murder) without intention to kill. Category Four consists of
those who looted and/or destroyed property. The law also provides
for regulations on compensation and reparation procedures.[10]

Thus, while domestic genocide trials began in 1996, limited resources prevented the ministry from alleviating the pressures posed by the very large number of detainees. Ministry of Justice sources indicate that only 2,000 cases were tried during a two-year period (1996–98). Various alternatives were tested, including group trials and the construction of specialized judicial facilities intended for use in genocide hearings in each province. But even the twelve tribunals were insufficient to deal with the 120,000-plus suspects, especially in light of the fact that more suspects were expected to surface. In addition, a law was passed in September 1996 stipulating that all genocide suspects' files be in order by December 1997, fixing the maximum permitted duration of detention at six months.

Three further initiatives were subsequently implemented. First, the Rwandan parliament extended the legal duration of detention from December 1997 to December 1999. Second, the ministry replaced the *commissions de triage* (selection commissions) in charge of creating case files with *groupes mobiles* (mobile groups), which proved more efficient in dealing with the problem of missing or non-existent files.[11] Third, beginning in August 1997, the government decided to release those genocide suspects suffering from incurable diseases (such as HIV/AIDS) and those who were elderly or minors during the genocide.

This was an unpopular decision. For the survivors' association Ibuka (Remember), it amounted to a declaration of amnesty, and some suggested that this represented an attempt to win votes in the upcoming local elections. A second wave of releases (10,000 in total) in 1998 drew more criticism. While the Rwandan government defended the releases by arguing that it would be a violation of human rights and international law to keep suspects in prison for four years without formal charges, the Rwandan press countered that the government had acted only in response to foreign donors—who were paying three-quarters of the US$8 million required to feed the prisoners annually.[12]

The criticism about the release of certain suspects exemplifies the central dilemma of postconflict justice: balancing the inadequacies of the judiciary and security apparatus with the financial realities in the country. Rwanda's poverty and very limited government resources were aggravated by the destruction of its infrastructure. A related challenge lay in reconciling the deplorable prison conditions of the genocide suspects (mostly Hutu) with the needs and demands of hundreds of thousands of victims (mostly Tutsi) who were tortured, killed, raped, robbed, and humiliated by those same prisoners. An atmosphere of ethnic polarization and distrust easily results from such a situation. These challenges thus received high-level attention, as calls for justice before reconciliation issued forth from several quarters, including a Rwandan peace activist, Father Modeste Mungwararreba, who said in 1995:

> Justice is a precondition to reconciliation. There must be justice so that we can recover as individuals, so that we can reconcile as a nation. There must be justice so that the survivors do not continue to be victims. Because to be a victim also kills. You live in a situation of perpetual loss of bereavement and longing. In your personality you become a broken person. The result can be an overwhelming sense of despair. In such a situation it becomes easier to hate.[13]

The speedy conduct of genocide trials was thus widely perceived as a necessary condition of the broader reconciliation project. Support for a more rapid judicial process was also heard from within the prisons, where a number of suspected genocide perpetrators supported a more rapid judicial process to enable those who were innocent to clear their names as quickly as possible.

Two points are worth emphasizing here. First, there was a clear and widespread will among ordinary Rwandans to conclude the judicial process. This enabled the trials to continue despite all the problems, inconsistencies, and contradictions in their implementation. Second, the practical constraints (lack of infrastructure, personnel, funding, and so on) were very serious. Starting at a great disadvantage, the Rwandan judicial establishment slowly improved:

> Nonetheless, there has been an improvement in the quality of justice of genocide trials. We have the data for the first half of 1999, but the tendencies are clear: one can see an increase in acquittals and shorter sentences, a decrease in life sentences and an increase in parties represented by a lawyer.[14] (translation from French by Charles Mironko)

As of this writing, the Ministry of Justice, with the help of the donor community, has achieved remarkable progress, especially in terms of infrastructure development. By May 1999, 104 judges had been trained, and the legal staff numbered 1,800. In August 2000, those same judges were appointed to the special chambers of the court dealing with genocide, significantly augmenting the 74 who were in place in 1998.[15] However, by any standard of measurement the situation is still far from ideal. Even after the 1997–98 amnesties (which saw some 14,000 prisoners released), the number of suspects still confined to the overburdened prison system remained intolerably high. While roughly 5,800 of the remaining 116,000 suspects were tried between 1998 and 2001, and 30,000 genocide suspects had confessed, at this rate it would still have taken over a century to process every person accused of genocide.[16] Clearly, an alternative judicial mechanism was required, and this chapter now turns to an examination of two such initiatives.

The International Criminal Tribunal for Rwanda

Besides recommending the use of foreign judges in Rwanda's domestic genocide trials, the international community also sought to make a contribution to the postgenocide judicial process by forming an ad hoc United Nations–sponsored tribunal. The International Criminal Tribunal for Rwanda (ICTR) was established by Resolution 955 of the UN Security Council under Chapter VII of the Charter of the United Nations on November 8, 1994, and is located in Arusha, Tanzania. The mission of the tribunal is to prosecute individuals who committed genocide and violations of international humanitarian law in Rwanda and neighboring states between January 1 and December 31, 1994. The ICTR is modeled on the International Criminal Tribunal for the Former Yugoslavia (ICTY) in The Hague.

The ICTR made several positive contributions to the implementation of international law with regard to ensuring accountability for genocide. The court's 1998 verdict on Jean-Paul Akayesu was the first-ever conviction by an international court on the crime of genocide. The 1999 conviction of Jean Kambanda represented the first time a former prime minister was convicted of the same charge. Furthermore, the tribunal's strong position on rape as a crime against humanity has made a marked contribution to the struggle to estab-lish the importance of gendered crimes in international humanitar-ian law.

Yet the overall performance of the ICTR has not been propor-tionate to its high profile and ample resources. In its first eight years, despite an annual budget of US$86 million, the tribunal processed remarkably few cases, handing down only eight convictions and one acquittal between 1994 and 2002. This perceived slow pace was to become a significant factor in Rwandans' perceptions of the ICTR. Although the tribunal had received far less in the way of resources and profile than its European counterpart, the ICTY, its low regard among Rwandans was due not to "the long-standing negative image and neglect of the African continent in the global media," as K. C. Moghalu claims, but rather to its apparent failure to match even the output of the overloaded Rwandan domestic/indigenous judicial sys-tem.[17] This unfavorable comparison has persisted; as of March 2005, the ICTR has handed down seventeen judgments involving twenty-three accused, including one prime minister, four ministers, one pre-fect, five burgomasters, and several others holding leadership positions during the genocide of 1994.[18] Twenty of them were convicted and three acquitted.

A further problem for the ICTR is the widely held perception among Rwandans that it is remote and extravagant. With its trials initially held outside the country, Rwandans saw the court more as an insincere expression of international guilt about the genocide than as a practical effort to achieve justice. Once some trials began in Kigali, the ICTR's impressive building there struck many poor Rwandans as excessive, especially since it housed only three trials in its first years. Despite the ICTR's efforts to disseminate information about its activities in Rwanda, negative opinions regarding its rele-vance persist. One interviewee, an ordinary Rwandan citizen, for instance, said, "What is the Arusha tribunal? Come on, it is useless! Arusha does not exist!"[19]

The ICTR has also generated significant tensions between Rwanda's postgenocide government and the international commu-nity. For example, Rwanda's domestic laws carry the death penalty for the crime of genocide, but the United Nations' ICTR does not.

Consequently, even the most senior génocidaires, when convicted by the ICTR, will receive lighter sentences than lower-level perpetrators convicted by Rwandan courts. In addition, ICTR detainees enjoy better prison conditions in Arusha (even after conviction) than detainees within the domestic system and, indeed—given the country's ongoing difficulties—most ordinary Rwandans. Survivors' groups such as Ibuka and AVEGA (Association des Veuves du Génocide d'Avril, primarily composed of widows) have become the voice of such dissatisfactions, also accusing the ICTR of being culturally insensitive to the witnesses from Rwanda during the trials, especially with regard to victims of rape.

Rwanda voted against the creation of the ICTR in the UN Security Council in 1994, defending its decision in terms of the principle of noninterference in internal matters of state. Although this decision was reversed when the Rwandan government agreed to cooperate with the tribunal after its formation, Rwanda suspended its cooperation with the tribunal in 1999 after the appeals court based in The Hague released Jean-Bosco Barayagwiza (one of the primary architects of the genocide) because of procedural technicalities.

Despite the handful of high-profile convictions and precedent-setting decisions, the ICTR has failed to convince Rwandans that it is doing more than scratching the surface of justice for the great crime of a generation's memory. Some, such as K. C. Moghalu, claim that broad and numerous investigations are not the responsibility of the ICTR and that its work is correctly limited to pursuing "big fish," or Category One suspects.[20] However, the list of Category One suspects contains 2,898 names, according to the Rwandan government.[21] Given its stated plan to cease operation in 2007, the ICTR's contribution to postgenocide justice in Rwanda will be much too little and far too late. The search for justice within Rwanda eventually led to an alternative process based on Rwanda's own traditional institutions. This process is called *gacaca* (on the grass, from *umucaca*, a type of grass in Kinyarwanda), a dispute resolution and management mechanism that dates to the precolonial period in Rwanda.

In the following sections we describe the adaptation of traditional gacaca as a means of conflict resolution after the genocide.

Based on interviews with perpetrators, on preliminary gacaca proceedings in Rwandan prisons, and on preliminary polling data of the
Rwandan public, we believe that gacaca courts have the potential to
meet the needs of a wider range of constituents within Rwanda and
to promote a more durable, peaceful coexistence among Hutu, Tutsi,
and Twa than either domestic or international courtroom trials.[22]

Ancient *Gacaca* (Gacaca ya Kera)

In precolonial Rwanda, there were two basic paths to formal conflict
resolution. Before the more formal route (a petition to the king)
could be explored, plaintiffs were asked whether they had taken their
case to the council of elders on their hill or village (gacaca). If they
had not consulted the elders, they were sent back to their hills, and
their mistake became a source of prejudice in their case.[23]

   Traditionally, gacaca was used at the local level to resolve disputes within one family or between close families. Gacaca dealt with
social as well as economic conflicts, ranging from property claims
and distribution of cattle among heirs to misunderstandings between
spouses. The basic unit of gacaca was the council of elders, with all
adult members of the community as observers. Although judgments
were reached by elders, and not necessarily by popular vote or consensus, the principle behind each judgment was the restoration of
social harmony, the reestablishment of order, the reintegration of
the offender, and the reconciliation of the two parties. The judgment handed down by a gacaca council thus usually took the form
of affordable reparations being paid by the guilty party to the
wronged party.

   In the unusual event that someone refused to obey the decision
of gacaca, severe punishments could be meted out, including banning
the offender from the community. However, if the offender agreed to
apologize, or one of the offender's family members intervened on his
or her behalf, the gacaca process could be invoked to reintegrate that
person into the community.[24] Thus, traditional gacaca put great
emphasis on promoting understanding and reconciliation between
the parties and existed as the most powerful and authoritative dispute
resolution technique at that time.[25] Although traditional gacaca lost
its prominence with the introduction of Western judicial practices, it

continued to be used at the local level among people in the hills of Rwanda, especially in resolving family disputes.

Administrative Gacaca (1962–94) and New Gacaca (Gacaca Nshya)

The gacaca process has undergone two reinventions since the precolonial period. During the Hutu ascendancy that culminated in the establishment of the Habyarimana regime, gacaca acquired a reputation for being more a tool of government officials than a local-level institution aimed at preserving unity among the population. C. Ntampaka claims that, during this period, traditional gacaca was reduced to an administrative jurisdiction operating at local levels.[26] At this level, gacaca heard and recorded witness testimony before sending the case file to the lowest-level court *(canton)*. He adds that family members stopped participating in these trials because administrative agents gave arbitrary sentences. Consequently, people simply took their cases straight to the courts. Following the genocide in 1994, at a time when most communities in Rwanda were totally devoid of any formal judicial mechanisms, the precolonial form of gacaca was deliberately resurrected at the community level in several locales. Elders and community members once again began to preside over cases and hand out judgments independent of any national or local governmental oversight.[27]

According to research conducted in 1996, Kibuye was the first prefecture to institutionalize this latest form of gacaca. The research findings suggest that while gacaca in Kibuye operated independently of governmental structures, it reported its activities to local authorities at the cell level. The head of this new gacaca was a chairman or head of family (*umutware w'imiryango* in Kinyarwanda). Following this innovation in Kibuye, new gacaca continued to operate at the cell level in the rural areas, while in towns it worked within groups of *nyumbakumi* (ten houses). The gacaca committee is usually composed of family heads (or deputy family heads as replacements), a secretary, and advisers. The role of the family heads (and their deputies) is to receive grievances, which they hand to the secretary in order to formally invoke gacaca. They also chair the debates and pronounce gacaca decisions.

Despite this increasing formalization, new gacaca until recently dealt with only minor to midlevel conflicts (such as theft, fights, looting, family abuse, land redistribution, and debt administration) and social issues (such as problems of health, welfare, and security, as well as educational and socioeconomic problems). Significantly, it did not deal with murders or genocide, which remained a sensitive matter in many communities. Furthermore, human rights researchers working on gacaca indicated that new gacaca did not enjoy universal appeal owing to perceived divisions and a general lack of trust between the survivors themselves, that is, between returnees from the diaspora and those who were in the country during the genocide. This may have contributed to difficulties in implementing some gacaca decisions. In some provinces surveyed by human rights researchers, communities were considering restoring the policy of banishment *(guhabwa akato)* for disobeying gacaca decisions; in other places, "compulsory social works" were being discussed as an option.

Despite these difficulties, the ad hoc resurgence of gacaca soon came to the attention of the Rwandan government, which began to investigate the possibility of modifying traditional gacaca for the purpose of judging genocidal crimes. In May 1998 several problem-solving "town meetings" occurred between then president Pasteur Bizimungu and members of civil society, including local elders. After these consultations, the president instructed the Ministry of Justice to begin designing a new gacaca format along these lines—so-called genocide gacaca.[28]

Genocide Gacaca—Jurisdiction and Site of Appeal

By 2002 gacaca courts had been set up throughout the country in accordance with the plea-bargain program introduced as part of the 1996 Organic Law to reduce sentences for those accused of genocide. According to the law, only crimes falling within Categories Two, Three, and Four can be heard in gacaca courts; those listed in Category One must be tried in the domestic genocide courts or by the ICTR. Suspects accused of Category Two crimes are tried at the district level and, if they plead guilty, can receive from twenty-five years to life imprisonment. Those who pleaded guilty before the 1996 law took effect receive sentences reduced by twelve to fifteen years, with half of the remaining sentence served by community service. Category Three suspects are judged at the sector level and can receive five to seven years if they pleaded not guilty and are found guilty, or three to five years if they pleaded guilty—with, once again, half of the sentence served through community service in this case. Category Four suspects are judged at the cell level with no possibility of appeal and are sentenced to pay restitution of damaged property unless an amicable agreement between the perpetrator and the victim is reached in arbitration. Categories Two and Three appeal to the provincial-level gacaca courts.

Organization of Gacaca Jurisdictions

Gacaca jurisdictions are administered by the Department of Gacaca, a division of the Supreme Court, and consist of three main divisions at each level of administration: each cell, sector, district, and province is thus represented by a General Assembly, Seat, and Coordinating Committee. General Assemblies consist of all adult (ages eighteen and up) members of the community; at the cellular level of administration, the nineteen-member Seat is then constituted by vote of the General Assembly, and some of the "persons of integrity" thus elected are sent up to the next administrative level as delegates from their cell.[29] Thus, at the district and provincial levels, the Seat consists of a minimum of fifty persons, including delegates from smaller administrative sections.

Judges

As in traditional gacaca, judges are called *inyangamugayo* (literally, people who don't like to be viewed as dishonorable), meaning people of integrity. Gacaca judges are thus meant to be Rwandans of high moral standards, who are elected by the population because of their reputations as constructive forces in their communities. They must be at least twenty-one years old and must have never been sentenced to more than six months in prison or accused of genocide. About 254,000 judges (roughly one in every twenty adults in the country) were publicly elected by their communities in October 2001 and were given a six-day orientation in basic principles of law, focusing on gacaca law, in April 2002.

Duties and Responsibilities

The process of judging genocide suspects in gacaca courts occurs in three stages, each one open to the public. The first stage involves gathering information regarding the victims of, and suspected perpetrators of, massacres at the cellular level. This work is conducted by the General Assembly of each cell. The information gathered, in the form of three main documents (a list of people who died in that cell, a form for each victim who lived in the cell before the genocide, and a list of suspects), is then transmitted to the courts by each cell's elected Seat. In the second stage, the courts gather information on each suspect and classify each according to the four categories of responsibility outlined in the Organic Law. Finally, following this classification, the cases are redistributed to courts at the appropriate level for the categories of genocide involved, using the jurisdictional guidelines detailed previously, and the trial process begins.

Criticism of the Implementation of Gacaca

The use of gacaca courts for genocide began amid many worries, suspicions, and critiques, as was perhaps to be expected in such a highly politicized situation. Many of the concerns revolved around legal or technical issues, such as the prominence given to eyewitness testimony in the gacaca system. Some fear untruthful testimony in the proceedings, or that genocide survivors will not testify because they fear revenge, or that victims of rape might refuse to testify in public because of the stigma associated with rape in Rwandan culture. In those places where there are no survivors left, it may also be possible to give false testimony without the fear of being exposed by other witnesses. Further legalistic critiques include the concern that the government is opting for expediency at the expense of due process and fairness. The UN General Assembly, for instance, has asserted that gacaca "do[es] not follow either a judicial process nor the principle of contradiction."[30] The two most important legal challenges to gacaca on the grounds of fairness are the International Covenant of Civil and Political Rights (Article 14.1) and the African Charter on

Human and Peoples Rights (Articles 7.1 and 26), both ratified by Rwanda.[31] The African Charter states that

> every individual shall have the right to have his case heard. This comprises: (a) the right to an appeal to competent national organs against acts of violating his fundamental rights as recognized and guaranteed by conventions, laws, regulations and customs in force; (b) the right to be presumed innocent until proved guilty by a competent court or tribunal; (c) the right to defense, including to be defended by counsel of his choice; (d) the right to be tried within a reasonable time by an impartial court or tribunal.[32]

And the Dakar Declaration, adopted on September 11, 1999, stipulates that traditional courts are not exempt from the provisions of the African Charter relating to fair trial.[33]

Over and above these legal concerns, some have also identified the use and configuration of gacaca as problematic in and of itself. Some of these critics focus on the government's prominent involvement in a process that has always been local and autonomous, expressing concerns that government officials could interfere with gacaca courts by intimidating or bribing judges or participants.

Others point out that institutions based in pregenocide Rwandan culture may no longer be relevant to Rwandans today, even going as far as to point out that had gacaca been efficient in building bonds of community at a grassroots level, genocide should not have happened in the first place.

Criticisms of the second form are, obviously, harder to address than the technical issues raised by the legal infrastructure in which gacaca is embedded, and thus various constructive suggestions have been made to achieve a form of gacaca more consistent with international legal norms. The European Union, for instance, has suggested that gacaca trials be based on the principle of amnesty to avoid violations of international human rights. However, criticisms such as those leveled by Amnesty International in its 2000 report, which states that "fundamental aspects of the gacaca proposals do not conform to basic international standards for fair trials guaranteed in the international treaties which Rwanda has ratified," can be useful only if they are accompanied with practical alternative solutions to problems such as the overburdened prison system in Rwanda. Beyond delivering criticisms of gacaca, external actors have done very little to develop an alternative system of justice applicable to the Rwandan situation.[34]

Expected Outcomes: Can Gacaca Deliver?

The Rwandan government has stated four main objectives of the new gacaca genocide courts: to establish a true account of the genocide, to speed adjudication of genocide suspects, to eliminate impunity in the country, and to reconstruct Rwandan society.[35] Although Rwandan authorities and nongovernmental groups examined the experience of the South African Truth and Reconciliation Commission, many believed that the events of the Rwandan genocide were not as shrouded in mystery as the crimes of apartheid in South Africa. They therefore emphasized the importance of seeking the justice that gacaca might deliver rather than solely establishing a record of flagrant and openly committed acts of genocide.[36]

Another source of concern relates to the possible social outcomes of the gacaca process. Could gacaca courts incite hate instead of solving problems if they do not function well? Will there be revenge violence against those who are acquitted? Or will those acquitted attempt to kill survivors? Some have argued that by using amnesty- or reconciliation-oriented gacaca courts, the government will undermine the seriousness of the crime of genocide within the Rwandan public imagination, sowing the seeds for future violence.

Officials in charge of gacaca courts are aware of these shortcomings. According to them, the solutions to these problems lie in the "sensitization" of the population through an information campaign to describe the process and to emphasize that no viable alternatives exist. They also expect that the law will need to be amended to deal with certain problems as they arise in the process.

The Prisons as a Source of Support for Gacaca

While arguments about gacaca are conducted on the international and domestic levels, it is significant that according to interviews conducted with about one hundred genocide suspects in six Rwandan prisons in 1998 and 2000, many confessed perpetrators were eager for

gacaca hearings to start. Although the enthusiasm of some respondents can be explained in terms of their having lost any hope of having their cases heard through regular channels, this was not the sole
motivation expressed by those interviewed; neither was it a simple
desire to demonstrate innocence or implicate associates who had not
joined them in prison. In the preliminary gacaca proceedings in
Rilima prison and in the testimonies of confessed perpetrators from
Ruhengeri prison, rather, many genocide suspects were looking forward to gacaca for reasons more closely related to community-level
outcomes than personal ones:

> We feel that we support this question of reconciliation. If gacaca
> courts will take us [to gacaca proceedings in the communities] as
> they say, we also support that idea. After all we have already started
> gacaca in prison. We take people from each cell separately, each
> sector, by commune.[37]

Already, there have been some unpublicized positive cases. For example, in Gitarama, where some Hutu prisoners pleaded guilty in prison-
sponsored gacaca,[38] they asked their Tutsi neighbors for forgiveness.
The Tutsi accepted their apologies and visited them in prisons, often
bringing food, according to Rwandan custom. According to some of
these confessed perpetrators, the victims' family members were waiting for gacaca courts in order to support their confessions officially.

Thus, despite the justified concerns outlined previously, there is
some evidence that gacaca permits perpetrators and victims to face
one another in a neutral space—a critical step toward peaceful coexistence and possibly reconciliation. Furthermore, if the government
takes adequate measures to reintegrate released prisoners into their
communities, there is a reasonable hope for a highly positive outcome from gacaca courts in terms of social reintegration. Suspects
acquitted by gacaca courts are likely to be more easily reintegrated
into their communities than those acquitted by the ordinary courts.
The Roman Catholic Church has already started a form of gacaca
(*Synode gacaca or Gacaca Nkirisitu*) to encourage Christians who
were involved in genocide to confess.

Table 6-1. Public Opinion of Gacaca

Awareness of Gacaca Courts

- 82.4 percent of the respondents have already heard about gacaca courts (men: 89.9 percent, women 75 percent).

- Less than 4 percent of the respondents are aware that their community members will elect their judges.

- 18.8 percent of the respondents have no idea about gacaca courts.

- 22 percent of the respondents have limited knowledge of gacaca courts.

- 47.6 percent of the respondents have an average knowledge of gacaca courts.

- 10 percent of the respondents have a good knowledge about gacaca courts.

Perceptions about Gacaca Courts

- The majority of Rwandans are hopeful and in favor of gacaca courts despite their limited knowledge on the subject.

- 57.6 percent of the respondents said that they are confident gacaca courts will be able to solve problems related to genocide.

- 53 percent of the respondents are certain gacaca courts will promote a lasting peace in the country.

- 75 percent of the respondents have no specific involvement in gacaca courts.

Willingness to Participate in Gacaca Proceedings

- 95 percent of the respondents are willing to participate in gacaca proceedings.

- 87 percent of the respondents are ready to give testimony.

Source: Summary findings of a joint research project conducted by the Center for Conflict Management, University of Rwanda, together with the Johns Hopkins Center for Communication Programs and the Rwandan Ministry of Justice (2001) on gacaca courts.

As table 6-1 shows, in 2001 a great majority of Rwandans (95 percent) were ready to participate in the gacaca courts. These high levels of perceived legitimacy for gacaca are the result of the system's deep roots in the communal world of the Rwandan people; in contrast to "foreign" Western-based programs, conflict resolution presided over by local wise men is an essential part of Rwandan culture and history.

In 2002, 751 village-level pilot gacaca courts were launched. In 2004 about 60,000 detainees confessed to the crime of genocide. In February 2005 investigative gacaca hearings were conducted in 8,262 courts, and in March 2005 trials authorized to hand out sentences started. In reaction, about 5,000 people fled to Burundi to avoid trials. Some of these refugees returned to Rwanda following negotiations between the Burundi and Rwandan governments.[39]

Summary of Justice Reforms

The Rwandan judiciary has undergone a great deal of change in the country's short history. Never fully independent of the ruling party, it has often served the political needs of the regime in power more than the requirements of the people for truth and justice. Unstable, politicized, and weak, the Rwandan judiciary now faces a task that would challenge even the most sophisticated and experienced of legal institutions: conducting national genocide trials involving more than 100,000 suspects. Partly out of pragmatism and partly out of philosophical commitment, the Rwandan government has turned to a traditional Rwandan conflict resolution mechanism to help address the backlog of genocide cases.

For the sake of justice, as well as long-term social and political reconciliation in Rwanda, gacaca courts represent a worthwhile experiment. As long as the Ministry of Justice is willing to remedy flaws as they emerge, to oppose gacaca may be to oppose Rwanda's only hope for averting yet another crisis. Since gacaca courts will involve all Rwandans and their elected judges in each local community, perhaps this system of justice will be not be seen as "victors' justice," a term used by some to describe the Western-style criminal courts that are trying other genocide cases in Rwanda.

In the end, courtroom trials that conform to Western standards may satisfy human rights advocates, but the inevitably slow pace satisfies neither alleged perpetrators awaiting trial nor survivors awaiting justice. The ICTR may conform to standards of due process in trying the genocide's "big fish," but the Rwandan people derive little social or legal satisfaction from these proceedings or their apparently unjust outcomes. Gacaca's focus on long-term social reconstruction and reconciliation may make certain constituencies nervous, but it is Rwanda, after all, that must live with the consequences of this experiment.

POLICE AND SECURITY IN RWANDA

Overview

Like the judiciary, the Rwandan police force has a history of favoring the interests of the regime rather than those of the overall population. Even within this context of politicized policing, the 1994 genocide stands out as an extreme breakdown of attempts to serve the public good. The civil war and the 1994 genocide led to a total breakdown of institutions and socioeconomic infrastructure and to staggering loss of life, with dire consequences for law, order, and security, at both the state and human levels.

After the genocide, the maintenance of civil order was further hampered by four main factors: first, the huge number of refugees both within the country and across its borders;[40] second, the practice of cross-border raiding by some elements of these displaced communities; third, an increase in the frequency of computer crimes, money laundering, counterfeiting, and other cross-border crimes following an influx of technologically skilled expatriates; and finally, the collapse of state machinery in the Democratic Republic of the Congo (formerly Zaire) in 1998, which prompted an increase in the trade in illegal arms and drugs throughout the Great Lakes region.

As with the judiciary, the police were hampered by a lack of skilled and experienced staff, scant financial resources, and lack of essential equipment. In addition, the security organs responsible for policing were administered by three different government ministries, making coordination difficult. The establishment of a consolidated National Police agency in 2000 was intended to help the country deal with some of its pressing security problems. However, this project required a renegotiation of the police force's contract with civil society—a renegotiation made necessary by policing's biased record in Rwanda. An outline of this record and of postgenocide attempts at internal security reform follows.[41]

The Rwandan Army

One of Rwanda's founding pieces of postindependence legislation was Legislative Order No. R/85/25 of May 10, 1962, related to the creation of the Rwandan army. While Article One of this order

establishes that "[t]he order and the defense of the Rwandan territory are ensured by the Rwandan army," Article Four grants the president the power to take officers from the national police and put
them in the national army as necessary. Thus, in the early days of
Rwanda's independence, there was little separation between the army
and the police. The two institutions were initially placed within the
same government department—the Ministry of the National Guard
and Police—but were placed in separate ministries in 1969. However,
this separation was reversed by presidential order on June 26, 1973—
exactly eight days before the coup d'état that brought General
Juvénal Habyarimana (then minister of defense) to the presidency. It
has been widely speculated that the reintegration of the police into
the army contributed to the coup. Habyarimana was one of the fore-
most proponents of integration and may have intended to thereby
circumvent potential resistance by returning the police to Ministry
of Defense control.

The army and police were, however, only two of the four law
enforcement agencies operated by the postindependence government. In fact, shortages of personnel within these forces had led to
the creation of a third arm of law enforcement, the Communal
Police, as early as 1963. The Communal Police was intended to
ensure security at the subprefecture level and reported to the Commune Head rather than the National Police. While statistics on the
number of Communal Police officers before the 1994 genocide do not
exist, it seems that recruits were chosen on ethnic grounds.

The fourth arm of law enforcement, the paramilitary National
Gendarmerie, was established by decree on January 23, 1974. While
the ostensible functions of the Gendarmerie were to conduct criminal investigations and support the actions of the courts, this decree
also provided for broader operations in support of "order," including
"preventive and suppressive measures at the same time." As will be
discussed, this open-ended declaration of function was to result in an
intensive use of the Gendarmerie in support of genocidal actions
during the 1994 crisis.

Crisis of Security—the 1994 Genocide

How did the country's security forces come to play such a central role in the genocide? The answer lies in the politicized and segregated nature of the country's security forces. The government of Rwanda before 1994 was characterized by ethnic discrimination at all levels. In the Gendarmerie, ethnic divisiveness was pervasive, from the recruitment phase to the service phase. Few, if any, Tutsi (reliable figures do not exist) were integrated into the Gendarmerie. The majority of recruits were Hutu who originated from certain regions of the country or who had links to members of the country's political elite.[42] Furthermore, former members of the Rwandan armed forces and the Gendarmerie have indicated that the few Tutsi who were recruited sometimes had to interrupt their training owing to harassment, intimidation, and stigmatization by their instructors, school administrators, and classmates.

In many ways, therefore, the structure of the Gendarmerie contained a more virulent form of the same divisions that ran through Rwandan civilian society. This state of affairs complicated relations between the Gendarmerie and members of the public and further established it as an instrument of the ruling cliques rather than an organization devoted to public service. Illegal detention was also common, with an ad hoc system of short-term detention without trial operating openly at the brigade level. In its use as a political instrument, the Gendarmerie was also active in the harassment of opposition politicians and parties, such as the PL (Parti Liberal) and the MDR (Mouvement Démocratique Républicain).

This already unstable relationship between the Gendarmerie and its ostensible role was aggravated after the start of the civil war in 1990, when extremists began to agitate for all Tutsi and moderate Hutu to be treated as potential RPF supporters. During this phase of the civil war, large numbers of "suspects" were rounded up by the Gendarmerie and the Criminal Investigative Department (CID). More than 10,000 were incarcerated in Kigali's Amahoro Stadium in October 1990 alone, with many of these suffering prolonged incarceration or even extrajudicial execution in the CID's holding cells. The intelligence system, including the military and Gendarmerie intelligence departments and the intelligence unit of the president's office, also fell prey to the divisionist political agenda, further weakening the legitimacy and accountability of law enforcement in pregenocide Rwanda.

While there are no reliable statistics concerning the extent of the police force's participation in the genocide, that it took part is evident from the numbers of former police officers now in prison charged with genocide and from the fact that out of a force of about 500 officers before the war, fewer than 50 reported for duty after the genocide ended.[43] This pattern was repeated at higher levels of the law enforcement infrastructure; according to a World Bank report, "most of the Burgomasters who, in addition to the administration of the communes, also carry out judicial police functions (i.e., the right to arrest), were alleged to be closely involved with the training and mobilization of the militia and might be guilty of genocide."

Postgenocide Police Reform: International Aid and Local Efforts

Immediately after the 1994 genocide, national security rested solely in the hands of the RPF's armed wing, the Rwandan Patriotic Army, while the National Gendarmerie (newly formed from the few remaining officers of the Gendarmerie who had reported for duty and who had not been implicated in the genocide) was responsible for providing police services. This remained so until the Communal Police was restored in 1995.

The establishment of the two institutions, the Gendarmerie and the Communal Police, was itself a recommendation of the 1993 Arusha Peace Agreement. Furthermore, when the new Government of National Unity came into power it entered into a training agreement with UNAMIR (United Nations Assistance Mission in Rwanda), which had been present in Rwanda since 1993 and sought to create a new Rwandan police force. In August 1994 UNAMIR began the Rwandan Police Training Program, which continued to operate until December 1995. During that time, 919 gendarmes and 750 police officers received training.[44] Various training manuals were prepared and given to the Rwandan authorities to ensure sustainability of the project. However, according to the United Nations Development Programme (UNDP) report, "inadequate CIVPOL [civilian police] trainers, lack of French-speaking personnel and insufficient resources hampered the training initiative." Furthermore, the report also notes that the components of UNAMIR that were involved in human rights monitoring "had no human rights training or guidance for this role."[45] As a result of these difficulties, and ongoing friction in UNAMIR's relationship with the Rwandan government, the relationship was formally terminated in May 1996.

Parallel to the UNAMIR efforts (although integration between the programs was limited or entirely absent) was a similar program fielded by the United Nations Human Rights Field Operation for Rwanda (HRFOR) aimed at training a new generation of Gendarmerie officers. The HRFOR operation also faced a great many challenges related to its operations in Rwanda. According the UNDP report, "it was heavily criticized, at first, for: a broad and ambiguous mandate, poor pre-deployment preparations, limited logistics and support, poor leadership, absence of a coherent strategy, insufficient coordination between headquarters and field staff, turf disputes within the UN system . . ."[46] The HRFOR mission was closed in 1998 following a dispute between the Office of the High Commissioner for Human Rights at the United Nations, which wished to retain HRFOR's function as a monitor for human rights, and the Rwandan government, which felt there should be a greater emphasis placed on capacity building, technical cooperation, training, and education.

In addition to the UNAMIR and HRFOR initiatives, several other international initiatives were put in place to assist in police reform. The UNDP sponsored various activities to strengthen local security forces (RWA/95/B16, RWA/96/B10, RWA/97/B40), including the renovation of the training facility at Ruhengeri as well as the provision of training, administrative materials, uniforms, transportation, and communication equipment to the Rwandan authorities. In addition, USAID financed the recruitment of police trainers from Uganda, who "assisted in the development of a detailed training curriculum for both the Gendarmerie and the Communal Police, and provided training for criminal investigators, and organizational development and training for mid-level police officers."[47]

Finally, several other African and European countries made efforts to support Rwandan police reform. Among Rwanda's regional allies, Uganda and Tanzania have been noteworthy in this regard. Teams from the United Kingdom's Bramshill Academy have been to Rwanda to assess the training needs of the Rwandan National Police (RNP) within the framework of institutional cooperation. The government of the Netherlands implemented a project aimed at renovating living quarters and offices that had belonged to the defunct Communal Police, and the Danish government provided human rights training for the National Police. These two projects, both operated through the UNDP trust, were perceived as positive by Rwandan authorities.

Amid these international efforts, certain domestic initiatives aimed at increasing policing efficiency and allowing for the better management of human, material, and financial resources led to the fusing of the historically divergent arms of the law enforcement services into one body, the RNP, in 2000. The RNP was formed by bringing together personnel from the National Gendarmerie (Ministry of Defense), the Communal Police (Ministry of Internal Affairs), and the Department of Judicial Police (Ministry of Justice).[48]

The RNP's mission statement declares that "the RNP is committed to friendly relationships and reassurance and dedicated to delivering a high quality service, working in partnership with our communities and being accountable to them for safeguarding the human rights of all people in Rwanda, upholding the law firmly and fairly, protecting people and their property and defeating offenders." Furthermore, Article Two of the Police Act stipulates that police services shall be delivered to the people on the basis of the following principles:

- The importance of safeguarding the fundamental rights guaranteed by law
- The need for cooperation between the police and the communities they serve
- The responsibility to account for their activities to the community

These reforms are a clear departure from the militarized and partisan actions of the postcolonial police force. Measures such as strong anti-corruption drives and the training of a new corps of officers equipped to educate their peers in issues pertaining to human rights are like-wise steps toward a "new model" for policing in Rwanda. The four foundations of this new model are response, targeted action, partnerships (with government and the public), and local focus. The RNP is more ethnically inclusive than any previous police force.

Finally, gender equality is a stated goal for the Rwandan government, and women are prominently represented in high-level posts and at all levels of government (thanks to laws regarding candidacies, the legislature in 2004 boasted the highest portion of women in the world). The RNP is working toward gender equity as well. Of the 4,000 people who made up the RNP in early 2003, only about 5 percent were women, with a large percentage of these concentrated in a single department—the Department of Judicial Police.[49] This distribution reflects the fact that current police officers came mostly from the prereform Gendarmerie and Communal Police, where women were very few. However, subsequent efforts by the new administration have been directly aimed at reversing this situation. In July 2002, 106 women graduated from the new Police Training School[50]—effectively doubling the number of women on the force.

This initiative, it is hoped, will have an effect on the continuing and serious problem of rape in Rwanda, which has become a pressing concern to the government; more than 505 cases of rape were recorded in 2001, and many more undoubtedly were unreported. Necessary resources, including more female police officers, have been made available to help locate and arrest offenders as well as to mobilize victims to work with medical experts in the Ministry of Health.

Implementation, Results, and Challenges

As a new institution, the RNP is still in the process of establishing itself. However, successes have been achieved, partly based on increasing amounts of information provided by the public. The immediate postgenocide period, for instance, was characterized by an increase in crime, especially armed robberies, with 115 cases reported in 2001. The proliferation and illegal possession of firearms was seen as an aggravating factor in this regard. Following a nationwide drive by the RNP based on tips provided by the community, more than one hundred small arms were confiscated in 2001, and those found in possession were tried. Although these figures seem small, they are significant for Rwanda's national-level institutions.

The increase of patrols in major towns, the reduction of reaction time by police officers (estimated at ten minutes in 2002), and improvements in mobility (owing to an increase in the number of motorcycles and other vehicles) and communication equipment have all helped to reduce the fear of crime. Emergency telephone numbers have been launched, aiding a quicker response time to public calls for help, despite the relatively low number of households with telephones (1 percent).

Finally, the arrest and detention of offenders has been a major factor in instilling greater confidence in the population. Unfortunately, no hard statistical information is available on the rate of improvement of police relations with the community. The police therefore judge the quality of their relations with the community through anecdotal sampling of public opinion conducted by officers in the field and through direct feedback from the community. Indeed, the existence and increasing strength of community interactions of this kind are in themselves an indication of improved community/police relations since 1994.

Coordination between Security Forces

In the context of the need to create a favorable environment for economic growth and development in Rwanda, the primary mission of the Rwandan armed forces remains the defense of the country's territorial integrity and national sovereignty. This leaves the internal security of the country to the National Police. Because the targets for police strength have not yet been met, the police still require occasional assistance from the armed forces. While the combined efforts of the police, the armed forces, the intelligence services, and the civilian population have been harnessed to bring an end to cross-border attacks into Rwandan territory by insurgents operating out of the Democratic Republic of the Congo (DRC), various initiatives have also been launched to provide alternative means for controlling this phenomenon. Regional and international cooperation, for instance, has become a prominent means for ensuring the security and stability required for trade, investment, and interaction in the area. Rwanda is a member of the East African Police Chiefs Committee (EAPCCO), in which ten East African member countries cooperate for the purpose of security and capacity building; indeed, from September 2001 to September 2002, Rwanda held the chairmanship of the EAPCCO.

Crime Detection and Criminal Justice

An important factor to consider with regard to police reform in cases such as Rwanda's is the effect of more efficient channels for the reporting of crimes where none existed previously. In the case of Rwanda since 1994, reported crimes have greatly increased. In Kigali, for instance, total crimes reported increased from 1,247 in 1999 to 1,801 in 2001.

If the challenges and successes of the Rwandan law enforcement situation just detailed were not taken into account, these figures would be of clear and pressing concern to the relevant authorities and international onlookers alike. However, it is critical to consider the particularities of the Rwandan context when analyzing crime figures. For example, since 1994 arrest and detention rates have increased. Measures were put in place to ensure the speedy follow-up of reported crimes. Wide-ranging efforts were introduced to respond more quickly to emergency calls and to use improved methods of investigation. Most important, the flow of information from the population to the police has emerged as a critical asset in the investigation of crimes. The RNP leadership (correctly, in our view) thus interprets the figures cited earlier not only as a sign of increased police efficiency but also as a firm indicator of growing public confidence in the capacity of the police to ensure public security.

Similarly, crime data demonstrate Rwanda's efforts to combat the regional problem of drug trafficking, a pressing cross-border issue that requires (and responds well to) intensive regional cooperation of the type discussed. Quantities of illegal drugs seized and the number of trafficking and drug abuse arrests in Rwanda increased in 2001 over prior years. Once again, while the increase appears to reflect growing criminal activity in these areas, it is more likely, given Rwanda's new and central role in bodies such as EAPCCO, to represent improved police performance and data gathering. These figures highlight the complexity of assessing police reform in the early days of a reconstructive program. The provision of resources for effectiveness surveys is critical if increased police efficiency is not to be mistaken for increasing lawlessness.

Role of the Police in the Preparation of Genocide Case Files

We earlier mentioned the serious problem of missing or nonexistent case files for many of the alleged genocide perpetrators in Rwandan prisons. Police reforms have also been undertaken to address this serious problem. During a two-month period, police officers and prosecutors prepared more than 14,000 case files for the genocide suspects. In addition, the police force had a major role to play in gacaca proceedings, being expected to participate fully during all three phases of gacaca. In the first phase (pretrial), the police fill out the forms of genocide cases using information available from the individuals' files. A total of 114 police officers were assigned to this work. Gacaca trials started in June 2002 and a total of 84,057 forms were to be completed by that time.

Other areas in which the new police force has had an impact include the Rwanda Revenue Authority (RRA), the government institution responsible for customs operations and tax collections. In the past, fraud was common among the majority of Rwandan traders and foreigners working in Rwanda; inadequate controls led to reduced revenue. At the request of the RRA, the RNP assigned a group of officers to the Revenue Protection Department. As a result, income increased by 250 percent between April 2001 and mid-2002, and importers found that they risked sanctions if they tried to smuggle goods.

Ongoing Challenges

Although much was achieved between 2000 and 2002 in maintaining and consolidating internal security and stability, constraints and challenges remain. These include insufficient personnel, lack of skills and equipment, a case backlog, illegal arms and drugs coming into Rwanda from other countries, corruption, and rapid urbanization.

The Rwanda National Police adopted a five-year plan for the period 2003–07, called Focus 2007, to try to meet many of the challenges described in this chapter.

CONCLUSION

Perhaps more than in any other sector, the specific challenges to the judiciary and the security apparatus in a postgenocidal context are monumental. In Rwanda, the judiciary and the police were historically unstable and highly politicized. With a radical regime change in 1994, these sectors practically had to be built from scratch at the very moment they were most critically needed. Although the Ministry of Justice had very few qualified legal professionals available to begin to address the judicial aftermath of genocide, within the police/security sector, there were ways to integrate personnel from organizations like the Communal Police, the Department of Judicial Police, and the Gendarmerie into the newly formed Rwanda National Police. Funding and infrastructure problems aside, the task of amassing the resources needed to do the work of trying cases and ensuring public safety may have been the most difficult challenge of the postgenocide period.

In a fragile political context such as that of a postconflict country under military rule, even the concepts of justice and security are highly politicized and subjective. Justice for whom, to what end, and according to whose standards? What exactly is being secured, and against what/whom? The process of organizing an effective judiciary and running a police force is anything but straightforward in such a context. While a great deal of attention is paid to the quality and pace of justice being administered in the genocide cases, there is still a need for people to feel secure in their homes and safe from mistreatment at the hands of the police, and to be able to seek recourse for the mundane wrongs that occur in everyday life. Some people allege that Hutu have not received fair and equal treatment. Under such strained circumstances, however, it is difficult to satisfy these ordinary needs for justice and security as well as the extraordinary needs of a postgenocide population for truth, justice, reconciliation, and restored social harmony. The Rwandan government has therefore made choices and set priorities. In the realm of justice, it has chosen to deal with the overwhelming caseload of genocide suspects by adapting a traditional mechanism of dispute resolution to the needs of genocide trials. In the realm of security, the RNP has decided to focus its resources on key areas of need and to work progressively toward a more comprehensive service.

Local institutions clearly play an important role in reforming the security and justice sectors in Rwanda. The RNP has been working hard to increase the public's trust in the police force to maximize the public's ability to participate in crime prevention and reduction. Many improvements have resulted from this approach. In the judicial sector, the government's decision to try genocide suspects within the framework of gacaca is another example of local resources being used to enhance the capacity of the government to fulfill its obligations to its citizens. There is a strong experimental component to this approach, but Rwanda's leaders have shown again and again that they would prefer to risk doing it their own way and suffer the consequences than to rely on an international community many see as capricious and hypocritical. The enduring lesson may be that resorting to local-level resources and institutions in the search for justice and security ought not to be the result of extreme violence, extreme poverty, or a defiant attitude toward international cooperation. It may prove useful, cost-effective, and pragmatic to seek models of conflict resolution and human security in indigenous practices and traditions no matter what the political or economic context. Rwanda may be learning this the hard way, but it would be wrong for outside observers to reject or, conversely, romanticize or "exoticize" this situation and overlook what lessons might apply to other situations around the world.

NOTES

1. The Supreme Court was reestablished through Organic Law No. 7/96 in 1996.

2. Human Rights Watch, *Human Rights in Africa and U.S. Policy.* HRW A606 (New York: Human Rights Watch, July 1, 1994), 20.

3. World Bank, *Rwandese Republic Emergency Recovery Project Technical Annex* (Washington, D.C.: World Bank, 1995), 13.

4. Embassy of the Republic of Rwanda to the United States, Washington, D.C., http://www.rwandemb.org (accessed July 4, 2003).

5. Similar information appeared in other Rwandan prisons that Charles Mironko visited in 1999, including Ruhengeri, Rilima, Butare.

6. Gérard Prunier, *The Rwanda Crisis, 1959–1994* (New York: Columbia University Press, 1995), 366.

7. Larry Minear and Randolph C. Kent, "Rwanda's Internally Displaced: A Conundrum within a Conundrum," in *The Forsaken People: Case Studies of the Internally Displaced,* ed. R. Cohen and Francis M. Deng (Washington, D.C.: Brookings Institution Press, 1998), 91.

8. Prunier, *The Rwanda Crisis,* 365.

9. Minear and Kent, "Rwanda's Internally Displaced." The distrust felt for France at this point, given its close collusion with the Habyarimana regime, was almost certainly an aggravating factor in the Rwandan decision.

10. *Official Gazette of the Republic of Rwanda* 40, no. 6, March 15, 2001.

11. P. Rutazibwa, ed., *Les Crises des Grands Lacs et la question Tutsi: Réflexions sur l'idéologie du génocide dans la sous-région* (Kigali: Rwanda News Agency, October 10, 1998).

12. Ibid., 123. This confrontation between the reconstruction agenda and public opinion was to become more pronounced over time, as the Rwandan News Agency began to expose what it identified as incompetence and corruption in the Rwandan justice system. For example, it pointed out some government ministers who were implicated in the genocide as well as officials who interfered with the judicial process in order to release their parents and friends from prison. The RNA even cited some officials of the Ministry of Justice (prosecutors, magistrates, and police investigators) individually involved in the genocide, and "538 files of genocide cases stolen or with missing testimonies."

13. Father Modeste Mungwarareba, speech delivered in Butare, Rwanda, January 18, 1995, *African Rights*, n.d.

14. P. Reyntjens, *L'Afrique des Grand Lacs, Annuaire 1999–2000* (Paris: L'Harmattan, 2000), 113–114.

15. J. Sarkin, "Gacaca Courts and Genocide," in *Rwanda and South Africa in Dialogue: Addressing the Legacies of Genocide and Crime against Humanity,* ed. C. Villa-Vicencio and T. Savage (Johannesburg: Institute for Justice and Reconciliation, 2001), 70, 73.

16. Jean de Dieu Mucyo, minister of justice, quoted in Villa-Vicencio and Savage, *Rwanda and South Africa in Dialogue.*

17. K. C. Moghalu, "Image and Reality of War Crimes Justice: External Perceptions of the International Criminal Tribunal for Rwanda," *Fletcher Forum of World Affairs* 26, no. 2 (Summer–Fall 2002): 21–47.

18. International Criminal Tribunal for Rwanda, http://www.ictr.org (accessed June 5, 2005).

19. Rwandan citizen, interview with Charles Mironko, Kigali, 2001.

20. Moghalu, "Image and Reality of War Crimes Justice."

21. *Official Gazette of the Republic of Rwanda* 40, special issue, March 19, 2001.

22. Peter Uvin and Charles Mironko, "Western and Local Approaches to Justice in Rwanda" (unpublished draft paper, 2003).

23. S. Sebasoni, personal communication with authors, 2002.

24. C. Ntampaka, "Le Gacaca Rwandais, une justice répressive partici-pative," in *Actualité du droit international humanitaire* (Leuven, Belgium: La Charte, 2001).

25. Ibid., 7.

26. Ibid.

27. This was the case in 20 of Rwanda's 147 "sectors," with a sector being a formal territorial-administrative designation encompassing multiple cells but itself forming one component of a larger "commune"—with multiple com-munes organized into "prefectures." See Christian P. Scherrer, *Justice in Transition and Conflict Prevention in Rwanda* (Tegelen, The Netherlands: ECOR [Ethnic Conflicts Research Project], 1997).

28. *Ministère de la Justice:Aide-mémoire des Principes de Base de l'Institut des Juridictions Gacaca conçu pour l'explication à la population* (Kigali: Gvt. of Rwanda Printer, November 2000), 4.

29. Documents dated 2000 from the Ministry of Justice mention that a five-member coordinating committee was sent to a higher level, but the gacaca manual (2001) simply mentions "some" members.

30. S. Vandeginste, "Les Juridictions gacaca et la poursuite des suspects auteurs du génocide et des crimes contre l'humanité au Rwanda," *L'Afrique des Grands Lacs, Annuaire 1999–2000*, ed. P. Reyntjens (Paris: L'Harmattan, 2000).

31. Ibid.; and Sarkin, "Gacaca Courts and Genocide."

32. Sarkin, "Gacaca Courts and Genocide."

33. Vandeginste, "Les Juridictions gacaca et la poursuite des suspects auteurs du génocide et des crimes contre l'humanité au Rwanda," 90; and Sarkin, "Gacaca Courts and Genocide," 82.

34. The only exception is Penal Reform International, which has been helping the Rwandan government to adapt gacaca for adjudicating genocide

cases through field research and technical assistance. See http://penalreform.
org.

35. Cour Suprême, Département des Juridictions Gacaca, *Manuel expli-
catif sur la loi organique portant création des juridictions gacaca* (Kigali: Gvt. of
Rwanda Printer, 2001).

36. Drawn from remarks made at a conference titled "Rwanda and South
Africa in Dialogue: Addressing the Legacies of Genocide and a Crime against
Humanity," held in Cape Town, February 2001.

37. Confessed prisoner, interview with Charles Mironko, Gitarama
prison, 2000.

38. Gacaca proceedings were conducted in prisons to determine their
feasibility for the country as a whole; in Rilima prison, the prisoners began
organizing gacaca hearings even before they were institutionalized.

39. IRIN News, March 10, 2005.

40. It is estimated that some one million people were displaced internally, with an additional 2.5 million displaced across the Rwandan border,
during this period. These figures represent over a quarter of Rwanda's total
population.

41. Apart from a few foreign military advisers, domestic (i.e., Rwandan)
control of the apparatus of law enforcement has been total ever since independence. Therefore, this study will focus exclusively on this (domestic) level.

42. Paul Magnarella, "Explaining Rwanda's 1994 Genocide," *Human
Rights and Human Welfare* 2, no. 1 (Winter 2002):26.

43. World Bank, *Rwandese Republic Emergency Recovery Project Technical
Annex*, 1.

44. United Nations Development Programme, "UNDP Security Sector
Reform Assistance in Post-conflict Situations: Lessons Learned in El Salvador,
Guatemala, Haiti, Mozambique, Somalia and Rwanda" (draft report prepared
for the UNDP Emergency Response Division by Laura Chinchilla and Luis
Salas, New York, June 20, 2001).

45. Ibid.

46. Ibid.

47. Ibid.

48. See Articles 54, 56, and 57 of law no. 09/2000 of June 16, 2000. This
law was preceded by a revision of the fundamental law of April 19, 2000.

49. This division is itself headed by a woman.

50. Founded in 1995, this facility can accommodate up to 1,000 recruits
at one time.

Part III
The Balkans
and Beyond

7

Too Little, Too Late?

Justice and Security Reform in Bosnia and Herzegovina

MICHAEL H. DOYLE

WITH THE CONCLUSION OF BOSNIA'S THREE-AND-A-HALF-YEAR bloody war in 1995, the international community embarked on an exercise in peacekeeping and state-building, guided by the U.S.-brokered Dayton Peace Accords. Still ongoing in 2005, this process had yielded important lessons applicable to the reconstruction of societies following ethnic conflict. One of the most important lessons was that holding elections before the establishment of an independent judiciary and police force undermines efforts to create a functioning democracy.

At the time of this writing, ten years after the Dayton Peace Accords put an end to the 1992–95 Bosnian war, internationally led security and justice reforms were still incomplete. Since the peace agreement failed to spell out a coordinated and comprehensive strategy of judicial and police reform, a panoply of international agencies deployed after Dayton only gradually evolved strategies and mandates necessary to establish the rule of law. Police and judicial institutions, often subject to undue political influence, tempted by corruption, or fearful of retribution, allowed rampant corruption and the flourishing of organized crime. Ethnically motivated violence, to which police, prosecutors, and courts had long turned a blind eye, appeared to be diminishing. However, the fragmented and broken policing system was ill equipped to deal with rising "everyday" criminality, including violent crime. The International Criminal Tribunal for the Former Yugoslavia (ICTY) had made inroads in bringing to justice those who perpetrated war crimes, but the fact that Radovan Karadžić, Ratko Mladić, and other indictees accused of complicity in genocide remained free made a mockery of international justice, bred cynicism among those who identified with their victims, and transformed national heroes into legends.

While the international community only belatedly realized the need to invest serious energy in thoroughgoing and integrated police and judicial reform, progress was eventually made starting in 2000. The Bosnian experience had demonstrated the need for a two-pronged strategy in establishing the rule of law in societies following ethnic conflict. In addition to undertaking long-term and difficult reforms of the institutions, links between organized crime and nationalist parties and individuals must be broken to remove from power individuals who have a vested interest in seeing that reforms fail.

The extraordinary powers of Bosnia's high representative, including the authority to remove elected officials, enact legislation, and establish new institutions, had been used robustly to erode the power of nationalist and corrupt spoilers and to accelerate the pace of judicial and police reform. However, Bosnia's long-term status as a quasi protectorate had put politicians in the habit of passing responsibility for difficult reforms to the Office of the High Representative (OHR) and other agencies, while raising questions about the accountability of the international presence. In 2005 it was still too soon to judge the long-term impact of efforts to establish sustainable public security and judicial institutions, or to see if reforms would survive the eventual withdrawal of international civilian agencies and military forces.

THE CONFLICT AND PEACE AGREEMENT

The 1992–95 Bosnian War

The Bosnian war began in April 1992, when units of the Yugoslav National Army (JNA), along with Bosnian Serb paramilitaries armed by Radovan Karadžić's Serb Democratic Party (SDS) and paramilitary units established and controlled by Serbian state security forces, attacked several Bosnian cities and towns, including Sarajevo. War came just a month after the results of a referendum on independence from Yugoslavia were announced. Although an overwhelming majority of Bosnian Muslim (Bosniak) and Croat citizens had voted in favor of an independent and multiethnic state, the SDS had "encouraged," through propaganda, intimidation, and armed roadblocks, the Bosnian Serb population to boycott the poll.[1]

The Yugoslav and Bosnian Serb operations were designed to divide Bosnia and establish ethnically "pure" Bosnian Serb territories to join with Mother Serbia. Paramilitary units from Serbia, perhaps the best known being Arkan's infamous Tigers, led the brutal "ethnic cleansing" of non-Serb civilians—mostly Bosniaks and Croats— from these areas, shattering decades of multiethnic coexistence. Locally established SDS war crisis staffs, composed of Serb representatives of the police, judiciary, military, and political establishments, organized terror campaigns that included massacres, executions, detention in concentration camps, torture, systematic rape, destruction, and confiscation of property and deportation of the non-Serb population.[2]

The hastily assembled Bosnian Army, which in larger towns like Sarajevo was multiethnic at the start of the war, found itself outgunned by the Serbs, who had the Serb-dominated JNA and its artillery behind them. Serbian president Slobodan Milošević eventually ceded to increasing international pressure and ceased attacks on Bosnia, now a sovereign country. But the "withdrawal" of JNA units amounted to leaving behind soldiers, weapons, and equipment for the Bosnian Serb Army (VRS), now the official army of the newly declared Republika Srpska (RS).

In the first year of war, the Bosnian Army fought several fronts in alliance with a separately formed Bosnian Croat militia, the Croat

Defense Council (HVO), and the Army of Croatia proper. This alliance broke down in the first year of war, and by 1993 a full-scale war between units of the HVO and the Bosnian Army raged in the northern Posavina region, central Bosnia, and Herzegovina. The main Croat political party, the Croat Democratic Union (HDZ), the Bosnian wing of Croatian president Franjo Tudjman's party, had gradually come under the control of a group of radical nationalist Croats from Herzegovina, led by Mate Boban. Whereas in the early days the HDZ and most Croats had supported the idea of a unified Bosnia, the HDZ and the HVO now fought for the glory of Herceg-Bosna, a separate Croat territory in areas bordering Croatia, envisioned as an ethnically pure addition to Croatia.

In 1994 the United States helped to broker a cease-fire between the HVO and the Bosnian Army, which led to the signing of the Washington Agreement in March 1994, creating a Bosniak-Croat Federation. At the time, it was envisioned that breakaway Serb areas would join the Federation under a later peace deal. This was not to be.

As war continued, the international community maintained its misguided policy of imposing a general arms embargo. This continued to favor the Bosnian Serbs, who had inherited weapons from the JNA and continued to receive support from Yugoslavia, in the form of supplies and occasional rotations of military units to the Bosnian front. The tide turned in the summer of 1995, when a series of attacks by the Croatian Army in western Bosnia, a major Bosnian Army offensive, and long overdue NATO air strikes forced the Serbs to the negotiating table.

United States envoy Richard Holbrooke spearheaded negotiations in Dayton, Ohio, in November, which ultimately led to the signing of the General Framework Agreement for Peace in Bosnia and Herzegovina, or the Dayton Peace Accords (DPA) in Paris in December 1995.[3]

During the course of the war, some 200,000 Bosnians were killed and 2.2 million persons, about half the population, fled their homes.

Contradictions of the Dayton Peace Accords
The agreement created a new state, now called Bosnia and Herzegovina (Bosnia or BiH), consisting of a weak central government

and two powerful entities, the Bosniak-Croat Federation (already negotiated into existence by the 1994 Washington Agreement) and the Republika Srpska. The Federation was further subdivided into ten cantons, eight of which were constitutionally defined as Bosniak- or Croat-majority and two of which were "mixed." Real power remained in the hands of the entities—and in the case of the Federation, the cantons—which retained near-exclusive control over revenue collection, separate police forces, and separate judicial systems. While technically putting the armed forces under the control of the three-member state presidency, the DPA allowed for the continuation of the three ethnic armies with separate chains of command.[4] This administrative chaos represented the appeasement of Bosnian Serbs and, to a lesser extent, Croat separatists, who counted on the eventual collapse of Bosnia's common state structure and union with their respective "homelands."

Against the ethnically divisive nature of the entities and cantons, the DPA contained provisions meant to bring about Bosnia's gradual reintegration into a full-fledged state. The state was given nominal control over ten areas, including foreign policy, foreign trade policy, customs policy, monetary policy, immigration, and interentity criminal law enforcement.[5] For several years after the peace was struck, however, entity and canton governments stubbornly resisted giving authority and legitimacy to the common state institutions.

Perhaps most important, the DPA sought to undo the effects of ethnic cleansing by guaranteeing refugees and internally displaced persons the absolute right to return to their prewar homes, devoting an entire annex of the agreement to this issue.[6] Besides upholding the right of individuals to return, the DPA obligated the Bosnian authorities to uphold "the highest level of internationally recognized human rights and fundamental freedoms."[7] Annex 4 of the agreement, the BiH state constitution, insisted that the rights and freedoms enumerated in the European Convention for the Protection of Human Rights and Fundamental Freedoms, its Protocols, and a number of other human rights treaties would have "priority over all other law."[8] Annex 6 established a special Commission on Human Rights, consisting of an Office of the Ombudsman (charged primarily with investigating and reporting on human rights violations) and a Human

Rights Chamber (a court of fourteen judges that would receive complaints and issue judgments), and was weighted with foreign judges.[9]

Dayton also created lead roles for multiple intergovernmental organizations under no single unambiguous authority, initially crippling the effectiveness of the international community. NATO's Implementation Force (IFOR), which later became the Stabilization Force (SFOR), was mandated to oversee implementation of military aspects of the agreement and provide a safe and secure environment for international civilian agencies. The Organization for Security and Cooperation in Europe was given responsibility for overseeing the conduct of the first "free and fair" elections. It also took on the task of conducting human rights monitoring. The UN Mission to Bosnia and Herzegovina (UNMIBH) and its International Police Task Force were to oversee local police forces. The UN High Commissioner for Refugees was to be the lead agency in refugee issues, including their return.

Perhaps most significantly, the DPA created the post of an internationally appointed high representative, whose task was to monitor the implementation of the DPA and coordinate the activities of the other agencies. In December 1997, at a meeting in Bonn, Germany, Bosnia's Peace Implementation Council decided to substantially increase the powers of the high representative, who was now authorized to use "his final authority in theatre regarding interpretation of the Agreement on the Civilian Implementation of the Peace Settlement in order to facilitate the resolution of any difficulties as aforesaid 'by making binding decisions, as he judges necessary' on certain issues including 'measures to ensure implementation of the Peace Agreement throughout Bosnia and Herzegovina and its Entities.'" At the time of this writing, the high representative had used this authority broadly to review and remove elected officials, impose legislation, amend entity constitutions, and create new institutions.

Nationalists Retain Control over Decentralized and Fragmented Institutions

The de facto recognition of partition between the entities, further legitimized by internationally sponsored elections that reappointed the nationalist SDS, HDZ, and Party of Democratic Action (SDA) within their respective enclaves, crippled early international efforts to help refugees return and to realize Dayton's promised human rights protections. These parties retained an interest in thwarting aspects of the DPA designed to create a functional and stable state.

The interests of the nationalist parties in stressing Dayton's divisive provisions and obstructing its integrative ones were not merely ideological but also financial. The three principal parties, the HDZ, SDS, and SDA, had forged strong links with organized crime during the war, partially out of the need to fund and equip the war effort and partially out of greed. Three self-contained political structures relied on ethnically divided public utilities and other enterprises to feed their networks of patronage, as well as control over judicial and police institutions to permit the unchecked robbing of public coffers.

Too naive, timid, or unwilling to acknowledge that corruption and links to organized crime were feeding these parties' anti-Dayton agendas, the international community waited some six years to use its powers to vigorously attack corruption and combat nationalist obstruction to reform.

SUCCESSES AND FAILURES OF POLICE REFORM

International Police Task Force (IPTF)

Annex 11 of the DPA called on the Bosnian authorities "to provide a safe and secure environment for all persons in their respective jurisdictions, by maintaining civilian law enforcement agencies operating in accordance with internationally recognized standards and with respect for internationally recognized human rights and fundamental freedoms."

The DPA and several subsequent UN Security Council resolutions created an International Police Task Force (IPTF), under the auspices of UNMIBH, to "assist" the local police in meeting this standard. The IPTF remit included

- Monitoring, observing, and inspecting law enforcement activities and facilities, including associated judicial organizations, structures, and proceedings

- Advising law enforcement personnel and forces
- Training law enforcement personnel
- Facilitating, within the IPTF's mission of assistance, the parties' law enforcement activities
- Assessing threats to public order and advising on the capability of law enforcement agencies to deal with such threats
- Advising governmental authorities in Bosnia and Herzegovina on the organization of effective civilian law enforcement agencies
- Assisting by accompanying the parties' law enforcement personnel as they carry out their responsibilities, as the IPTF deems appropriate[10]

Throughout UNMIBH's tenure in Bosnia, the IPTF's activities formed the core of its role in the country. Unarmed, possessing a weak mandate, and lacking a clear strategy, the IPTF relied on the goodwill of the local authorities to carry out difficult police reforms. Sanctions against the parties if they defied the authority of the IPTF were vague and toothless.[11] NATO's Implementation Force, with some 60,000 troops, could have provided, in theory, the muscle to back police reforms that challenged the interests of the ruling parties, but it was unwilling to do so in the early years after Dayton.[12] Thus, the agreement left ultimate responsibility for providing security to the local authorities.

This was a tall order for a police force now asked, in many areas, to assist in the return of the same refugees it had helped to terrorize and expel. In the case of Republika Srpska, many police administrations and officers had participated in brutal wartime "ethnic cleansing" operations. In Prijedor, for instance, the police had been directly involved in torturing and executing civilians and establishing concentration camps,[13] while in Bratunac, the local police assisted in the massacre of some 7,000 Muslim men and boys, following the fall of Srebrenica in July 1995.[14] Police had also been implicated in war crimes in Croat-held areas of Herceg-Bosna and in areas under the control of the wartime Republic of Bosnia and Herzegovina, though on a less systematic scale.

The Evolution of the IPTF Mandate

Despite these early obstacles, UNMIBH/IPTF did evolve into a more robust and focused instrument of police reform during the next seven years, with noticeable effects by 2000. A turning point came in 1997, when NATO's Stability Force (SFOR, the heir to IFOR) agreed to assist the unarmed IPTF in its tasks.

The major reforms initiated by UNMIBH/IPTF included establishing ethnic recruitment targets for police, vetting police personnel, downsizing police forces, and establishing a registry of authorized police officers. The Petersburg Declaration of April 1996 set the stage for these reforms, authorizing the IPTF to oversee changes to the Federation police, including the reduction of the force by two-thirds. Force reduction was achieved by vetting officers on the basis of educational qualifications and prior policing background and through training courses in human rights and democratic policing. The RS Police Restructuring Agreement, signed in 1998, allowed for similar reforms in that entity, though it set less robust restructuring requirements than in the Federation.

The IPTF defined its mandate further in 1999 with the announcement of a new three-point plan to achieve "democratic policing" through

- More postcommunist, postparamilitary restructuring
- More rigorous training, selection, certification, and decertification procedures
- More democratization by establishing depoliticized, impartial, accountable, and multinational police forces dedicated to the principles of community policing[15]

The most important reforms introduced under this scheme, and their effectiveness, are discussed later. However, it should be noted that the overall task of creating a democratic police force suffered as a result of the period of several years between the end of the war and serious attempts at restructuring, vetting, and professionalizing the police. This was particularly the case in Republika Srpska, where international timidity in opposing nationalist opposition to reform allowed that entity to lag well behind the Federation. In addition, piecemeal reform within Bosnia's divided police forces could go only so far in overcoming the lack of coordination and cooperation between Bosnia's thirteen police forces.

European Union Police Mission

On January 1, 2003, the European Union Police Mission (EUPM), equipped with a three-year mandate, succeeded the United Nations as the primary agency for police reform in Bosnia. At the time serious problems plagued Bosnia's police forces. Up until the very end of the UN mandate, IPTF intervention remained a necessary prerequisite for compelling the police to carry out sensitive investigations in many parts of the country; interentity policing cooperation was still problematic; lower-level officers had not been comprehensibly screened; and a number of other important reforms remained for the EUPM to complete. Nevertheless, the United Nations was eager to declare Bosnia's police reform a success. "Bosnia and Herzegovina now has 'a police force fit for Europe' firmly based on international standards of democratic policing and in the service of all citizens of Bosnia and Herzegovina. It represents a major stride forward towards European integration."[16]

From the start, the EUPM was limited by a weak, nonexecutive mandate to monitor, advise, and inspect high- and middle-ranking police. The idea was to achieve results comparable to those of the IPTF with fewer staff and resources.[17] However, within Bosnia, the mission and its work have been the subject of some criticism. One major problem is the fact that the contributing nations ultimately decide whom they will send to which positions in the mission, sometimes sending junior police officers or officers not qualified for the positions they will fill. A more serious complaint, made by EUPM employees themselves, is a lack of regional experience among upper management and a lack of strategic direction. This lack of strategic direction, coupled with a weak mandate and a flawed management model, means that the technical expertise that does exist within the mission is not optimized.

Police Reforms

Reducing the Police

By the end of its mandate, UNMIBH had overseen a dramatic reduction in police from 40,000 officers immediately after the war to some 16,000 regular civilian police in December 2002.[18] This reduction still left the ratio of police to citizens above the European average of 1 to 330. A functional review of the Bosnian police forces, financed by the European Commission (EC) and published in 2004, recommended a further reduction of about 3,000 authorized police officers and 2,000 administrative staff throughout the country. Such reductions would need to be accompanied by social programs and reeducation to ensure that sacked officers would not become disgruntled and turn to criminality. Remaining staff would need to be more rationally deployed, and a certain number transferred to understaffed state-level police agencies.[19]

Paying the Police

Low police salaries, often distributed months in arrears, plagued attempts at reforming Bosnia's police, leaving them open to taking bribes and engaging in corruption and organized crime. Differences in police salaries among the entities and cantons and even within cantons with separate ethnic budgetary structures helped to perpetuate ethnic segregation. These problems revealed mismanagement and corruption within the Ministries of the Interior, as well as the financial fragility of a system that duplicated administrative and support functions thirteen times, in a country of less than four million inhabitants, possessing a weak economy.

Training

Bosnia's police were subjected to a plethora of training courses by UNMIBH, the EUPM, and other agencies to raise professional competence and sensitivity to human rights and to improve relations between the police and the public. Special courses and on-the-job training included management skills, evidence recovery techniques, forensic crime scene management, economic crime investigation, antiterrorism techniques, community policing, and effective cooperation with prosecutors. In 2005 it was still unclear how effective this training had been at increasing the overall professionalism of the police.

On-the-job training of police, through the "colocation" of international officers in local stations throughout the country, formed the backbone of the IPTF mission. If nothing else, the presence of international monitors, when backed by sanctions for dereliction of duty, served to keep the police on their best (or at least better) behavior. The EUPM continued the practice of colocation, with fewer monitors, focusing on management and the newly created state policing agencies, the State Border Service (SBS) and the State Investigation and Protection Agency (SIPA).

Screening and Registering the Police

The power of the IPTF to "de-authorize" police officers, revoking their right to perform policing functions, was a crucial tool for weeding out individuals with poor credentials or dubious pasts and for pressuring the police to carry out sensitive investigations, including of war crimes and violence against returning minorities. For example, when the Trebinje police chief refused to initiate criminal investigations against the participants and organizers of anti-Muslim riots in 2001, the IPTF removed him. IPTF "assistance" in the case of a sixteen-year-old Bosniak returnee to Vlasenica, murdered in her home by a sniper in 2001, revealed an RS police force unwilling to follow obvious leads against the perpetrators of ethnically motivated violence. However useful IPTF intervention was, the ongoing need for such intervention pointed to its shortcomings as a means of permanently severing undue influence of politics on policing.

UNMIBH also attempted a more comprehensive vetting and registration of police, subjecting all serving officers and new cadets to a two-step process of "provisional authorization" and "final certification," which lasted until the end of its mandate in December 2002. Provisional authorization was granted largely on the basis of information provided by the officers themselves, and "final certification" was to follow only after more extensive background checks, particularly of high- and middle-ranking police. However, it was not until early 2001 that UNMIBH began to examine the wartime activities of serving officers, in response to criticisms that some "provisionally authorized" police in the RS were allegedly complicit in war crimes.[20] A major weakness of the system was that "de-authorizations" only covered officers engaged in law enforcement, allowing corrupt, incompetent, and nationalist personnel to be transferred to administrative or political positions, where they continued to wield power. In addition, local prosecutors almost never followed up on "de-authorization" with criminal indictments.[21]

Unfortunately, UNMIBH did not complete comprehensive investigations of lower-ranking officers before its mandate expired. Moreover, since vetting criteria used by the United Nations were not given the force of law, local authorities were not compelled to continue the process. Worst of all, the United Nations did not hand the database of registered police to the EUPM or the local authorities, creating a gap of several years of personnel changes in the local police forces unrecorded in the registry. As of 2005, the EUPM had just created a new police personnel database from scratch, based on reporting from the various police agencies. At the same time the international community was trying to introduce a national police identification card linked to this database, which would allow for a fully accurate picture of all serving police in Bosnia.

Creating a Multiethnic Police Force

RS and Federation police restructuring agreements established hiring targets for so-called minority police officers. These quotas were to serve a few purposes: to encourage returns by undoing the "ethnic cleansing" of Bosnia's police, to provide employment and a sustainable existence to minority police officers and their families, and to break up the nationalist monopolies within law enforcement. Incremental reintegration had been achieved through police academies admitting primarily minority recruits and through voluntary redeployment of serving officers.

However, the process was tainted from the start by the application of a double standard in the two entities. While Federation police targets were based on the ethnic composition of municipalities according to the last prewar census, less stringent RS quotas followed the proportion of non-Serb elected officials in the 1997 municipal councils. The international community essentially accepted the refusal of Bosnian Serb authorities to undo the wartime ethnic cleansing of its police forces. As of 2005, figures for minority recruitment remained comparatively low, particularly in the RS.

The reasons for low minority recruitment were manifold and included insufficient housing, political obstruction, and in the RS until about 2003, lack of personal security.[22] Another significant deterrent for officers in the Federation to relocate to the RS was the lower police salaries that prevail in the poorer entity. In addition, once recruited, minority officers encountered a host of difficulties in performing their duties. In some municipalities, minority officers were not issued firearms and badges or were relegated to menial tasks.

Some have used the limited success of minority police recruitment to argue that its goals are unrealistic. However, in creating the new State Border Service and State Investigation and Protection Agency from scratch, the international community has succeeded in meeting multiethnic quotas. This implies that a more comprehensive policy of rehiring or redeploying would have been more successful had the international community been prepared to shoulder the financial costs and political risks of such a policy.

Limiting Inappropriate Political Influence over the Police

Before, during, and after the war, political influence over the work of the police was embodied in the politically appointed ministers of the interior, who possessed broad authority over the day-to-day operations of the police within their respective jurisdictions. However, modern policing systems in the countries of the European Union institute a clear division between the functions of strategic planning and policymaking in public security and the everyday operations of the police. UNMIBH led a project to create a senior operational post for each of Bosnia's police agencies, functionally independent of the respective minister. The Federation and Republika Srpska "directors of police" and the "police commissioners" of the ten cantons would be accountable for the everyday operations of their respective police, while the ministers would control overall policymaking. A specific division of authority between these two senior officials, the director of police (or police commissioner) and the minister of the interior, was derived from precedents and legal opinions in New Zealand and Northern Ireland.[23]

Running counter to the interests of parties in parliament and the various ministers of the interior, the project encountered significant local political resistance. UNMIBH appointed interim directors and commissioners, while the parliaments of the entities and cantons dragged their feet in adopting the necessary changes to police legislation. After these appointments, ministers of the interior reportedly used special advisers or other officials to circumvent the authority of the commissioners. In 2005 ministers of the interior still remained the de facto heads of police operations in some cantons and in the RS, where the minister of the interior made little effort to conceal his complete control over the RS police.

Cross-Entity and Canton Coordination and Cooperation

The Dayton Peace Accords left Bosnia's police forces divided. Each of the two entities, the Republika Srpska and the Federation, maintained its own police under the control of its Ministry of the Interior. While policing in the RS was divided among regional public security centers, which oversaw municipal police forces in their area, a clear hierarchy put ultimate police authority in the hands of the RS Ministry of the Interior. The Federation, on the other hand, was divided into cantons that maintained virtual administrative autonomy from the center and from one another, each possessing its own Interior Ministry separate from the Federation ministry. These provided the administrative framework for the ethnic division of Federation police into Bosniak and Croat forces. The situation was further complicated until 2002 by the so-called mixed cantons, in which Croat and Bosniak police administrations and forces existed in parallel form, defying integration. In addition, with the final arbitration award creating the special Brčko District under temporary, international administration, in 1999, this small territory gained its own autonomous police force, answerable to the mayor and the district assembly. Cooperation among these various police forces remained sporadic at best in 2005, as indictments issued in one entity had little force in the other.

State-Level Policing Agencies

Within this context, the institutions of the common Bosnian state retained very little police power. The DPA granted authority to the central state over "international and inter-Entity criminal law enforcement, including relations with Interpol." By 2005 the international community had established two state-level policing agencies, the State Border Service (SBS) and the State Investigation and Protection Agency (SIPA), and a state Ministry of Security, charged with providing political oversight and accountability for these policing agencies. UNMIBH built up the SBS from scratch in 2000 to police the country's borders, and the OHR and the EUPM played a dominant role in developing SIPA into the police agency to combat interentity crime and complex crimes falling within the jurisdiction of the Bosnian state court, including terrorism, war crimes, money laundering, and human trafficking. The institutional development of SIPA was ongoing as of August 2005.

Comprehensive Police Restructuring

Despite the efforts of UNMIBH/IPTF, the EUPM, and other international agencies to train, vet, register, and advise the police within the existing police structure, by 2004 the emerging consensus was that systemic deficiencies in the overall structure of policing prevented the police from operating effectively and efficiently. Divided along ethnic and political lines, the various police forces did not work within a single legal framework that would compel them to cooperate, resulting in a fragmented and ineffective system of law enforcement, in which criminals enjoyed more freedom of movement than police. Thirteen local and two state-level police agencies, operating with separate administrative apparatuses, forensics capabilities, crime databases, communications systems, procurement services, recruitment bodies, and other support functions, as well as two separate police-training regimes, were proving financially unsustainable within Bosnia's weak economy.

These considerations prompted the EC to include "structural police reform with a view to rationalizing police services" as one of sixteen requirements set out in its so-called *Feasibility Study* of 2003, a document outlining the reforms necessary for Bosnia to enter the first phase of formal negotiations on entering the European Union (EU).[24] As part of its overall review of public administration in Bosnia, the EC financed a comprehensive study of the Bosnian police agencies, published in 2004. This study confirmed many of the systemic weaknesses described earlier, pointing to the fact that current policing arrangements were not financially sustainable.[25]

Two successive EU enlargement commissioners further defined the meaning of the EU requirement for police restructuring. In a letter to the chair of the Bosnian Council of Ministers, then commissioner Christopher Patten explained: "The EU has a direct stake in this matter, because if BiH is not able to tackle crime effectively, that has a bearing on crime elsewhere in Europe, including the European Union. . . . The EU also has an interest in making sure it has effective law enforcement partners in BiH with which it can deal—police counterparts at the state level, with broadly the same competencies as their counterparts elsewhere in Europe. The current policing structure does not provide for this."[26]

The high representative initiated the first steps to making comprehensive police restructuring a reality in July 2004 by establishing the Police Restructuring Commission (PRC), made up of international and domestic public security officials and experts and mandated to propose a "single structure of policing" for Bosnia, under the political oversight of a state-level ministry. As part of its mandate, the PRC was also charged with drafting the legislation needed to implement whatever recommendations it made. The PRC deliberated for six months, analyzing the weaknesses of the Bosnian policing structure in the light of modern European best practice in policing.

The work of the commission resulted in a proposal that the central state exercise exclusive competency for all police legislative and budget matters, with police organized within a single Police Service of Bosnia and Herzegovina. The state Ministry of Security would exercise policymaking functions for all police agencies in Bosnia. Operationally, policing would be organized at the national level (SIPA and SBS) and at the local level, through ten new police regions. Support functions like procurement, forensics, recruitment and training, crime databases, and communications would be centralized, eliminating the costly duplication inherent in the current arrangement. Institutional mechanisms such as a Conference of Directors and Commissioners and a police director for all local police regions would ensure the cooperation and coordination currently lacking among police agencies.[27]

Because this proposal would mean transferring responsibilities and competencies related to policing, which currently belong to the cantons, entities, and Brčko District, to the state level, the RS mounted opposition to it, both within the commission and following the publication of the commission's report. As of August 2005, representatives of political parties in the parliaments, as well as state and entity representatives, were still negotiating a final political deal on the future structure of policing, the last hurdle for Bosnia to begin formal negotiations toward EU membership. The EC had clearly stated that any proposal for restructured police would have to be endorsed by the country's parliaments and would have to conform to three principles:

- The state would have exclusive competency for all police matters, including passing legislation and establishing a budget.
- The new system would have to severely limit the inappropriate influence of politics on policing.
- The police regions would have to be drawn up on the basis of technical policing criteria, rather than slavishly following entity or cantonal borders.

It remained unclear at the time of this writing when Bosnia's politicians would agree on a new, more effective single structure of policing, facilitating the country's eventual integration into the EU.

SUCCESSES AND FAILURES OF JUDICIAL REFORM

The wartime institutional divisions confirmed at Dayton left Bosnia with nearly twice the number of courts it had before the war, saddled with a backlog of tens of thousands of cases stemming from clumsy and easily abused procedures.[28] Nevertheless, the DPA reflected no serious commitment to judicial reform on the part of the international community, focusing instead on disarming the combatants, holding elections, establishing common state political institutions, and providing for refugee return.

Annex 11 of the DPA gave the IPTF the mandate to monitor, observe, and inspect "law enforcement activities and facilities, including associated judicial organizations, structures, and proceedings," but this was the only mention of anything even approaching judicial reform. A mix of international organizations initiated small projects to address the rule of law, but these efforts were ad hoc, uncoordinated, and inadequate. Successive meetings of the Peace Implementation Council in 1997 and 1998 confirmed the need for expanded and coordinated judicial reform efforts to be led by the OHR, but the OHR did not develop a comprehensive strategic judicial reform plan until July 1999.

In the meantime, the nascent UN mandate defined in Annex 11 led to the creation of the UN Judicial System Assessment Programme (JSAP) in November 1998. JSAP deployed officers to the field to monitor court proceedings, provide support to local judges, and collect information for a series of detailed assessments on the state of the judiciary. When the JSAP concluded its mandate at the end of 2000, the international community endeavored to establish a follow-on mission under the auspices of the OHR. Unfortunately, the International Judicial Commission (IJC) was not up and running until March 2001, leaving a gap of more than six months between the significant drawdown of JSAP efforts and the establishment of a follow-on body.[29]

With the appointment of Lord Paddy Ashdown as Bosnia's high representative in May 2002, the international community embarked on a "reinvigorated judicial reform strategy." In the run-up to the October 5, 2002, elections, the OHR drafted a public strategy for reforming Bosnia's economic sector and judiciary and urged local politicians to sign up for its noble if rather vague tenets, expressed in the brochure title *Jobs and Justice: Our Agenda*.[30] Implicitly acknowledging the shortcomings of previous judicial reform efforts, the brochure noted that "this country has many laws and many judges, but it does not have the rule of law."[31]

During the first months of his mandate, Ashdown and the OHR spearheaded a significant judicial reform effort. The most important reforms included the establishment of Independent Judicial and

Prosecutorial Councils for appointing and reviewing judges and prosecutors, a new state-level Criminal Code and Criminal Procedural
Code, laws on witness protection, and the law establishing a new BiH
central state court. Unfortunately, the legislation required to initiate
these changes had to be imposed by the high representative, since
Bosnian parliaments could not muster the votes to make these needed
reforms themselves.

Professionalizing the Judiciary

During and after the war, nationalist political establishments in Bosnia's three ethnic enclaves appointed an unknown number of unqualified and politically amenable judges and prosecutors. Reports of
corruption were supported by the inability of Bosnia's courts to con-
vict public officials suspected of abusing their positions for financial
gain. Political influence was demonstrated by the common practice
of prosecutors initiating corruption investigations exclusively against
members of the outgoing regime when elections brought new parties
to power. Frequent failures by the courts to professionally try suspected war criminals and perpetrators of violence against returning
"minorities" showed that many judges did not administer "ethnically
blind" justice. During the war, some of these judges presided over
sham trials against members of the "wrong" ethnicity, reviewed
detention facilities where prisoners were mistreated or "disappeared,"
or were otherwise complicit in violations of international humanitarian law.[32]

The Failed Policy of Judicial Review

Lack of public confidence in the judiciary was revealed in 2002 polls
showing that more than 20 percent of citizens believed the practice
of taking bribes to be "very common."[33] While many serving judges
and prosecutors were competent and conscientious, Bosnia's postwar
judiciary needed an effective process for separating the wheat from
the chaff, taking judicial appointments outside the sphere of politics,
and providing for ongoing review of judicial personnel.

As a comparative lesson, Bosnia had the advantage of having
tried one form of ineffective judicial review and eventually scrapping
it in favor of another. In 2000 special entity-level commissions and

councils of serving judges and prosecutors were convened to vet their colleagues under a process of "comprehensive peer review," initiated by the international community and carried out under the close supervision of the international IJC. Detailed reviews of serving judges and prosecutors could be initiated on the basis of a preliminary review, on a well-documented complaint by a member of the public, or on information provided by international organizations monitoring the judiciary.

During the eighteen-month process of review, the commissions and councils processed 1,145 judges and prosecutors in both entities on the basis of some 1,594 citizen complaints against incumbents. Disappointingly, only five post holders were removed, thirty-two were subjected to other disciplinary procedures, and a handful resigned.

The reasons for failure were manifold, but an unavoidable short-coming of the process was the expectation that "a highly politicized, nationally divided, financially dependent and institutionally deficient judiciary" could "transform itself into a competent, freedom-loving and disinterested bastion of democratic values, human rights and civil society."[34] Peer review was a contradiction in terms, asking the judiciary to correct the system it was perpetuating.[35]

General Reappointment of Judges and Prosecutors

Mounting criticism finally convinced Bosnia's international Peace Implementation Council to discard the comprehensive peer review model in February 2002, essentially acknowledging that the international reform project had failed. Several commentators argued that the review bodies should be replaced with permanent independent high judicial councils, based on the model used throughout continental Europe, which would appoint, discipline, and remove judges and prosecutors. The first task of these councils would be to reopen all judicial posts, forcing current judges and prosecutors to compete for their jobs against all other interested and qualified applicants. This model was successfully used in East Germany following reunification and in Georgia.

A successful example of so-called general reappointment also existed in Bosnia itself, in the Brčko District. In Brčko, the entire process of judicial reform was completed in two years under the aegis of a single agency, the Brčko Law Revision Commission. While judicial reform in the rest of Bosnia was floundering under a lack of coordination and vision, the Brčko Law Revision Commission managed to establish an independent judiciary, appointed, reviewed, and disciplined by an independent judicial commission and equipped with streamlined criminal codes and procedures. Using the general reappointment model, the judicial commission replaced 80 percent of judges and prosecutors in Brčko, and a sizable majority of appointees were returning refugees and other applicants from outside the district.

Having given up on comprehensive peer review, the OHR launched a "general reappointment," establishing High Judicial and Prosecutorial Councils (HJPC) at the BiH and entity level. From March 2003 to March 2004, the HJPCs appointed nearly 900 judges and prosecutors (or 91 percent of positions) through a staggered application process.[36] Moreover, the three HJPCs had been merged into a single state-level council charged with applying uniform standards in the appointment and discipline of judges and prosecutors throughout Bosnia.

Initial evaluations of the success of countrywide reappointment were mixed. The fact that more than 80 percent of appointed judges and prosecutors were incumbents raised concerns that the process had not successfully weeded out corrupt or politically influenced officials. At the same time, however, 30 percent of judges and prosecutors serving prior to the process were not reappointed. The process also succeeded in significantly restoring ethnic balance on the bench and in prosecutors' offices, in both entities.[37]

Court Restructuring

In 2001 Bosnia's court system was bloated and financially unsustainable. In comparison to countries of similar size in Western Europe, Bosnia had more than twice the number of judges, amounting to one judge per 4,000 citizens. Moreover, the irrational distribution of lower courts meant that judges in different jurisdictions had widely varying caseloads.

Beginning in September 2002, the IJC and local authorities embarked on a downsizing of courts and court personnel, resulting in a reduction of first-instance courts from fifty-eight to twenty-eight in the Federation, and from twenty-five to nineteen in the RS. Amendments to the HJPC laws, imposed by the high representative in August 2002, gave these bodies the authority to determine the staffing levels for judges in lower courts and appeals courts, whose ranks were reduced by 28 percent, from 868 to 629.[38]

Criminal and Procedural Codes

After much delay, in August 2000, the international community, headed by the OHR, began a comprehensive and uniform overhaul of Bosnian criminal law at the level of the state, the entities, and the cantons and in the Brčko District.[39] The strategy after 2000 was to start at the state level and to harmonize legislation at lower levels, basing new laws and procedures on European models, including those in Germany and Sweden.

Local criminal law suffered from three main weaknesses. The first was a complicated set of procedures creating abundant opportunity to delay proceedings indefinitely. The second was the failure of the law to define certain crimes, particularly economic ones, such as corruption and money laundering. Finally, the law lacked mechanisms to restrict these crimes, such as confiscation of illegally earned profits.

The major changes introduced to judicial proceedings were the abolition of the investigative judge and the curtailment of the institutional independence of the police in carrying out investigations, putting full control over investigations in the hands of prosecutors. The role of expert witnesses, previously open to abuse, was limited, and parties were permitted to call their own experts. Changes to trial procedures, including the recording of trials, were aimed at reducing the chances of judges misrepresenting trial proceedings to stenographers. A requirement designed to streamline the process was that a trial begin within 120 days after an indictment was issued. Another major reform was the introduction of witness protection legislation, essential to tackling cases of corruption, organized crime, and war crimes.

Establishment of a State Criminal Code and State Court

From November 2000 to May 2003, the Office of the High Representative walked Bosnia's entity and state governments through a series of legislative and administrative steps needed to establish a state-level court competent to try sensitive and complex criminal cases, including ones involving organized crime and corruption, money laundering, human trafficking, trafficking in weapons and drugs, terrorism, and war crimes. A significant measure in the fight against organized crime was the decision to include both national and international judges and prosecutors on a new panel in the Prosecutor's Office, the Special Organized Crime, Economic Crime, and Corruption Department. While the representatives of Bosnia's main political parties participated in the drafting of necessary laws and repeatedly voiced their commitment to the creation of the court, the state parliament was unable to make good on their promises, compelling the high representative to impose the law establishing the court, subsequent amendments to the law, legislation on the writ of the state Prosecutor's Office, the state Criminal Code, the state Criminal Procedure Code, and a law on witness protection.

The Bosnian state court officially opened on January 27, 2003, and received its first indictment in April. A joint operation conducted by SFOR and the RS Ministry of the Interior led to the arrest of a prominent RS underground crime figure involved in trafficking in women in May 2003, also indicted by the court. As of mid-2005, forty-eight cases involving organized crime, commercial crime, and corruption were in various stages of procedure, including the high-profile trial of a former member of the Bosnian presidency.

DEALING WITH THE PAST: JUSTICE FOR WAR CRIMES

International Criminal Tribunal for the Former Yugoslavia (ICTY)

In response to serious violations of international humanitarian law perpetrated during the Croatian and Bosnian wars, the United Nations Security Council established the ICTY in The Hague in May 1993.[40] The tribunal's jurisdiction extended to crimes committed anywhere in the territory of the former Yugoslavia since 1991, and indictments were issued for war crimes committed during the Croatian, Bosnian, and Kosovo wars, though the majority were related to the Bosnian conflict. As of July 2005, the ICTY had issued public indictments against 162 individuals, as well as an unknown number of "sealed" indictments.[41] At this time, 126 suspects had appeared before the tribunal, and 39 had received sentences ranging from three to forty years.[42]

Lacking its own police, the ICTY relied on the cooperation of the local Bosnian, Serbian, and Croatian authorities to arrest and transfer suspects to the court, except in cases where suspects turned themselves in. In the initial years following the peace agreement, Croatia, Yugoslavia, and Bosnia's Republika Srpska refused to recognize the writ of the tribunal and did not arrest suspects in their jurisdictions. In 1997 NATO's SFOR began arresting ICTY indictees, becoming increasingly proactive in this regard in the following years. The authorities in the Federation, Croatia, and finally Serbia began arresting their citizens and transferring them to The Hague, the most celebrated transfer being that of Yugoslav president Slobodan Milošević in June 2001.

In the RS, inadequate cooperation with the ICTY continued into 2005. In 2004 it was revealed that General Ratko Mladić, indicted by the ICTY for genocide for his role in the Srebrenica massacre, had been on the RS military payrolls as recently as 2002 and that he had taken refuge in an underground RS military complex in Han Pijesak in 2004. NATO rejected Bosnia's bid for membership in the Partnership for Peace Program in July 2004 and again in December 2005, in large measure for the failures of the RS to make progress in arresting Karadžić and Mladić. In a speech delivered in November 2004 to the UN Security Council, the ICTY chief prosecutor linked the failure of the RS authorities to apprehend war crimes suspects to systemic weaknesses in police structures. "[T]hat nine years after Dayton, the authorities of Republika Srpska have not apprehended a single individual indicted by the ICTY . . . confirms the existence of fundamental systemic weaknesses built into the law enforcement and security structures of BiH, and in particular Republika Srpska."

Overwhelming pressure from the international community, including removals of SDS and RS officials by the high representative, freezes on the local and international bank accounts of SDS members, and threats of further sanctions, compelled the RS to take incremental steps toward cooperation in 2004 and 2005. These included convincing a number of ICTY suspects to surrender, partly with cash awards to them and their families (in effect rewarding alleged ethnic cleansers), handing over documents subpoenaed by the ICTY years earlier, and arresting eight suspects on war crimes arrest warrants issued by courts in the Federation. As of July 2005, however, the RS police had yet to arrest a single ICTY indictee.

The political polemics and legal proceedings surrounding the Srebrenica massacre of July 1995, in which Bosnian Serb military and civilian police forces rounded up and executed some 7,000 Muslim men and boys, demonstrate the crucial role that war crimes proceedings must play in coming to grips with the past. The ICTY publicly indicted Karadžić and eleven officers of the VRS and RS police for their alleged role in the massacre, yet many Serbs in the RS continued to downplay the massacre or deny that it took place, a view reinforced in a spurious official report of the RS Government Bureau for Cooperation with the ICTY, released in September 2002.[43]

In May 2002, however, the ICTY scored a major victory in setting the record straight, when a high-ranking officer of the VRS, indicted for genocide and other war crimes for his role in the Srebrenica tragedy, made a full confession of guilt. Momir Nikolić, a former schoolteacher from neighboring Bratunac, gave details about the decision within the VRS to execute the men and boys, logistical plans to assemble and murder them at agreed-on sites, and the massacre itself.[44] Moreover, Nikolić admitted to organizing, in cooperation with local SDS civilian authorities, the destruction of documents implicating the army in the massacre and the transfer and cover-up of mass graves, carried out by members of the army, military police, and civilian police.[45] NATO surveillance had pointed to the transfer of mass graves in 1995 in the area, though Bosnian Serb authorities vigorously denied the accusation. Soon after Nikolić's confession, one of his coaccused, Dragan Obrenović, also admitted guilt, further implicating members of the police and army.[46]

Immediately following Nikolić's admission, the reaction in Bosnia's Republika Srpska was surprisingly muted. Local media did little to cover the plea, RS politicians kept silent, and most citizens of the

RS were reportedly unaware of his confession. As one article on the case noted, official silence may in part reflect the fact that Nikolić's plea implicated members of the current RS military and political establishment in the Srebrenica massacre.[47]

Official disdain toward the ICTY seems to have resonated with the RS public, generally suspicious of the tribunal as anti-Serb. An independent poll conducted in November 2002 found that 74.4 percent of respondents in the RS disagreed with the statement "All citizens who are indicted of war crimes should be tried in The Hague." The same question put to a random sample in the Federation elicited the opposite response: 80 percent agreed that all those indicted should be tried by the ICTY.[48]

However, by 2005 the RS establishment and public had shown signs of coming to terms with the massacre committed ten years previously in Srebrenica. The president of the RS and the prime minister of Serbia both attended the ten-year anniversary commemoration ceremony for the victims, acknowledging the terrible crime committed by Serb forces. Even if such admissions seemed designed primarily to satisfy international critics, they formed a crucial first step in reconciliation.

Domestic War Crimes Trials

The Bosnian case has shown that an international war crimes tribunal is a necessary component for ensuring justice for war crimes, having a residual effect of bringing the truth about crimes committed into public discourse and differentiating collective from individual guilt. It has also made clear that such a tribunal is insufficient in itself, without a parallel process in the domestic courts. This is necessary to cover the potentially thousands of "small fish" who cannot be tried internationally,[49] and also to bring the proceedings closer to the public.[50]

According to the ICTY statute, the tribunal has concurrent jurisdiction with local courts but reserves the right to claim primacy over national proceedings at any stage of investigation, indictment, detention, or trial.[51] Moreover, Bosnian legal authorities were limited in the processing of war crimes cases by procedures set out in the 1996 Rome Agreement, known as the Rules of the Road. Designed to prevent arbitrary arrests on war crimes charges, which would inhibit freedom of movement, the Rules of the Road required Bosnian authorities to submit local indictments and evidence to the prosecutor of the tribunal for review and approval before an arrest could be made locally.

Under the Rules of the Road, the ICTY approved some 846 cases for domestic courts between 1996 and September 2004.[52] According to information collected by the Organization for Security and Cooperation in Europe, only fifty-four of these approved cases, against ninety-four defendants, reached trial phase, with only two of these occurring in the Republika Srpska.[53] Before the establishment of the state court in 2003, most war crimes tried by domestic courts could be described as failures of justice.[54]

Perceiving that the courts of the entities and cantons, dominated by one of the three ethnic groups, could not be expected to try cases locally, the international community placed its hope in a new special chamber of the state-level court, created largely through international funds, with local and international judges and prosecutors, using new criminal codes and procedures. The War Crimes Chamber of the State Court of Bosnia and Herzegovina was officially established in January 2005 and charged with trying some ICTY cases for which indictments had been issued or were being prepared, as well as Rules of the Road cases deemed too sensitive for trial in the entity or cantonal courts.[55] As of August 2005, the War Crimes Chamber had not yet begun trials; however, nine cases, involving fourteen accused, were planned for transfer from the ICTY, while some thirty war crimes cases were under investigation by the Bosnian state prosecutor for possible indictment.[56]

Despite progress made in establishing a functional War Crimes Chamber of the state court including international judges and prosecutors, it was still the case in August 2005 that the majority of war crimes cases would be tried in entity and cantonal courts, many lacking the financial capacity, expertise, or sufficient judicial independence to meet the task. "[I]t has been confirmed by the BiH Prosecutor's Office that the Chamber will only hear the most serious, *'highly sensitive'* cases, as it will have *'neither the resources nor the time to try all war crimes cases.'*"[57] A report issued by Amnesty International in November 2003 called attention to the shortsightedness of pinning the hopes of all domestic prosecutions on a single court in the capital. The authors argued that most cases relating to the thousands of unsolved disappearances would still need to be tried in the courts of the entities and cantons, where no international judges and prosecutors were foreseen.[58]

The inability of almost all domestic courts to address war crimes, particularly those linked to individuals who are still in positions of authority or power in the Republika Srpska, demonstrated the limited progress made in establishing the rule of law in Bosnia. It points not only to fundamental weaknesses in the judicial system, including problems with witness protection, training of judges and prosecutors in war crimes law, and limited finances, but also to inadequacies within the police. Despite a 2002 law compelling the police in all entities and cantons to respect and act on warrants, decisions, and judgments from courts and prosecutors throughout the country, local prosecutors complain that this law remains largely unimplemented and is often not respected, particularly by the RS police.[59] This deficiency points to the need for more comprehensive police restructuring, which would bring all police in the country under a single legal, procedural, and disciplinary regime.

INDICATORS OF THE RULE OF LAW IN BOSNIA IN 2005

Public Perceptions

Public confidence in the police remained low in 2004 and 2005, and one survey found that as many as 55 percent of citizens believed that most or almost all police officers were involved in corruption.[60] This same survey revealed similar views among the public about the judiciary: 36.7 percent of citizens in the Federation and only 23 percent in the RS believed the judiciary to be fair and impartial.[61]

Despite this generally low level of confidence, the survey suggested that public perceptions of the work of courts and prosecutors were improving, perhaps an indication that comprehensive judicial reform was bearing fruit. The United Nations Development Programme, in a 2004 study, expressed a similar view that "[p]ublic support for the judicial system (and the police), as measured by our polls during 2004, is higher than for any other public institution, which suggests that reform in this area has been moving in the right direction."[62]

Ethnically Motivated Violence

Another positive development in the rule of law was a decline in the incidence of violence against displaced persons and refugees who had returned to areas where they were now in the "minority." The Helsinki Human Rights Committee in Bosnia and Herzegovina summarized the situation: "In comparison with previous years, the security situation has improved. It does not mean that in 2004 we did not register occurrences of discriminatory behavior based on ethnicity. There were cases of physical assault on returnees, their property, and national and religious monuments."[63]

Until about 2003, ethnically motivated violence was a serious problem in Bosnia. Statistics on violent incidents compiled by SFOR in early 2002 revealed that while 1 in 3,500 persons in BiH had been the victim of a violent crime, such as bombing, rape, stoning, assault, arson, or murder, for Bosniaks in certain parts of Republika Srpska, 1 in 220 could expect to be a victim of one of these crimes.[64] In 2003 the Helsinki Committee for Human Rights noted an increase in ethnically motivated attacks since the nationalist victory in the October 5, 2002, general elections.[65]

These problems were a clear reflection of a lack of independence and fairness in the work of prosecutors, police, and judges, particularly in the RS. In 2001 and 2002 several high-profile cases demonstrated that the police and judiciary of Republika Srpska would investigate and try attacks on Bosniaks and Croats only when subjected to significant international pressure. One such case involved organized riots in the RS towns of Trebinje and Banja Luka in May 2001, during which police stood by and permitted the rioters to wreak havoc, and after which the police and courts refused to conduct serious investigations and trials.[66]

Given the appalling record of police and courts in the RS up until 2004, it was still too early to determine whether improvements in the security situation reflected true improvement in the professionalism of these institutions or a temporary reaction to extreme pressure from the international community on the RS, linked to its failures to cooperate with the ICTY. Improved security for returnees may also have been a reflection of the fact that while almost all Bosnian refugees or displaced persons had succeeded in reclaiming their prewar property, only about 20 percent of those persons no longer in the dominant ethnic group chose to physically return to their prewar homes.[67] Thus the incentive for organized violence against returnees had been diminished since ethnic cleansing had in large measure proved successful.

"Classic" Crime and Organized Crime

Nearly ten years after the conflict, security problems in Bosnia no longer revolved primarily around issues directly linked to the war, as seen in the downward trend in ethnically motivated violence. At the same time, the poor economic situation and fragmented institutional arrangement created by the peace agreement had resulted in progressively higher levels of "classic" crime and organized crime.

Although overall crime statistics had not been collected on a systematic basis at the time of writing, this picture can be pieced together from various sources, including statistics provided by the various Ministries of the Interior and human rights groups. For instance, in its 2004 report, the Helsinki Committee for Human Rights in Bosnia and Herzegovina noted a steady increase in juvenile delinquency, with the age of perpetrators getting lower and lower. The committee cited 1,288 reported criminal offenses by minors in the area around Sarajevo over a ten-month period, while juvenile delinquency in the RS was reported to have increased by 44 percent over the previous year.[68] The report also claimed an increase in domestic violence against women and children, citing one estimate that 55 percent of women suffer from some kind of violence in the family, while also acknowledging that reliable statistics on this issue are woefully lacking.[69]

In terms of organized crime, human trafficking was also identified as a serious problem. The report noted a trend in Bosnia from being primarily a country of transit for trafficked women to becoming a country of origin for victims of sexual exploitation.[70] By 2005 organized crime was universally acknowledged as the most serious public security threat in Bosnia. As the high representative explained, "Organized crime in BiH feeds off, and is protected by, the weak and fractured State, by institutions and officials compromised by corruption, and by the extensive gray economy which obscures criminal activity."[71]

International efforts in imposing the state criminal code, creating the state court and prosecutor's office, and creating the State Investigation and Protection Agency, a police agency with jurisdiction to battle organized crime throughout Bosnia, reflected these concerns. In the area of police restructuring, however, the commitment of the local authorities to the fight against organized crime would again be put to the test in 2005.

Corruption

Stories accusing functionaries, politicians, and political parties of robbing public coffers appeared almost daily in the Bosnian press in 2005. According to one independent survey, corruption was the second most worrisome issue among Bosnia's citizens, after unemployment.[72] One estimate put the revenue losses to corruption in the customs and tax administrations alone in 2002 at 1.2 billion KM (approximately US$740 million),[73] three times the budget of the state.[74]

The inability and unwillingness of local police and courts to investigate and try corruption cases were demonstrated by the ever-increasing role international organizations assumed in tackling the problem. For instance, Bosnia's international high representative used his powers of decree to establish internationally staffed special auditor offices in both entities, charged with examining the accounts of public institutions and companies.

The stated purpose of the special auditors was "to protect the public funds, so that citizens' tax revenue is spent on schools, hospitals, roads and other legitimate items, and does not disappear into the pockets of dishonest bureaucrats, politicians or businesspeople."[75] In December 2002 the OHR announced its intention to conduct comprehensive investigations of fictitious companies established to launder money and evade taxes and to remove judges complicit in the establishment of such companies.

As much as these actions revealed a new resolve within the international community in Bosnia to address corruption and its links to prominent politicians and parties, they also revealed the ineffectiveness of judicial and police reform to date. It remained to be seen whether Bosnia's courts could successfully try politicians and functionaries implicated in corruption by Bosnia's international protectors.

CONCLUSION

One of the most interesting aspects of international efforts to reform security and justice institutions in Bosnia has been the fact that almost ten years after the peace deal was signed, the international community has found it increasingly necessary to perform judicial and security tasks itself, under the auspices of NATO's SFOR and the Office of the High Representative.

The original mistake in Bosnia's postwar reconstruction effort was the failure to recognize that nationalist political establishments lived off of networks of patronage founded on the absence of the rule of law and on control over the police and judiciary. The Dayton-anointed ethnic and administrative division of the country created political and economic incentives for the three nationalist political parties to thwart the creation of a stable and functioning state. Lacking a comprehensive and coordinated strategy for reforming Bosnia's institutions, the international community naively left this task to these same parties during the first five years of the peace process.

Thus the primary lesson of the Bosnian experience is that reforms of the judiciary and police must take place concurrently and immediately to establish the rule of law. Elections should take a backseat to such reforms, as they risk giving the stamp of democratic legitimacy to societies that do not uphold democratic values and human rights protections. Parallel to difficult institutional reforms, international mandates should be used to take financial and political power away from political elements that thrive off organized crime and the breakdown of order. Moreover, a process for removing elements of the security forces, police, and judiciary implicated in war crimes and criminal activity should be enacted immediately.

Bosnia's international guardians have belatedly learned this lesson, but at a price. Bosnians increasingly view their police and courts and the international presence itself with a certain cynicism and suspicion. A series of democratic elections have appointed leaders who seem to hold the fate of their country less and less in their own hands, deferring difficult decisions to the international high representative. After the West's intervention to stop the Bosnian war and to broker a peace agreement that acknowledged the existence of a single Bosnian state, many Bosnian Serbs and Croats viewed the international presence with suspicion. One indicator of growing dissatisfaction with international actors in 2005 was increased criticism among the Bosniak media, which traditionally supported the international quasi protectorate.

As of 2005, the rule of law in Bosnia hung in the balance. No one could reasonably claim that Bosnians did not enjoy a measure of increased security after signing the peace accord. Nor could it be said that Bosnia's police and courts were fully professional, efficient, or independent. Whether it came to providing security for returning refugees, arresting and trying war crimes suspects, combating organized crime, or indicting corrupt officials, justice still depended on the intervention of Bosnia's international guardians.

NOTES

1. For a detailed account and analysis of the rise of nationalism in Yugoslavia and the Slovenian, Croatian, and Bosnian wars, see Laura Silber and Allan Little, *The Death of Yugoslavia* (London: Penguin Books, BBC Books, 1995), accompanied by a BBC documentary television series. For a précis of the events of 1992–95, in the overall context of the history of Bosnia over the past few hundred years, see Noel Malcolm, *Bosnia: A Short History* (London: Macmillan, 1994).

2. For a description of these ethnic cleansing campaigns, see the Amended Indictment against Radovan Karadžić, International Criminal Tribunal for the Former Yugoslavia (ICTY), http://www.un.org/icty/.

3. For a detailed account of the negotiations at the Wright Patterson Air Force Base leading to the final agreement, see Richard Holbrooke, *To End a War* (New York: Random House, 1998).

4. The Bosnian Serb Army (VRS) remained accountable to, dependent on, and institutionally linked to the army of neighboring Yugoslavia, while the Croat component of the Federation Army maintained close ties with the Croatian Army.

5. The authority of the state institutions is outlined in the BiH constitution, General Framework Agreement for Peace, Annex 4, Article III, paragraph 1.

6. Ibid., Annex 7. Article II of Annex 7 called on all local authorities to "create in their territories the political, economic, and social conditions conducive to the voluntary return and harmonious reintegration of refugees and displaced persons, without preference for any particular group." For the full text of the agreement, see the Office of the High Representative, http://www.ohr.int.

7. Ibid., Annex 6, Chapter One, Article I.

8. Ibid., Annex 4, Article II, paragraph 2.

9. Ibid., Annex 6.

10. Ibid., Annex 11, Article III, paragraph 1.

11. According to the General Framework Agreement for Peace, Annex 11, Article V: Failure to Cooperate, "Any obstruction of or interference with IPTF activities, failure or refusal to comply with an IPTF request, or other failure to meet the Parties' responsibilities or other obligations in this Agreement, shall constitute a failure to cooperate with the IPTF. . . . The IPTF Commissioner will notify the High Representative and inform the IFOR Commander of failures to cooperate with the IPTF. The IPTF Commissioner may request that the High Representative take appropriate steps upon receiving such notifications, including calling such failures to the attention of the Parties, convening the Joint Civilian Commission, and consulting with the United Nations, relevant states, and international organizations on further responses."

12. Dayton's chief architect, U.S. diplomat Richard Holbrooke, identified the weak IPTF mandate as one of the agreement's greatest flaws. Holbrooke, *To End a War,* 362.

13. The Prijedor chief of police and a number of other officers were indicted by the ICTY for their role in the ethnic cleansing of Prijedor. See Indictment against Simo Drljača and Milan Kovačević, International Criminal Tribunal for the Former Yugoslavia. For all public indictments, see ICTY, www.un.org/icty/.

14. The role of Bosnian Serb police and military units in the Srebrenica massacre is detailed in Jan Willem Honig and Norbert Both, *Srebrenica: Record of a War Crime* (London: Penguin Books, 1996).

15. UNMIBH developed principles of democratic policing drawing on input from U.S. policing expert David Bayley and *Principles and Procedures in Democratic Policing,* a booklet prepared by the government of the United Kingdom (1997).

16. UNMIBH, press release, "End of a Mandate," December 31, 2002.

17. European Union Police Mission, *EUPM Overview,* December 20, 2002, http://ue.eu.int/eupm/pdf/EUPMoverview.pdf.

18. UNMIBH, press release, "End of a Mandate."

19. *Financial, Organisational and Administrative Assessment of the BiH Police Forces and the State Border Service, Final Assessment Report* (Sarajevo: Ministry of Justice of Bosnia and Herzegovina Office of the Coordinator for Public Administration Reform, 2004).

20. International Crisis Group, *War Criminals in Bosnia's Republika Srpska,* Balkans Report No. 103 (Sarajevo/Washington/Brussels: International Crisis Group, November 2, 2000), http://www.crisisweb.org.

21. A report issued in January 2003 found that out of some sixty-four officers suspended by the United Nations between October 2002 and January 2003 for suspected involvement in war crimes, not one had been brought to justice, while most had never even been investigated by local prosecutors. *Bosnia: Police Blamed for War Crimes* (London: Institute for War and Peace Reporting, January 2, 2003).

22. In eastern Republika Srpska, the homes of returning Bosniak police officers were attacked with hand grenades, and some Bosniak officers admitted to UNMIBH that they did not feel secure. International Crisis Group, *Policing the Police in Bosnia: A Further Reform Agenda,* Balkans Report No. 130 (Sarajevo/Washington/Brussels: International Crisis Group, May 10, 2002), 42, http://www.crisisweb.org.

23. For a detailed account of the Police Commissioners Project, political obstructions to it, and compromises made by the United Nations, see International Crisis Group, *Policing the Police in Bosnia.*

24. European Commission, *Report on Bosnia's Readiness to Negotiate a Stabilization and Association Agreement,* 2003.

25. European Union, *Financial, Organisational, and Administrative Assessment of the BiH Police Forces and the State Border Service, Final Assessment Report.* (Sarajevo, June 2004)

26. Christopher Patten, then European Union commissioner for enlargement, letter to Adnan Terzić, chair of the Council of Ministers of Bosnia and Herzegovina, November 16, 2004.

27. *Final Report on the Work of the Police Restructuring Commission of Bosnia and Herzegovina,* December 2004, http://www.ohr.int.

28. The average German judge hears three times as many cases per year as the average Bosnian judge. International Crisis Group, *Courting Disaster: The Misrule of Law in Bosnia and Herzegovina*, Balkans Report No. 127 (Sarajevo/Washington/Brussels: International Crisis Group, March 25, 2002), 13, http://www.crisisweb.org.

29. For an excellent review and critique of international judicial reform efforts up until the end of 2001, see Charles Erdmann, *Assessment of the Current Mandate of the Independent Judicial Commission and Review of the Judicial Reform Follow-on Mission for Bosnia and Herzegovina*, November 2001, http://www.esiweb.org/bridges/bosnia/Erdmann_IJC.pdf.

30. The officially released document *Jobs and Justice: Our Agenda* billed itself as an agreement among the international community, the BiH Council of Ministers, and the entity governments, but it was clearly crafted by the international community. Between January 1 and May 25, 2003, the high representative had imposed fifteen decisions in the sphere of judicial reform.

31. Office of the High Representative, *Jobs and Justice*, 19.

32. International Crisis Group, *War Criminals in Bosnia's Republika Srpska*, Balkans Report No. 103 (Sarajevo/Washington/Brussels: International Crisis Group, November 2, 2000), http://www.crisisweb.org.

33. UN Development Programme, *Early Warning System, Bosnia and Herzegovina*, quarterly report, July–September 2002, http://www.undp.ba.

34. International Crisis Group, *Courting Disaster*, 37.

35. For a full analysis of the shortcomings of judicial peer review in Bosnia, see Erdmann, *Assessment of the Current Mandate of the Independent Judicial Commission and Review of the Judicial Reform Follow-on Mission for Bosnia and Herzegovina*.

36. *Final Report of the Independent Judicial Commission, January 2001– March 2004*, November 2004, http://www.hjpc.ba/reports/pdf/final_report_eng.PDF. This report describes in detail the implementation of general reappointment, the establishment of the HJPCs, the restructuring of the court system, and legal reform of court procedures.

37. Ibid.

38. Ibid.

39. Bosnia has three basic levels of elected government above the municipality: the central state, the two entities (the Republika Srpska and the Federation), and the ten cantons of the Federation. Each of these has its own legislature. This means that, including the assembly of the internationally administered Brčko District, Bosnia has fourteen lawmaking bodies. Thus the first obstacle to countrywide judicial reform has been the need to pass analogous laws in all of these largely independent parliaments. To speed the process of legislative harmonization, the high representative frequently imposed identical laws at all the different levels of government, allowing the parliaments to "ratify" these laws in their own good time.

40. The ICTY was established by UN Security Council Resolution 827. For more background and information about ICTY proceedings, see http://www.un.org/icty.

41. "Key Figures of ICTY Cases," July 27, 2005.

42. Ibid.

43. This report was amended in 2004, under significant pressure from the OHR.

44. International Criminal Tribunal for the Former Yugloslavia, Joint Motion for Consideration of Plea Agreement between Momir Nikolić and the Office of the Prosecutor, Annex A, "Statement of Facts and Acceptance of Responsibility," May 6, 2003.

45. Ibid.

46. Judith Armatta, "Srebrenica Guilty Pleas May Have Repercussions," Coalition for International Justice, May 21, 2003, http://www.cij.org.

47. Stacy Sullivan, "Bosnian Serbs Refuse to Confront Past" (London: Institute of War and Peace Reporting, May 15, 2003).

48. "Saradnja sa Tribunalom," *Reporter*, January 28, 2003.

49. As part of its strategy to close the proceedings of the court by 2008 (excluding appeals), the UN Security Council decided on a strategy to transfer the cases of all low- and mid-ranking indictees to domestic courts.

50. In a 2002 report, Amnesty International pointed to the 17,000 unsolved "disappearances" from the 1992–95 war, calling on the EUPM and other international agencies involved in justice reforms to make the resolution of these cases and the prosecution of their perpetrators a priority. Amnesty International, *Bosnia-Herzegovina: Honouring the Ghosts: Confronting Impunity for "Disappearances,"* March 5, 2003, http://web.amnesty.org/library/Index/EN GEUR630042003?open&of=ENG-BIH. "Aside from awarding long-overdue justice to all victims, prosecuting the perpetrators of concrete cases of 'disappearances' will be the real litmus test for the comprehensive, lengthy and costly process of reform of the Bosnian judiciary and law enforcement agencies." Amnesty International, press release, "Bosnia-Herzegovina: Time to End Impunity for 'Disappearances,'" March 5, 2003.

51. Statute of the International Criminal Tribunal for the Former Yugoslavia, Article 9.

52. An additional 3,021 were sent back because of insufficient evidence or inability to determine the sufficiency of evidence. Statistics cited in Organization for Security and Cooperation in Europe (OSCE), *War Crimes Trials before* the Domestic Courts of Bosnia and Herzegovina, Progress and Obstacles, March 2005, http://www.osce.org/press_rel/2005/pdf_documents/03-4802-bih1.pdf.

53. Ibid.

54. OHR official engaged in legal reform, interview with author, Sarajevo, May 5, 2003.

55. Office of the High Representative, press release, "Joint Preliminary Conclusions of OHR and ICTY Experts' Conference on Scope of BiH War-Crimes Prosecutions," January 15, 2003.

56. Information was provided by the State Court of Bosnia and Herzegovina.

57. Cited in Organization for Security and Cooperation in Europe, *War Crimes Trials before the Domestic Courts of Bosnia and Herzegovina, Progress and Obstacles.*

58. Amnesty International, *Bosnia-Herzegovina: Shelving Justice—War Crimes Prosecutions in Paralysis* (Amnesty International, November 2004).

59. Cited in Organization for Security and Cooperation in Europe, *War Crimes Trials before the Domestic Courts of Bosnia and Herzegovina, Progress and Obstacles.*

60. Boris Divjak, ed., *Corruption Perception Study 2004* (Banja Luka/Sarajevo: Transparency International BiH, 2004).

61. Ibid.

62. UN Development Programme, *Early Warning System*, annual report 2004.

63. Helsinki Committee for Human Rights in Bosnia and Herzegovina, *Report on the Status of Human Rights for Bosnia and Herzegovina (January–December 2004)* (Sarajevo: Helsinki Committee for Human Rights in Bosnia and Herzegovina, 2004).

64. SFOR intelligence official, interview with author, Sarajevo, July 2002.

65. Joint press release of the Helsinki Committee for Human Rights in Bosnia and Herzegovina and the Helsinki Committee for Human Rights in Republika Srpska, February 28, 2003.

66. Helsinki Committee for Human Rights in Bosnia and Herzegovina, *Report on the Status of Human Rights for Bosnia and Herzegovina (January–December 2002)* (Sarajevo: Helsinki Committee for Human Rights in Bosnia and Herzegovina, 2002).

67. Ibid.

68. Helsinki Committee for Human Rights in Bosnia and Herzegovina, *Report on the Status of Human Rights for Bosnia and Herzegovina (January–December 2004)*.

69. Ibid.

70. Ibid.

71. Paddy Ashdown, address to London Conference on Organised Crime, November 25, 2002.

72. UN Development Programme, *Early Warning System: Bosnia and Herzegovina*, quarterly report July–September 2002, table IV, 35.

73. The Bosnian convertible mark is pegged to the euro (1 KM = 0.51 EUR) so its value in U.S. dollars fluctuates with the dollar/euro conversion.

74. Paddy Ashdown, address to the BiH House of Representatives, December 17, 2002.

75. Office of the High Representative, press release, "High Representative Issues Decisions on Special Auditor for the Federation and RS," August 1, 2002.

8

From Elation to Disappointment

Justice and Security Reform in Kosovo

Colette Rausch

WHEN CALLED ON TO RESTORE STABILITY TO POSTCONFLICT regions, policymakers often restrict their reforms to the judges, prosecutors, and law enforcement personnel and institutions that make up the judicial system. However, in doing so they disregard the political, economic, and cultural environment in which the justice and law enforcement reforms take place. This can put the entire reform project in jeopardy. Further, sustainable reforms require not only a context-sensitive approach but also the genuine, informed, and coordinated efforts of all participants, whether domestic or foreign.

BACKDROP TO WAR AND REFORM

In 1999 the Serbian government of President Slobodan Milošević launched a campaign of ethnic cleansing that drove roughly half of the majority ethnic Albanians from the province of Kosovo. NATO's seventy-eight-day war ousted Serbia's state presence entirely from the province in June 1999. In response, the United Nations Security Council created the United Nations Interim Administration Mission in Kosovo (UNMIK), which would act as the transitional authority for administering the territory. Although Kosovo remained under Serbia's juridical sovereignty, the United Nations exercised de facto state authority.

Milošević's actions were the culmination of more than a decade of oppression designed to strengthen his own political position by stoking Serbian nationalism while quelling Kosovo Albanian aspirations of independence.[1] In March 1989 Milošević rescinded Kosovo's status as an autonomous province of Serbia and a federal unit of Yugoslavia and amended the constitution to place the police and courts under Serbia's control. Previously, the people of Kosovo had enjoyed some autonomy in the selection and administration of their own systems of justice and policing. The Milošević regime forced many Kosovo Albanians from jobs in the public sector, including most Kosovo Albanian police and judicial personnel, although ethnic Albanians made up 90 percent of the territory's population. Moreover, international observers found that "Serbian authorities in Kosovo were responsible for the torture and killing of ethnic Albanians in detention," as well as a high number of arbitrary arrests, prosecutions, and incarcerations.[2]

Kosovo Albanians initially responded to these difficulties in two ways. First, a passive resistance campaign emerged, orchestrated by Ibrahim Rugova, leader of the Democratic League of Kosova (LDK) political party. Second, the LDK led in the establishment of a parallel government with a taxation mechanism, parliament, university, law school, and health care system, alongside traditional conflict resolution mechanisms based on customary practices.[3]

With the signing of the Dayton Peace Accords to end the war in Bosnia and Herzegovina in 1995, Kosovo Albanians hoped the international community would begin to address their plight. Believing the accords rewarded Serbian aggression by recognizing the self-declared and Serb-dominated Republika Srpska (RS) within Bosnia and Herzegovina, some Kosovo Albanians thought that violent tactics were necessary to gain autonomy. The Kosovo Liberation

Army (KLA) was formed in the early 1990s, and Serbian police posts and patrols came under increasing attack. Following unrelated civil unrest in Albania, arms depots were raided and many of the arms ended up in Kosovo in 1997. With the influx of arms, KLA attacks increased, eliciting a strong response from Belgrade in early 1998. Belgrade's aggressive military and police crackdown led to accusations of widespread human rights violations and atrocities, ranging from looting and arbitrary arrests to rape, torture, kidnapping, and summary executions.[4]

In 1998 the Organization for Security and Cooperation in Europe (OSCE) sent monitors to Kosovo as part of the Kosovo Verification Mission (KVM). Despite this mission and several efforts to sustain peace negotiations (most notably the proposed "Rambouillet Agreement," signed by the Kosovo Albanian delegation but not the Serbian delegation in Rambouillet, France, in February 1999), in March 1999 Serbian offensives led to a punitive air campaign by NATO, the first war in the alliance's fifty-year history.

Planning and Organizing the International Mission

Before the NATO air campaign ended in June 1999, much debate took place among the international community over who should be responsible for rebuilding Kosovo at the conflict's end. Although the United Nations seemed to be a natural choice for overall control and coordination of the civilian mission, some opposed giving it the full civilian mandate because of its perceived failures in other missions.

Ultimately, member states and organizations involved agreed to create a UN mission, but also to provide roles for the OSCE and the European Union (EU), as well as for the United Nations High Commissioner for Refugees (UNHCR). NATO, not the United Nations, would have full and exclusive operational control over the Kosovo Force (KFOR), the mission's military presence. After the NATO-led air campaign, the UN Security Council passed Resolution 1244[5] authorizing the secretary-general to establish an international civil presence in Kosovo. This presence was directed to provide an interim administration for Kosovo under which the people of Kosovo could enjoy substantial autonomy within the Federal Republic of Yugoslavia (FRY). It was also directed to provide a transitional administration while establishing and overseeing the development of provisional democratic self-governing institutions to ensure conditions for a peaceful and normal life for all inhabitants of Kosovo.[6] UNMIK would be led by a special representative of the secretary-general (SRSG), who was given executive and legislative power to run Kosovo.[7]

According to its mandate, UNMIK's responsibilities included

- "performing basic civilian administration functions"
- "organizing and overseeing the development of provisional institutions for democratic and autonomous self-government pending a political settlement, including the holding of elections"
- transferring administrative responsibilities to these institutions "while overseeing and supporting the consolidation of Kosovo's local provisional institutions and other peace-building activities"
- "maintaining civil law and order, including establishing local police forces and in the meantime, through deployment of international police personnel to serve in Kosovo"
- "protecting and promoting human rights" and "assuring the safe and unimpeded return of all refugees and displaced persons to their homes in Kosovo"[8]

To accomplish these duties, four "pillars" were created under the umbrella of UNMIK with the SRSG at the helm. Under Pillar I, the UNHCR was responsible for managing the humanitarian assistance programs.[9] Pillar II, known as the Civil Administration pillar, was assigned to the United Nations. Its functions included establishing the local judiciary, international police, and correctional system as well as providing utilities and water services, paying government employees, and issuing license plates and business licenses. Pillar III was assigned to the OSCE, responsible for institution- and capacity-building functions, such as providing local judicial and police training and development, supporting democratization activities, developing the media, conducting elections, and monitoring, reporting on, and educating the public on human rights issues. Pillar IV, Economic Reconstruction, was assigned to the European Union.

When the FRY armed forces left Kosovo in June 1999, so did nearly all ethnic Serbian police and judicial personnel, creating a vacuum. Had the Rambouillet Agreement been in force, the Yugoslav security forces would have had a continued presence with an international police force. Furthermore, the existing judicial system would have continued, with reforms providing for equitable treatment of all inhabitants of Kosovo. However, Resolution 1244 significantly altered the role envisioned for KFOR and the international police as they became the entire administrative and security apparatus, rather than a part of it, as provided for in the Rambouillet Agreement.

When Milošević abruptly agreed to stop his military campaign, KFOR and the civilian mission faced additional challenges not covered by the Rambouillet Agreement, including displaced populations, the investigation of war crimes, violence and retaliation by Kosovo Albanians against ethnic minorities (in particular, Serbs and Roma who were seen as collaborators with the Kosovo Serbs), and infrastructural damage.

Resolution 1244 was developed while decisions on the civilian planning side were being made with little reliable information about the condition of Kosovo's courts and the number of judges, prosecutors, and defense attorneys willing to return to Kosovo. The possibility of using foreign nationals in this process was also raised. While the use of international judges and prosecutors was ultimately rejected, it was decided that international civilian police (CIVPOL) would be used to provide security until local police could be trained and deployed. Within this general framework the United Nations, with KFOR engagement, began the task of rebuilding the Kosovo judicial and law enforcement system and structures.

REBUILDING THE JUDICIAL SYSTEM

Overview

When KFOR and a small number of UNMIK civilian personnel arrived in June 1999, they faced the daunting task of trying to maintain security in an environment filled with violence and ethnic hatred. The unexpectedly swift return of approximately 800,000 Kosovo Albanian refugees, plus a surge in violence directed against ethnic minorities, posed immediate challenges. Through either force or intimidation, many members of these minority groups were evicted from their homes and businesses, until the number of ethnically mixed villages decreased to the point that most Kosovo Serbs were congregated in "Serb enclaves" protected by KFOR soldiers. They had to be escorted by the KFOR troops to get supplies or visit their families. By mid-June the majority of Kosovo Serbs had fled the province. The existing organized-crime groups—many now linked to the former KLA—were quick to exploit the judicial and security vacuum. As a result, several concerted efforts to force Serbs out of Kosovo, attributed to former KLA members, were rooted in financial motives as well as ethnic hatred.

These conflicts, as well as jurisdictional clashes between the United Nations and the OSCE, UNMIK's slow deployment of CIVPOL, and various other time-consuming political battles, constituted the main challenges for KFOR and UNMIK in their efforts to rebuild Kosovo's disintegrated judicial and security system.

Personnel shortages dogged the UN mission from its inception, leading to violations of international human rights standards (through extended detention without trial) and thereby undermining the legitimacy of the international mission.[10] As public faith eroded in the absence of effective control of crime, KFOR's credibility suffered and investigations were further hampered. When judges issued summons, requested that evidence be gathered, or directed that witnesses be questioned, KFOR had difficulty performing the tasks, especially before CIVPOL began patrols in August 1999.

These problems contributed to increased lawlessness, which continued even after CIVPOL began assuming responsibility for law-and-order policing activities in the province. Attacks on Kosovo Serbs increased, organized-crime activities against Kosovo Albanian businesses increased, Kosovo Serb judges resigned citing intimidation and threats, and accusations of Kosovo Albanian judges showing bias against Kosovo Serbs became the norm. Some Kosovo Albanian arrestees were allegedly released when former KLA members, sometimes in uniform, intimidated judges; one prosecutor was threatened with execution if he did not secure the release of three detainees.[11] KFOR, having witnessed or been the victim of the criminal activity itself, complained that the local judges were releasing dangerous suspects, including some accused of attacking KFOR soldiers, and well-founded reports of corruption began to spread. These were the challenges that UNMIK and KFOR faced in the first few months of the mission.

The Beginning of Reforms

This section addresses implementation and progress of reforms from June 1999 through March 2002.

Legal Framework: Applicable Law and Legislative Reform

UNMIK Regulation 1999/1 established that laws applicable in Kosovo as of March 24, 1999, to the extent they did not conflict with internationally recognized human rights standards, would continue to be enforced. This was interpreted to mean that the FRY and Serbian laws would be in effect, but not the Kosovo Criminal Code because it had, in effect, been repealed by Milošević when he eliminated Kosovo's autonomy in 1989. This interpretation was strongly protested, especially by the Kosovo Albanian judges and prosecutors, who argued that the Kosovo Criminal Code should still be in effect because Milošević's elimination of autonomy was illegal. At this point, Kosovo Serbs made up but a small handful of the prosecutors and judges. Kosovo Albanian judges refused to implement the regulation they saw as embracing the Serbian government's repressive laws. Eventually, the United Nations acquiesced and passed Regulation 1999/24, which adopted the Kosovo law as it existed in 1989 before Milošević eliminated Kosovo's autonomy, thus allowing the Kosovo Criminal Code to be applied. In practice, however, the few remaining Kosovo Serb judges continued to apply the 1999 law, thus resulting in the prosecution of individuals under different "applicable laws" depending on the ethnicity of the judge handling the case.

Although this particular dispute had now been resolved, many legal and practical issues remained. For example, innumerable challenges confronted the international law-and-order apparatus that had assumed responsibility overnight. KFOR legal officers educated themselves as best they could but struggled to convey this knowledge to the soldiers themselves. Thus, KFOR initially concentrated on addressing only serious crimes (principally ethnic violence and the incitement of public disturbances) and allowed member nations to set the tone for maintaining law and order in their designated sectors,

despite the inevitable contradictions and discrepancies this occa-
sioned.[12] Similarly, the slow-to-deploy CIVPOL contingent had little
or no familiarity with local laws and inconsistent understanding of
international human rights law, relying instead on its own disparate
legal traditions. Last, the vast majority of KFOR, CIVPOL, and
international civilian staff were unable to speak the local languages
and thus relied on interpreters, who had varying levels of competency, in all justice matters from patrols to investigations and from
questioning witnesses to trials.

The United Nations, acting as a territory's sole executive and
legislative authority for the first time in its history, encountered difficulties of its own. Initially, the United Nations did a poor job of making laws and regulations accessible. Copies of applicable law and
international human rights standards were not readily available to
CIVPOL in English, let alone in Albanian and Serbian. In addition,
UN departments, including the UN Department of Judicial Affairs,
renamed in 2002 the UN Department of Justice, issued "circulars"
that provided clarification or interpretation of regulations but failed
to disseminate them consistently. Although the United Nations produced an "Official Gazette" [13] containing translated versions of many
regulations issued through 1999, the "Official Gazette" for 2001 and
2002 could be found only in English on the UN website, clearly inadequate for widespread usage in Kosovo. In the legal realm, meanwhile, several bilateral donors, multilateral actors, and international
NGOs worked together to try to assist the United Nations, with
varying degrees of success. For instance, realizing the lack of a UN
lawmaking process, representatives from the American Bar Association's Central and East European Law Initiative (ABA CEELI) and
the United States Department of Justice (U.S. DOJ) sent the SRSG
a memo discussing the need to resolve the applicable law issue and
the importance of securing local input into the legislative reform
process.[14] In August 1999 the SRSG established the Joint Advisory
Council for Legislative Matters (JAC/LM), composed mostly of local
experts with representatives from the United Nations, the OSCE,
and the Council of Europe.

However, efforts to involve local experts in legal reform fared
poorly. The JAC/LM's vision was to prepare and suggest reform pack-

ages in the areas of criminal law, property law, civil law, administrative law, and commercial law. Thus the JAC/LM's first priority was to prepare a revised criminal code and criminal procedure code in compliance with international human rights standards. Of particular concern were arrest procedures, detention, and access to counsel. Unfortunately, the JAC/LM's vision never came to fruition because of a combination of political, organizational, and resource issues. At the same time, a variety of working groups, composed almost entirely of international actors, convened to draft various regulations, including one to address detention and access to counsel issues. These working groups often failed to coordinate or consult with the JAC/LM, whose criminal procedure code draft was addressing the same issues.

Compounding the problem of lack of local involvement and coordination in legal reform efforts, the United Nations often chose to rely almost exclusively on its own legal advisers and outside experts who submitted various draft regulations. As a result, much of the legislative work was done in an ad hoc fashion: local input was marginalized, JAC/LM participants were expected to rubber-stamp UN proposals, and some controversial regulations[15] were signed by the SRSG without consulting the JAC/LM. Consequently, some of the criminal provisions were inconsistent with the local legal system, some international human rights experts argued that they were inconsistent with international standards, and local judges and prosecutors did not always interpret them consistently.

Despite the obstacles it faced, the JAC/LM finally produced reformed criminal and criminal procedure codes, which were submitted to the United Nations for legal review in 2001. However, as of April 2002, they had not moved beyond this stage.

The Courts, Judges, Prosecutors, and Defense Attorneys

Immediately after the war, Kosovo was divided into five sectors (American, British, French, German, and Italian), and KFOR took on law-and-order functions. In what became known as the emergency phase, the SRSG created the Joint Advisory Council on Provisional Judicial Appointments to make recommendations to the SRSG for appointments of judges and prosecutors for three-month terms.[16] On June 30, 1999, a small number of appointments were made, and beginning in July, a team of judges and prosecutors traveled around Kosovo holding detention hearings. KFOR provided the transport and logistical support and conducted the initial arrests, investigations, and detention proceedings according to each sector's military procedures. KFOR then turned over the detainees to the local civilian emergency judicial system for detention hearings. From June 30 to October 1999, the SRSG appointed a total of fifty-five judges and prosecutors. Of these, thirty-six were criminal law judges, five were civil judges, and fourteen were prosecutors; seven were Serbs. By October, however, none of the Serbs remained,[17] having either resigned or departed, some after receiving threats. In fall 1999 CIVPOL began assuming law-and-order duties alongside KFOR.

In September 1999 the Advisory Judicial Commission (AJC) was created to replace the Joint Advisory Council on Provisional Judicial Appointments.[18] It began its work on October 27, 1999, and on December 13, 1999, submitted to the SRSG a list of recommendations for new appointments. The list contained 328 judges and prosecutors and 238 lay judges.[19] The OSCE reported that the insufficient number of judges and prosecutors and the lack of multiethnic participation presented serious challenges to the proper functioning of a judicial system.[20] Nevertheless, on December 29, 2000, the SRSG appointed 296 judges and prosecutors and 238 lay judges, including two Serbs and eight other minorities (six Bosniaks and two Turks) as judges and one Serb and two other minorities (one Roma and one Turk) as prosecutors.[21] However, one Serb judge refused to travel to court, citing security concerns. By September 2000 the number of judges and prosecutors had increased to 405, but the lack of Serb participation in the judiciary continued. The OSCE provided basic training on international human rights standards to the newly appointed judges and prosecutors.

Largely inactive after its first few months of work, the AJC was criticized by international and local actors, who concluded that its members had appointed judges based on personal relationships and ethnic background (in this case, Kosovo Albanian) rather than merit. In addition, the AJC did not discipline a single judge or prosecutor for bias or corruption, despite eligible cases. Thus, in April 2001 the Kosovo Judicial and Prosecutorial Council (KJPC) replaced the AJC, with the authority to advise the SRSG on the appointment of judges, prosecutors, and lay judges. The new council also oversaw discipline and removal proceedings to assure the independence, competence, and impartiality of the judiciary.

On May 10, 2001, the KJPC's nine members were sworn in. The new panel consisted of five internationals and four locals: all current or former judges, prosecutors, lawyers, and legal professionals with human rights experience. Given the prior allegations of threats and intimidation, the United Nations decided that internationals would make up the majority of the KJPC for the short to medium term. It operated alongside a Judicial Inspection Unit (JIU) within UNMIK that in 2001 began investigations of alleged wrongdoing by judicial personnel.

Despite an ever-present lack of resources and a backlog of cases caused by caution within the KJPC, both the KJPC and the JIU functioned more successfully than their predecessor, the AJC. Their success is believed to have been largely due to the input of local officials in developing the KJPC and the JIU, and the mixture of international and local perspectives within the KJPC.

The new arrangement was not without its detractors, however. The OSCE questioned the lack of independence of the KJPC, charging that (1) the members of the KJPC were appointed by the same executive body, the SRSG, responsible for appointing the judiciary; (2) the KJPC could only recommend problematic officials' removal from office—the SRSG had to order the removal; and (3) judges and prosecutors had no right to a review of disciplinary actions lodged against them as there were no appellate procedures.[22] Nonetheless, by January 2001 UNMIK's Judicial Investigative Unit was conducting investigations of alleged judicial and prosecutorial misconduct and referring cases to the KJCP. As of January 2002, the KJPC had removed four judges from office and reprimanded two.[23]

Turf battles continued over assistance to the judiciary. Partly because the OSCE had a presence in Kosovo before NATO's air campaign, its Rule of Law Division handled tasks that arguably could have been within the responsibilities of the United Nations. In addition to training the judiciary and monitoring for human rights compliance (tasks that would be considered clearly within the OSCE's

mandate), the OSCE's Judicial Support Section (JSS) provided logistical support for the judiciary and helped interview and identify
judicial candidates. In practice, the OSCE carried out these tasks
because UN resources were insufficient. As the United Nations mission acquired more staff and became better able to assist the local
judiciary, the OSCE disbanded the JSS and turned over its tasks to
the United Nations' Department of Judicial Affairs in spring 2001.

As in many postwar situations, the courts had limited resources.
In addition, a few courts were not operational under UNMIK owing
to a lack of either security or facilities. In the first several months of
the mission, international organizations, including the United
Nations, sometimes took over court buildings and refused to vacate
them. Moreover, judges and prosecutors lacked basic equipment,
office supplies, and regular pay. Protests from various quarters soon
led to a reversal of these shortcomings, including by providing the
judiciary with "quick-start" packages (cars, generators, computers,
and other supplies). Still, salaries proved inadequate, and many judges
and prosecutors left to go into more lucrative private practice.

Despite a recruitment campaign,[24] the UN mission had a difficult time filling the vacancies and, as of March 2002, continued to
seek qualified candidates because of the departure of existing judiciary combined with a dearth of qualified lawyers owing to a ten-year
absence of bar exams in Kosovo. Attracting minority judges and
prosecutors also proved difficult. Kosovo Serb officials were reluctant
to accept appointments, because of either security concerns or the
fear that they would lose their pensions from Belgrade. Negotiations
through early 2002 had not resolved these issues, as Belgrade argued
that UNMIK could not provide the security and money needed to
attract the judges.

War Crimes and Ethnic Bias in the Judiciary

The prosecution of war crimes was discussed early in the mission,
and some thought that the International Criminal Tribunal for the
Former Yugoslavia (ICTY), created in 1994 in the wake of the Bosnian war, would hear all such cases. However, the ICTY made it clear
that it would prosecute only a handful of cases, leaving the remainder to the Kosovo court system, although, since the majority of war

crimes defendants were expected to be Serbs, and the Kosovo judiciary was nearly all Kosovo Albanians, the fairness of trials was questionable. As time went on, it became evident that Kosovo Serb suspects had neither sufficient access to counsel nor any prospect of a fair and unbiased hearing for their cases.[25]

At the same time, KFOR grew increasingly concerned that the judiciary was releasing dangerous Kosovo Albanians. Seeing no alternatives given the state of the judiciary, KFOR instituted "COMKFOR holds," a procedure whereby the commander of KFOR could approve continued detention, despite a release order from the local judiciary, if he believed the judiciary had acted improperly. The OSCE argued that since CIVPOL had primacy throughout Kosovo and a functioning judicial system was in place, there was little, if any, justification for COMKFOR holds. The OSCE further argued that "in the exceptional case where 'holds' are used, in line with international standards, there must be a legal mechanism whereby the detainee can challenge the lawfulness of his detention."[26]

A series of tragic events in February 2000 propelled UNMIK to scramble to find a more concrete solution to the injustices plaguing the local judiciary. A UNHCR bus of Serbs was attacked by a rocket near Mitrovica, prompting outbreaks of violence across the predominantly Serb enclave, in which at least eight people were killed and many more Kosovo Albanians driven into flight. After the judiciary released a group of ethnic Albanians accused of shooting at KFOR and at Serb apartments in Mitrovica, UNMIK sprang into action. According to William O'Neill, "Overnight, the UNMIK Legal Department, which often took months to issue the simplest regulation, presented Regulation 2000/6 for SRSG Kouchner's signature."[27] This regulation allowed for international judges and prosecutors to be appointed in the Mitrovica district. It was later amended by Regulation 2000/34 to allow appointment of international judges and prosecutors to all districts and the Supreme Court. Regulation 2000/64, passed in December 2000, permitted the creation of three-judge panels composed of a majority of international judges to handle sensitive cases.

National and international actors criticized both the substance and the process of approving Regulation 2000/64, while the United Nations defended the regulation as urgently needed, arguing that it could not wait for additional consultation. The Supreme Court and local judiciary complained that the measure had been implemented without consultation, that it infringed on the independent Kosovo judiciary, and that it had not been implemented through the proper channels (i.e., JAC/LM). The OSCE, which had been involved in the early stages of the drafting process, further argued that the regulation failed to establish criteria defining the applicability of the regulation to a certain case. It suggested that, to ensure judicial independence, an independent appointment committee or other mechanism, rather than the SRSG or UNMIK DOJ, appoint judges and prosecutors. However, despite these concerns, further modifications to Regulation 2000/64 to implement safeguards against interference by the executive branch had not been implemented by mid-2002.[28]

Beyond these procedural hurdles, several practical issues associated with the use of international judges and prosecutors also became factors: varying degrees of competency, different legal backgrounds, inadequate English-language skills, and lack of proficiency with the applicable law. Further complicating the mission were the short rotation times of a typical assignment in Kosovo. Each UN appointment term lasted for only six months, and thus many international judges and prosecutors left after completing just one term. Finally, a reduction in pay levels made it difficult to fill vacancies with qualified personnel.

In May 2001 UNMIK Pillar I, Police and Justice, was created. It brought together the police and justice sectors, which were previously under the authority of the civil administration (Pillar II). This action was aimed at linking the components of the judicial system (police, justice, and prisons) under one umbrella, allowing a consolidated approach to address security issues, including those involving organized crime and extremism. In addition to facilitating coordination within UNMIK, Pillar I was designed to facilitate coordination among the OSCE, KFOR, and other international organizations in Kosovo. However, as discussed later, from the beginning of the mission the division of responsibility between the OSCE and the United Nations for development of the local police force was not always clear and coordinated. The creation of Pillar I did not resolve this. In September and December 2001 joint meetings were held between UNMIK and KFOR to enhance law enforcement cooperation regarding organized crime, an overdue and important step in civil-military collaboration.

Under the Constitutional Framework promulgated on May 15, 2001,[29] most government functions were transferred to provisional Kosovo authorities elected in November 2001.[30] However, the justice and police sectors remained under the control of the international community via Pillar I. Some of the functions of the judicial system were transferred to the Ministry of Public Services; however, these functions were mainly administrative. Furthermore, although the Constitutional Framework envisaged that the Kosovo Assembly would be able to create laws, the SRSG held the ultimate authority to strike down any law. It was likely that the criminal justice sector, including legislative authority, would remain under the United Nations for some time to come. This situation clearly exemplified the tension between international goals of capacity building on the one hand and order maintenance on the other, in the face of threats to security such as organized crime and extremism.

In Kosovo, where the international community struggled to mount its own unprecedented interim administrative reforms, it largely failed to adequately prepare for handing over justice and security responsibilities to local authorities. Although the mandate of Pillar I included preparing for the eventual handover to local officials, there was no handover strategy as of mid-2002. For example, there was no bridge between local and international efforts, which operated in a parallel fashion. There was no vision for a future Kosovo Ministry of Justice or even a UNMIK-led Department of Justice that included local officials. As part of incorporating locals into governance, a local cohead of the Department of Justice position was in existence; however, this post was eliminated once elections occurred and the department reorganized.

As discussed later, UNMIK police had developed a strategy for the handover of policing to the Kosovo Police Service. Unfortunately, developments in the judiciary seemed to be moving in the opposite direction. As international police prepared to transfer functions to local police, the judicial system moved toward increased levels of international control.

Bar Exam and Judicial Training

Becoming a judge, prosecutor, or lawyer in Kosovo required success-ful completion of the bar exam followed by a period of apprentice-ship. However, the Milošević regime's elimination of the law school and the bar exam in the Albanian language after 1989 made finding qualified judges, prosecutors, and lawyers difficult.

In an effort to improve the qualifications of the local judiciary, the OSCE established the Kosovo Judicial Institute (KJI). Modeled after the system used by France, Italy, and Albania, the institute would serve as a magistrate's school, offering a program that candi-dates for judicial posts would be required to complete before gaining eligibility for appointment. It would also provide continuing legal education to judges and prosecutors.

Initially, the new institute focused on short-term, remedial training, emphasizing humanitarian law and international standards. The OSCE decided to staff it primarily with nationals to enhance its sustainability. After posting a public announcement and carefully screening and interviewing candidates, the OSCE selected some of the local judiciary's most respected members, including a local judge as codirector of the institute. However, despite this prestigious start, the KJI's development into a full-scale professional training institute rather than one providing ad hoc training courses lagged. The devel-opment of the Kosovo bar exam, however, moved forward in 2001, a perfect example of how ensuring sustainability through local partici-pation and ownership of judicial reform requires patience and con-cessions. It took UNMIK two and a half years to hold the first bar exam, the delay the result of a debate between UN officials and local members of the judiciary. To avoid possible bias, UN officials argued that the test must be administered by internationals under certain conditions. Members of the Kosovo legal community argued that it should be administered by locals according to applicable law. The sides became polarized and refused to compromise. These delays began to affect the drive to fill a growing number of vacancies in the judiciary. Eventually, an intermediary was brought in, and after lengthy negotiations, the first bar exam—administered by UNMIK-trained locals—took place in December 2001. It would be repeated every three months for sixty candidates.

Effective Assistance of Counsel

Early on, KFOR had to figure out how to deal with the issue of access to counsel by defendants. Many individuals claiming to be defense attorneys demanded access to their "clients." At the time, KFOR had no way of determining the validity of such claims. Equally frustrating was the difficulty KFOR encountered trying to provide legal counsel for those detained without representation. Making matters more difficult was the fact that, while the international community had focused almost entirely on judges and prosecutors in its reform efforts, little attention was given to defense attorneys. As a result, defense attorneys had few options for improving their skills. To remedy this, in April 2001, the Criminal Defense Resource Center (CDRC) was created by the OSCE and began working in a limited capacity from the OSCE headquarters in Pristina. The goal of the CDRC was to support the Chamber of Advocates, a local bar association that boasted 186 paying members. It received nongovernmental status from UNMIK in May 2001 and moved into its own office space in October 2001 after receiving funding from the United States.

The CDRC came to serve as an invaluable resource for local defense counsel, providing access to relevant international instruments and research material related to the rights of accused, case preparation and research, and help challenging violations of international standards in criminal matters. Initially, the CDRC met with some resistance. Some believed that the CDRC was a thinly veiled attempt to create a parallel system to represent Kosovo Serb defendants in war crimes cases or that it would be staffed with international lawyers who would push aside the local lawyers and actually represent clients in court. This resistance persisted until it became clear that the CDRC aided all defense attorneys and accused, regardless of ethnic origin, and that the international lawyers who staffed it would be acting in an advisory capacity only.

Legal System Monitoring

To implement its human rights monitoring mandate, the OSCE established the Legal System Monitoring Section (LSMS) in July 1999. It quickly grew from an organization with just a few staff members to one with international monitors in every district, supported by a headquarters in Pristina. The LSMS became a tool for monitoring progress in the judicial arena. Its report reviewing the second six months of the mission, from February 1 to July 31, 2000,[31] noted several problems, including lack of knowledge of human rights standards; limited, weak, and ethnically biased access to defense counsel; and inadequate prosecution of sexual violence.

The report gave rise to tensions between the OSCE and the United Nations, sparking a debate about the appropriate role of the OSCE's monitoring and whether its reporting should be made public. Eventually tensions eased, a joint OSCE and United Nations working group was established to address the LSMS report recommendations, and new reports were issued in April and October 2001.[32] These reports acknowledged progress made as well as pointing out continuing deficiencies, such as the need for greater emphasis on alternatives to pretrial detention of juveniles, appropriate detention facilities for mentally ill individuals, and improved access to defense attorneys.

However, these reports also claimed that the United Nations lacked the resources and motivation to combat problems of organized crime in Kosovo, especially the growing problem of illegal trafficking in women.[33] Despite aggressive antitrafficking provisions, the creation of a CIVPOL Specialized Unit, and redoubled effort by law enforcement, the resulting impact on trafficking in women was minimal. Rather than arrest traffickers during brothel raids, CIVPOL would sometimes round up these trafficked women instead, revictimizing them and leaving free their captors. Compounding the problem, judges and prosecutors often took a casual approach to cases of sexual crimes and resisted prosecuting them effectively.

The LSMS report also raised concerns about the ongoing problem of extrajudicial detentions by KFOR. Originally, in 1999, COMKFOR holds had been intended as a temporary stopgap measure to support the fledgling judicial system. KFOR, however, had begun to use the practice in 2001 to prevent hostilities from escalating in the Former Yugoslav Republic of Macedonia (FYROM) and southern Serbia by restricting the flow of insurgents across Kosovo's borders. KFOR justified the holds by arguing that Resolution 1244 mandated that it ensure a safe and secure environment in Kosovo. The LSMS maintained that nothing could justify indefinitely detaining a large number of persons without independent review. Finally, the LSMS had also expressed concerns about SRSG executive orders authorizing extrajudicial detentions. The SRSG had sometimes issued executive orders to detain even after a court, and in some cases a court composed of international judges, had ordered an individual released for lack of evidence. The LSMS argued that such executive orders violated the principle of judicial independence. Further, executive orders to detain lacked basis in local or international law when they failed to provide for judicial review.

The Council of Europe, Amnesty International, the UN Office of the High Commissioner for Human Rights, and other international organizations raised concerns over the human rights issues involved. The Ombudsperson Institution in Kosovo issued a report concluding executive orders to detain "do not conform with recognized international standards."[34] As criticism of these executive orders mounted, the United Nations convened a special panel of internationals with appropriate security clearances to review sensitive evidence in a case against four suspects and determine whether continued detention was warranted.[35] The goal was to provide enough time for the regular investigation to continue so that evidence admissible in court could be obtained, the point being that eventually the suspects would be tried in a court and that executive orders to detain would be a temporary measure. The Ombudsperson Institution in Kosovo argued that establishing the commission did not remedy the situation and that the detention was still contrary to international standards.[36] The special panel determined that there was enough evidence to continue to hold the suspects for a specified amount of time, but eventually the investigation failed to obtain enough court-admissible evidence to try three of the four suspects, so the three were released. As of March 2002, no further executive order to detain had been issued.

International Civilian Police

As outlined previously, the United Nations' and member countries' lack of adequate deployment capabilities hampered the introduction of CIVPOL into Kosovo. Further complications were introduced by the more ambitious scope (in terms of jurisdiction and primacy over local police forces) of the Kosovo operation compared with previous CIVPOL missions.

The United Nations responded positively on a number of fronts. Its recruitment and deployment of CIVPOL resources were accomplished faster than ever before. To address its legacy of quality control problems, the United Nations also sought to prescreen candidates from some countries, recruiting better-qualified candidates than it had for previous missions. Finally, special units deployed specifically for riot control and area security helped fill a gap usually left between military troops and civilian police.

However, these positive moves were not enough. The "accelerated" recruitment process for CIVPOL remained slow. By March 2000 only 2,000 of the authorized 4,700 positions for UNMIK had been filled.[37] Despite the screening, some CIVPOL officers still proved incompetent and had to be repatriated. Beyond these difficulties, other factors also adversely affected CIVPOL formation; for instance, the requirement that CIVPOL officers carry arms for their executive functions dissuaded some countries from contributing police officers.[38] A few CIVPOL officers complained that some of their colleagues were assigned to the mission because they were politically connected or were unwelcome at home, and others complained that most of CIVPOL's work was being done by a small number of highly motivated individuals, instead of by everyone carrying his or her fair share. As of 2002, the disparity between those with adequate motivation, training, or experience and those without such qualities continued. Kosovo Albanians and Serbs freely commented on the contrast between those CIVPOL officers whom they viewed as committed and helpful and those they did not. They confessed trust in officers coming from countries with a history of professional and democratic policing and resented the presence of those from countries known for corruption and/or abuse.

The first CIVPOL contingent arrived on June 28, 1999, but it was only an advance team to plan and prepare for the arrival of the larger CIVPOL force. The first joint KFOR/CIVPOL patrol did not take place until the first week of August 1999. CIVPOL assumed primary responsibility ("primacy") for law enforcement in Pristina on August 27, 1999. At this time, there were just 774 CIVPOL officers, with 663 in Pristina. Although CIVPOL strength was to reach slightly more than 1,000 by September 7, 1999, and grow steadily from there to more than 4,400,[39] policing operations in many parts of the country still required substantial personnel support from KFOR in 2002—a situation regarded as problematic by KFOR planners.

In addition to pure numerical strength, the task of sustaining law and order in Kosovo required specialization on the part of the CIVPOL contingent. One such specialized arm was CIVPOL's Central Investigation Unit (CCIU), originally established to investigate homicide. The mandate of the CCIU was expanded in November 1999 to include assaults, arsons, bombings, burglaries, intimidations, rapes, robberies, and other serious crimes committed prior to UNMIK's presence. Under the new mandate, the CCIU also investigated war crimes not falling under the jurisdiction of the ICTY and other investigations as directed by the police commissioner. Former KLA members also fell under CCIU jurisdiction, including many Kosovo Protection Corps[40] members and Kosovo Police Service (KPS) officers accused of committing serious crimes during the war.

Prostitution and trafficking, as mentioned previously, continued to be a problem for CIVPOL, especially after a number of CIVPOL officers were found to have solicited the services of women working as prostitutes or being held as sex slaves. To improve its record against this kind of crime, CIVPOL established the Trafficking and Prostitution Investigative Unit (TPIU) in September 2000. Its primary function was to investigate and prosecute human trafficking, while the International Office of Migration (IOM) and the OSCE assisted with repatriation. The new unit and UNMIK's antitrafficking regulation signaled a crackdown on trafficking; however, implementation was inadequate and reports of trafficking persisted.

The short rotations for CIVPOL personnel also posed a number of challenges, including maintaining the continuity of ongoing investigations. Long-term cases, especially those requiring cultivation of local informants, proved particularly difficult. Moreover, Kosovo's applicable law initially did not contain the law enforcement tools necessary for combating the types of crimes faced by police, for example, witness protection programs, electronic surveillance, and mechanisms for using informants.

The struggle to assert responsible and effective policing in Kosovo provides several important learning points. First, given the character of the conflict, it should have been possible to anticipate postwar ethnic-related and organized crime. However, the United Nations took more than a year to promulgate regulations and mechanisms to address these crimes; these measures remained inadequate as of 2002. Future missions should anticipate the types of crimes that peacekeepers will likely encounter and develop strategies to secure personnel with the right legal background and expertise. Second, cooperation between civilian and military authorities is critical in ensuring that investigations are not conducted at cross-purposes. In Kosovo, a lack of coordination between KFOR and UNMIK led to incidents in which brothels under investigation by CIVPOL were raided by military personnel unaware of the ongoing investigation. KFOR and CIVPOL improved their collaboration, especially in the area of organized crime, where it is essential to ensure that military intelligence can be converted into arrests and evidence that will be admissible in court.

Kosovo Police Service School

To help bolster the policing capabilities of the local authorities, the OSCE established the Kosovo Police Service School (KPSS) in June 2001.[41] Early on, the school was mired by political infighting, staff shortages, and general infrastructure shortcomings.[42] Time pressures, inadequate entrance exams, and insufficient screening and background investigations of the school's first 32,000 applicants also proved problematic. The testing and screening instruments for the candidates, for instance, had not been deployed in the cultural environment before their use, and the process was frustrated by a lack of official documentation of education and other background information. In addition, the former KLA representatives insisted on a role in vetting applicants. UN officials and powerful donors ultimately agreed that former KLA members could make up 50 percent of new police cadets at the basic level.[43]

This was not the only way in which the KLA's influence became problematic. At the time, former KLA members were revered as war heroes and wielded their influence accordingly. Partly because of the

KLA's perceived excessive influence and partly because qualified males without past experience in the police or insurgency had access to only 10 percent of KPS slots, the application process was restructured in spring 2001, ending the quota and preferential consideration for ex-KLA candidates.

The basic training program consisted of a twelve-week academy course (500 hours of lecture and practical application) followed by a fifteen-week (originally seventeen-week) mentoring program under the guidance of field training officers (FTOs) from CIVPOL. Academy training consisted of five major components: human rights and democratic policing, traffic and patrol procedures, legal affairs, report writing and interviewing techniques, and crime investigation. Instruction also included operational skills training in the use of force, firearms safety and procedures, major incident response, the use of batons and handcuffs, and mine awareness. Field training included written performance evaluations that became part of the officer's permanent record. As of January 2002, deployment of KPS officers had been primarily in traffic enforcement and patrol, while a limited number of KPS officers had received specialized training and were integrated into UNMIK police ranks. In addition, forensics and narcotics training were provided to some officers. Promotions in the supervisory levels were made in 2001, including first-line sergeant, colonel, and lieutenant colonel.

As of January 2002, KPSS staff comprised 244 nationals and 111 internationals from twenty-four nations. The varying legal systems and policing styles and techniques of contributing nations posed interesting challenges for the school; it was essential that students be taught the law as applied by judges and prosecutors. One example of the difficulties of creating coherence out of a multinational mission is that U.S. instructors, in accord with their own doctrine, instructed students never to use warning shots. Meanwhile, CIVPOL's policy manual permitted warning shots under certain circumstances, a practice followed by many European countries.

From the outset, the curriculum of the KPSS also failed to incorporate many standard international practices. For instance, a human rights component originally included general principles but not how to apply them in day-to-day operations. However, this was remedied by mainstreaming human rights principles into each area of performance, including searches, detention, and use of force. Eventually, the KPSS established a training program for FTOs and created primary field training officers (PFTOs), to provide more and higher-quality training to students. A combination of high turnover and inconsistency in training methods, as well as the fact that some FTOs did not want to mentor their local charges, resulted in the KPSS training program for FTOs falling short of expectations in 2002.

Overall, despite these challenges, the KPS and its school are often cited as success stories in Kosovo. If there is one lesson KPS officers learn, it is the ability to adapt to the ever-changing situation and legal framework. The KPSS showed a willingness to cooperate and engaged in cross-training on investigative techniques with the Kosovo Judicial Institute. Through this and similar programs, the gap between the police and judiciary steadily narrowed. The United Nations set the goal that by 2006 the KPS would replace CIVPOL, providing an indigenous, multiethnic, and professional police force, operating under democratic principles and representing the community in terms of ethnic and gender proportions. As of January 2002, the KPSS was making progress toward this goal. Of those who graduated, 23 percent were police officers, 37 percent were military personnel, 17 percent were women, and 16 percent were minorities (8 percent Serb and 8 percent others), maintaining the KPS's goal of 15 percent minority representation.[44] These efforts formed part of a broader attempt to increase cooperation between police officers who would normally be on opposite sides of ethnic or gender divides, and to foster a close working relationship during schooling that would be continued into the field. Despite progress in these areas, difficulties persisted; reports of harassment of Serb KPS officers existed, and discrimination against women officers remained widespread.

An immediate goal for the KPSS was to increase the number of KPS officers and to have the first promotions to KPS captain, as well as to have the KPS assume operational responsibility for police station management and supervision by the fourth quarter of 2002. To meet the 2006 deadline, the KPS would begin transitioning officers into positions traditionally occupied by CIVPOL officials, with first-line transitions in 2004, middle-management transitions in 2005, and executive management transitions in 2006. There also remained the need for the KPS to have budget and administrative training so that it could take over these and other responsibilities from UNMIK.

Many in the international community believed that the 2006 time line was overly ambitious. While they acknowledged great progress in traffic and enforcement, they argued that the KPS lagged in developing capacity to combat organized crime and political or ethnic crime. A contributing factor to this concern is a difference in opinion about what constitutes "organized crime." The international community views crimes such as smuggling cigarettes as serious offenses, as they can provide funding for organized criminals. However, this view is not generally shared by the people of Kosovo, and thus by extension the KPS officers themselves. Instead, cigarette smuggling is viewed more as a part of the "gray economy" that comprises untaxed goods. As much of the Kosovo economy is driven by such transactions, local officers do not generally act aggressively against them.

Culturally based perceptions like these are an ongoing challenge to policing in Kosovo. For instance, while interviews with internationals and locals revealed an overall favorable impression of KPS officers, the longtime mistrust of police and lack of respect in general will likely take a generation to modify; historically, the police have been viewed as oppressors and bribe takers in Kosovo. As of 2004, the KPS included highly motivated police officers endeavoring to learn and develop on the job, as well as some who chose to take the path of least resistance. KPS officers are perceived as being more effective than CIVPOL in some instances (such as individual disputes, car accidents, and minor offenses) since they know the language and culture of Kosovo. Some locals have lamented that still more needs to be done to remedy the matter of unqualified people who were originally selected due to the quota-based system and a selection process tainted by favoritism in the early stages. The majority of KPS officers had functioned only within the limited range of activities outlined previously. Both internationals and locals expressed concern about whether the KPS would be able to withstand the inevitable pressures when confronted with organized crime or blood feuds within families.

Like many institution-building efforts, the KPSS faced time constraints. Unfortunately, resources and international interests often overrode the principles of institution building. The success of a mission cannot be measured in dollars spent or calendar days passed. In the case of the KPSS, from the beginning the deadline to recruit, train, and deploy a local police force was an arbitrary one. Little consideration was given to factors like preexisting prejudices and practices that took generations to develop and cannot be changed overnight. If the handover of policing authority to the KPS is rushed to meet artificial external deadlines rather than to reflect actual police readiness, then the Kosovo government is unlikely to be able to counter economic, political, or financial crimes.

Detention Facilities and Prisons

In planning its mission, the United Nations failed to address the creation of correctional services. So, just as it had done earlier for the judicial and policing functions, KFOR found itself overseeing initial detention responsibilities. KFOR made do with the resources it had on hand. In the U.S. sector, detainees were held in tents. In the German sector, a former prison was used. In all areas, facilities were limited and only the most serious offenders were usually held.

Most donor nations did not understand the critical importance of effective correctional systems in maintaining order and upholding human rights standards. Only after an assessment of Kosovo's dismal correctional system by Canadian and British experts did the mission form the Penal Management Division (PMD) in October 1999. The PMD's staff consisted of one UN representative and personnel donated by Canada and the United Kingdom. In November the Kosovo Correctional Service (KCS) was established under the authority of UNMIK. Since the United Nations had not budgeted for detention or correctional services, the PMD/KCS was forced to seek donations from other countries, only to learn that most nations simply were not interested in funding prisons. So the staff of the PMD/KCS was reduced to circulating "wish lists" among donors, requesting basic necessities like blankets, food, and clothing. Finally, in February 2000 the United Nations created a realistic budget based on operational requirements and allocated money to the PMD/KCS.

International corrections officials also made policy on an ad hoc basis. They decided to apply the UN minimum standards for treatment of prisoners and European standards and structures to the emerging correctional system. How these standards would apply to postconflict Kosovo was another question. Gradually, between November 1999 and early 2001, the PMD/KCS began assuming responsibility for corrections from KFOR and CIVPOL. In May 2000 it opened the Lipjan facility to house juveniles, women, and the mentally ill. By November 2000 a total of 599 KCS staff members had been trained by the PMD and posted in facilities overseeing 227 prisoners. Because of security concerns, a few facilities were still maintained by KFOR or CIVPOL as late as January 2002.

Most international observers viewed the PMD's performance as successful, despite the slow and inadequate initial response of the international community in establishing Kosovo's correctional system. The PMD assumed control of corrections, improved conditions, and helped ensure compliance with some minimal standards of treatment. In 2002 the PMD sought the creation of mechanisms for probation and parole to ease the burden on the prison system while still maintaining the safety of the community. This measure required new funding and changes to the applicable law to permit alternative sentencing, such as fines or community service.

During its first year and a half, the PMD experienced difficulties coordinating with the judicial system. The legal/procedural dimension of the challenges in the judiciary has already been discussed, but these challenges all had practical effects in terms of corrections as well. For instance, the problem of illegal detention was exacerbated by infrastructural problems in relaying hearing schedules and release orders from courts to detention facilities. Liaison with the judiciary greatly improved the situation. Another challenge was that the law did not allow the court to issue alternative penalties (e.g., community service in lieu of prison time), resulting in a higher-than-desired prison population. To address these challenges, the PMD adopted a progressive approach and willingness to cooperate with other justice sector components to work through issues. Such cooperation led to vast improvements in the way mentally ill[45] and juvenile offenders are treated within the Kosovo judicial system. The PMD provided advice on legislation related to detention of juveniles and the mentally ill and formed a working group with the OSCE and others to suggest recommendations regarding treatment of mentally ill prisoners. Yet despite these efforts, as of 2002, Kosovo still lacked a clear legislative and operational regulatory framework covering mentally ill persons in the correctional system. Staff shortages in juvenile prisons led to the broad rehiring of members of the previous regime's prisons system without sufficient training. Consequently, the level of care and treatment did not meet international standards.

In the foreseeable future, the largest challenge facing the correctional system will be one of resources and oversight. Through the KCS, the PMD developed a local capacity for corrections, with correctional officers attending a four-week Corrections Officer Course at the Kosovo Police Service School. Some 700 officers had been trained and deployed as of January 2002. The challenge is ensuring that sufficient numbers of international officers and other resources are available to continue with training once in the facility. The leadership of the PMD was consistent from the beginning, greatly assisting its own development and that of the KCS. When problems occurred, it looked to solve the problems constructively with those involved rather than be defensive or evasive. The PMD also benefited from the hard-learned British lessons in Northern Ireland in terms of dealing with difficult situations and hunger strikers. By striving to maintain positive relations with the prisoners, for instance, by simply taking time to explain the process and rules and what could be expected in detention as well as in court, the PMD managed to overcome many of the challenges of a very high guard-to-prisoner ratio while still maintaining an unarmed or lightly armed warder force.

CONCLUSION

The tension between establishing order and upholding international human rights standards emerged early in the Kosovo mission and persisted. Many argue it would have been better to declare a public emergency (some refer to this as martial law) at the beginning of the mission, thus allowing limited derogation from certain human rights standards as permitted under international law.[46] Yet the United Nations was not willing to declare a public emergency, which would have laid bare its inability to provide security. In the end, the international presence in postwar Kosovo succeeded on neither side of this purported trade-off, providing insufficient public security and failing to deliver justice in compliance with international rights standards.

A more workable strategy would have included addressing the applicable-law challenges early on so that the most critical provisions could be readily amended or gaps filled to meet international standards and respond to realities on the ground. Instead, KFOR and CIVPOL arrived in a volatile Kosovo amid a raging debate over the applicable law, followed by disagreements about how to apply and adapt the law to international standards. KFOR entered the mission with the incorrect assumption that the civilian authorities would take over law-and-order duties in short order. In retrospect, it would have been preferable for KFOR to be prepared to handle certain law-and-order functions until CIVPOL could adequately assume them. Some human rights advocates argued for standards that others believed were impossible or unnecessary under international law. These debates contributed to inconsistent international policies and tensions between the human rights community, CIVPOL, and KFOR. In future circumstances, international human rights experts with field experience should join international military and law enforcement experts to forge a viable plan and an applicable law that meets international standards. Effective law enforcement is not inconsistent with human rights standards, as long as these interests are properly balanced.

Some believed the UN mission in Kosovo had it all: a full executive mandate and more resources than many previous UN post-conflict missions. It was even referred to as the "perfect mission" by some, in that it was like a petri dish for the international community to do the ultimate in nation-building, top to bottom, left to right. Yet those who viewed it this way lost sight of the fact that Kosovo representatives should have been part of the process from the beginning. The international community largely excluded local input, failing to distinguish between obstructionists and those who were constructive and added value to the process. Moreover, those who excluded

Kosovar locals' participation were often themselves incompetent in their jobs.

Lawlessness, organized crime, political extremism, and ethnic retaliation thrived at the beginning of the mission because of the security vacuum and persisted as of late 2002. The justice system is but one component of a stable society. Conflict continued to be played out through politics and violence; intraethnic violence plagued the Kosovo Albanian political parties, and interethnic violence against Serbs and other minorities was unceasing. These types of crimes are unlikely to be completely eradicated, considering that many developed countries continue to struggle with the same issues. The goal should thus be to limit the expansion of such crimes, disrupt their operations, and limit their influence over the political process and civil society.

If the international community cannot demonstrate that criminal activity will not be tolerated, the consequences will be dire for future international efforts. Despite this urgency, UNMIK entered its third year in 2002 facing a number of serious challenges, including a 15 percent reduction in UN personnel and a continued decline of member state focus and funding. It is important for the international military leadership to understand that in the absence of a judicial system, including police, judges, prosecutors, and corrections personnel, the military will need to step in to fill the gap in certain circumstances if it expects to be able to leave.[47] This, of course, assumes that the military forces will be properly trained to handle law-and-order duties in accordance with international standards and be subject to a system of accountability. At a minimum, the military may need to provide support to the civilian authorities in areas such as security and logistics. Some countries, like the United Kingdom, fully embraced this broader role in Kosovo, realizing that mission success depends on it. U.S. and British KFOR legal officers did a commendable job considering the circumstances and readily engaged in outreach and coordination activities with civilian authorities. Military field officers clearly saw that if they did not step in, things would only get worse, as the civilians could not assume control seamlessly. However, they often ended up doing so "on the fly" without the benefit of an accepted widespread headquarters policy embracing this role.

To some extent, even the limited success shown by the UN mission to this point is not universally appreciated. While most Kosovo Albanians would agree that the overall judicial situation in Kosovo was better in 2002 than it was for the preceding ten years, and also that it was better in 2002 than when KFOR and UNMIK first deployed in Kosovo, they still do not have trust in the UMMIK-run judicial system. Most Kosovo Serbs, however, would say that ever since the Serbs pulled out and KFOR and UNMIK took over administration of Kosovo, things have deteriorated precipitously and failed to improve. They have no faith in the legal system in Kosovo, regardless of whether or not it is run by the United Nations, with or without international prosecutors and judges.

One lesson of the Kosovo experience is that leadership and morale among international staff matter. For the first year and a half (roughly through February 2001) internationals and Kosovo Albanians had high morale amid plentiful resources. The SRSG and the director of the Department of Judicial Affairs were engaged, and the SRSG was respected by most Kosovo authorities, who saw him as caring, though unorthodox. Kosovo Albanians remained grateful for the international military intervention. Despite mistakes and misdirected efforts, important judicial and police reform activity began.

Yet, as with most peace operations, goodwill between international staffers and the local community eroded over time. Morale was at an all-time low in January 2002, both for the internationals working in the judicial area and for the Kosovo Albanians and Serbs. Some of the latter viewed the international police and members of the OSCE and the United Nations as an occupying force, drawn to Kosovo merely for the money.

It is thus too early to judge the outcome of security and justice reforms in Kosovo. The conflict ended, and the reconstruction of physical infrastructure and new governance structures occurred. Three years after the NATO campaign ended, the progress in institution building looked impressive considering the dire situation in 1999. Yet as long as the final status of the province remains undetermined, the international community remains deeply involved in governance, and no solid plan exists for turnover to locals in the judicial area, the gains achieved are uncertain and even artificial.

Their consolidation depends on a number of factors: whether Western capitals remain financially and politically engaged, whether (and how) local expertise and authority are included in building the justice system and overseeing public security, whether organized crime is effectively confronted, and whether Kosovo's leaders act in the interests of the entire populace or in furtherance of their own personal and factional interests. The final chapter on Kosovo's judicial and policing systems will reflect both broader considerations about Kosovo's political fate and the international community's engagement and the choices made by international actors and Kosovo's leaders.

Postscript: 2003–05

This chapter focuses on the early years of the justice and security reform efforts in Kosovo, from the end of NATO's war in 1999 to 2002. From 2003 through 2005, reform efforts get a mixed report card. New Kosovo criminal and criminal procedure codes were promulgated, training and reliance on local police continued, and the number of skilled criminal defense attorneys increased. Notwithstanding these important advances, the political factors that plagued the mission from the beginning continued.

While the rhetoric of the international community has been "partnership," "local ownership," and "self-government," the reality, particularly in the justice and police spheres, was that direct and sole control continued to be maintained by international personnel. Although local judges and prosecutors handled the great majority of criminal and civil cases, the United Nations continued to deem some cases, such as serious ethnic violence and organized crime, too sensitive for local prosecutors and judges to handle alone. Thus, international prosecutors initiated investigations in these cases and international judges held the deciding votes. In addition, internationals held the key decision-making positions in the justice and security sectors. Furthermore, with three exceptions, no international prosecutor has coprosecuted with local prosecutors. Although the UMMIK website claimed that the international and local judges and prosecutors were "integrated," in practice, they were only colocated; nonintegrated parallel systems operated. International judges and prosecutors have international supervisors who control their case assignments completely apart from the local judiciary.

Most worrisome, there continued to be no Kosovo Ministry of Justice or Ministry of the Interior, though international officials suggested that creation of such institutions would begin by early 2006 and UNMIK would begin to hand over authority to local actors. As a result, little progress was achieved in supporting sustainable local institutions that could administer both the interior and justice ministries in a manner that fostered legitimacy across diverse ethnic groups. Nor were local actors afforded the space to carry out such responsibilities within the presence of the United Nations' technical assistance and its eye toward enhancing accountability against abuse and corruption. In terms of ethnic representation, as of June 1, 2005, only 14 of 362 judges and 2 of 58 prosecutors were Serb, although problem-plagued parallel Serbian judicial institutions operated.[48] Not only were local actors excluded from many aspects of the justice system; they were also excluded from the process of reforming their own justice system. A real danger existed that the international community might suddenly confer responsibility on local institutions without sufficient capacity-building or oversight mechanisms in place.

One positive sign is that the principal deputy SRSG stated in February 2005 that the debate on reforms must include judges, prosecutors, and the wider Kosovo legal profession. Some UN officials also indicate that such consultation is occurring. After the United Nations failed to engage in meaningful consultation before issuing a new criminal procedure code, that code was once again being revised, this time with the involvement of the Kosovo legal community and a broader array of international actors.

In police institutional development, the Kosovo Police Service continued to grow and to carry out everyday security tasks, but under the de facto and de jure control of UNMIK. As of March 2004, 5,700 KPS officers had been trained and deployed. In Serb-dominated regions of Kosovo, KPS units tended to be almost entirely Serb, whereas in Albanian-dominant areas, KPS units had virtually no minorities.[49] As of late 2003, KPS officers had received only one uniform each and lacked minimal antiriot gear such as tear gas and shields. The controversial Kosovo Protection Corps, many of whose members were selected from the remnants of the demobilized KLA, had an unclear role in security and was marginalized in major public order disturbances by KFOR. Partly because international KFOR forces and UNMIK's police continued to be evaluated on the basis of their ability to provide order, rather than on institution building, the Kosovo Police Service had little responsibility for planning, implementing, or managing crisis response or public order problems, being relegated to more everyday security tasks.

In mid-March 2004 Kosovo was rocked by a series of violent riots involving mobs of Kosovo Albanians, primarily young adults and teenagers who attacked minority enclaves inhabited mostly by Serbs. The rioting was sparked by a media report that Serbs had caused the deaths of three Albanian children. The spontaneous demonstrations that followed were exploited by a small handful of people who seized on the opportunity to stoke violence for their own ends by orchestrating the outbursts.

A number of factors underlay the violence, including persistent ethnic tensions, the uncertain final status of the territory, and a stagnant economy. Simply existing in a limbo state sparks frustration with certain issues, such as the lack of passports and identification cards. For those who have only United Nations travel documents and no official passport, getting visas to travel to other countries is a challenging, and sometimes impossible, endeavor. The riots revealed both the public's frustration and UNMIK's and KFOR's lack of preparedness, evidenced by their inability to curb the violence until after nineteen people had been killed, more than nine hundred people injured, and more than eight hundred houses and some twenty-nine churches and monasteries burned.[50] UNMIK and KFOR were criticized for not sharing information, while KFOR in particular was blamed for viewing itself as responsible for traditional military functions of thwarting an invasion rather than being prepared to engage in appropriate peacekeeping/law-and-order activity, such as protecting against civil violence, disturbances, and ethnic violence.[51] NATO had to rush in an additional 2,000 troops to quell the violence.[52] French KFOR, long distrustful of Albanian-dominated KPS units in the area, blocked the KPS from carrying out its duties during the riots and reportedly considered burning down its police station.[53]

The riots prompted soul-searching on the part of the international community. The issue of status, a topic that had long been avoided, was finally brought to the fore of international discussions. To some, the international community rewarded the tactic of violence as a means to an end by moving forward on the issue of status. To others, it had waited too long and therefore had created the situation that allowed violence to be used in the first place. Eight standards of reforms, including establishing democratic institutions, ensuring minority rights, and maintaining an impartial legal system, were set as prerequisites for status discussions to take place. The standards were made public in December 2003, while the Kosovo Standards Implementation Plan was published on March 31, 2004. In May 2005 the SRSG reported that progress had been made toward establishing a multiethnic democracy in Kosovo and recommended a comprehensive review of the eight standards of reform over the summer. Should there be sufficient progress, negotiations could begin to determine Kosovo's status and whether it should remain part of Serbia. Belgrade claimed that the SRSG's assessment was unbalanced as the minority Serbs in Kosovo continued to face ongoing security problems.

Observers speculate that if Serbs and Albanians are unable to agree on Kosovo's status, the UN Security Council may decide. Serbs warn that if Kosovo achieves independence absent Serb consent, extreme nationalists will win power in Belgrade and plunge the region into chaos. At the same time, Kosovo Albanians argue that if they do not get independence, extremists on their side will take matters into their own hands and cleanse the remaining Serbs from Kosovo. Given what happened in March 2004, that is not an unrealistic scenario. Although achieving final status is fraught with dangers, the March violence is only the latest reminder that inaction also risks violence.

The International Crisis Group (ICG) issued a report in May 2005[54] stating that UNMIK had little credibility among local people in Kosovo and had been in a "six-year holding pattern" in which it had ignored major challenges to democracy and the rule of law. "Rather than state-building, UNMIK is now mainly working on its own escape strategy, passing on unresolved problems that will haunt

Kosovo for years to come," said ICG Kosovo project director Alex Anderson. "Corruption is being transferred intact." The report further stated, "Recent weeks have seen an escalation in tension between [the two main ethnic Albanian political parties] so bitter that it risks spiraling into killings."[55]

Should status be resolved, there is debate about how the United Nations would phase out and whether other institutions, such as the European Union and the OSCE, would take over. It will be critical for continued institution- and capacity-building activities to take place, assuming, of course, that such activities are properly devised to accomplish the intended goals.

In terms of transitional justice, the ICTY has jurisdiction over war crimes and crimes against humanity arising from the Kosovo conflict, but so far it has chosen to exercise its jurisdiction in only a few instances. Its most sensitive efforts regarding Kosovo involve indictments of former KLA members. Aside from the Slobodan Milošević indictment, the ICTY essentially left prosecution of Serbs to the local court systems, with the involvement of international judges and prosecutors. In 2003 the ICTY indicted and arrested Kosovo Albanians Fatmir Limaj, Isak Musliu, and Haradin Bala. In November 2005, Limaj and Musliu were acquitted, while Bala was sentenced to thirteen years in prison for executing nine prisoners in the woods in July 1998.

In March 2005, the ICTY indicted former KLA commander and recently elected prime minister Ramush Haradinaj for war crimes and crimes against humanity. It also indicted two former KLA commanders, Idriz Balaj and Lahi Brahimaj. Observers were relieved that Kosovo Albanians did not engage in rock-throwing demonstrations, as had happened with earlier arrests of Kosovo Albanians. Instead, Haradinaj resigned and called for calm as he voluntarily surrendered to the ICTY. Observers noted that this shows the sway political leaders can have over the public in inciting or quelling violence. All three are pending trial as of December 2005.

In mid-2005 a number of factors were contributing to skepticism and uncertainty about the ability of Kosovo institutions to provide security and justice, especially for ethnic minorities. These factors included the volatility of the process of defining Kosovo's final status, Kosovo political parties' partisan battles, and international actors' strategy and skill for institution building in the coming months and years. Thus far, institution building in security and justice has been surprisingly limited, reflecting many of the same limitations and neglect exhibited by other UN missions. As previously indicated, many international state-builders arrived with optimism about the chance to create functional justice and security systems, given the high degree of influence of external actors at the war's end. Kosovo's experience suggests some common deficiencies among international actors' approaches to postconflict construction of security and justice systems, but it also suggests that building justice and security systems is simply difficult, no matter how war ends or how much leeway international organizations wield vis-à-vis local political elites. Changing institutionalized patterns remains deeply challenging, no matter how much authority external actors hold, how one-sided their victory, or how generous the rules of engagement granted to peace-keeping forces.

NOTES

1. Many Kosovo Albanians had long favored a Kosovo republic in Yugoslavia rather than a subordinate role within Serbia. By this time, there was an Albanian consensus for independence. See William G. O'Neill, *Kosovo: An Unfinished Peace* (Boulder, Colo.: Lynne Rienner, 2002).

2. Quoted in Human Rights Watch, *Yugoslavia: Human Rights Abuses in Kosovo 1990–1992*, http://www.hrw.org/reports/1992/yugoslavia/. See also the Organization for Security and Cooperation in Europe (OSCE), *Kosovo/ Kosova as Seen, as Told: An Analysis of the Human Rights Findings of the OSCE Kosovo Verification Mission October 1998 to June 1999* (Warsaw: Office for Democratic Institutions and Human Rights Watch, 1999), http://www.osce. org/documents/mik/1999/11/1620_en.pdf.

3. Kosovo Albanians had long resolved disputes through customary law. The practice began during the Ottoman period, when Kosovo Albanians, desiring to avoid the involvement of Ottoman or other foreign officials, turned to village elders. A body of law developed that came to be known as the Kanun of Leke Dukagjini. Unwritten at first, it later became codified. Over time, and especially following World War II, its use diminished. However, it continued to be used periodically in limited circumstances, especially in rural villages or when the public viewed the court system as unreliable or unfair. For an account

of the movement and all the cases in Kosovo in 1990–91, see Anton Çetta, ed., *Pajtimi I Gjaqeve: 1990–91* (Pristina: ERA, 2001).

4. OSCE, *Kosovo/Kosova as Seen, as Told.*

5. UN Security Council Resolution 1244, June 10, 1999, http://www. un.org/Docs/scres/1999/sc99.htm.

6. Ibid. par. 10. Independence for Kosovo was not supported by most members of the Security Council, who, concerned about setting a precedent for independence movements in other parts of the world, opposed any border changes brought about by force or armed conflict.

7. Following the October 2001 elections, a parliament was established with authority to pass laws. However, the SRSG still held reserved powers and the final authority over what laws were ultimately promulgated.

8. UN Security Council Resolution 1244, par. 11(k).

9. In early 2001, having completed its mandate, the UNHCR was no longer under Pillar I. A new Pillar I was created, called the Justice and Police pillar.

10. OSCE Legal System Monitoring Section (LSMS), *Expiration of Detention Periods for Current Detainees*, Report No. 3 (Pristina: OSCE, March 8, 2000), 1; and OSCE LSMS, *Update on the Expiration of Detention Periods for Detainees*, Report No. 4 (Pristina: OSCE, March 18, 2000), 1.

11. OSCE LSMS, *The Development of the Kosovo Judicial System*, Report No. 2 (Pristina: OSCE, December 17, 1999) (hereafter OSCE Report No. 2).

12. See Captain Alton L. Gwaltney III, "Law and Order in Kosovo: A Look at Criminal Justice during the First Year of Operation Joint Guardian," in *Lessons from Kosovo: The KFOR Experience*, ed. Larry Wentz (Washington, D.C.: Command Control Research Program Publication Series, 2002), 233–268.

13. For all regulations, see United Nations Mission in Kosovo, "Official Gazette," http://www.unmikonline.org/regulations/index.htm.

14. Starting in 1999, ABA CEELI (with the OSCE's help) also attempted to address the poor circulation of legal materials described here, compiling and distributing applicable laws. Nonetheless, as of March 2002, many regulations adopted by the SRSG had not been translated into Albanian or Serbian.

15. These regulations included UNMIK Regulation No. 2000/64, December 15, 2000, discussed later.

16. UNMIK Emergency Decree No. 1999/1, June 28, 1999, provided for the establishment of the Joint Advisory Council for Provisional Judicial Appointments (JAC/PJA), and UNMIK Emergency Decree No. 1999/2, June 28, 1999, appointed members of JAC/PJA.

17. OSCE, *Kosovo/Kosova as Seen, as Told*, 10–11.

18. UNMIK Regulation No. 1999/7, September 7, 1999.

19. See OSCE Report No. 2. In the Kosovo legal system, citizens are appointed as lay judges to sit with judges on the trial panels of serious cases.

20. Ibid.

21. *Kosovo Judicial Assessment Mission Report* (assessment mission conducted by U.S. DOJ, U.S. DOS, and USAID), April 2000, 19, http://www.pristina.usmission.gov/jud.pdf.

22. See OSCE, *Review of the Criminal Justice System, September 2001–February 2002*, issued by the OSCE Department of Human Rights and Rule of Law (DHRRL), April 2002 (hereafter OSCE Fourth Review), http://www.osce.org/kosovo/documents/reports/justice/criminal_justice_eng.pdf.

23. These statistics are according to records of the UN DOJ.

24. Ibid. As of February 2002, of the 420 judges and prosecutors authorized by the budget for the Kosovo judiciary and prosecutorial services, 341 officials had been appointed (296 judges and 45 prosecutors). Of those, there were 62 women judges and 6 women prosecutors. The group included four Serbs (three men and one woman), seven Turks (three men and four women), ten Bosniaks (seven men and three women), and two Romas (males).

25. See generally OSCE LSMS, *The Treatment of Minorities by the Judicial System*, Background Report (Pristina: OSCE, March 2000); OSCE LSMS, *Access to Effective Counsel—Stage 1: Arrest to the First Detention Hearing*, Report No. 7 (Pristina: OSCE, May 23, 2000); and OSCE, *Access to Effective Counsel—Stage 2: Investigative Hearings to Indictment*, Report No. 8 (Pristina: OSCE, July 20, 2000).

26. OSCE DHRRL, *Review of the Criminal Justice System, February 1, 2000–July 31, 2000* (Pristina: OSCE, October 18, 2000) (hereafter OSCE First Review).

27. O'Neill, *Kosovo*, 90.

28. See OSCE Fourth Review.

29. UNMIK Regulation No. 2001/19, May 15, 2001.

30. This coalition government consisted of Ibrahim Rugova's LDK and the more militant Democratic Party of Kosovo (PDK) and Alliance for the Future of Kosovo (AAK), both of which were led by former KLA commanders.

31. See OSCE First Review.

32. See OSCE DHRRL, *Review of the Criminal Justice System, September 1, 2000–February 1, 2001* (Pristina: OSCE, April 2001).

33. Women, primarily from Bulgaria, Moldova, Romania, Russia, and Ukraine, are increasingly present in Kosovo's illicit "coffee bars" and brothels, catering to clients who include international police and civilians. Many of these women arrive after being approached in their home countries by traffickers posing as employers and promising them jobs abroad. Once in Kosovo or neighboring areas, the women find their passports and papers withheld until a "debt" is paid off, essentially becoming sexual slaves.

34. Ombudsperson Institution in Kosovo, *On the Conformity of Deprivations of Liberty under "Executive Orders" with Recognized International Standards*, Special Report No. 3, June 29, 2001, http://www.ombudspersonkosovo.org/reports_special.htm.

35. UNMIK, "On the Establishment of a Detention Review Commission for Extra-judicial Detention Based on Executive Order," UNMIK Regulation No. 2001/18, August 25, 2001.

36. Ombudsperson Institution in Kosovo, *On Certain Aspects of UNMIK Regulation No. 2001/18 on the Establishment of a Detention Review Commission for Extra-judicial Detention Based on Executive Orders*, Special Report No. 4, September 12, 2001, http://www.ombudspersonkosovo.org/reports_special.htm.

37. See *UNMIK at Nine Months: Report of UN Mission in Kosovo*, March 8, 2000, http://www.un.org /peace/Kosovo/pages/9months.html.

38. With a single exception, CIVPOL missions had never before been required to carry weapons.

39. In October 2000, the Security Council authorized a total force of 4,718 CIVPOL officers for UNMIK, plus an additional 1,100 special police, making it possible for CIVPOL to take primacy of Prizren in October, Gnjilane/Gjilan in May 2000, and Peć/Peja in June 2000. By January 2002, with its headquarters in Pristina/Prishtine, and 32 police stations over five regions, CIVPOL had expanded its ranks to 4,407, including 980 special police, which deployed as intact units from Pakistan, India, Jordan, and Poland. The special units were separate from Mobile Support Units composed of French gendarmerie and Italian carabinieri who deployed as part of KFOR.

40. The Kosovo Protection Corps (KPC), an unarmed civilian agency composed of former members of the Kosovo Liberation Army, is charged with protecting Kosovo citizens and assisting in Kosovo's rebuilding. However, some KPC members have been accused of continuing to engage in interethnic violence, causing much of the international community to view the KPC as a destabilizing force.

41. Information was obtained from the OSCE Kosovo Police Service School, including from its 2000 annual report and interviews with the school's director and other officials, January 2002.

42. Many of the school's budgetary difficulties still persist. Between 2001 and 2002, the KPSS budget was cut by more than 30 percent and its international staffing decreased by 41 percent. Concurrently, the United Nations reduced CIVPOL funding by 15 percent.

43. An additional 20 percent of seats were set aside for women applicants, and another 20 percent for former police officers dismissed following Kosovo's loss of autonomy in 1989.

44. Kosovo Police Service School (KPSS), "Welcome to the OSCE Department of Police Education and Development," Powerpoint presentation, Kosovo, January 2002.

45. See OSCE Fourth Review.

46. See O'Neill, *Kosovo,* 75–76.

47. For an excellent discussion of the military's role in peace operations, see Edith Wilkie, Beth C. DeGrasse, and Colonel Richard W. Roan, *A Force for Peace and Security: U.S. and Allied Commanders' Views of the Military's Role in Peace Operations and the Impact on Terrorism of States in Conflict* (Washington, D.C.: Peace through Law Education Fund, 2002). The report, available at http://www.ptlef.org/reportshtm, contains interviews of more than thirty top U.S. and Allied military commanders.

48. UNMIK Department of Justice, weekly report, May 31–June 1, 2005. Women made up 27 percent of judges.

49. Human Rights Watch, *Failure to Protect: Antiminority Violence in Kosovo, March 2004* (July 2004), http://www.hrm.org/reports/2004/kosovo0704/.

50. Ibid.

51. Ibid.

52. Although KFOR had 18,500 troops in the territory during the riots, roughly two-thirds of those were dedicated to logistical support. As of June 2005, KFOR totaled 17,00 troops. See Stefan Ratzenberger, "6th Anniversary of KFOR Ceremony," KFOR, press release, June 13, 2005, http://www.nato.int/kfor/inside/2005/06/i050613a.htm.

53. See Human Rights Watch, "Failure to Protect."

54. See International Crisis Group, *Kosovo after Haradinaj,* Report No. 163, May 26, 2005, http://www.crisisgroup.org/home/index.cfm?1=1&id=3474.

55. Ibid.

9

Lawyers, Guns, and Money

Justice and Security Reform in East Timor

RONALD A. WEST

ON MAY 20, 2002, EAST TIMOR BECAME A NEW COUNTRY amid a ceremony marked by speeches, balloons, and fireworks. The foreign flavor of the celebration closely resembled the character of the UN Transitional Administration in East Timor (UNTAET), which preceded the current government of the Democratic Republic of East Timor. International actors tended to emphasize the appearance rather than the substance of change, which demanded getting one's hands dirty during a sustained period at the local level, something that never happened.

This chapter analyzes one aspect of the international community's efforts at building a new state—the construction of a system of justice and security following the termination of occupation and conflict in East Timor. I will argue that reconstruction and the initial batch of postreconstruction reforms in East Timor have done little beyond assembling a justice bureaucracy—the Timor-Leste Police

Service (TLPS), a judiciary, and the Timor-Leste Prison Service. Partly owing to insufficient attention to informal, traditional mechanisms of justice and security, neither the United Nations nor other actors have succeeded in establishing a strong institutional basis for the future systemic provision of internal security and justice. I rely not only on primary documents and analysis of the United Nations' unusual experience as an interim government but also on personal experience as I managed two USAID-funded programs in East Timor. One program involved rural public information outreach through large public meetings that provided villagers and justice system officials an opportunity to discuss national and local level development of police, courts, and prisons.

PORTUGUESE ADMINISTRATION OF EAST TIMOR

East Timor, at 12,400 square miles roughly the size of Belgium or the state of Maryland, constitutes one-half of an island located approximately 270 miles northwest of Australia. Seventy-five percent of Timorese live outside the country's two cities, Dili, the capital, and Baucau.

Knowing where so many Timorese live is important to understanding how they live. Outside the cities, the typical village is the center of most political, religious, economic, and social transactions. It has maintained this status for far more than four centuries, since well before the first Europeans stepped ashore to build a trading base.

East Timor was ruled by Portugal from 1642 to 1974, and according to vivid accounts of those who spent some time in the colony, the colonial administration was "miserable" and "oppressive."[1] Timorese males were frequently drafted into the Portuguese colonial force and served as a labor force for the colonial administration, which relied on allied local leaders to maintain order within their spheres of influence.[2] While the administration exercised some responsibility for security and order maintenance in the colony, local leaders exercised much greater control. In the kingdom of Aileu, for instance, the *liurai* (king of the land) maintained order and enforced local custom through the deployment of agents who would be equivalent to a kingdom police force.[3] These police officers were authorized to take prisoners upon evidence of wrongdoing within the kingdom and to present them to the *liurai* for judgment.

Leaders were responsible for finding just solutions to a range of communal problems. The informal process differed across kingdoms and independent villages, and in some places, where Catholicism had been preached or was actively practiced by Portuguese, tradition became suffused with a belief that church law, particularly that part based on Old Testament biblical principles, informed the structure of dispute resolution and sanctions meted out to guilty parties.[4] To this day, local leaders retain their preeminent role as the arbiters of conflict and as community problem solvers, thus fulfilling a basic social priority for justice and security.

Indonesian Annexation

Indonesia launched an invasion of East Timor on December 7, 1975, following the emergence of Frente Revolucionaria do Timor-Leste Independente (FRETILIN) as the dominant political faction and subsequent to the sudden abdication by Portugal of colonial rule.[5] It is estimated that some 200,000 civilian Timorese were killed during the next four years and more than 1,000 during the 1980s and 1990s.[6]

Indonesian administration was driven by the priorities of the Armed Forces of the Republic (TNI), which sought to pacify all resistance and socialize East Timor into Greater Indonesia.[7] Mass murder, forced resettlement, and torture were employed by Indonesian forces to terrorize men, women, and children and to undermine support for FRETILIN's armed-resistance wing, Forças Armadas do Libertaçao Nacional do Timor L'Este (FALINTIL). A creation of the post-August civil war street fighting in August 1975, FALINTIL was composed of many Timorese who had undergone training in the Portuguese colonial army, including former noncommissioned officers in that service.[8]

Indonesian forces in the territory were composed of regular military, military Special Forces known as KOPASSUS, police (POLRI), and militias made up of Timorese who had undergone selection and training by the armed forces.[9] Despite the overwhelming force, the occupation did not go smoothly for the Government of Indonesia.

Although some inroads were made in limiting FALINTIL's capacity for striking government targets, the ongoing resistance was a continual source of frustration for the occupiers and led to a number of atrocities against civilians. In the twenty-five-year conflict between Indonesian forces and FALINTIL, upward of one-fourth of the Timorese population may have been killed.[10]

Administration of justice was, of course, subsumed by the military priority of crushing the active insurgency. Indonesian police (POLRI) reported to TNI and were deployed throughout East Timor in the thirteen districts and sixty-two subdistricts, often alongside TNI forces within military posts.[11] POLRI handled traffic control, managed cases of a serious criminal nature, and responded to low-level threats to public order with riot control units.

Courts and prisons were similarly used as tools of the occupation regime. Courts provided the stage whereon guerrillas and their suspected civilian allies could be publicly branded as traitors or criminals, and prisons and jails facilitated the indefinite holding and extrajudicial punishment of suspects. With such a history, it is hardly surprising that Timorese society and cultural practices offer intensely local replacements for centrally administered justice.

Foxes Guarding the Chicken Coop: Indonesian Security and the Referendum

In May 1999 the Government of Indonesia agreed to allow a UN-monitored referendum on the status of East Timor (a de facto choice between autonomy and independence) and committed to safeguard that process.[12] The decision to conduct a popular consultation stemmed from several factors: the fall of Suharto in May 1998, certain restrictions on the role of the military in governance by the new Indonesian leadership, and decades of lobbying by international activists and such well-known Timorese as 1996 Nobel Peace Prize winners Dr. José Ramos-Horta and Bishop Carlos Filipe Ximenes Belo, as well as an active student movement and simmering problems within other Indonesian provinces.

The UN Assistance Mission in East Timor (UNAMET) and twenty-three international observer groups monitored the vote. The referendum was held on August 30, 1999, in an increasingly unstable security environment.[13] Despite international inability to stymie obstruction by Indonesian forces, some 98.6 percent of the eligible population participated in the referendum, and 78.5 percent voted for independence from Indonesia in a process deemed "free and fair" by UNAMET.[14]

The following weeks were marked by a deluge of savagery per-petrated by the military and affiliated militia units, which moved toward the territory's border with West Timor, killing, raping, pillag-ing, and burning buildings. When the Government of Indonesia agreed to withdraw TNI, KOPASSUS, and POLRI, Indonesian forces destroyed or removed 70 percent of all infrastructure, includ-ing physical parts of government buildings and private residences, as well as data, communications, and consumable items. The orgy of violence claimed several hundred lives and led to the forced emigra-tion of nearly one-quarter of the population and the flight of tens of thousands more into mountainous areas within East Timor.[15]

INTERFET AND INTERNATIONAL ADMINISTRATION IN EAST TIMOR

The ensuing international outcry forced Indonesia to request assis-tance on September 12 and mobilized the UN Security Council to pass Resolution 1264 on September 15, 1999, which authorized a multinational force under the robust provisions of Chapter 7. The UN resolution mandated the force to act under a unified command, to protect and support UNAMET, and, when possible, to facilitate humanitarian assistance to the Timorese.[16] Australia led the Inter-national Force in East Timor (INTERFET), which landed on Sep-tember 20 and had deployed 11,000 troops by November. INTERFET ultimately succeeded in reestablishing order and preventing further violence in East Timor from pro-Jakarta militias still operating in the territory.

In late October 1999 the UN Security Council established UNTAET, which would hold all executive and legislative authority, including the responsibility for assuring law and order in the territory. UNTAET was also mandated to establish national justice institutions, including a civilian police force, an independent judiciary, and a correctional system.

CONSTRUCTING A POLITY

INTERFET restored order, and its multinational forces were deployed strategically throughout the territory. The UN assumed responsibility for peacekeeping in February 2000, but the first wave of UN officials returning to East Timor in late October 1999 found an appalling environment in which to begin their work. Their challenges were made more difficult by the fact that funding requirements for reconstruction and extensive shortfalls in the budget with which to conduct humanitarian relief were not discussed until after a World Bank and International Monetary Fund assessment, conducted by an equal number of East Timorese and international representatives, was completed in mid-November 1999.

Donors meeting in Tokyo on December 17, 1999, pledged slightly more than US$522 million, of which $149 million was allocated to humanitarian relief and $373.47 million to development and reconstruction.[17] The World Bank, in coordination with the Asian Development Bank, administered the East Timor Trust Fund; priorities for spending were established jointly by the World Bank, the Asian Development Bank, a National Consultative Council, and donors.

Sergio Vieira de Mello, the special representative of the secretary-general (SRSG), found himself pleading with the Security Council several months later as the East Timor Trust Fund was slow in absorbing and disbursing donor funds.[18] The UN Consolidated Inter-agency Appeal of October 27 had previously urged donors to release much-needed funds for humanitarian assistance, but that call had gone largely unheeded. Ongoing problems, such as a large number of still-displaced persons, militia activity on the border, shortfalls in available food and shelter, and high unemployment, combined to create security challenges. As the euphoria of freedom gradually subsided, people began to realize that it was going to take more than a large square of canvas and a bag of rice to take the place of burned-out homes and unharvested fields.

UNTAET AND CONSTRUCTION OF A NATIONAL JUSTICE SYSTEM

Timorese elites contributed to rebuilding a new central administration. In July 2000 the East Timor Transitional Administration (ETTA) was established as a local replacement for UNTAET's internationally staffed Governance and Political Administration branch. In the arrangement, five Timorese political figures were selected by the international administration to serve on the nine-member advisory cabinet within the executive office of the SRSG. This coincided with an expansion of the National Consultative Council, established the preceding November, comprising thirty-six unelected officials handpicked by the international administration to form a quasi-legislative body known as the National Council.

UNTAET officials consulted frequently with the de facto Timorese leadership—people like Ramos-Horta and Xanana Gusmão, who had been leaders during the resistance—as well as with the Conselho Nacional da Resistencia Timorense (CNRT) before its dissolution in 2001, but consultations were seldom public or open, and government authority was largely confined to Dili.

Because the United Nations was unaccustomed to functioning as the sovereign state of a territory (it had assumed similar powers in Kosovo only five months earlier), it had difficulty finding and deploying the appropriate personnel, especially in the administration of security and justice. INTERFET operated with police powers until February 2000, and its Detention Management Unit (DMU) included military lawyers who handled the detention and judicial hearings of arrestees.[19] Recruiting the necessary numbers of police, given concurrent demands in the UN missions in Kosovo and in Bosnia, proved difficult.

Because of the dearth of qualified local justice personnel, UNTAET was forced to recruit international jurists and judicial personnel, encountering the same problems as with police recruitment. But a small number of prosecutors, defense attorneys, and judges were eventually pooled to constitute a judiciary. Two prison complexes were staffed by UN Civilian Police (CIVPOL) as the DMU was phased out.

Finding staff, whether police, jurists, or prison guards, to flesh out the UN bureaucracy was one challenge. Assembling the equipment and tools with which to make that bureaucracy operational was another. CIVPOL suffered from a lack of vehicles, station houses and lockup cells, and basic office equipment; jurists lacked law books and courtroom facilities. Transitional institutions capable of providing justice services were meager and underresourced well beyond the early days of UNTAET. Still, as peacekeepers were deployed throughout the territory and most of the local population was busily engaged trying to locate loved ones, find work, or rebuild, the main emphasis was on dealing with the atrocities of the referendum period, not disorder and crime.

Despite these problems, UNTAET made some important early contributions to security and justice reforms. CIVPOL provided helpful mentoring and advice to top TLPS officials at CIVPOL National Headquarters, and the military peacekeeping forces adequately provided for internal and external security, especially on the border. These troops enjoyed widespread local respect, perhaps higher than that given to any other international detachment in East Timor. Moreover, neither the United Nations nor other international organizations interfered with traditional mechanisms of justice, which continued to function in many areas.

Police

Responsibility for CIVPOL as of January 2000 lay in the hands of José Luis da Costa e Sousa, a Portuguese police commissioner with previous UN service in Bosnia. Da Costa reported to the deputy SRSG, Jean Cady, whose portfolio included security for East Timor.

By fall 2000 an increase in numbers of CIVPOL officers theoretically permitted international police to enforce law in the territory. UNTAET had existed for one year, and the CIVPOL administration was still studying how best to operationalize a police style that would meet the exigencies of life at the village level. The original plan was drafted by CIVPOL during the UNAMET period and relied on consultations with Timorese POLRI officers, who could have had very little to offer those planning a new approach to policing.

Out in the districts, some commanders and dedicated international police had already begun working with community leaders to maintain order and solve problems at the local level. The lack of foresight in building a new police institution was so great that UN Headquarters had to respond to an emergency request from the field to get equipment shipped to Dili for the first class of sworn officers.[20]

Ongoing planning was the purview of the TLPS Policy and Planning Unit, which was operational by mid-2000. The unit was charged with designing a policing strategy and planning for institution building. One element of the planning was known as the Koban Strategy for Community Policing, which drew on the model innovated in Japan and later adapted by the Singaporean police. The intention of the plan was to coordinate police enforcement activities with preexisting local customary practices as managed and directed by the village hierarchy.[21] Since the first batch of TLPS recruits had just graduated from the National Police College and the new force was only at partial strength and not yet authorized to take any enforcement actions, the plan was to be implemented first by international police and later by the TLPS.

Peter Miller arrived to take charge of CIVPOL in early spring 2001. Implementation of most of CIVPOL's paper plan for development of the TLPS was months behind schedule. Miller, who had served as director of police training for the United Nations in Haiti, adopted a centralized approach in administering the police.

Under Miller's direction, the community policing program was moved into the Operations Branch at National Headquarters. Law and Order Committees were designated in each district and were composed of community policing officers and local leaders. The two-fold purpose of committee meetings was to elicit feedback from local communities and to transmit public service information back to local communities via the source of information trusted most by citizens, local leaders.[22] Like the Koban plan, Law and Order Committees were designed to create a police-community partnership even though that frequently took the form of *one* CIVPOL or TLPS officer solving local problems through the good offices of a local leader.

In January 2002 CIVPOL created the East Timor Police Service Development Plan, which provided for transitional policing and shared authority after independence. Until January 1, 2004, when TLPS commissioner Paul Martins assumed full command of the joint service, the chain of command terminated at the UN police commissioner.[23] CIVPOL numbers immediately before independence in 2002 stood at 1,288, a level maintained during most of the mission (bolstered by 6,281 peacekeepers).[24] Meanwhile, traditional political and social cleavages within Timorese society gradually began to surface during the UNTAET period. CIVPOL lacked an appreciation of the environment in which it was both planning for a new police force and acting as a transitional police agency.

TLPS Recruitment and Training

The National Police College in Dili opened in March 2000. Instructors were assigned from CIVPOL, while the U.S. International Criminal Investigative Training Assistance Program provided supplementary training in areas like police management, crowd control, and civil disaster management. CIVPOL instructors came from all nations, but particularly Australia, Norway, Portugal, the United Kingdom, and the United States. They provided instruction mainly in Portuguese and English through interpreters, which posed difficulties since most of the recruits did not speak or understand these languages.

UNTAET worked with the CNRT in the selection and vetting process for the first wave of police recruits.[25] Subsequently, the entire recruitment process consisted of four stages. Applications were disbursed to subdistrict stations and collected by a district-level CIVPOL recruitment coordinator, who then interviewed candidates using a format that awarded points for language ability, past work experience, and basic physical fitness. Applications and the resulting interview sheets were forwarded to National Headquarters in Dili, where the vetting and evaluation of candidates took place. In the case of former POLRI, initial vetting often occurred at local stations. Once the vetting was complete, CIVPOL posted the list of all candidates approved by Dili in subdistrict stations, permitting local villagers, through their leaders, to inform CIVPOL if any of the recruit candidates had committed past criminal offenses or taken part in militia activities. The names cleared through this village-level process were then resubmitted to Dili for selection.

The first TLPS class of 50 officers graduated in June from a three-month training course. Roughly 20 percent of the TLPS were women. Ex-POLRI, who numbered just under 350 (some 12 percent of the force) as of June 2002, were provided one-month abbreviated academy training that mainly emphasized human rights while providing refresher training on other topics. Key technical skills such as training and qualifying with force-issued Glock 9mm pistols were also emphasized in the abbreviated academy session. The firearms course proved difficult for the older men of POLRI, who were accustomed to revolvers from their previous service.[26] CIVPOL planned for the further training and deployment of 180 officers for special TLPS units and 200 officers to serve in Border Patrol. Training and technical assistance to Border Patrol continued through spring 2005.

After independence, CIVPOL and the TLPS were administered and operated as a joint police service. According to the turnover plan, joint command for "routine policing" was established in phases, district by district, following UN certification of Timorese police in a district and accreditation of the district or unit operational command and control. At that time, decisions made by TLPS commanders were to be effective upon the countersigning of a CIVPOL commander, and CIVPOL would operate only in an advisory capacity.[27] Force levels (mixed service) through February 28, 2005, were 138 CIVPOL and 2,830 Timorese officers.[28] The government also sought to recruit some ex-resistance civilians to balance out the POLRI percentage.

TLPS special police units (SPUs), totaling 180 officers, were stationed in Baucau and Dili and reported through the regular police chain of command. The primary mandates of SPUs were order maintenance and tactical response; those serving in the units participated in technical training programs in such subjects as crowd control, civil disaster management, use of force, use of firearms, building and person searches, human rights, the constitution, and law.[29]

Total expenditures for internal security, comprising both police and military, were 22 percent of East Timor's budget for 2003–04.[30] A shortfall in donor assistance and a longer-than-expected period for payout from exploitation of oil resources will significantly alter the amount of available resources from 2005 onward.

Establishing Justice as a Formal Process

UNTAET Regulation 1999/1 established the applied law of the land by recognizing Indonesian law insofar as it was consistent with international law.[31] That decision was made with an eye toward providing a legal framework that would guide interim justice services and assure that the small pool of trained Timorese lawyers would not be overburdened with the added weight of learning a completely different legal system.[32] There was no general consultation on the matter.

Several hurdles remained that thwarted the efficacy of national law in the short term. These included poor infrastructure; a lack of suitably trained or experienced Timorese legal personnel; little extensive knowledge of Indonesian legislation governing the law, which required translation and research; and uncertainty over necessary amendments to supplement Indonesian law.[33]

As part of an effort to overcome these obstacles, UNTAET enacted Regulation No. 1999/3 on December 3, 1999, which established a Judicial Service Commission, chaired by Bishop Belo and composed of three Timorese and two international jurists. The commission, as a first step toward assuring a local voice and nonpartisan selection of judicial nominees in an independent state, was empowered to make merit recommendations to the SRSG on judicial candidates.[34]

While a number of Timorese judges were eventually seated to hear criminal cases, all failed an examination of their competencies in January 2005. Formal training at the Judicial Training Centre, which is funded by the UN Development Programme (UNDP), was being carried out in early 2005 to enhance the skills of judges, prosecutors, and public defenders. Meanwhile, hearings in criminal matters have become the responsibility of international judges, who were hastily brought in to prevent a complete logjam in the courts.[35]

Between 2004 and early 2005, some important steps were taken toward formalizing legal codes and procedures, including the passage of a draft criminal code, draft code of criminal procedure, draft law on public prosecutors, and draft law on accreditation of private lawyers.

Total expenditures for courts and personnel (judges, prosecutors, and public defenders) were slightly more than 1 percent of the government budget through June 2002 but would drop to 0.70 percent by June 2004. Once again, the shortfall in donor assistance past 2004 was likely to undermine judicial staffing and operations.

Crime Trends

It is difficult to accurately calculate the level of crime in the months following the referendum; crime statistics for the period are marked by underreporting on the part of Timorese and poor recording on the part of CIVPOL. Serious offenses such as murder and rape are more frequently reported to international police than other crimes.[36]

A noticeable rise in all types of crimes followed INTERFET stabilization of the territory. The year 2001 was marked by an increasing number of attacks against UN and expatriate personnel, including several rapes, assaults, and home break-ins. This crime trend continued into 2002 with an additional rise in Timorese gang activity. Gangs sometimes operated along clan or political lines and in the Baucau-Viqueque area, usually fronted as martial arts clubs. The burning of the mosque in Baucau and attacks on the Timorese district administrator and other UN staff in March 2001 by members of the Council for the Defense of the Democratic Republic of East Timor (CPD-RDTL) and former members of FALINTIL made international headlines.

Organized crime as both a feature of internal criminal activity and a link to transnational crime emerged in the first two years after the withdrawal of Indonesian forces and was believed likely to worsen in subsequent years. East Timor, situated in a zone that sustains the highest incident rate of sea piracy in the world, will have a maritime unit, but it will not be equipped or funded to deal with this category of crime. The Australian Federal Police (AFP) noted that there was "compelling evidence" of organized criminal activity, including drug trafficking, fraud, and money laundering, being conducted in and around East Timor.[37] Markets along the border with West Timor support black marketeering and have thus far been underregulated. In other instances, local leaders negotiated directly with smugglers to procure cheaper gasoline.[38]

After independence, crime statistics continued to be problematic. Anecdotal accounts indicated that crime seemed to have risen in most categories, with no perceptible decline in any category.

Homicides tended to be either gang related or to stem from family feuds. Arson was used as a tool to send a political message.

If international and national police capacity to address these threats was low, international police did make inroads against domestic violence. Domestic violence cases posed a special dilemma to CIVPOL, especially in the early months of the UN administration, as there is no statute within Indonesian criminal law codifying it as an offense. While UNTAET, empowered by Security Council Resolution 1272, eventually passed some regulations covering loopholes in Indonesian law, domestic violence remained prevalent.

By mid-2001 both the local population and its leaders were more aware that domestic violence was a priority issue for CIVPOL and foreigners. (In many cases local leaders permitted CIVPOL to exercise their powers of arrest, though just as often incidents simply weren't reported to police.) This may have been partially due to a media campaign by CIVPOL's Vulnerable Persons Unit and the Human Rights Unit as well as pressure by some police commanders on local leaders to comply with new laws. In subdistricts commanded by a CIVPOL member who did not deem domestic violence worthy of arrest, the practice of turning victims away or ignoring popular reports of crime continued with little change.

"Serious Crimes"

Recognizing the recently committed atrocities by Indonesian forces, UNTAET made provision for the prosecution of what were termed "serious crimes"—that is, cases of genocide, war crimes, crimes against humanity, murder, sexual offenses, and torture committed against the civilian population between January 1 and October 25, 1999.[39] UNTAET Regulation No. 2000/15 of June 6 established "Panels with Exclusive Jurisdiction over Serious Criminal Offenses" and also the exclusive jurisdiction of Dili District Court to hear such cases. The Office of the General Prosecutor and a Serious Crimes Investigation Unit (SCIU) were established shortly thereafter.[40] Before the inception of the SCIU and the serious crimes panels, some argued for passing serious crimes cases on to local dispute resolution processes,[41] but UNTAET officials did not take those arguments seriously. International prosecutors and police staffed the

SCIU and the Office of the General Prosecutor. Governments sec-onded personnel to UNTAET, and CIVPOL filled vacant posts. Investigators relied heavily on Timorese local staff to assist in trans-lation and interpretation.

The UN Mission of Support in East Timor (UNMISET), which succeeded UNTAET upon independence in May 2002, retained the authority to investigate and prosecute serious crimes. In carrying out its mandate through May 2005, the SCIU has been training Timorese police counterparts in investigations in a manner more akin to field training than realized previously by CIVPOL.

The SCIU received funding from UNTAET and voluntary contributions that enabled operations into 2005. Still, prosecution staff frequently operated without enough vehicles, computers, inter-preters/translator staff, or forensic scientists. The territory's sole morgue was located in the Dili compound of the SCIU and consisted of a container equipped to keep bodies cool. On one occasion, UNTAET cut the power supply and an SCIU investigator reportedly complained directly to the SRSG that "you should at least respect the dead even if you don't respect our work. The evidence is begin-ning to smell." Power was quickly restored.[42]

Public satisfaction with the prosecution of alleged perpetrators of the events that took place between January and October 1999 has been muted, partly owing to the uncooperative stance of the Gov-ernment of Indonesia, which has steadfastly refused to indict or extradite many high-ranking military officials. Indonesia signed a Memorandum of Understanding with UNTAET in April 2000, promising to cooperate fully with investigations into human rights violations and to turn over evidence and witnesses to the SCIU when requested. However, the Indonesian government has been less than forthcoming, arguing that it will try perpetrators itself.[43] More recently, the United Nations selected three international judges to determine how much progress has been made in bringing perpetra-tors of the postreferendum violence to justice.[44] At the same time, the governments of East Timor and Indonesia have established a Commission on Truth and Friendship, the purpose of which is to encourage "truth telling" by perpetrators in exchange for amnesty and the waiver of future prosecution.[45]

While Indonesia has refused to extradite suspected perpetrators to East Timor for trial, Indonesian courts have heard cases against Indonesian military, police, and civilian officials. Some consider these trials a whitewash. Indonesia's Ad-hoc Tribunal for Human Rights Violations in East Timor had, as of March 2003, acquitted eleven defendants charged with atrocities in East Timor and convicted and sentenced four officials.[46] These included East Timor's former civilian governor, Abilio Soares, who was found guilty of crimes against humanity in an Indonesian court and sentenced to three years in prison for failing to control his subordinates, and Brigadier General Noer Muis, TNI commander of East Timor, who received a five-year sentence for failure to act in connection with the Suai church massacre of September 6, 1999. Yet, as of April 2005, none of the sixteen military personnel tried by the Indonesian tribunal had served a day in jail, as either they were acquitted or their sentences were overturned on review.[47]

The purpose of serious crimes prosecutions was to forestall impunity. However, for many instances in which lower-ranking members of militia had carried out orders that did not include the killing of innocents, an alternative was sought. A Commission for Reception, Truth, and Reconciliation (CRTR) was established on July 15, 2001, partially modeled on South Africa's Truth and Reconciliation Commission. The UNDP, the World Bank, and several governments supported the commission. As of January 2005, the largest donor was Japan, which pledged nearly US$1 million. Yet projected needs for the commission exceeded US$5.6 million.[48]

The broad purpose of the truth commission was to promote national and community-level reconciliation through publicly airing cases, conducting inquiries, facilitating data collection, reporting findings, and making policy recommendations.[49] The transitional administrator appointed seven commissioners, who were selected by a special panel. Representation was drawn from various political parties, the church, and NGOs and included men, women, and youth.[50]

Promoting a Prison Industry

The treatment of pretrial detainees and sentenced prisoners has been a difficult matter in post-conflict reconstruction around the world.

UNTAET established a prison system in East Timor by enacting Regulation No. 2001-23 on August 28, 2001. That regulation created the Timor-Leste Prison Service and three penal institutions—Dili, Baucau, and Gleno—and provided for additional prisons. Correctional officers from Australia and New Zealand were seconded to UNTAET and continued service under UNMISET. As of March 2003, Dili held 215 prisoners, Baucau held 20 prisoners, and Gleno held 80 prisoners, numbers that included pretrial detainees, convicts, and juveniles.[51] A 2003 report by the UN Commissioner for Human Rights noted that incidents of assault on prisoners by prison guards and other prisoners had risen, though it remained low.[52] In addition, pretrial detainees made up an inordinately high portion of the prison population—some 80 percent.[53]

Training of Timorese prison staff by officers by the New Zealand Department of Corrections is the result of a grant from that government to the Consolidated Fund for East Timor. Total expenditures for prisons were slightly more than 1 percent of the total budget through 2002 but would likely suffer cutbacks owing to shortfalls in available government resources.[54]

Local Mechanisms of Justice

Many Timorese continued to prefer resolving problems without foreigners. Foreigners not only were largely incapable of fully understanding matters brought to their attention but often failed to respond to requests for assistance. When foreign administrators and police acted, moreover, family members and neighbors would vanish from the village for extended periods of time.[55]

Forced disappearance often occurred during the Indonesian occupation, which helps explain why Timorese typically do not favor incarceration for most offenses. During both the Portuguese colonial period and the Indonesian occupation, prison was used to contain threats to the government, an arbitrary device not necessarily part of a fair and impartial judicial process.

At the local level, conflicts are treated the same as marriages, funerals, or trade agreements. A premium is placed on discussion between two parties in the transaction, who follow a common set of rules in participating in a process that has broad social consensus. In a typical case, a man steals a bull from a family in a neighboring village. A member of the victim's family learns where the bull is being kept and a confrontation occurs among family members or (more likely) between the heads of the families about who is the proper owner of the bull. If the bull is not returned and the heads of the family are unable to work out the problem, they both go to elders within one of the villages and present their versions of the case. If the elders are unable to resolve the problem, the matter is then taken to the *suco* chief, who is above the village headmen. The penalties for these offenses are typically financial, and the suspected thief, if found guilty, is forced to pay the victim's family. The victim's family may be permitted to pick from among the offending family's livestock a large animal that will be slaughtered and become the centerpiece of a *suco* ritual, in which a mixture of animal blood and dirt signifies the purging of the offender's shame. Afterward, a large, open feast may be held to reconcile the two families and resolve the conflict completely.[56] Both the economic nature of the penalty structure and the reconciliation that is encouraged and later solidified through a communal feast are characteristic of how conflict over many issues is resolved in East Timor to this day.[57]

Reconciliation may be the centerpiece of successful arbitration by local leaders of disputes that pit individuals and usually families against one another. The process by which reconciliation is achieved derives great legitimacy from the fact that it is local, respects traditional values, and is implemented by recognized authority figures. Local leaders enforce rules, review incidents, find guilt or innocence, and impose sanctions when necessary, and the people generally acquiesce with both the concept and its implementation. This partially explains the difficulty in substantiating national institutions at the local level.

Analysis

CIVPOL and Police Reform

Postconflict construction of a Timorese justice system focused on the triad of institutions that make up such systems in other democratic states—that is, definable police, judicial, and penal institutions. While the right amount of money can buy the police cars, pay builders to construct courthouses, and renovate prison complexes, what relevance do the institutions together and separately have for security and justice at the village level? The enduring relevance of informal, local security practices in the postreferendum period can be directly linked to the inability or unwillingness of UNTAET to provide formal alternatives through local governance.

CIVPOL programs aimed at facilitating enforcement of national law by tying the legitimacy of first CIVPOL and then the TLPS to the recognized authority of local leaders. The Koban Community Policing Plan for East Timor incorporated the proclivity of central officials to relegate more authority to local leaders. It had several core strengths: (1) establishing a police presence within villages rather than at the subdistrict level, (2) incorporating police development into larger community development, (3) providing local commanders with greater autonomy to carry out projects, and (4) promoting efficiency in terms of case intake by courts. In these respects, the Koban plan was rather progressive as it offered a key government service at the village rather than subdistrict level, which was where the rest of UNTAET slowly set up shop.

Nevertheless, the plan suffered from several weaknesses. It confronted a change in CIVPOL administration, reshuffling of officials at CIVPOL headquarters, and budget limitations. Perhaps the central weakness of the plan was that it would have officially sanctioned a relationship between local police and a small number of unelected community leaders in many security-related matters, a mode at odds with the key tenets of community policing. This relationship would have preceded the formation of representative local government as well as any legislation according to which that government would be administered. As it turned out, the successors to the Koban plan, the Law and Order Committees, were essentially implemented in much the same fashion, emphasizing the resolution of problems through a reliance on the authority of local leaders.

CIVPOL received insufficient resources to properly ensure security. While resource limitations encouraged police to consider local practice and known traditions, they also permitted excesses and clear instances of injustice. Peacekeepers and CIVPOL often allowed village headmen to handle less serious problems, such as vandalism, destruction of property, and theft, which had consequences for both security and justice. This "hands-off" approach to such manifestations of disorder all too frequently characterized police responsiveness to more serious incidents. Eighteen months after the referendum, political violence and nonpolitical violence were cited in a survey conducted by the Asia Foundation (TAF) as the top two problems facing East Timor. In the TAF survey, conducted in March and April 2001, the question, "In your view, what are the biggest problems facing East Timor?" elicited the following responses:[58]

Violence	29%
Political conflicts	29%
Economy/prices	25%
Health/education	12%
Reconciliation	8%
Unmet local demands	8%
Ethnic differences	5%
Don't know	18%

Only 10 percent of respondents cited improved security in answer to the question, "What, if anything, has improved in East Timor?"[59] More than one year after the Asia Foundation's survey, focus group discussions held by the National Democratic Institute found a perception that the security situation was worsening, not improving.[60]

Suspected witches were attacked by local populations in Ermera and Lautem districts in late 2001 and early 2002, resulting in one confirmed death and perhaps others.[61] In March 2001, CIVPOL did nothing to stop a rampaging mob from Baucau from burning a portion of Viqueque town and killing a youth from a rival clan, who was himself implicated in a murder. The truce eventually brokered by a locally respected priest testified to the power of local mediators rather than to the justice and security services of UNTAET.[62]

Security inadequacies were not limited to rural villages. Intra-clan violence in Viqueque in March 2001 met with no police inter-vention whatsoever. In Dili and Baucau, where local leadership was weak or fragmented, no informal arrangements prevailed between police and local leaders, and police action was either overreactive or nonreactive in the face of serious security threats. A melee that erupted out of popular protests against police actions in Baucau (November 2002) and Dili (December 2002) left a number of protes-tors beaten or dead and the house of Prime Minister Mari Alkatiri in ashes.[63]

After a series of militia incursions from West Timor at Atsabe resulted in seven deaths in early 2003, there was a marked increase in political and public support for cooperative agreements between the police and the military. The East Timor Defense Force (ETDF) had taken over all military duties from peacekeepers in Lautem Dis-trict in July 2002 and progressively assumed these duties district by district across the island through 2004.[64]

The demand for order grew louder. Local leaders, cognizant of the presence of large numbers of unemployed youth in their villages, often set up village guard units composed of former Joventude youth or demobilized ex-FALINTIL. Unable to provide a modicum of secu-rity and order maintenance in most parts of the new state for threats that were beyond the capacity of village security organizations to handle, police ceded institutional responsibility for security and law enforcement to the ETDF, who were authorized to arrest suspects during operations.

At a more elemental level, CIVPOL never truly demonstrated how a "democratic" police force should be managed. Many of the most serious problems, such as police lack of reaction or overreaction to public disorder and the infrequency and inefficiency with which basic services were rendered, were interrelated. Lack of mobility for police also left some areas with no law enforcement coverage. The mobility issue was particularly serious given that police could not respond to some villages when weather made some roads impassable for days or weeks at certain times of the year. In mountainous areas, Timorese have traditionally used ponies to carry goods to market and for basic travel needs. A Royal Canadian Mounted Police officer trained the TLPS assigned to his station in mounted patrol, but such innovation was limited to individual CIVPOL and was not characteristic of CIVPOL policy and planning.

Neither CIVPOL nor bilateral agencies successfully implemented a comprehensive or regimented national field training program for the TLPS. As in the case of Haiti, the emphasis on the specialization of basic police functions, such as crowd control, within smaller units took precedence over broader force development that might have included greater attention to the operating standards at local station houses. Centralization of key police functions limits the capacity of local police stations to react appropriately to local disturbances and provide adequate law enforcement services, thereby widening the credibility gap that police often experience in a post-conflict environment.

Administrative guidelines held slim sway over the various nationalities represented within CIVPOL. Abuse of police powers and the use of excessive force were also CIVPOL problems requiring more internal discipline and the promulgation of enforceable rules. Within weeks of Peter Miller's arrival, for example, a commander at Manatuto District Station was removed from duty for allegedly demonstrating to TLPS rookies how to torture detainees.[65] During the same period, two CIVPOL officers were arrested in Dili for allegedly raping a young Timorese hotel worker.

There were also problems with information flow within the CIVPOL structure, specifically in the gathering of statistical data on crime. CIVPOL commanders and staff reported incidents from subdistrict station houses to the CIVPOL National Headquarters. Gathering data locally and methodically reviewing it at all command levels (national, regional, and local) simply did not take place, nor was the purpose of such rigor imparted to the TLPS. No uniform crime index existed to accurately record incidents, and the quality of station reports that would have contributed to such an index varied greatly. The combined lack of radio equipment, transport resources, and data management, mainly a result of inadequate and shortsighted planning, prevented CIVPOL and the TLPS from providing more than hit-or-miss law enforcement coverage outside main villages.

Removed from daily contact with the local population, CIVPOL commanders, especially at higher administrative levels, were able to ignore the widespread public perception that recruitment of the TLPS had been conducted unfairly. Timorese often felt strongly that youth who had either fought with FALINTIL or served the clandestine resistance in Joventude deserved preference in recruitment. Government job opportunities that did not demand special education (law, politics) or previous experience (FALINTIL) were in short supply for most Timorese.

Villages were well aware of how many young people, whose names CIVPOL vetted through local leaders to screen out possible militia, were recruited and which ones were not. The underrepresentation of some villages in the first batches of recruits as well as CIVPOL's decision to recruit several hundred ex-POLRI members only amplified perceptions of unfairness or corruption. The recruitment of ex-POLRI officers, when eligible youth who had actively resisted the Indonesian occupation regime remained jobless, generated anger among Timorese.

Even though both commissioners da Costa e Sousa and Miller had served in prior CIVPOL missions, CIVPOL's organizational deficiencies, so visible in those previous missions, continued to plague police administration in East Timor with little evidence of innovation to suit East Timor's environment. The repressive tendencies of mobile order maintenance units; the inability of international police to establish firm, transparent relationships with a wide cross section of people at the local level; the lack of adequate resources; and inadequate investigations all undercut accountability. As a result, citizens were less willing to report criminal incidents to UN police.

Weak mechanisms for hearing complaints and oversight further undermined the legitimacy of both CIVPOL and later the TLPS. The fact that a majority of neither CIVPOL nor peacekeeping troops spoke one of the local languages, coupled with a dearth of suitable interpreters and translators, might have contributed to the frequency with which Timorese took complaints to their leaders as opposed to police, though the stringent guidelines of local leaders were certainly the main reason. In other instances, CIVPOL and the TLPS under their charge routinely referred complainants back to village leaders.

When victims/complainants were told to seek out their local leader, no complaint was ever recorded.

Some local leaders insisted that villagers consult them before going to the police. As one *chefe de suco* declared, "I am responsible for security here. Nobody can go past me to the police."[66] For their part, international police, unable to fully provide law enforcement services, simply reinforced customary authority. To the public, less concerned with democratic theory and development of justice institutions, the old ways of doing business seemed much more likely to guarantee a resolution of problems and were much less risky than circumventing local leaders.

The creation of Law and Order Committees was intended to address the gap between the institutional mandate of police and the actual provision of police services. The infrequency with which meetings were conducted, and the fact that they were poorly promoted and misunderstood by both police and local leaders, did little to accomplish the intended objective. This was part of a wider government tendency to transmit information through local and traditional hierarchies rather than through grassroots, direct consultations. As one leader remarked, "We don't need *malay* [foreigner] committees. We solve problems our own way."[67]

Judicial

The slow process by which national law and complementary UNTAET regulations were publicly promulgated hindered the building of a foundation for the national justice system. It wasn't uncommon for some CIVPOL members to believe that there was no body of law governing their operations, leaving any incident to police discretion or within the proper but often murky jurisdiction of local leaders.[68] In addition, CIVPOL had inadequate preparation for criminal investigations, especially given language limitations.

Local understanding of national law was similarly slight. For instance, a civil offense was widely deemed among Timorese to be any bad act committed within a dwelling or between family members. Thus, domestic violence, assault, and even rape were matters for family heads to resolve. Even with the passage of UNTAET law and proactive police activity to encourage victims to report offenses, police often had difficulty locating complainants. Obviously, without a complainant a case would never be heard in court.

A principal dilemma for UNTAET and the government was tensions between customary practice and evolving national law. Judges, the police, corrections officers, local leaders, and the public did not fully understand the rules of the game—do all domestic violence cases get taken to the police and courts? What is the law of property? This quandary continued through the time of writing, as exemplified in one case in October 2004 in which an investigating judge at Dili District Court facilitated an informal settlement in an action well outside his mandate.[69] International officials and national counterparts have recognized the predicament but have thus far been unable to address it.

Apart from the policy dimension, courtroom adjudication of cases, already a slow process, fell off sharply both in 2002, when judges went on strike and during training exercises, and in early 2005, when all the judges failed to pass an evaluation. During late August 2002 a prison assessment by UNDP concluded that nearly 30 percent of the inmate population was being held in violation of due process.[70] The district courts at Suai and Oecussi did not reopen until March 2005, and cases under their jurisdiction had previously been heard in Dili District Court.

The backlogs and overcentralization of judicial processes had damaging ripple effects for the justice system. Training programs sponsored by international organizations were often presented in Dili, further assuring that the quasi-functional Baucau Tribunal would have to close its doors periodically. At one point in 2002, police in Viqueque were unable to locate an investigating judge in Baucau and were forced to transport a suspect to Dili, five hours distant, to present the case to an investigating judge. This required three CIVPOL members to be away from an understaffed subdistrict for more than two days.[71] Baucau Tribunal had regular hours of operation (twice a week) only beginning in late 2004, and then only because three Portuguese-speaking jurists from abroad were recruited to serve as judge, prosecutor, and court clerk.

Serious crimes cases were plagued throughout the UNTAET period by similar problems of backlog, lack of resources, and insufficient personnel during hearing phases as well as lax case file management and government oversight. The inherent fairness of proceedings was questioned owing to the inexperience of defense attorneys, who were facing more experienced public prosecutors, including international trial lawyers.[72]

There were additional problems. Most hearings were held at Dili District Court even if the cases were based on incidents occurring elsewhere in the territory. Courts failed to announce hearing dates to the public, and in some instances CIVPOL barred members of the public from entering the court for open hearings.[73] In mid-2004 Timorese police blocked access to a hearing at Dili District Court that was open to the public and concerned the alleged rape of an eighteen-year-old female by a group of police officers.[74] Generally, there were few outreach efforts that served to keep victims and witnesses apprised of the status of serious crimes cases.[75] As of spring 2005, the court clerks were still not using a whiteboard that was put up expressly for the purpose of notifying the public of hearings.[76] Public understanding of serious crimes prosecutions, whether in East Timor or Indonesia, is colored by the belief that crimes committed before January 1, 1999, many of them gross violations of human rights by Indonesian forces, will never be fully investigated or properly adjudicated by the formal system.[77]

As of February 2004, the SCIU had filed ninety-five indictments, including for all ten priority cases. The February 24, 2003, national indictment charged the former Indonesian minister of defense, the former governor of East Timor, and a number of high-ranking Indonesian military commanders with crimes against humanity. The SCIU's final indictments were filed in December 2004, mainly against suspects outside East Timor, and the office was scheduled for closure in May 2005 despite the fact that hearings and trials were still on the docket of the Special Panel for Serious Crimes.[78]

The CRTR

The CRTR hearings were characterized by confessions that were part of simple local events as well as larger ceremonies wherein groups of perpetrators acknowledged past crimes. In a successful reconciliation hearing, an agreement was signed by victims and perpetrators and submitted for signing by a judge as a formal court order that would grant immunity to the perpetrator, much like a plea bargain. If, during the hearing, new evidence came to light of acts that would fall into the category of serious crimes, the hearing would be referred back to the prosecutor.

In April 2004 the CRTR officially ended its work, having conducted 8 national hearings and 216 community reconciliations for 1,403 deponents. The CRTR also facilitated assistance to the victims of human rights violations and atrocities committed during the occupation and conducted public information outreach in refugee camps in West Timor.[79]

The threat of sanctions by the formal justice system in the form of prison sentences packaged together with the incentives of formal reconciliation was sufficient to make many perpetrators step forward. However, the weakness of institutions such as courts and police to deliver the sanctions in the likely event of a violation could seriously undermine the long-term impact of the CRTR's efforts. Many district courts continued to function irregularly, thus placing the burden of taking action against violations of community reconciliation agreements on the overtaxed courts that were functioning. Police had low capacity to protect victims and witnesses who participated in the hearings. Inaction by the formal system would ultimately decrease the motivation of perpetrators or communities to abide by the terms of reconciliation agreements. There was ample evidence that not everyone was pleased with the outcomes of reconciliation.[80] As one restaurant owner in Lautem District noted, "Nobody is really satisfied with the reconciliation process. We will square our debts once the internationals leave."[81]

The Prison System

Though UNTAET completely revamped prisons in East Timor, Timorese remain nonplussed about the social benefits of incarceration and fearful of what happens to prisoners. Deeper than tradition, perhaps, is the fear that exists across all age groups of government-administered justice, especially when it comes to talk of prisons.

For their part, local chiefs were concerned that a police arrest of which they were not informed could pose a problem once the suspect returned to the community, particularly if the arrest led to a detention outside the police station (such as at a prison in Dili). No matter how the case proceeds in court, or even when it doesn't, the only means by which an offender and his family may be reconciled with a victim and his family is a local process. A man who murdered his wife during the occupation, believing she had committed adultery, was reportedly required to undergo examination by village elders during a public ceremony after he had returned from prison.[82] On other occasions, local leaders stated publicly that returning convicts would face local processes if they wished to live in the community.

A communal economic rationale informs the sanctions meted out to offenders in customary law. The ultimate goal of full restitution within the community serves the community's interest by protecting the family and village unit from economic hardships due to a loss of labor. If part of the labor force is depleted by incarceration, then fewer people are available to farm village land and to provide village security and income to a family. When prisoners are moved far away from family and friends, the question arises of who will provide them with food and other basic goods given inadequate resources within the prisons.

The interest of Western donors and criminal justice experts in emphasizing the development of East Timor's prison institution is noteworthy and important inasmuch as it is imperative to establish a trained and professional prison service whose managers and guards respect the rights of prisoners and operate according to international standards for prison administration. But prisoners cited increasingly austere conditions in 2002 as motivating the escape of 181 persons from the Becora prison in August 2002.[83] Budgetary goals through fiscal year 2005 for spending on the prison system did not reflect a wide appreciation within the government of the actual costs of administering and operating such a service in accordance with international standards.[84]

No matter how advanced those prisons become, however, the justice system will have failed to deliver on its mandate if prisoners are well treated but incarcerated despite infringements on their due process rights or the existence of a valid legal order. The bottleneck in the system was with the judiciary, which influences how police use their discretion and the frequency with which people are held in extended, unlawful detention. As noted previously, lack of a clear line between formal and informal customary law contributes to the systemic malaise.

CONCLUSION

The 2003 population of East Timor stood at 800,000, with an estimated 30,000 persons remaining in refugee camps within West Timor proper.[85] Actors constructing a justice system in East Timor that was modeled on similar systems found in continental Europe encountered a variety of problems, some of which were evident in similar endeavors elsewhere. A number of these problems might have been forestalled through better mission design. Others, such as the mandate of CIVPOL and the prosecution of war crimes, are structural in nature and demand intense consideration by donors and the United Nations. In May 2005 UNMISET's mandate was set for extension partly because of the continued weakness of critical justice system institutions. Several issues highlight the usefulness of East Timor's experience for postwar societies.[86]

Imperfect Information

From the outset and through the early independence period, there was a lack of information or understanding of information by key players (CIVPOL, donor governments, international jurists, etc.) regarding the society within which the new institutions of police, a judiciary, and a prison service would be established. A common misunderstanding was to lump Timorese into two categories, pro- and anti-independence, when, in fact, social and ethnic cleavages dating back centuries underlay relatively recent political divisions. The barrier to effective planning and implementation posed by the information deficit was only reinforced by the time constraints typical of postconflict situations. Such problems encouraged the transfer of inadequate approaches from other development missions or contexts.

Deficiencies of CIVPOL

Maintaining order while a professionally trained, appropriately equipped police force is developed should be the job of international police. CIVPOL often fails to fulfill this task because its officers lack either the skills or the will to do their job. Ill-defined guidelines and policies along with bad management and political interference contribute to the failure. It is unrealistic to expect that a multinational police agency will function cohesively when police having vastly different levels of experience and training are thrown together in a place where they do not speak the language or understand the customs, much less laws. The learning curve for such an agency in a postconflict environment under rapidly changing conditions is simply too high for effectiveness. Adding the responsibility for training the new national force is detrimental to the future integrity of the new national force. As the UN Mission of Support in East Timor (UNMISET) continued to grapple with structural defects caused by faulty building blocks laid during the UNTAET period, including more recent allegations of misconduct by East Timorese police,[87] it was poignantly clear that problems left unresolved will not simply vanish of their own accord.

TLPS Development

A major flaw in the postconflict development of local police forces was the amount of discretionary authority given to inexperienced officers. Their actions were de-linked from the accountability normally provided by courts and civilian authorities. The common lack of a field training protocol, or even in-service training, meant that rookie police received no further guidance in how to carry out their tasks effectively. Under UNMISET, inexperienced TLPS officers were assigned to CIVPOL partners, a process referred to as field training. However, simply by comparing numbers of CIVPOL officers to numbers of TLPS members and without judging the competencies of the CIVPOL officers charged with such a responsibility, it is clear that this field training cannot meet international standards for field training programs. Performance standards should be high, not low, despite the urgency to deploy police on the street and maintain public order. This points to a need both for donors and host country nationals to agree on a realistic time frame for the development program and for greater rigor in promulgating standards once initial training has ended.

A lack of in-service training is just one indication of skewed priorities. The overspecialization of police weakens police command and control, tends to prevent local stations from delivering necessary services to local clientele, and may encourage excess by specialized officers, who are not subject to the same social controls as locally stationed officers. People simply will not take problems to the police if police fail to provide some measure of service to complainants, particularly if making a complaint violates local norms and risks sanctions from local leaders. Furthermore, it is implausible to expect the development of quality police criminal intelligence when there is so little public trust in police capacity to react appropriately, especially in a traditional society accustomed to repression.

Integrated Systems

Institutions may be built in stages, but not so systems. Police and courts must be linked at the beginning of postconflict reconstruction. In a civil law system, judges and prosecutors exercise more authority over police than in a common-law system. Perhaps mobile courts are one solution. The authority to review police decisions and cases without undue delay must be placed squarely within the mandate of tribunals, and any necessary resources should be committed up front to make sure that such reviews take place. If there are fewer judges by ratio to police, it would make more sense to bring the courts to the police. Spending more money on the courts would be a first good step toward establishing a fundamental role of courts, which is to oversee and review executive authority. It would also ensure that detainees are accorded due process rights in line with international standards and prevent stagnation of cases from choking the system.

But the integrity of a new justice system is not all about personnel and resources. It is also incumbent on donors and implementing actors to remember that in traditional societies, local rules often have as much legitimacy as law. Efforts to institutionalize those rules or otherwise reconcile international legal standards and local customary practice must be undertaken as soon as possible if law is to be accepted as the final authority over social conflict.

Budgets, Planning, and Initiatives

Peacebuilding operations operate on limited funds. Realistic budget priorities, given the environment, should be tied to tangible objectives that will guide strategic planning. New governments have limited resources, casting in doubt the sustainability of overly technology-dependent institutions once peacekeeping operations conclude. Police stations without electricity do not require computers. Assuring sustainable transportation and communications and promoting sensible data management appropriate for local conditions should be priorities both for international police and for new police institutions.

Furthermore, public impressions are important. In a society where weighty matters are often discussed and resolved publicly, efforts must be made to conduct important activities as openly as possible from the outset. The legitimacy of a police force will often hinge on the level of public acceptance of "who" will do the job and a broader understanding of "how" they will perform.

For the other pillars of a justice system, the costs of maintaining an adversarial justice system should receive as much consideration as the goals of that justice system, particularly when existing sociocultural practices support an alternate process. In developed countries, alternative dispute resolution is gaining ground for the very reason that the costs of trying every case and incarcerating every felon are simply too high.

How should a postconflict society undertake to provide justice for past crimes when progress toward developing a formal system is likely to be slow and the institutions administering justice likely to be weak? How can justice and security services be provided fairly and efficiently? Whether or not and how these questions are answered may greatly affect the degree to which the public accepts institutionalized justice and security as a monopoly enterprise of the state.

NOTES

Research for this chapter was assisted by the Social Science Research Council's Program on Global Security and Cooperation. In addition to the SSRC, the author wishes to express his appreciation to the following people, who provided useful commentary and criticism from several perspectives during earlier draft versions: Chuck Call, Jim Della-Giacoma, Edie Bowles, Roy Licklider, Karen West, and Violet West.

1. Alfred Russell Wallace, *The Malay Archipelago: The Land of the Orang-Utan and the Bird of Paradise* (London: MacMillan and Co., 1880).

2. Jill Jolliffe, *East Timor: Nationalism and Colonials* (St. Lucia, Queensland: University of Queensland Press, 1978).

3. I use the term "kingdom police force" based on Traube's account of local security in the colony. See Elizabeth Traube, *Cosmology and Social Life: Ritual Exchange among the Mambai of East Timor* (Chicago: University of Chicago Press, 1986), 111–112.

4. From comments of participating headmen at Freedom House's "Conference on Community Police and Justice," Laleia Subdistrict, April 25–28, 2001. To that end, the local priest could sometimes play a role in finding a settlement to conflict.

5. FRETILIN, originally the Social Democratic Association of East Timor (ASDT), was founded by José Ramos-Horta, Nicolau Lobato, and Mari Alkatiri, among others. See Jolliffe, *East Timor*, 63. Alkatiri was East Timor's first prime minister, and Ramos-Horta the first minister of foreign affairs.

6. James Dunn, "Crimes against Humanity in East Timor" in *Masters of Terror: Indonesia's Military and Violence in East Timor in 1999* (Canberra: Strategic and Defence Studies Centre, 2002).

7. See Robert Lowry, *The Armed Forces of Indonesia* (St. Leonards, New South Wales: Allen & Unwin, 1996.) The Indonesian military was referred to by its acronym, ABRI, until restructuring in April 1999. We use the subsequent acronym, TNI, for simplicity.

8. Jolliffe, *East Timor*.

9. See Lowry, *Armed Forces of Indonesia*, 111–112. See also Michael G. Smith with Moreen Dee. *Peacekeeping in East Timor: The Path to Independence* (Boulder: Lynne Rienner Publishers, 2003), Annex A.

10. Dunn, *Masters of Terror*. 2002, 65.

11. Wairoa-Harrison, 2000. Unpublished working paper circulated within UNTAET (Dili).

12. See UN Security Council Resolution 1246, June 11, 1999.

13. See reports in Sue Downie and Damien Kingsbury, eds., "The Independence Ballot in East Timor," Monash Asia Institute Working Paper 113 (Victoria, 2001).

14. United Nations, press release, "People of East Timor Reject Proposed Special Autonomy, Express Wish to Begin Transition to Independence, Secretary-General Informs Security Council" (New York: United Nations, September 3, 1999).

15. See World Bank, *Report of the World Bank Sponsored Joint Assessment Mission to East Timor* (Washington, D.C.: World Bank, December 1999); and Amnesty International, *Report on East Timor* (Amnesty International, July 2001).

16. See UN Security Council Resolution 1264, September 15, 1999.

17. See Kofi Annan, *Report of the Secretary-General on the United Nations Transitional Administration in East Timor,* 26S/2000/53 (New York: United Nations, January 26, 2000).

18. UNTAET, press release, "Funds Needed Urgently to Avert Strife in East Timor, Head of UN Mission Tells Security Council" (Dili: UNTAET, February 4, 2000).

19. Hansjoerg Strohmyer, "Policing the Peace: Post-conflict Judicial System Reconstruction in East Timor," 24 University of New South Wales Law Journal, 171, 2001.

20. "A Review of Peace Operations: A Case for Change," The International Policy Institute, King's College, London 2003. Reference taken from Part 2.G.1, Sec. 91; http://ipi.sspp.kcl.ac.uk/index.htm/ (accessed June 2003).

21. See Paul Pommerville, Ph.D., director of Timor Lorosae Police Service Policy and Planning Unit, and Inspector William Wairoa-Harrison, "Feasibility Study for Community Policing Based on the Koban System," September 13, 2000. Unpublished working paper circulated within UNTAET (Dili).

22. Asia Foundation, "Timor Loro Sa'e National Survey of Citizen Knowledge 2002" (Washington, D.C.: Asia Foundation, 2002). Fifty-four percent of respondents claimed that they preferred to receive political information from their *chefe de suco.*

23. UNMISET, "East Timor Police Service Development Plan," July 24, 2002.

24. See http://www.un.org/peace/etimor/UntaetF.htm (accessed April 2005).

25. The CNRT was established in 1986 for the purpose of coordinating resistance between local and national leaders. It was dissolved in June 2001.

26. A number were forced to undergo the training three and four times and still had difficulty passing. CIVPOL national firearms instructor, conversation with author, Lautem District, February 21, 2002.

27. UNMISET, "Supplemental Arrangement between the United Nations Mission of Support in East Timor and the Government of the Democratic Republic of East Timor on the Transfer of Police Responsibilities to the East Timor Police Service," May 20, 2002.

28. UNMISET, updated version of "East Timor Police Service Development Plan," July 24, 2002. See also UNMISET facts and figures as posted at http://www.unmiset.org (accessed April 2005).

29. Ibid., 5.

30. Aicha Bassarewan, vice minister for planning and finance, Government of East Timor, presentation at Second Regional PRS Conference, Phnom Penh, Cambodia, October 16–18, 2003, http://lnweb18.worldbank.org (accessed April 2005).

31. See Strohmeyer, *Policing the Peace*, 173.

32. Ibid., 174. Most of East Timor's lawyers underwent law studies in Indonesia and were thus familiar with that system.

33. Ibid.

34. Ibid., 176.

35. Judicial System Monitoring Programme, "Overview of the Justice Sector: March 2005," http://www.jsmp.minihub.org (accessed April 2005).

36. See also David Mearns, "Variations on a Theme: Coalitions of Authority in East Timor." Australian Legal Resources International, December 2001.

37. Mick Keelty, commissioner of AFP, cited in Desmond Ball, "The Defence of East Timor: A Recipe for Disaster?" *Pacifica Review*, 14, no. 3, October 2002, 11.

38. Author's field notes from visits to Manatuto and Bobonaro districts, spring 2001.

39. See also the recommendations of the International Commission of Inquiry (UN Doc. S/2000/59, January 31, 2000) and the UN Commission on Human Rights resolution of September 27, 1999 (UN Doc. 1999-4/1).

40. UNTAET Regulation No. 2000/16.

41. Strohmeyer, *Policing the Peace*, 179, 20n.

42. SCIU investigator, conversation with author, Dili, April 2001.

43. Amnesty International, *East Timor: Justice Past, Present, and Future* (New York: Amnesty International, July 2001).

44. See Terms of Reference for Committee of Experts, http://www.etag.org (accessed April 2005).

45. CIIR Email News, Catholic Institute for International Relations, "East Timor: Truth Commission Appointed to Settle Events of 1999," March 21, 2005, http://www.jsmp.minihub.org (accessed April 2005).

46. See Associated Press, "Indonesian Army General Sentenced to 5 Years in Prison," March 12, 2003.

47. Eduardo Gonzalez, "Timor Leste: Time for Action," *Jakarta Post,* April 2005, http://www.globalpolicy.org/intljustice/tribunals/timor/2005/0414 residual.htm (accessed May 17, 2005).

48. For other facts and figures, see Commission for Reception, Truth, and Reconciliation (CRTR), http://www.easttimor-reconciliation.org.

49. UNTAET Regulation No. 2001/10, Section 14.1.

50. Ibid., Section 4.3(a).

51. Amnesty International, *East Timor: Justice Past, Present, and Future* (July 2001) http://www.amnesty.org (accessed December 2002).

52. Ibid.

53. Ibid.

54. The Democratic Republic of East Timor Combined Sources Budget, 2002–2003.

55. Carter Center's "Conference on Community Police and Justice," Lospalos Subdistrict, February 21, 2002.

56. Freedom House's "Conference on Community Police and Justice," Cailaco Subdistrict, July 11–12, 2001. The illustration was provided by village headmen from the subdistrict.

57. According to a participant at the Carter Center's "Conference on Community Police and Justice," Viqueque Subdistrict, March 4, 2002, "When we solve the problem locally, we kill animals and have a big feast afterwards and everybody is happy. After a court makes a decision, everybody comes back to us anyways and there is no peace."

58. Responses combined all problems cited by 5 percent or more of respondents. See Asia Foundation, *East Timor National Survey of Voter Knowledge (Preliminary Findings)* (Washington, D.C.: Asia Foundation, May 2001), 23.

59. Ibid., 20.

60. See National Democratic Institute, *Government within Reach: A Report on the Views of East Timorese on Local Government* (East Timor: National Democratic Institute, 2003).

61. UNTAET Human Rights Office, conversation with author, Gleno (Ermera), February 5, 2002.

62. Father Adilindo, conversation with author, Laleia Subdistrict, December 15, 2001.

63. Reuters Wire, "UN Troops Mobilized as 5 Said Killed in East Timor," December 4, 2002.

64. The ETDF force projection is a 1,500-member light battalion and 1,500 reservists. As of April 2005, nearly 1,500 troops had completed training and were deployed throughout the state. See UNTAET Press Office, "Fact Sheet 16," April 2002.

65. UN Human Rights officer, conversation with author, Dili, December 2002.

66. Xaime F. Gonzales, *chefe de suco* of Umacit (Viqueque), conversation with author, Umacit, January 2002.

67. Alfredo Moniz da Costa, FRETILIN party representative, interview with author, Cailaco Subdistrict, December 14, 2001.

68. Manatuto Subdistrict station commander, private conversation with author, February 2001.

69. See Judicial System Monitoring Programme, "Justice Update," Issue 8/2004, October 5, 2004, http://jsmp.minihub.org (accessed April 2005).

70. UN Development Programme, "Timor-Leste Correctional Service: Setting the Course," August 2002.

71. Viqueque commander (CIVPOL), private conversation with author, January 23, 2002.

72. See Amnesty International, *East Timor: Justice Past, Present and Future.*

73. Ibid.

74. See Judicial System Monitoring Programme, "Justice Update," Issue 5, June 1–18, 2004, http://www.jsmp.minihub.org (accessed April 2005).

75. Efforts by local organizations like Yayasan HAK and the East Timor Jurists Association were exceptions, not the rule.

76. Judicial System Monitoring Programme, "Overview of the Justice Sector: March 2005," http://www.jsmp.minihub.org (accessed April 2005).

77. From participants' questions and comments at Freedom House's "Conference on Community Police and Justice," Cailaco Subdistrict, July 11–12, 2001.

78. Office of the Deputy General Prosecutor for Serious Crimes Timor-Leste, "Serious Crimes Unit Update," February 2004, http://www.scu-dili.org (accessed April 2005).

79. CRTR (CAVR [Comissão de Alcolhimento, Verdade e Reconciliação]), "CAVR Update, February–July 2004," http://jsmp.minihub.org (accessed April 2005).

80. Chris McCall, "Old Grievances Fester as the Justice System Stalls," *South China Morning Post,* March 13, 2003, http://www.jsmp.minihub.org.

81. Businessman, conversation with author, Lospalos Subdistrict, February 22, 2002.

82. From a participant's statement at Freedom House's "Conference on Community Police and Justice," Laleia Subdistrict, April 25–28, 2001.

83. UN Commission on Human Rights, *Question of the Violation of Human Rights and Fundamental Freedoms in Any Part of the World: Situation of Human Rights in Timor-Leste,* Report of the UN High Commissioner for Human Rights, March 4, 2003, http://www.unhchr.ch/pdf/chr59/37AV.pdf.

84. See UN Development Programme, "Timor-Leste Correctional Service." The UNDP estimated that approximately 77 percent of all prisoners were awaiting trial.

85. As for refugees, see Human Rights Watch, *World Report 2003: East Timor* (New York: Human Rights Watch, 2003).

86. See "U.N. Security Council Tipped to Approve New Mission for East Timor," http://www.jsmp.minihub.org (accessed April 2005).

87. Ibid.

10

Engendering Justice and Security after War

TRACY FITZSIMMONS

FROM HAITI AND BOSNIA TO EAST TIMOR AND AFGHANISTAN, peacebuilding has become the central challenge in regions emerging from civil war or political instability. Peacebuilding in recent postconflict settings is essentially about two things: first, establishing and maintaining security, and second, constituting and buttressing a democratic political system.[1] With regard to the former, security efforts cluster around demilitarization and ridding the country of ethnic and politically motivated violence. In oversimplified terms, international organizations, governments, and nongovernmental organizations claim peacebuilding success when there is a reasonable degree of certainty that armed conflict will not recur, when free and fair elections are held, and when a person's skin color, religious persuasion, or political party affiliation is not likely to get him killed.

I say "him" because gender is largely absent from discussions of postconflict peace. Postwar victories are claimed even as women experience increasing levels of some forms of physical and sexual violence and economic and political isolation. For many women, the end of war does not mean the advent of security. War can provide pockets of peace and opportunity for women, whereas peacetime,

351

paradoxically, can yield increasing violence, insecurity, and economic and political constraints for them. Women's groups in El Salvador, for example, report that after that country's civil war ended in 1992, levels of domestic violence increased, partly because thousands of men returned home with few job opportunities and twelve years of experience with violence. In Bosnia, women claim that men, unsatisfied with the outcome of the most recent ethnic conflict, continue to fight in their homes, using the weapons of sexual and domestic violence.[2]

In search of stabilization, the United Nations as well as local leaders reinforces, perhaps inadvertently, visions of country, home, and family that domesticate and subordinate women.[3] Despite a publicized focus on gender and women's issues in postwar operations, issues such as nonpolitical rape and domestic violence tend to get lost in peacebuilding missions. At the authors' workshop in preparation for this volume, a Rwandan scholar exclaimed, "If you have 120,000 people in jail waiting to be tried for genocide and thirty-six judges in the whole country, how do you expect courts and police to concern themselves and deal effectively with things like domestic violence?"[4]

In postconflict settings, institutions charged with providing security to all offer that security unequally and unevenly to women—if at all—owing to limited resources and competing needs. At the heart of this problem are two conceptual problems. First, international actors, including the United Nations, ineluctably privilege threats to *international* security, including stabilizing a society from future warfare, over threats to *human* security. Pacifying unruly global neighborhoods drives UN Security Council decisions to create peacekeeping missions and to fund peacebuilding operations far more than concerns about security from "everyday" violence, which fall outside the Security Council's view of its authority. Second, conceptions of security—in theory and in practice, at the international level and at most local levels—are gender biased.[5] Despite genuine achievements in advancing women's rights in some postwar contexts (most notably in post-Taliban Afghanistan, where the benefits remain highly uneven), the special challenges, needs, and context of women's security are insufficiently incorporated into Western peacebuilding efforts and even academic conferences on postwar security.[6]

In this chapter, I offer some theoretical reflections as well as policy prescriptions concerning the integration of women and women's issues into conceptions and mechanisms of domestic security and justice in postconflict settings—in particular with regard to the United Nations Civilian Police (CIVPOL). In doing so, I draw on personal field research completed in Haiti, Central America, and the former Yugoslavia during UN peace operations, as well as on the case studies in this volume.

CIVPOL AND WOMEN AFTER WAR

Most would agree that women experience war and conflict in a different way than men. Feminist theorists long ago began arguing that reactions to war, to demilitarization, and to protection of home and family are gendered, so it is unremarkable that women also experience peacetime differently than men. But what some may find surprising, and disquieting, is how international and domestic actors may be setting women up for an *unpeaceful* transition toward democracy and peacetime. Levels of domestic violence, nonpolitical rape, and sexual harassment may actually increase in postconflict periods as returning soldiers, who are overwhelmingly male, redirect their aggression to their households, demanding a return to prewar societal patterns of interaction and responsibilities. Yet the law and its enforcers offer little protection to women during this period, as they instead focus their energies on political and ethnic violence, riot control, and demilitarization and disarmament. Even when they seek to address nonpolitical violence, their concerns privilege higher-profile organized crime, street crime, homicides, and political corruption. Women may have made great gains across many cultures, but the ways in which international actors conceive of, train, and supply new police forces and judicial systems in transitional societies create a gendered sense of peace and security for women.

Transitions from war offer unique opportunities to reshape domestic norms, institutions, and practices, especially in the realm of internal security and policing.[7] Yet peace treaties, peacebuilding missions, and new civilian police forces are designed first to ensure international security, second to ensure national-level *public* stability, and third to guarantee private peace *in the realms that are most visible to the public.* In all cases, peace is largely measured by men of men.

How should we examine issues of gender in postconflict international activities, especially with regard to security? I herein focus on the increasingly accepted use of United Nations international police personnel in peace operations. Known as CIVPOL, these forces grew from 35 in 1988 to 3,500 in 1997 to nearly 8,000 in 2001 (then deployed mainly in Bosnia, Kosovo, and East Timor) before dropping back to 6,700 in December 2004 (deployed largely in Kosovo, Liberia, and Haiti).[8] Officers are recruited from UN member states and serve on short-term contracts of six to eighteen months. Their activities (and whether the officers are armed or have arrest powers) vary from mission to mission, depending on the mandate approved by the Security Council.[9] Increasingly, the international community relies on CIVPOL not only to monitor local police forces after wars but also to train and "mentor" new or reformed local police forces. Although bilateral and regional organizations engage in police education, training, and advice, CIVPOL is the main vehicle for police monitoring and field training in most postconflict settings, and its salience continues to grow as of this writing.

And while peace operations are still a very male domain, there *has* been an improvement, or learning across cases, with regard to the integration of women into new civilian police forces and the parallel role of CIVPOL. By way of example, I compare two cases in which CIVPOL was highly involved in the creation and training of the new civilian police: Haiti (focus on 1994–97) and Kosovo (focus on 1999–present).

Haiti

Following the ouster of Haiti's democratically elected president Jean-Bertrand Aristide in 1991, the United States led a UN-authorized multinational military force that restored him to power in September 1994.[10] The military force, accompanied by international police monitors under U.S. command, was replaced by a United Nations peacekeeping operation in February 1995. The UN Mission in Haiti (UNMIH) was the first ever whose mandate explicitly included creation of a new police force.[11] The Aristide government decided to disband the Haitian armed forces, replacing them with a 5,000-member Haitian National Police (known by its French acronym, HNP), to be trained at a new police academy in Haiti initially run by the U.S. Department of Justice. The law creating the HNP was adopted by the Haitian parliament and signed by President Aristide in late 1994. President Aristide's return to the presidency signaled the end of a coup regime under which, as in Bosnia and Sudan, rape was used as a political tool. For the many Haitian women who had been terrorized by the former military forces, the civilian HNP provided a ray of hope that security under the new regime would include women and protect them from violence.

In February 1995 the first class of police cadets began training at the new police academy. There were no specific efforts to recruit women into the force, nor did the United Nations or the HNP set target goals for the number of women officers. By the end of the deployment of the last of the first round of classes, only 7 percent of the HNP were women officers, many of whom were relegated to serving as desk officers and traffic cops. Within the first year of deployment, and reportedly under the urging of some CIVPOL personnel, some police stations endeavored to begin a system whereby women complainants could report crimes to women officers, but the practice was far from institutionalized.

CIVPOL officers participated in classroom training and served as the field trainers for the HNP during the two and a half years of the UN operation.[12] For the first classes through the academy, all the instructors were men. The four-month-long training course for all new Haitian police officers, designed and run by a U.S. Department of Justice agency, included less than half a day on rape and domestic sexual violence, and nothing more generally on gender issues or the treatment of women. Two women police cadets reported in interviews with the author that much of that half day was spent with the male recruits making snide and sexually explicit comments. In 1996, in response to the secretary-general's concern that the four-month basic training course was "widely considered insufficient," the training program added training centers in each of Haiti's nine *départements* to focus on six priority areas: crowd control, criminal investigation, collection and analysis of information and operations, traffic, personnel management, and management of resources. Issues related to women and gender were noticeably absent from the list as well as from the course content.[13]

This lack of enthusiasm for women's involvement in policing in Haiti was unfortunate, as women proved to be responsible members of the HNP. Research shows that across many cultures, women police officers use force less frequently than their male counterparts, are less authoritarian in their interactions with citizens and with officers of lower rank, possess better communication and negotiation skills, and are more likely than male officers to defuse potentially violent situations.[14] Among the Haitian police force, these studies were borne out in practice. At the end of the first six months of the HNP's deployment, the inspector general's office was bogged down investigating complaints of police misconduct—but not one of those cases was filed against a women officer, a statistic probably boosted by the institutional reluctance to deploy women on the street. Nor had the inspector general received any complaints of improper use of force or firearms by women officers; yet during the same period several male officers were under review for improper use of firearms. Despite this positive performance, women officers received a less than warm welcome in Haiti; men officers frequently refused to go out on patrol with women partners, or to share sources or leads with them.[15]

The assistant inspector general in Haiti, in response to questions on women, policing, and violence in Haiti in 2000, replied to the author, "This study is silly. Crime and politics are the most important [issues] in Haiti now. All you want to know about is women. They are not so important."[16] In Haiti, women are seen as inferior and outside the realm of politics and crime—and therefore unimportant in discussions of security. Addressing the Security Council in December 1996, Haiti's permanent representative at the United Nations, Pierre LeLong, reported that "the specific needs of the National Police had been identified, and before the end of the year, the force would be able to guarantee peace and security throughout Haiti"[17]—at a time when more than 40 percent of the population reported experiencing rape or domestic violence.[18] At the end of 1997, after nearly two years of CIVPOL's involvement in Haiti, women officers made up less than 6 percent of the HNP, no women's police stations existed, and remnants of a Napoleonic Code still did not criminalize all forms of violence against women. As recounted in more detail in the Haiti case study in this volume, the entire security reform effort had become plagued with problems and failure by the time of the U.S.-pressured resignation of then-reelected president Aristide in 2004. Efforts to promote gendered security in Haiti since that time are beyond the scope of this study, but women's security was marginal in the UN-led approach to police reform in the mid-1990s.

Kosovo

After NATO's bombing campaign in response to the displacement of hundreds of thousands of Kosovo Albanians in 1999, an agreement with the Federal Republic of Yugoslavia (FRY) permitted a NATO-led Kosovo Force (KFOR) to occupy Kosovo. As part of this process, the Yugoslav armed forces, as well as almost all police forces and judicial personnel, withdrew from the territory of Kosovo, leaving a vacuum in policing, justice, and other local administration.[19] Under UN Security Council Resolution 1244, the United Nations acquired unprecedented powers over the territory, assuming the full range of government functions, including taxation, administration of justice, administration of postal service, banking regulation, and payment of all public employees at the municipal level. The total absence of any recognized Kosovar organization specializing in policing or justice led the Security Council to grant unprecedented executive authority to CIVPOL. Deployed beginning in summer 1999, the CIVPOL mission would grow to the largest in history at roughly 4,500 officers in 2001, and more than half of that number is still in Kosovo as of this writing. A central part of the UN mission was the creation of a new Kosovo Police Service (KPS), to consist of 6,000 members trained in a police academy run by the Organization for Security and Cooperation in Europe (OSCE).[20]

Unlike with the cases of Haiti and Bosnia, rape was not widely used as a political tool in Kosovo, although there are reported individual cases of the Kosovo Liberation Army military police participating in sexual violence against teenage girls, and of FRY soldiers raping ethnic Albanians in Kosovo. But a United Nations Development

Fund for Women (UNIFEM) survey found that 23 percent of women in Kosovo have experienced domestic violence.

In the five years between the founding of Haiti's HNP and Kosovo's KPS, some advancement can be noted with regard to the international community's commitment to gendered policing. The UN Mission in Kosovo (UNMIK) and the OSCE mandated a target of 20 percent women for the KPS. UNMIK's stated objective was that "[t]he recruitment and selection process for the Kosovo Police Service should strive to include no less than 20% *females*. The degree of interest received during recruitment will influence the gender composition. However, specific strategies will be developed to encourage the participation of women."[21] OSCE planning documents likewise underscore the importance of including women in the KPS as a way to "enhance the capabilities of the organization and provide a balance between the agency and the population it serves."[22] UNMIK and the OSCE also encouraged increased research into violence against women and attempted to strengthen the laws criminalizing such violence. The training of the KPS, designed by U.S. Department of Justice International Criminal Investigative Training Assistance Program (ICITAP) personnel in collaboration with the OSCE, included more modules on domestic violence, rape, and women's issues than heretofore seen in a UN mission. Of the first 16 classes graduating into the KPS, 18 percent of the trainees were women—a percentage higher than in any postconflict peace force involving the United Nations, and also higher than the average percentage in U.S. police forces. And the presence of women seems to be sustaining: as of April 2005, 15.85 percent of the KPS was women.[23] In September 2000 UNMIK's joint administrator for civil society, Vjosa Dobruna, chaired a multiethnic strategic planning session on the integration of women throughout the mission.[24] At about the same time, UNMIK created a Trafficking and Prostitution Investigative Unit. In the secretary-general's report of December 31, 2003, women accounted for 25 percent of judges and 17 percent of prosecutors in Kosovo.

However, from a women's rights perspective, the deployed KPS and the role of internationals in its founding still leave much room for improvement. Initially, only 1.5 percent of UNMIK police officers were women; that percentage had increased only to 5.5 percent as of

April 2005. After finding it difficult to recruit enough women to fill 20 percent of the KPS slots, UNMIK reduced the target number to 15 percent—a goal that has been met. In the institutional structure of the KPS, there are no women's police stations and no separate sections dealing with crimes against women and children. And while international actors aimed appropriately high in the initial target of 20 percent women in the KPS, they neglected to institutionalize any mechanisms that would protect women officers from being sidelined into the low-profile policing areas of personnel, traffic, and administration. Furthermore, despite the solid numbers of women in the judiciary, OSCE reports state that the legal system in Kosovo lacks "a mechanism and means to prosecute sexual violence cases and protect the victim," which also holds true for trafficking cases (see chapter 8). A 2001 OSCE assessment of the justice sector in Kosovo found that "[t]here has been no practical training of judicial, police or social services personnel on issues of sexual violence, including heightening sensitivity towards alleged victims. Over the past six months, the average sentence for sexual violence cases has declined from three years to one year."[25] In February 2005 the secretary-general critiqued the gender balance in Kosovo, saying, "The new Government has . . . not yet taken steps to promote gender equality, including through the development of policies and strategies to address gender gaps, the establishment of an office for gender equality, harmonization of law with the principles of gender equality and the allocation of funds for the action plan for gender equality. . . . Women are underrepresented at all levels."[26]

LESSONS FOR GENDERING POSTCONFLICT SECURITY

The case studies in this chapter underscore the importance for peace operations of taking more deliberate and far-reaching steps toward adopting a framework of gendered policing in which the peacekeepers and the new civilian police forces do not or are not perceived to sustain, permit, or participate in violence against women. Gendered policing in peace operations, while clearly making some significant inroads between the Haiti mission and the Kosovo mission, is still insufficient and subject to reversal in most postconflict societies. This

study of gender and the role of CIVPOL in postconflict civilian policing yields several lessons for how to work toward institutionalizing a
more gendered conception of policing and justice.

First, *peacekeeping policymakers should focus more on violence and
less on crime.* Because violence is a principal and direct concern of
peace operations, and because some violence, especially domestic
violence, may not be criminalized, an emphasis on reducing violence
rather than fighting crime may augment security from physical
harm.[27] Violence against women should be classified as a "crime" and,
as such, should be dealt with in criminal court. But in Kosovo, the
law did not define rape within a marriage as a criminal act. In the
absence of appropriate laws and social services, the KPS and international police officers "have been mediating cases involving domestic
violence, either facilitating a reconciliation between the parties or
admonishing the husband because the wife recants her statement."[28]
In less than half of the Latin American countries does violence
against women automatically fall under the penal code; in the rest of
Latin America, allegations of violence against women (or children)
go before a criminal court judge only in cases of extreme injury,
death, or threat of death.[29] Violence against women "in defense of
honor" is still permitted in many posttransition countries, as well as
the requirement that women establish their virtue before being
allowed to bring rape or sexual violence charges against a man. In
many cases, the law suggests or requires mediation or reconciliation
measures before a criminal or civil case involving domestic violence
can be brought to court—which is tantamount to prescribing mediation for an assault or attempted homicide case.

Second, *timing and impetus are crucial.* Gendering police forces
at their moment of founding or significant reform can minimize a
zero-sum identity game. If gendered policing is introduced when a
police force and its identity as "masculine" are not already established, the entrance of women and gender issues into the force is less
likely to be perceived as a loss of identity and power for the male
officers. The key is to emphasize that there are mutual interests—
not an ensured loss—in gendering a new or reformed police force.
Such benefits extend not only to the women officers but also to male

cops, the police institution at large, and democratization processes more generally.

The same can be said for judicial systems. As postconflict transitions nearly always involve a rewriting or redefinition of constitutions, penal and civil codes, and judicial norms, efforts should be made to introduce pro-women legislation, women judges, and gender sensitivity training for justice system personnel from the beginning of the reform process. Where this has occurred, it has marked a contribution to improving institutionalized protection of women's rights. Likewise, the training, composition, and leadership within CIVPOL operations should recognize and seek to address issues of gender imbalance right from the start of the mission.[30]

The case of East Timor suggests that a Gender Affairs Unit that is well placed and started early in a peacebuilding mission raises the level of future participation and integration of women: more than 30 percent of the Timorese Police Service are women, 50 percent of the members of the Village Development Councils are women, and legislation has been passed that addresses violence against women and equal participation of women in the political process.[31] The United Nations Mission in Support of East Timor (UNMISET) and the national civilian police also launched a Vulnerable Persons Unit that opened the way for a tripling in the number of reports of violence against women. The late Sergio Vieira de Mello, former special representative of the secretary-general in East Timor confessed, "I was against the creation of a Gender Affairs Unit for the United Nations' Transitional Authority in Timor-Leste. I did not think a Gender Unit would help rebuild institutions from the ashes of what the militia left. I was wrong."[32]

Third, *coalitions are necessary for security reforms.* No Latin American country has made progress toward gendering its civilian police force without the existence of coalitions—within and between civil society, international funding agencies, and women officers. In highly patriarchal and sexist societies, police forces see little incentive or justification to "de-masculinize" their institutions without receiving pressure from outside domestic coalitions. In the Brazilian case, it was a joint effort between women's organizations, human rights organizations, and state-level Ministries of Justice that led to the opening of women's police stations and the doubling of the number of women cops.[33] In Guatemala, the women's movement joined forces with the indigenous movement to demand representation in a new civilian police force. But in Haiti, where few organizations and no coalitions sustained a focus on gendered security during the creation of new police forces, the percentage of women police officers and the number of police programs aimed at gendered crimes fell between 1995 and 1999. International funding and training agencies such as ICITAP and CIVPOL have yet to learn that their few efforts to gender postconflict police forces will fail if they do not also train civil society groups to work with the police and act as watchdogs of the police, as well as encourage other societal groups that are underrepresented within the criminal justice system to forge alliances with women in gendering the new police forces.[34] Furthermore, community-policing models likely mean little for women's rights and gendered policing if there are no women's organizations extant or involved in the community.[35]

Fourth, *gendered policing cannot occur in a vacuum.* The United Nations and others who work in postconflict settings must begin to see the totality of the security issue. Too often, those responsible for constructing a domestic security system include one or two powerful, pro-women ideas—that is, changing divorce laws, allowing women to enter the police force, offering psychological counseling to rape survivors. But without gendering the entire system, each of these changes makes very little impact. In combating violence against women, policing must be just one link in a solid chain uniting the courts, the prisons, the lawmakers, and civil society. And while this is nothing new, it bears repeating: peacekeepers and police units must see physical, political, and economic violence against women as a crime *and* as a human rights abuse. Human Rights Watch argued that in the South African case, "violence against women has not achieved the sort of high-level political attention that the more general political violence, for example, has been given both during the transition period and under the new regime."[36] The same could be said for the way in which CIVPOL approached the training and oversight of the new civilian police forces in El Salvador, Haiti, and Bosnia.

Fifth, *training and transparency cannot be shortchanged*. In Bosnia, 60 percent of women surveyed said that they would never go to the courts, police, or Center for Social Work to report domestic violence because of their fear of the institutions, fear of not being understood, or the perceived inability of the institutions to do anything. According to one study, "No woman can report a rape, sexual assault or incident of domestic violence and expect the police to investigate it fairly. Police—predominantly male—have little or no training in investigating sexual offenses in general, or domestic violence in particular, and can themselves be an obstacle by embarrassing women or making women feel that they are partly or wholly to blame."[37] Yet the training of the Bosnian police force, which did not include gender issues, was at least initially a CIVPOL-conceived set of courses.

Sixth, *development agencies must incorporate gender more into their antiviolence and security programs*. The U.S. and British government aid agencies have bilaterally undertaken some training in domestic violence and gender crimes, but not to the extent needed. Similarly, growing violence reduction efforts by the World Bank have included some domestic violence programming but emphasized other categories of violence, such as gang violence and armed assault. Although the importance of women to most development agencies makes these agencies a promising mechanism for engendering security, among major institutions only the Inter-American Development Bank has embraced a holistic notion of violence reduction that reflects the importance of reducing gender violence.[38] It has funded projects to combat domestic violence in several Latin American countries.

Seventh, *statistics are important—and must be generated on local and national levels*. Throughout the first five years of the new Haitian National Police, crime statistics were kept and compiled irregularly. In one police station in southern Haiti, the author interviewed the police chief, the head of investigations, the head of reporting (of crimes), two police officers, and one CIVPOL officer; each gave her different statistics for the number of rapes and domestic abuse cases reported, the number of arrests, and so on. And the numbers not only varied wildly within the police station but also differed from the number recorded with the French gendarmerie advisers to the Haitian police. Such statistical chaos was also present, but to a lesser extent, for nongender-specific crimes of homicide and armed robbery. It is difficult to fight crime and to get donor support for antiviolence programs if reliable statistics are unavailable.

Eighth, *numbers matter.* Societies need not just numbers in the form of statistics but also numbers of women, en masse, involved in policing at all levels. In October 2000 the Security Council (Resolution 1325) called for greater inclusion of women in peace operations in the field—noting specifically the importance of women in the military and police; that same year the European Parliament issued a call for at least 40 percent of all peacekeeping posts to be filled by women. These international institutions are headed in the right direction. If women suffered violence at the hands of a prior security force (such as the military or police), they are unlikely in the postconflict period to be suddenly trusting and willing to report violence committed against them to the new, supposedly democratic police force. And in the postconflict period, the issue is about not just what new violence is inflicted on women but also the physical and mental trauma associated with past violence that went untreated. According to South African government reports, more than 97 percent of rapes went unreported in 1994. Having a threshold number of women officers so that the new police force is not identified as "masculine," and having women officers take police report statements from women crime survivors, will contribute to women being more willing to report crimes against them.[39] The importance of numbers also applies to agencies and units dealing with trafficking, where it is very important that women who have been sold and prostituted by men be able to tell their story to female investigators. While women are increasing in number in CIVPOL and in new civilian police forces, it was not until 2003 that the United Nations' first female police commissioner assumed the highest in-country post, in East Timor.

Ninth, *representativity is necessary but not sufficient.* Infusing new police forces and justice systems with lots of women personnel will alter some practices and perceptions but will fall far short of delivering gendered security. Doing more than adding representativity to police forces is in the spirit of Article 7 of the 1994 Inter-American Convention on the Prevention, Punishment and Eradication of Violence against Women, which calls on states parties to "take all appropriate measures . . . to modify legal or customary practices which sustain the persistence and tolerance of violence against women."[40] International and domestic actors should seek to (re)structure police forces and redefine policing practices and norms such that the police do not, or are not perceived to, sustain and permit violence against women. In countries where state violence against women, or tolerance of it, has been institutionalized, a concerted effort (e.g, public relations campaign) may be necessary to assure that public perception of the women-friendly nature of the police or judiciary keeps time with the implemented changes. Above all, protection of female victims is not enough; prevention of violence should be the goal. One model of gendered security is that of South Africa's establishment of an independent Commission on Gender Equality, an attempt to get beyond just numbers to use participant observation to assess the level of gender advances in security, politics, and social realms.[41]

Tenth, *progressive policing does not usually come from international peacekeepers.* CIVPOL missions bring together a group of mostly male police officers, hailing from diverse countries that often have their own forms of institutionalized sexism, to train a mostly male local police on how to protect citizens. It should not be surprising that the end result is less than women centered. For example, one of the more progressive innovations in gendered policing during the past two decades has been the creation of women's police stations or women's sections within police stations. Studies show that women's police stations encourage higher reporting levels and more citizen confidence in the police.[42] Yet, of the more than twelve countries in Latin America that have women's police stations, not one was the result of a mission of the United Nations or the Organization of American States. Most notable in postconflict women's policing is the case of Nicaragua, where without the aid or guidance of international peacekeepers, the Nicaraguans managed to construct a system in which women officers and gender sensitivity are woven into policing, not set apart in a marginalized office.

Eleventh, *police officers and international peacekeepers should be held accountable* for the violence they commit or are complicit in against women. Promoting security that is offered equally to women is exceedingly difficult if those doing the teaching or enforcing do not model the behavior themselves—particularly when it is as egregious as the sex slave trade. One UN report charges that "law enforcement is often complicit, either overtly or by silence and failure to act" in the trafficking of women.[43] Unofficial reports abound in Bosnia and Kosovo of domestic and international peacekeepers having sexual relations with minors, buying sex in brothels, harboring trafficked girls, and allowing or participating in trafficking women. CIVPOL, the KPS, the International Police Task Force, and Dyncorp have all reportedly dealt, in a very quiet way, with personnel who have participated in such acts.[44] In an interview with the author, one CIVPOL officer in Bosnia claimed that such behavior "is common, more common than anyone will admit." Pressed to explain why she didn't demand prosecution or go public with this information, she told the author that "the old-boys network works just as well or better here than it does at home"—officers fear dismissal and therefore are unwilling to report such behavior. An International Crisis Group report found that the local police in Bosnia were a "major user group" of trafficked women.[45] Public denunciation and prosecution of such cases not only are legally mandated and just but would do much for furthering the public's perception that peacekeepers are committed to an equal peace for all citizens. The United Nations Mission in Bosnia-Herzegovina Special Trafficking Operations Program is a step in the right direction.

CONCLUSION

A security and justice system biased against women and their rights is, of course, not a problem particular to postconflict societies. The United States, India, and Germany have all had their individual challenges with recruiting high numbers of women police officers and with providing women with supportive spaces and structures in which to report abusers. However, a bias against women becomes even more exacerbated by conflict, digging deep, gendered trenches in a society that can then become frozen in the newly formed political institutions. And nothing damages the chances for a successful political transition more than the perception that people can get away—in public or in private—with the same impunity under the new democracy as they did under the former regime or under war, particularly when that perception is held by more than half of the population—even if it is the disempowered female half.

To return to a variation on the question posed in the introduction to this edited volume, *Can societies emerging from armed conflict create systems of justice and security that ensure basic rights, apply the law effectively and impartially, and enjoy popular support?* In that introduction, the volume's editor contends that the answer is "Yes, but." However, in the case of women's security, the case studies presented in this chapter, and the lessons thereof, suggest that the answer may be somewhat less positive. While there have been learning and subsequent improvements in gendered policing and justice between Haiti and Kosovo, where gender is concerned the answer to the question is more appropriately "No, not fully." A central challenge in these societies is how to transition the culture while also transitioning the political system. For some, gendering policing is tantamount to undermining the security of men; at which point does that then undermine the peace?

NOTES

Portions of this chapter have been reprinted, with publisher's permission, from the author's chapter, "The Postconflict Postscript: Gender and Policing in Peace Operations," in Dyan Mazurana, Angela Raven-Roberts, and Jane Parpart, eds., *Gender, Conflict and Peacekeeping* (Boulder, Colo.: Rowman Littlefield, 2005).

Many thanks to Charles T. Call, Nadine Jubb, and Maria Cecilia dos Santos for their very helpful substantive and editorial contributions to this chapter, to Katie Torrington for research assistance, and to Dyan Mazurana, Angela Raven-Roberts, and Jane Parpart for their insightful critiques of earlier versions of this work.

1. First given broad exposure in UN secretary-general Boutros Boutros-Ghali's 1992 *An Agenda for Peace* (New York: United Nations), the term "peacebuilding" is still used in multiple ways.

2. Members of women's organizations, interviews with author, El Salvador (1995, 1998) and Bosnia (1999).

3. This is a variation on an argument made by Elaine Tyler May in *Homeward Bound: American Families in the Cold War Era* (New York: Basic Books, 1988) about middle-class families in the United States in the 1950s.

4. His data come from the Rwandan Ministry of Justice, October 1994.

5. From a gender perspective, postconflict security can be seen as a different kind of "protection racket." See William Stanley, *The Protection Racket State: Elite Politics, Military Extortion, and Civil War in El Salvador* (Philadelphia: Temple University Press, 1996). Charles Tilly's conception of a protection racket state refers to imaginary or self-induced threats from which a government "protects" its citizens, using the constructed threat as an excuse or means to consolidate its control. See Charles Tilly, "War Making and State Making as Organized Crime," in *Bringing the State Back In*, ed. Peter Evans, Dietrich Rueschmeyer, and Theda Skocpol (Cambridge: Cambridge University Press, 1985). In the case of postconflict security, the protection racket is that governments and international agencies react to very real threats of postconflict violence by constructing a citizenry that is male and essentially void of a sexual or gendered context.

6. The United Nations' Brahimi Report is a very recent and notable exception; however, its sections on gender are still largely waiting to be implemented. See the Brahimi Panel, *Report of the Panel on United Nations Peace Operations*, A/55/305 (New York: United Nations, 2000).

7. Charles T. Call, "War Transitions and the New Civilian Security in Latin America," in *Comparative Politics* 35, no. 1, October 2002.

8. Charles T. Call, "Institutional Learning within the U.S. International Criminal Investigative Training Assistance Program," in *Policing the New World Disorder: Peace Operations and Public Security*, ed. Robert B. Oakley, Michael J. Dziedzic, and Eliot M. Goldberg (Washington, D.C.: National Defense University, 1998); UN Civilian Police unit in New York, 2001; and http://www.un.org/Depts/dpko (accessed June 2005).

9. For more on UN CIVPOL, see Nassrine Azimi, ed., *The Role and Functions of Civilian Police in United Nations Peacekeeping Operations: Debriefing and Lessons* (Cambridge, Mass.: Kluwer Law International and UN Institute for Training and Research [UNITAR], 1997); Charles T. Call and Michael Barnett, "Looking for a Few Good Cops," *International Peacekeeping* (Fall 1999); and Tor Tanke Holm and Espen Barth Eide, eds., *Peacebuilding and Police Reform* (Boulder, Colo.: Lynne Rienner, 2000).

10. Although Haiti's conflict was not an armed uprising or war, it involved civil resistance to a brutal authoritarian regime and left in its wake a legacy of violence and posttraumatic stress. Furthermore, Haiti's international peacekeeping operation was very similar to other peacekeeping missions and was drawn on heavily in subsequent peace operations.

11. UN Security Council Resolution 940, passed July 31, 1994, authorized the UN Mission in Haiti, with a mandate (par. 9) of "(a) sustaining the secure and stable environment established during the multinational phase and protecting international personnel and key installations; and (b) the professionalization of the Haitian armed forces and the creation of a separate police force."

12. UNMIH was replaced by smaller, successive missions under different names through March 2000; a new, distinct UN mission in Haiti was opened in June 2004. On early efforts on police reform in Haiti, see Michael Bailey, Robert Maguire, and Neil Pouliot, "Haiti: Military-Police Partnership for Public Security," in *Policing the New World Disorder*. See also chapter 3 in this volume.

13. Boutros Boutros-Ghali, *Report of the Secretary-General of the United Nations*, 1996, http://www.un.org/Docs/s1996416; and Kofi Annan, *Report of the Secretary-General of the United Nations, Transition Mission in Haiti* (New York: United Nations, October 31, 1997).

14. Tracy Fitzsimmons, "Engendering a New Police Identity?" *Peace Review* 10, no. 2 (1998): 269–274.

15. Women police officers and male police personnel in Petionville and Carrefour stations, interviews with author, 1996, 1998.

16. Assistant inspector general, interview with author, Port-au-Prince, August 2000.

17. United Nations, press release, SC/6300, December 5, 1996.

18. Fitzsimmons, "Engendering a New Police Identity?"

19. For general information about Kosovo and the NATO war, see Ivo H. Daalder and Michael E. O'Hanlon, *Winning Ugly: NATO's War to Save Kosovo* (Washington, D.C.: Brookings Institution, 2000); Noel Malcolm, *Kosovo: A Short History* (New York: New York University Press, 2001); Tim Judah, *Kosovo: War and Revenge* (New Haven, Conn.: Yale University Press, 2000); and Julie Mertus, *Kosovo: How Myths and Truth Started a War* (Berkeley: University of California Press, 1999).

20. The target was increased from 4,000 initially to 6,000 by the end of 2002. See UNMIK, *UNMIK at Two*, UNMIK Report, 2001.

21. UNMIK, *UNMIK Police Strategic Planning Guide: Establishment of the Rule of Law and the Development of the Kosovo Police Service*, Section 12.4.2(b), 1999.

22. Ibid., Section 13.5.4.

23. Data for 2005 are from http://www.unmikonline.org.

24. Swanee Hunt and Cristina Posa, "Women Waging Peace," *Foreign Policy* (May–June 2001): 38–47.

25. Organization for Security and Cooperation in Europe (OSCE), untitled assessment of judicial sector reform in Kosovo, 2001, 60, author files.

26. Kofi Annan, *Report of the Secretary-General on the United Nations Interim Administration in Kosovo*, S/2005/88 (New York: United Nations, February 2005).

27. Charles T. Call, *Sustainable Development in Central America: The Challenges of Violence, Injustice and Insecurity*, report prepared for Centroamerica 2020, a project of the European Commission and U.S. Agency for International Development.

28. OSCE, untitled assessment, 67.

29. For more information, see the many research projects done by ICRW (e.g., ICRW and CLADEM, "Violence against Women in Latin America and the Caribbean") and Instituto del Tercer Mundo. One important point made by ICRW and the Instituto del Tercer Mundo is that there is some perversion in cases when the victim must choose between family and criminal court, thereby forcing the victim to shoulder the burden (and pressure from her community) of whether or not her husband/lover will perhaps go to jail.

30. The first iteration of this argument was made in Fitzsimmons, "Engendering a New Police Identity?"

31. International Alert, "Gender and Peace Support Operations: Opportunities and Challenges to Improve Practice," ed. Nicola Johnston (London: International Alert, 2001), 11.

32. UNIFEM, report dated May 2005, http://womenwarpeace.org/timor.

33. M. Cecilia MacDowell Santos, "Gender, the State, and Citizenship: Women's Police Stations in São Paulo, Brazil," in *Irrumpiendo en lo público* (San José: Costa Rica, 2000).

34. UN Development Programme, "Security Sector Reform: Lessons Learned from Bosnia and Herzegovina and Kosovo" (draft report based on a joint UNDP/DPKO mission in August 2001); and International Criminal Investigative Training Assistance Program, quarterly reports of activities (Washington, D.C.: U.S. Department of Justice, 2000–2001).

35. At the authors' conference in preparation for this volume, one of the contributors commented on the aftermath of war or major conflict, "All this nice stuff about community policing, but the reality is there are *no* communities afterwards."

36. Human Rights Watch and HRW Women's Rights Project, *Violence against Women in South Africa* (New York: Human Rights Watch, 1995), 4.

37. International Human Rights Law Group BiH Project et al., *Izvestaj nvo-a o zenskim ljudskim pravima u Bosni I Hercegovini* (Sarajevo: International Human Rights Law Group, 1999), 172–173.

38. See Mayra Buvinic and Andrew Morrison, "Living in a More Violent World," *Foreign Policy* 118 (Spring 2000): 58–72; and Inter-American Development Bank, http://www.iadb.org.

39. I say "contribute to" because in itself, the lack of women officers does not entirely explain women's unwillingness to report such crimes. Societal pressures that reflect cultural beliefs are perhaps a stronger factor in some societies (especially in Bosnia and Haiti); in such societies, rape or reporting a family member for domestic violence brings dishonor on the family.

40. The Inter-American Convention on the Prevention, Punishment and Eradication of Violence against Women of Belém do Pará is the only international treaty in the world specifically on violence against women. See Amnesty International, press release, "Tenth Anniversary of the Convention of Belém do Pará: Time for Action" (London: Amnesty International, June 8, 2004).

41. G. Seidman, "Strategic Challenges to Gender Inequality: The South Africa Gender Commission," *Ethnography* 2, no. 2 (June 2001): 219–241.

42. For a very useful analysis of the rise and contributions of women's police stations, see Santos, "Gender, the State, and Citizenship"; and Nadine Jubb, "Enforcing Gendering Meanings and Social Order: The Participation of the National Police in the Nicaraguan Women's and Children's Police Stations" (paper given at Latin American Studies Association international conference, March 2001). However, there is some question about whether women's police stations ultimately empower or weaken women's professional advancement; women police officers may get stuck in such stations permanently and find it difficult to transfer to the "regular" police stations, from which the likelihood of advancement to the most senior levels is the highest.

43. International Crisis Group (ICG), "Policing the Police in Bosnia: A Further Reform Agenda," Balkans Report No. 130 (Sarajevo and Brussels: International Crisis Group, 2002).

44. CIVPOL and International Criminal Tribunal for the Former Yugoslavia (ICTY) personnel, interviews with author, Bosnia, 1999.

45. ICG, "Policing the Police in Bosnia," 32.

Part IV
Conclusion

11

Conclusion

Constructing Justice and Security after War

CHARLES T. CALL

T HIS VOLUME OPENED BY POSING THE QUESTION, *Can societies emerging from armed conflict create systems of justice and security that ensure basic rights, apply the law effectively and impartially, and enjoy popular support?* Based on the diverse experiences of some of the most prominent transitions from war in the 1990s, the answer is "Yes, but." "Yes" because certain postconflict policing and justice services clearly improved in virtually every case examined. Consider El Salvador's new National Civilian Police, South Africa's Truth and Reconciliation Commission, Rwanda's adaptation of traditional *gacaca* courts to process genocide suspects, and the speedy construction of new systems of justice and security in Kosovo and East Timor. Contrary to what is expected by theorists of state-building and democratization who are pessimistic about quick, internationally supported processes, these state-building efforts resulted in clear and specific improvements over prior state institutions. In some cases, reforms played a crucial role in advancing broader peace and democracy.

"Yes, but," because of the widespread disillusion that ensued in each case. In all cases, reforms encountered obstacles, resource

shortfalls, and resistance. The populace unfailingly experienced high
levels of disappointment and frustration, often in unexpected areas.
New forms of violence emerged, and durable reforms seemed to require
relatively high levels of institutionalization among state agencies and
society. Despite experiencing "successes," none of these cases of justice
and security sector reform (JSSR) is considered a "success story" by its
author. Each author identifies some clear failures of reform efforts.
The disappointments are all the more striking given that conventional wisdom would suggest maximum chances for success in these
cases, whose wars had successfully ended (unlike with Angola in the
1990s and Iraq in 2003) and where international actors committed
resources and diplomacy to justice and security sector reform amid
some movement toward democracy (unlike with Kuwait in 1991).

The positive and negative aspects of virtually all these cases
elicit confusion. When are justice and security sector reforms possible? Which sorts of reforms are easiest? Which are toughest? Are the
constraints on reform immutable, or can a better understanding of
reforms lead to better outcomes for justice in the broadest sense?
What can we learn about justice and security reforms from some of
the most highly regarded peace processes and postconflict reconstruction efforts since the early 1990s?

Drawing principally on the eight case studies presented, this
chapter offers several generalizations and hypotheses about the processes and outcomes that international and national-level actors can
expect in postwar settings. The universe of such cases since the 1990s
is not large, nor can a brief chapter exhaust the issues and challenges
for postwar security and justice. However, by drawing heuristically
on several cases, the hypotheses offered are stronger than a single
case or two might suggest. Had they been heeded, several of these
findings—especially those emphasizing postwar insecurity, the overriding importance of developing sound national security forces, the
need to creatively rely on local informal mechanisms, and the links
between security and justice systems—might have made a positive
difference in the early and midterm state-building efforts in post–
Saddam Hussein Iraq.

The case studies collectively reveal several conceptually and
practically important empirical findings. This chapter is organized

into the following sections, with findings followed by implications and recommendations for international actors:

1. Postconflict crime and violence
2. Security reforms
3. Judicial reforms
4. War crimes and past human rights abuses
5. Traditional authority and customary law
6. Civil society and citizen participation

Although these topics are treated sequentially, the case studies underscore the importance of an integrated approach to "justice and security sector reform," one that links efforts to transform security and justice institutions and takes into account past injustices.

POSTCONFLICT CRIME AND VIOLENCE

Peace Produces New Sources of Insecurity

Perhaps the most salient empirical finding of this volume is the near-universal emergence of new forms of insecurity in the wake of war. Any serious attempt to transform security and justice systems must anticipate and address these challenges. Wars end, but violence in a society does not. Instead, the formal end of war transforms the nature of a society's violence. This maxim is true no matter whether war is deemed over on the day a regime crumbles or on the day a cease-fire takes effect.

In virtually every postwar case, public frustration about heightened violent crime and sensations of insecurity emerged within two years after the cessation of hostilities. The looting and breakdown of law and order in postwar Iraq was perhaps the most publicized instance of a crime surge in the first few days after war, but when one examines crime over months rather than days, medium-term increases in common crime and violence afflicted most of the cases examined here. Consider the following:

- Within two years of El Salvador's 1992 cease-fire, homicides tripled and kidnappings per year increased from 11 to 126.

Robberies quintupled within seven years. Common crime, virtually absent in previous opinion polls about the country's number one problem, suddenly zoomed to the top of the list, remaining there for ten years.

- One year after its transition in 1994, South Africa achieved the highest homicide rate in the world.[1] Muggings and armed robbery became commonplace, affecting even well-guarded government ministers.
- In Guatemala, kidnappings increased thirtyfold, and homicides went up 20 percent within two years of the cease-fire.
- In East Timor, "[a] noticeable rise in all types of crime followed INTERFET stabilization of the territory."[2]

Insecurity produced by common, violent crime was not limited to these cases. In Kosovo, Haiti, and even post–World War II Germany, the end of war coincided with the escalation of common crime and a sense of greater freedom to transgress the law. Given that we selected societies whose wars had already been successfully terminated, the cases represent something close to "best-case" scenarios.

Because postwar crime rarely focuses on foreign personnel or threatens to reignite war, it receives little attention from the international media. Yet postwar crime waves pose tremendous challenges for the reconstruction of state institutions, for the legitimacy of new democratizing regimes, and for the quality of justice and everyday life of the populace. It carries important political, economic, and social costs; insecurity can quickly undermine carefully negotiated constitutions, delicate power-sharing arrangements, foreign investment incentives, local development efforts, and human rights reforms. Common crime tends to weaken precisely what peace processes seek to achieve: consolidated peace, deeper democracy, justice, and reconciliation.

Social and/or Economic Violence Tends to Supplant Political Violence

Political violence declined dramatically in all the cases examined here—unsurprising since the cases were selected precisely because their armed conflicts had concluded. Since "postconflict" is generally equated with the end of organized, armed political struggle, we would expect political violence to fade amid peace. In most societies labeled postconflict, political violence indeed dissipates quickly. In some cases, especially successfully negotiated peace settlements like Mozambique, El Salvador, and Guatemala, the disappearance of political violence is so sudden it can create a silence that is strange to and mistrusted by a war-weary population.

However, the successful end of war tends to produce new forms of insecurity. This new violence and crime takes three forms: political (i.e., violence aimed at taking or undermining power to govern), economic (i.e., violence aimed at accumulating or protecting wealth or its sources), and social (i.e., violence aimed at reinforcing or protecting a collective identity).[3] Exceptions exist, of course, mainly in postrevolutionary or postliberation regimes whose victorious forces had acted as a counterstate in a territory before assuming full state power.

Political Violence

In some postconflict societies, political violence does not end but rather persists or mutates.[4] This occurs in two sorts of postconflict societies. First, persistent political violence occurs where one armed actor acts as a spoiler but is unable to retain or win state power. Examples include Iraq in 2003, Afghanistan after 2001, Cambodia in the mid-1990s, and Nicaragua after 1979. Cases of successful spoilers, like Angola, are generally not considered to be postconflict. Second, political violence can be said to mutate where certain ethnic groups or new actors (i.e., not the warring parties) carry out vengeance attacks on their defeated former oppressors. Examples include Rwanda and Kosovo in the 1990s and post-Taliban Afghanistan.

Economic Violence

More common, and less anticipated, is the rise of economic violence in the wake of war. Kidnappings, robberies, organized crime, and white-collar and other financially motivated crime increases in most societies. This economic violence also varies in form, intensity, and timing. In Bosnia and Kosovo, organized crime expanded over many months after the termination of armed conflicts, showing some similarities to the pattern in postsocialist states of the former Soviet

Union. Powerful political parties, in conjunction with armed groups and elements of the state, became involved in illegal smuggling of humans and goods.

The earlier examples of El Salvador, Guatemala, and South Africa also illustrate the rise of economic crimes. The statistics from these cases show dramatic increases in economic and social crimes, followed by a steady decline that began within three years of war termination. In all three cases, homicides, armed robberies, and kidnappings rose precipitously during the first two or three years of a peace process and then stabilized for a period of two or three years before declining. After that, crime increased in some cases, but the link to a peace process must be viewed as tenuous given that ten years had passed since war. In Afghanistan, the rapid resurgence of poppy cultivation and trafficking between 2002 and 2004 conformed to this trend. Unfortunately, crime statistics were flawed in virtually all these countries, sometimes showing wide variation across different reporting agencies (see chapter 4). Such problems render comparison of annual crime statistics across postconflict cases very difficult and frustrating.

In general, postwar societies can expect a decline in forms of violence associated with the former conflict (e.g., ethnic or political), but a noticeable increase in organized crime or common crime over the medium run. In addition, citizen perceptions will reflect a sense that insecurity is greater, partly because its sources become more diffuse and less predictable. In postwar states that have dramatically broken with the prior state and its supporting structures of power, people (especially the privileged) have a sense that they are vulnerable to robbery, carjacking, kidnapping, or extortion in new, unexpected ways. As mentioned earlier, where the collapse of a regime leaves a void in public security, as in Iraq and Panama, looting occurs in major urban areas. Generally, such looting can be checked by a few exemplary instances of suppression. Looting is usually a short-term concern rooted less in structural factors than in conjunctural decisions based on perceived absences of a modicum of public order. Yet its consequences for the legitimacy of a new or transitional government can be serious, as demonstrated by the U.S. debacle in Iraq.

Social Violence

Social violence, reflecting the desire to reinforce or protect collective identity, follows disparate patterns, the best known of which in a postconflict setting is ethnic violence. In places like Kosovo and Rwanda, members of an ethnicity favored by wartime security and justice systems "lose" under new security arrangements and find their lives endangered. In the case of Kosovo, "reverse" ethnic cleansing emerged and advanced apart from organized political struggles with little effective resistance by victorious NATO-led forces responsible for internal security. Kosovo Serbs suffered massive displacement, loss of property, and extensive loss of life and ill-treatment under postwar regimes declaring their commitment to international princi-ples of rights and inclusiveness. The case studies suggest that post-conflict ethnic violence and displacement are a particular danger where a government identified with one ethnicity falls in warfare, rather than in a successfully negotiated peace agreement.

A second form of social violence manifests itself in common crime and youth gang violence. The case studies indicate that such social violence especially affects postconflict environs where a large portion of the populace is displaced by war, and where rural social networks are broken and many young males are rendered unemployed and uninterested in returning to rural livelihoods. In South Africa, El Salvador, and Guatemala, common crimes reflected not just eco-nomic motives but social factors as well. The Salvadoran police esti-mated that 85 percent of violent crimes reported in 2002 reflected social violence such as bar fights, domestic violence, or disputes among neighbors and friends ending in gunshots.

A third form of social violence, family violence, often increases in the wake of war. "Social" family violence against women should be distinguished from political violence against women. In societies like Bosnia and Rwanda, rape was used as a horrific, deliberate, and wide-spread policy against women and girls for ethnopolitical purposes. The political targeting of women by armed groups generally declines after armed conflict ends, yet violence among couples and family members, usually against women and children, often increases after war. As Tracy Fitzsimmons shows, in Central America, Haiti, and Bosnia, women's groups reported that peace coincided with an increase in domestic violence, as demobilized soldiers returned home with limited job opportunities.

Postwar Insecurity: Implications for Theory and Practice

The near-universal rise in certain forms of economic and social violence after war holds important implications for peacekeeping theory and policy. The core works on postconflict reconstruction are based on peace processes (as in Central America, southern Africa, or Cambodia) or on occupations (like the Allied occupations of West Germany and Japan). Our understanding of violence in postconflict settings emphasizes the *political* dimension, which is the focus of wars and peace processes. "Security" in these contexts is often equated with the end of the political violence and heavily shaped by international security interests in ending the war at hand, rather than with local or national security interests in ensuring everyday security and preventing future forms of oppression or violence. A full understanding of postconflict security requires an analytic framework that encompasses a threefold notion of postconflict insecurity: political violence, social violence, and economic violence. Caroline Moser notes that postconflict societies often experience a combination of these types of violence that may be difficult to cleanly distinguish.[5]

As a matter of policy, intergovernmental organizations like the World Bank and the United Nations as well as national-level actors should be more aware of the likely emergence of new insecurities, deploying appropriate resources to prevent such violence and to reduce it as it emerges. International actors need to improve their tools for detecting and addressing new forms of violence. Several security measures might help, including deploying sufficient policing capability in the immediate aftermath of a military defeat or a negotiated ceasefire, seeking prior agreement about what law shall apply after war, preparing a judicial capability to operate in a postconflict environment until a more permanent judicial system may take root, developing a prior understanding of how local mechanisms of justice and conflict resolution might operate in the absence of a functioning central state, and having sufficient resources and organizational capacity to reintegrate demobilized combatants.[6] All such measures might involve international forces, national forces, or some combination thereof.

SECURITY REFORMS

In virtually all of the cases examined, reform of the security system was seen as an important component of efforts, not only to consolidate peace and prevent future conflict, but also to achieve most post-conflict liberal aims: prevention of human rights violations, reconstruction of the economy, attainment of justice for past atrocities, and establishment of the rule of law and a stable environment for everyday life and democratic consolidation. As presented in the introduction to this volume, numerous studies have set forth the elements of justice and security sector reform and the tasks deemed necessary for effective peace consolidation. Sustainable peace requires not simply demobilizing the parties to war but the existence of a functioning and legitimate state (a notion now widely equated with electoral democracy) as well as some degree of social reconciliation in ethnically conflictive settings.[7] Security reforms are only one component of this multifaceted endeavor. Rather than present yet another comprehensive catalog of the various elements of security sector reform, this section selectively highlights important findings from the case studies, treating demobilization/disarmament/reintegration (known as DDR) issues, military and intelligence reforms, and then police reforms.

Demobilization, Disarmament, and Reintegration (DDR)

Although peacebuilding goes well beyond demobilizing the warring parties, it requires the effective demobilization, disarmament, and reintegration of insurgent forces and that portion of government troops rendered unnecessary (or politically unpalatable) by peace. DDR programs, carried out in virtually every case examined, became widely accepted as a component of international postconflict packages during the 1990s. These programs generally consisted of supervised cantonment of irregular forces and some state armies, the handing over and destruction of some arms, registration of ex-combatants, and the provision of some sum of money and/or training in a trade or agricultural inputs and support.

International actors have improved their analysis and implementation of DDR programs through learning over time.[8] Two constraints afflict most DDR programs. First, a shortage of resources for DDR made it difficult to meet time lines and expectations, sparking angry demonstrations in several postconflict societies by people accustomed to wielding power collectively. Second, DDR resources alone cannot create long-term jobs. Even where DDR resources generously ensure the training and employment of an ex-soldier for one year, sustainable employment or farming depends on market forces outside the control of DDR projects. DDR programs are important for alleviating the immediate burden on postconflict societies, helping prevent ex-combatants from returning to war, turning to crime, or undermining the new regime. Nevertheless, a striking number of postconflict governments confronted well-organized demonstrations or protests by associations of ex-combatants, usually because of a perceived failure to deliver on promised severance or demobilization packages.

More important in DDR programs is *how* the process occurs: the timing of DDR among disparate groups, the timing with regard to elections, the sequencing of DDR with respect to the construction of a new security and justice system. In Angola, the failure to demobilize before elections is widely considered to have contributed to the failure of a negotiated settlement in the early 1990s. In El Salvador, the sweeping, swift cantonment of both sides left a public security gap that fueled criminal activity and damaged the legitimacy of the postwar government. The failure to prosecute certain Haitian ex-soldiers seems to have contributed to subsequent political instability there. Poor societies confront more challenges, since the market so rarely can absorb demobilized combatants sufficiently to prevent a problem of economic violence. Women combatants have different needs, which can have multiplier effects for reconstruction and reconciliation. In general, DDR is much more than a technical process. It must be carefully implemented in tandem with a political strategy following war. Recent analysis emphasizes how the growing DDR programs of the World Bank and the UN Development Programme (UNDP) must be better coordinated with international political and military actions.[9] The creation of a UN Peacebuilding Commission should assist this coordination.

Demobilization must be carried out in an integrated fashion, not only to alleviate the "security dilemma" of foes wary of trickery but also to ensure that demobilized combatants do not join informal private armies not covered by a DDR process, as occurred in Afghanistan after 2003. In contrast to irregular private armies, regulated private security companies can become a positive source of employment for ex-combatants. Private security agencies erected to protect businesses, people, and affluent neighborhoods must be carefully regulated to prevent their conversion into criminal enterprises or sources of political or social violence. Unfortunately, from South Africa to Rwanda to Central America and the Balkans, regulation of private security companies was either absent or woefully underenforced.

Military and Intelligence Reforms

Win, lose, or draw, the state where the fighting took place generally undertakes some significant transformation of its armed forces. "Military reform," like police reform, can encompass changes to the mission, size, composition, internal organization, and political supervision of the respective forces. Every postconflict case examined here, plus those in Panama, Iraq, Cambodia, Mozambique, and Afghanistan, included some significant effort to reform the armed forces that emerged from conflict, often under a purportedly democratizing regime.

The specific elements of military reform vary according to the regional and historical context, as well as to the terms of settlement, the interests of the victors, and the influence of international actors. After the wars of the 1980s, every country in Central America experienced important improvements in establishing civilian control over the military, shrinking the size and budget of the armed forces, and enhancing accountability for human rights conduct. Haiti and Panama joined Costa Rica as the only nonmicrostates without an army. In Bosnia and Kosovo, new armies were forged from parties to war, with efforts to integrate formerly warring ethnic groups. Victorious rebel armies, as in Rwanda and the Democratic Republic of the Congo, tend to seek to simply install their rebel structures in the state apparatus. Where foreign military forces have played salient roles in interventions, as in Haiti, Bosnia, Kosovo, Afghanistan, and Iraq, international actors will likely seek to carry out what might be called the 3-P program: professionalization, purges, and pluralism (of ethnic or political groups).

The case studies in this volume indicate that military reforms, often resisted, can have limited and important impact where commanders can ensure the compliance of subordinate troops—that is, where soldiers are unlikely to defy agreements and join new armed bands. The reduction of troop strength and budgets proceeded smoothly and swiftly in most of these (admittedly selected) cases. The elimination of Haiti's army is perhaps considered the signal legacy of the reforms instituted after the U.S.-led intervention. The incorporation of blacks into the senior ranks of South Africa's military forces and defense establishment proceeded remarkably smoothly. In places like Kosovo and East Timor, international military assistance created new armies in short order, largely in conformity with the 3 Ps. Peace largely removed the Salvadoran military from the political stage.

At the same time, formal improvements in professionalization, incorporation of former enemies, and downsizing rarely forge the behavior desired by international military reformers. In Bosnia, efforts to integrate three enemy armies into a single state military proved extremely frustrating and difficult. Kosovo's new Protection Corps failed to exhibit the ethnic tolerance sought by KFOR. Rwanda's army allegedly committed human rights atrocities as part of its campaign against Hutu deemed to threaten the country in the late 1990s. Perhaps as a fruit of its strategic superiority and political power at war's end, the Guatemalan military continued its internal security activities and retained significant political influence and strong de facto protection from charges of human rights violations. In addition, Guatemala is the only case examined where intelligence reforms received serious public attention, partly because of the important role played by intelligence agencies in that country's repression. The challenging reform of intelligence agencies, an area hidden from the public eye, is generally overlooked but is crucial for the humane and accountable performance of state forces.

In the end, institutional military and intelligence reforms can help prevent conflict and enhance human rights and democratic governance. These case studies point to several steps that can be taken to reduce the size and influence of military forces in the wake of war, as well as to enhance their accountability to democratic authorities. Yet political processes fundamentally shape the fate of institutional military reforms; if peace processes break down over political disagreements, technical programs of professionalization and democratic values are unlikely to prevent the incursion of military leaders and factions into renewed political disputes or warfare.

Police Reforms

Policing stands at the intersection of human rights, justice, and security, and police reform is one of the most important components of JSSR in postconflict societies. The case studies examined here demonstrate the possibilities and the difficulties of establishing civilian, accountable, representative, and nonpartisan police forces that respect human rights. In cases as diverse as South Africa, Central America, Kosovo, and East Timor, police reform figured prominently in postconflict state-building efforts, and international actors played an important role. International actors have learned across peace operations, improving programs and developing a robust list of tasks in police institutional development. One comprehensive study, for instance, calls for postwar reformers to "plan for the reorganization" of police forces, to recruit more "representative security forces," to vet them, to "develop training programs," to "professionalize" these forces, and to "develop community requirements" for them.[10] International actors perform some of these tasks, especially formal institutional modifications, more proficiently than others.

One of the most important findings of this volume is that successful police reform requires more than simply tinkering with policing organizations; it requires transforming the relationship between police institutions and society. Institutional modifications to police organizations—including merit-based selection criteria, more professional training, the inclusion of important ethnic and religious groups and women, and restructuring—are quite feasible and important in postwar settings. Unfortunately, efforts to transform police-society relations—including genuine collaboration between civil society or citizens and police agencies, community policing efforts, sensitivity to gendered crimes, and the elimination of ethnic bias—face considerably more obstacles and have met with less success. These findings— of progress in formal reforms alongside disappointment in informal

**Figure 11-1. Role of Formerly Dominant Groups
in Postwar Police Forces**

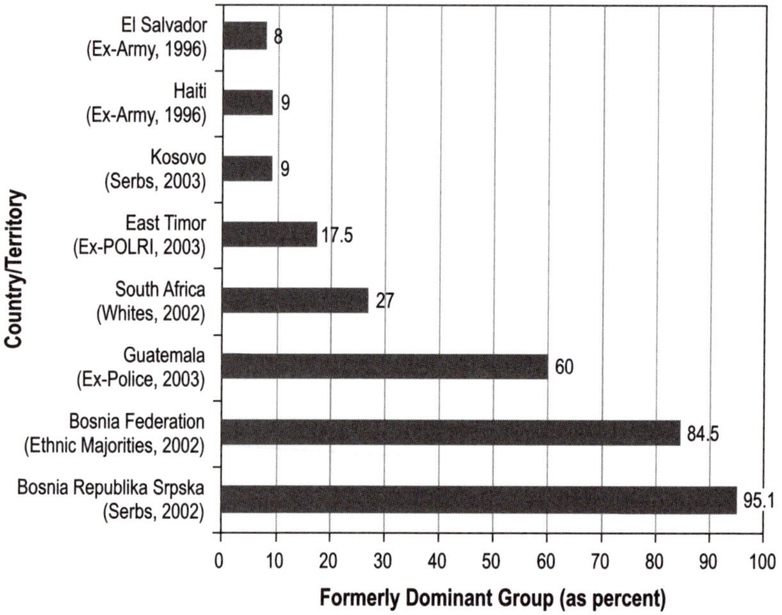

Country/Territory	Formerly Dominant Group (as percent)
El Salvador (Ex-Army, 1996)	8
Haiti (Ex-Army, 1996)	9
Kosovo (Serbs, 2003)	9
East Timor (Ex-POLRI, 2003)	17.5
South Africa (Whites, 2002)	27
Guatemala (Ex-Police, 2003)	60
Bosnia Federation (Ethnic Majorities, 2002)	84.5
Bosnia Republika Srpska (Serbs, 2002)	95.1

Source: Data culled from chapters in this volume.

practice—are elaborated in five important areas of police reform: composition of policing organizations, professionalization and restructuring, oversight of policing, gender issues, and citizen involvement.

Police Composition

One of the most celebrated successes of political reconstruction in Kosovo, Bosnia, and Central America was the incorporation of former enemies into new or reformed police forces. UN officials trumpeted the surprising ease with which former enemies trained together, formed collegial relationships, and effectively deployed together in patrol and investigative units. Police academies in El Salvador and Kosovo became routine stops for visiting international officials, diplomats, and journalists. In El Salvador, ex-guerrillas spoke movingly of the identities and missions as law enforcement officers they shared with their former foes. Kosovo Albanian police emphasized the value of their Serb colleagues, sometimes intervening to protect Serb policemen in danger of violence at the hands of Albanian citizens. Then U.S. secretary of state Madeleine Albright visited a police station in Sarajevo in 1997, proclaiming, "These are the heroes you don't hear about very often in Bosnia. . . . They are part of the first multiethnic [district] police force."[11]

Peace agreements and international interventions have enjoyed remarkable success in both integrating former enemies and excluding the most notoriously abusive individuals from new police forces. As figure 11-1 shows, countries such as Kosovo, El Salvador, and Haiti all experienced a turnover of a majority of police personnel within four years of transition.[12] Where new political actors come to power, they wish to ensure their own security (and reward their followers) by appointing loyalists to the police forces and, if possible, the military. Preserving the status quo ante of policing personnel (and judicial personnel) is a formula for failure for restructuring those forces to reflect the values of new, usually more democratic regimes.

Unfortunately, inclusion of formerly excluded groups does not mean their actual cooperation and integration in day-to-day operations of state institutions. As shown by the South African Police force's heavy reliance on black members during decades of apartheid, simple representation of ethnic groups in police forces does not necessarily ensure fair treatment or physical security for the groups represented. Nor does incorporation of specific groups in justice and security organizations automatically influence operational behavior. Despite the international enforcement of agreed-on quotas for incorporating minorities into the police forces of the Bosniak- and Croat-majority cantons of the Bosnian Federation, "integration" was largely a facade. Ethnic minorities operated largely on separate, parallel tracks. Croat personnel reported to the senior Croat interior ministry official, and Bosniaks reported to the top Bosniak official, with little cooperation and incomplete communication between these parallel informal structures. In addition, even where "holdover" police from wartime represent a low percentage of new police members, they are likely to occupy some of the key positions in the police force.[13] Including previously repressed groups in senior police positions cannot by itself overcome deep-seated ethnic prejudice and social stratification.

Police Professionalism and Restructuring

Professionalization represents another dimension of reform where formal institutional changes were both important and feasible yet fell short of meeting expectations about transformed police conduct. International advisers and local officials praise enhanced professionalism and better police structures in most cases, from East Timor to Haiti, Guatemala, Kosovo, Bosnia, Rwanda, and El Salvador. The UN secretary-general reported in 2001 that the leadership of the Federation's Interior Ministry had made "considerable strides in reintegrating Bosniac and Croat officers and reorganizing the Ministry."[14] The cases of Panama, El Salvador, Haiti, Kosovo, and East Timor show that the international community has become quite capable of establishing new police academies and promptly completing the recruitment and training of basic-level police cadets to deploy in new police forces.[15]

If we define "professionalism" as the degree to which career standards and protections are applied to members of the profession, and "restructuring" to mean changes to the organizational chart and the force's relations with other government agencies, then reforms along these dimensions were manifold and meaningful in the cases examined. In many cases, wholly new forces were created or police organizations enjoyed substantial reorganization. Clearer, more merit-based criteria for selection, for promotion, and for job retention were adopted in several postwar societies. In many cases, restructuring was used to weed out top leaders or rank-and-file personnel deemed unsuitable for security and justice systems under a new, democratic regime.

At the same time, efforts to professionalize and restructure police and judicial institutions often served as a ready substitute for deeper transformation of organizational cultures inimical to plural and liberal democracies. In the face of recalcitrant security and judicial officials, new national governments settled for reshuffling bureaucracies rather than rooting out incompetent, corrupt, or abusive personnel. International police advisers tend to identify with their local counterparts and seek to meet the latter's wishes, which often lie in the status quo and not in streamlining management, empowering junior patrol officers, or reaching out to communities. It is always easier to provide training ("professionalization") than to modify administrative and operational systems to ensure that good training is not wasted. Reshuffling bureaucracies, therefore, can serve as a poor substitute for thwarted reforms.

Oversight and Control Mechanisms

In most contemporary internal wars, coercive forces and judicial agents are party to appalling violations of human rights. Consequently, the development of mechanisms of oversight for security forces and judicial conduct is extremely important after armed conflict. Across the cases examined, new mechanisms of oversight and accountability encapsulate the mix of formal improvements and informal shortfalls apparent in postconflict justice and security sector reforms.

In virtually every case, formal organizational innovations brought oversight to a historic high, and constitutional and legal changes increased judicial adherence to international human rights treaties. Kosovo and El Salvador benefited from the creation of human rights ombudspersons. Aggressive police oversight offices ("internal affairs units" and/or "inspectors general") were installed or bolstered in Haiti, East Timor, Guatemala, and El Salvador. Legislatures play newly mandated roles fostering transparency and minimal oversight over security forces, while new judicial commissions oversee judicial conduct in some societies. Often unheralded, the growth of investigative journalism amid a freer press provides an independent, public check on police abuse. In Guatemala, South Africa, and Kosovo, newspapers spurred police investigations and cleansing of courts, exposing instances of corruption in ways that internal affairs units and legislative committees were unable to do.[16] Over time, international donors have placed greater emphasis on oversight mechanisms.

The cases also suggest that oversight mechanisms are often slow to be developed and function much less effectively than advertised. The internal oversight units of the new Salvadoran police were slow to emerge and failed to deter widespread criminal activity among police officers, leading to their revamping and the enactment of a special housecleaning law. Internal oversight mechanisms failed to control abusive forces in Haiti, Bosnia, and Guatemala. In these and other countries, new human rights institutions proved unable to accomplish their purpose, despite glowing initial reviews and high hopes. Interestingly, external oversight mechanisms such as investigative journalism, ombudspersons, legislators, and international scrutiny contributed more to prosecution for abusive behavior than internal affairs units.

Gender and Policing

Gender represents another dimension of police reform where impressive formal achievements coexist with unsatisfactory changes of informal practice. One of the most overlooked successes of recent postconflict police and justice reforms is their ability to enhance the formal inclusion of women and women's issues in policing and judicial institutions. Largely through the influence of international organizations and domestic women's groups, women have found new avenues of participation in policing.[17] In Haiti, Panama, El Salvador, and East Timor, women had never had the chance to become police officers, but after postwar police reforms they were admitted to new police academies and careers. In Kosovo, Bosnia, South Africa, and Rwanda, women achieved greater representation in police forces than they had prior to war termination. Except in Muslim-dominant societies, international donors encountered surprisingly little resistance to explicit incorporation of women in policing and judicial structures and to formal commitments to equal opportunities for women in legal education and employment.

Nevertheless, women's everyday security was changed less than institutional changes would indicate. As Tracy Fitzsimmons shows, family violence increased at the end of many wars; peace brought violence from the battlefield into the home. Domestic violence was aggravated by the lack of jobs for demobilized soldiers, by socialization to violence, and by resentment at the opportunities and the (usually obligatory) mobility women experienced during wartime. With the principal exception of some postcommunist countries, women police officers remained severely underrepresented in the upper ranks of most postwar societies and overly confined to traditionally female units such as domestic violence, community policing, traffic control, and youth prevention—that is, taking care of the house, the neighbors, and the kids. Police organizations failed to create the necessary units and staff them with qualified women and professionals necessary to effectively prevent, resolve, and ensure sensitive handling of gendered crimes.

Putting Citizens into Citizen Security

A recurring theme of security reform in postconflict societies since the 1980s has been transforming the relations between police forces and citizens. In El Salvador, Haiti, and South Africa, "community policing" was a widely publicized component of police reforms. Here again, formal organizational changes proved more feasible than redefining the way citizens relate to the police. The experience of postwar societies since 1990 shows that putting "citizens" into "citizen security" is among the most difficult aspects of security reform. In Guatemala and Haiti, popular frustrations with the lack of justice fueled vigilante killings for simple crimes like petty theft. Three successive experiments with community policing failed to take root in postwar El Salvador, while the "community policing" concept itself encountered difficulty in the Balkans, East Timor, Guatemala, and Haiti. Ronald West's chapter captures the multiple (and thus hardly meaningful) meanings of community policing in many postwar settings. In discussing UN reform efforts in East Timor, he claimed, "Community policing became a term within which to couch pronouncements on order maintenance, excoriate lawlessness or opine on the virtues of national unity by international officials and their local counterparts."[18] Even South Africa, which enjoyed a relatively committed government and open society, encountered great difficulty in implementing community-oriented programs. The collapse of community-police forums and the increasingly reactionary public discourses on crime in that country illustrate the obstacles to bringing communities into the process of setting policing priorities and changing the way police and society relate to each other.

JUDICIAL REFORMS

As seen earlier, judicial reforms conform to many of the patterns of police and military reform. Yet the process and challenges of transforming judiciaries differ in important ways from those of police reforms.[19] First, judicial personnel generally require more education than police officers; it is unrealistic to expect even lawyers to work effectively as judges or prosecutors with only several weeks of training. Second, judicial personnel are usually more removed from the actual commission of brutal human rights violations (though they are often responsible for ensuring impunity and protecting abusers). Consequently, it is not as easy to purge judges and other judicial personnel.

Third, the nominal independence of the judicial branch in most societies makes it more difficult for heads of state or legislatures to implement justice reforms. Judges seeking to resist changes can complain of executive interference. The most extreme example of this dynamic occurred in El Salvador, where a highly politicized Supreme Court chief justice, opposed to concessions granted in the peace agreements, resisted calls for his resignation by crying that "only God" could remove him from office. The nominal independence of the judiciary under El Salvador's constitution impeded reforms. It may be necessary to encroach on judicial independence in order to enact reforms aimed at greater judicial accountability, efficiency, responsiveness, and (ironically!) independence.

The main implication of these dilemmas is the need for promoting both judicial independence *and* accountability and for establishing mechanisms of accountability *before* judicial autonomy becomes entrenched. Transitional powers to modify the justice system may be especially necessary if that system threatens to act in a biased or arbitrary fashion. Kosovo illustrates the challenges of this apparent dilemma. Upon assuming transitional executive authority, the United Nations mission (UNMIK) permitted prior Kosovo Albanian judges, stripped of their posts by the Yugoslav government for ten years, to reassume their posts outside the executive branch but to be paid by UNMIK. When those judges began to decide cases in a manner that seemed to discriminate against ethnic Serbs, the United Nations appointed international judges to sit on panels. When that did not work, UNMIK appointed foreigners to appellate courts, where they played a determinant role in deciding ethnically charged cases. UNMIK also issued a decree permitting the UN head of mission to override judicial decisions in certain cases.

Kosovars charged the United Nations with violating the separation of powers and with abrogating the law in favor of Serbs. Moreover, just as the rest of territorial administration was being gradually handed over to local officials, the judiciary was increasingly taken away from Kosovars, calling into question the sustainability of institution building.[20] Perhaps if new mechanisms of accountability (e.g., a judicial commission) had been created before the full empowerment of Kosovo Albanian judges to dispense justice, the United Nations might not have found itself in the awkward position of second-guessing, even revoking, some judicial decisions and undermining its own claims of neutrality and commitment to democracy. In this way, both judicial accountability and independence might have been assured.

Most striking, the case studies reveal that judicial reforms have generally accomplished less than security reforms. They have tended to be less ambitious, less strategically planned, less coordinated, less swift, and less publicly understood and supported than security reforms. Despite claims to the contrary, they are usually poorly linked to police reforms, continuing the disaggregation of the "triad" of police, judicial, and prison reforms. They have focused on isolated elements of judicial performance rather than taking an integrated approach to multiple problems of the administration of justice. In countries where the state has been practically destroyed, restoring buildings, desks, information systems, and minimal security is a priority. In some established judiciaries, reformers have tended to stress training and purges, neglecting things like protection programs for witnesses and judicial personnel, improved access to courts, and alternative dispute resolution. In no case has judicial reform been deemed an unqualified success, and the difficulties encountered are notable.

Take the Bosnian case, where judicial corruption and blatant ethnic bias were frequent during the war. A UNDP report in 2002 concluded that "[t]he absence of any significant justice reform in BiH marks one of the missed opportunities of the mission thus far."[21] The United Nations' first try at judicial reform, after a delay of almost two years, resulted only in an unwieldy four-volume diagnostic that had no impact. A second reform effort launched in 2000, under the aegis of the International Justice Mission, convened sitting judges and prosecutors to vet their peers.[22] That disappointing effort led to the removal of only 5 officials out of 1,145 and was discontinued in 2002, "essentially acknowledging that the international reform project had failed." In the meantime, police reform had proceeded on a completely separate track. Given the resources and international attention dedicated to Bosnia's peace process, the poor plans, implementation, and results exemplify the continued shortcomings of judicial reform efforts in postconflict societies around the world.[23]

One important reason for the neglect of judicial reform is the primacy of order among the priorities of the international community. The maintenance of stability, both among states and within them, remains the major powers' top imperative, especially the United States'. Peace seems to offer easier, more immediate, and more prized benefits to powerful countries than the difficult provision of justice in divided societies. Part of the emphasis on the reform and development of military and police forces in postconflict societies, for instance, stems from donors' desire to limit exposure of their own peacekeeping troops. In Haiti and Bosnia, the U.S. Defense Department promoted police development in large part because it would alleviate the burden of peacekeeping duties and permit U.S. soldiers to return home more quickly.

In addition, legal and code reforms are a foundation for most postwar judicial reform processes. Constitutions under prepeace regimes in Serbia, South Africa, Central America, and Rwanda curtailed human and political rights and ensured impunity for the state and other elites. Changing these provisions was a necessary starting point for bringing security and fairness to the rule of law. The new criminal procedure codes in Central America and Kosovo lay the foundation for more transparent and efficient administration of justice, and nternational human rights protections guaranteed recourse to present and future victims. New constitutional formulas for representation are crucial to ensuring that major social groups have a stake in national-level governance. Constitutional reforms in South Africa, El Salvador, and Bosnia reflect these central changes.

Yet the on-the-ground experience of postwar societies demonstrates that excessive emphasis on constitutions, laws, and formal authority is misplaced. Legal reforms are insufficient without institutions that can guarantee rights, protect citizens, and enforce laws. Institution building of police, prosecutors, courts, bar associations, and relevant civil society actors is crucial to the perception and existence of justice. Written guarantees have done little to protect Serbs in postintervention Kosovo. In country after country, legal reforms have been hampered by judges and lawyers trained in the old system who cling to its privileges, its hierarchies, and its habits. Change requires transforming not just codes, but the very mind-set of the legal profession and institutions themselves. Without effective checks on state institutions, they are likely to continue to engage in discriminatory or corrupt behavior, despite laws to the contrary.

WAR CRIMES AND PAST HUMAN RIGHTS ABUSES

Practically every instance of war termination involves reckoning with war crimes and human rights abuses committed by prior regimes. In most wars, all sides commit some sort of violation of the laws of war, although one side's violations usually exceed the other's.[24] The case studies in this volume did not seek to examine in full detail efforts to address past war crimes and human rights abuses.[25] However, we sought to discern the impact of these efforts to deal with the past on the present-day legitimacy and efficacy of postconflict justice, including the judicial system. Several conclusions emerged from the cases that enrich existing knowledge about these issues.

Despite the persistent influence of victors in dispensing postwar justice, the case studies reveal an important trend in international humanitarian law (the "laws of war"): prior authoritarians have fewer and fewer possibilities to immunize themselves from criminal prosecution. During transitions of the 1980s, ruling elites were routinely able to pass amnesties for their atrocities. Over the past decade, however, local civil society pressures for judicial accountability found more echo in local media and political debate and in international diplomatic circles. International actors also developed more powerful tools to criminally prosecute war criminals. Between the international tribunals for the former Yugoslavia and for Rwanda, the International Criminal Court, and bilateral prosecutions by third-party countries such as Belgium and Spain, the net of transnational justice drew tighter between the 1980s and the early twenty-first century.

At the same time, a great variety of tools and options continued to be exercised in addressing past abuses, including diverse complements (sometimes used as alternatives) to trials. Postwar regimes in Sierra Leone and East Timor drew on prior experiences with trials and truth commissions elsewhere to adopt creative combinations of international assets and local resources and people. These cases and Rwanda's community-based trials demonstrate the active experimentation and learning across time that has occurred in the realm of transitional justice.

A second conclusion to be drawn from these case studies is that the link between past justice and future judicial systems is increasingly embraced in discourse and policy but remains elusive. Scholars and advocates of transitional justice have maintained that redress of past human rights abuses is necessary to lay a foundation for the rule of law and justice in new democracies. Deputy Secretary of Defense Paul Wolfowitz, for example, stated in 2003 after the U.S. war in Iraq began, "[T]he atrocities [of Saddam Hussein's regime] and the punishment of those responsible are directly linked to our success in helping the Iraqi people build a free, secure and democratic future."[26]

Yet this limited collection of cases failed to establish a robust, empirical connection between justice for past abuses and the quality and accessibility of justice in the future. No society examined enjoyed both successful prosecutions and a healthy system of postwar justice. In South Africa, famous for its innovative attempt to make amnesty for wartime abuses conditional on truth telling, popular faith in the justice system remained abysmal in 2003. Ironically, in El Salvador, where a comprehensive amnesty was adopted, the justice system underwent some significant reforms, despite continued shortcomings. The deficiencies of justice under new postconflict regimes varied greatly across the cases examined in this volume, but they seemed rooted in institutional choices, political decisions, and the context of war termination more than in the decision about how to deal with perpetrators of past atrocities.

Nevertheless, perceptions of justice for past abuses affected popular acceptance of present-day justice systems in some countries.

In cases where a large proportion of the population was affected by state violence and rights abuses, as in Rwanda, East Timor, and parts of Bosnia, popular perceptions of present-day justice are closely linked to the adjudication of those who committed past human rights abuses. Where perpetrators are viewed as "other" by one population, one segment of the population—the victims of abuse and those associated with them—will remain disenfranchised and disillusioned if some accountability is not exacted from those seen as responsible for directing the abuses.

TRADITIONAL AUTHORITY AND CUSTOMARY LAW

One of the most difficult tensions in democratizing postwar societies is addressing traditional authorities and local, informal mechanisms of justice. In many agrarian societies, leaders have been selected not through multiparty elections but through heredity, consensus, or an informal consultation process. These leaders often rule with few constraints, relying on informal consultations with elders or other community leaders. On the one hand, new central regimes (or transitional international administrations) cannot sweep aside such authorities without jeopardizing their own legitimacy, provoking violent resistance, or disarticulating the only known mechanisms of conflict resolution and order maintenance. Where central states or occupation forces have neither the knowledge nor the willingness to use sufficient military force, reliance on local authorities is a virtual necessity. Colonial administrations historically relied heavily on preexisting local chiefs, and some believe that present-day peacebuilders should adapt those experiences.[27]

On the other hand, nonelected local or traditional authorities often suffer from the same problems as the ousted authoritarian regime. They rule arbitrarily and without accountability, often discriminating against certain ethnic groups and women. Exclusionary structures were often the original cause of armed conflict. Reinforcing them only alienates some groups and deepens future sources of conflict.

The central governance dilemma is how to rely on traditional structures even while rejecting practices by local authorities that are antithetical to the principles of international organizations and donors. For postconflict policymakers, the quickest means of assuring short-term stability is to rely on extant structures. Yet can we say that popular empowerment or the rule of law exists if a local chieftain in East Timor can state, "I am responsible for security here. Nobody can go past me to the police."[28] Or if Kosovar judges of Albanian descent routinely act with bias against Serbs? Some measure of accountability and transparency is necessary for local authority to conform to minimal notions of liberal democracy, yet introducing liberal institutional measures risks destroying existing social constraints and expectations before an alternative has been debated, agreed on, explained, funded, and made operational. Eradicating local *suco* chieftains, for instance, would leave a vacuum of authority, security, and justice.

In some societies, traditional forms of authority and conflict resolution survived colonial rule. In societies such as Rwanda, East Timor, and parts of Guatemala and South Africa, justice reform requires fully understanding local society, customs, practices, and power structures. Ronald West argues that efforts to reconcile law and custom "must be undertaken as soon as possible if law is to be accepted as the final authority over social conflict."[29] Yet custom often entails ways of thinking that are anathema to Western legal traditions. In many rural societies, monetary compensation for the victims is considered sufficient punishment for perpetrators of theft, murder, and rape.

Rwanda's nationally monitored, locally run system for trying genocide suspects, gacaca, exemplifies several advantages of local or traditional conflict resolution mechanisms in postwar settings. First, gacaca has itself changed during past decades, illustrating Mahmood Mamdani's point that customary law is "not opaque but porous, not stagnant but dynamic."[30] Justice reformers must be conscious that customary law cannot be readily codified but evolves over time. Second, gacaca was not historically practiced in the way adopted after the genocide. Rather, the Rwandan government adapted and modified it for wide-scale use throughout the country toward new purposes created by circumstances. Just as societies can rarely be "reconstructed" after war (and certainly genocide), prewar judicial mechanisms are not necessarily appropriate for postwar conditions.

Finally, gacaca combines justice with reconciliation like few other justice tools. It seeks community reconciliation at the local level, mediated by local notables who received authority from the central state (in a country accustomed to high levels of central authority). At the same time, it not only aims at social reconciliation but also metes out justice, including punishment, which can include banishment and imprisonment. It may be that the community reconciliation that is often associated with traditional dispute resolution mechanisms may be most possible (or only possible) if accompanied by the capacity to determine guilt and mete out punishment.

This volume initially sought to identify multiple local or traditional conflict resolution mechanisms adopted in various postconflict settings. Yet few such mechanisms appear in the case studies, mainly because postconflict reformers tend to rely on formal institutional models and mechanisms in the judicial and security sectors. In Guatemala, East Timor, and the Balkans, formal judicial systems at the national level remained the centerpiece of judicial planning. Informal or traditional alternatives were viewed as incompatible with Western liberal values by the United Nations in Guatemala, for instance, and eschewed. Other countries, however, like Chad and Zaire, historically retained colonial judicial systems that combined customary courts with modern, centrally administered courts.[31] Rama Mani advocates this "legal pluralism" as a way for Western reformers to recognize and embrace local practices that are familiar and legitimate.[32] Even with preservation of "traditional" forms of justice, education of broader society will usually be necessary to ensure that those mechanisms become tools for neither impunity nor mass vigilante justice.

CIVIL SOCIETY AND CITIZEN PARTICIPATION IN JSSR

Many analysts of democracy insist on the importance of civil society and popular participation.[33] Indeed, participation has increasingly become a demand of mobilized groups and donors in postwar democracies. Yet one of the most striking outcomes of this volume is the absence, and difficulty, of citizen participation in military, police, or judicial reform processes after conflicts. Neither everyday citizens nor civil society organizations figure prominently in these accounts of justice and security sector reform. Postwar JSSR efforts are generally state initiated or externally directed, top-down reforms to state institutions that have marginalized citizen input. Two salient points of this chapter are that the end of war does not end violence and that formal institutional changes have generally failed to transform the daily practices of justice and security in postconflict societies. These points lay bare the central role of citizens and civil society, in conjunction with state agencies, in effective JSSR.

Three conclusions regarding roles for citizen participation emerge from the case studies. First, citizens should have an important voice, either directly in neighborhood meetings or through civil society intermediaries, in the design and implementation of justice and security sector reforms. International organizations, especially those concerned with short-term order rather than long-term development, have at times been egregiously remiss. Judicial reform processes focus on elites, often limited to a handful of international donors and a small circle of lawyers from the transitional society. Colette Rausch provides a detailed account of the inadequate and superficial efforts by the UN mission to consult even the most expert constitutional scholars and respected lawyers in Kosovo. Ronald West's most resonant theme regarding East Timor is the lack of international incorporation of local voices and participation in judicial decision making, police policies, and lawmaking. Across all regions, police reforms involved little public consultation. Although local legal professionals are often exclusionary or antiquated in their attitudes, international peacekeeping actors have not found creative, positive ways to incorporate local participation in the design and implementation of postwar judicial or security reforms. The limits of organizational reform suggest that some minimal local participation and ownership is necessary for sustainability.

Second, public education has been neglected in postconflict JSSR efforts. The difficulty in moving beyond formal police reforms to new police-society relations epitomizes the need for specific efforts to transform public attitudes and expectations. Creating more courteous, respectful police is insufficient if the public continues to view the police with fear or suspicion. In societies like Bosnia, Cambodia, and South Africa, many citizens' only experience of public policing was through repression and fear, as police had participated in horrible atrocities and routine torture. Changing this relationship proved harder than changing police attitudes. In Haiti, for instance, the new Haitian National Police found that the public held them in low regard because they were unwilling to use the "stick" to discipline suspects on the street. New governments rarely engaged in public education campaigns to reorient the public and transform their concepts and expectations of the police. Stimulating trust in judicial institutions poses an equally daunting challenge; public education aimed at creating new expectations of reformed security and justice organizations is indispensable for institutional reforms to take root.

A third conclusion about citizen participation is that civil society organizations in postconflict societies have been ill equipped to contribute to JSSR. This volume has focused on top-down, state-directed, externally driven institutional reforms rather than society-led initiatives, public education, or community-level projects, yet analysis points to the importance of the latter. In police reforms as well as judicial reforms, institutional changes have not transformed the everyday practices of justice and security to the extent desired or expected by most citizens. The need for reformers not only to heed but to strengthen civil society organizations in JSSR is apparent. Without new understandings of justice and security among the general population, institutional reforms will have limited and reversible impact. In Haiti, for example, achievements in depoliticization and accountability of policing began to be reversed long before the uprising that brought down the Aristide government in 2004. And without active, effective nongovernmental organizations helping to revise constitutions and codes, improve police procedure and conduct, enhance military doctrine, and improve criminal statistics and crime prevention, top-down institutional reforms will not prove sustainable.

Civil society bears some responsibility here. Many nongovernmental organizations have not sought a role in contributing to justice and security reforms, preferring instead to be external critics of internationally backed state efforts. The transition from persecuted critic to constructive partner of government is difficult for NGOs. Here international donors can shift resources to support civil society's capacity to serve as a long-term source of ideas, of human resources, of legitimacy, and of accountability for security and justice agencies. In addition, local-level initiatives in neighborhood watch groups, local-level reconciliation, and peacebuilding programs offer possibilities of generating citizen input and participation in justice and security sector reform. Although their aggregate impact is difficult to measure, new governments and donors have not fully exploited the contribution these programs might make to creating legitimate and sustainable security and justice systems. External programs to support NGOs working on security reforms, now in their infancy, will likely encounter many challenges, and civil society promotion will not serve as a panacea. Yet the findings of these case studies point toward the need for broadening citizen participation in JSSR to ensure sustainability.

CONCLUSION

Societies emerging from armed conflicts always face challenges of establishing security and providing justice. Suffering populations wearily seek order and safety, even as they warily hope that their aspirations for justice and a better life may be met under a new regime. In recent years, meeting these challenges has become more complicated. Mobilized populations demand safety and fair treatment; televised images magnify dissatisfaction and disorder; and international rights regimes impose an array of obligations. Multiple pressures confront actors ranging from local police officers and tribal chieftains to national justice ministers and human rights advocates to international development agencies and occupying armies. In the end, neither justice nor security will be delivered to everyone's satisfaction. Even in the most consolidated and peaceful democracies, disgruntlement with justice and security prevails among minority populations and, to some degree, throughout society.

The ambition of international organizations to refashion the military forces, the police forces, and the justice system of a nation reflects tremendous idealism and, indeed, hubris. These vital structures of a state rest on cultural and historical foundations whose features resist change. To some natives of any given society, those foundations seem immovable, and replacing them in a few short years appears ludicrous. Idealistic and often naive, thousands of globe-trotting police trainers, constitution drafters, and court advisers have been agents of the Western world order, even when they attempt to adapt that order to local realities and ease its entry.[34] That world order is not homogeneous, fixed, or fully liberal. However, many of its features are liberal: the establishment of basic rights to life and fundamental liberties, the end of political or ethnic violence, the realization of a formal judicial system that at least occasionally delivers justice, some recognition (if not retribution) for past acts of injustice, formal equal rights and opportunities for women, the enjoyment of physical security on the street (though less often in the home and family), and some expectation that the state will serve its citizens rather than exploit or abuse its subjects.

As we have seen, UN, European, U.S., and other external reform advocates have silenced naysayers in many cases. The skeletal structure of democracy has taken root in societies where it was once deemed impossible. In South Africa, no other form of government is conceivable, just as old-style military rule is highly unlikely in Central America. Women have achieved unprecedented opportunities in postconflict societies in every region, including in the Muslim-majority Bosnian Federation and Kosovo. Justice occasionally is served up where it was previously absent in Central America. Reform efforts have transformed what was once politicized state policing in the former communist world, militarized policing in Latin America, and ethnically exclusive policing in the Balkans. Japan, a culture considered alien to democracy in 1945, stands as a symbol of how imposed democracy can become consolidated democracy, and how notions of voice, participation, and demilitarization can find adherents in any society. Even in places like Bosnia and Kosovo, where statehood itself is not clearly tenable, the end of war paved the way for certain steps toward inclusiveness, professionalization, and some sense of justice for past atrocities.

Specifically, where cease-fires have borne fruit, it has proved possible in most cases to remove the most abusive and autocratic persons from justice and police institutions. It has proved possible to restructure police forces, judicial systems, military forces, security doctrines, and prison systems so that they respond to elected civilian officials and are subject to greater transparency. When we disaggregate police reforms into different endeavors, some (e.g., composition and restructuring) are easier than others (e.g., involving citizens and communities in policing). In some cases, state organizations formulated comprehensive criminal justice strategies that embraced interrelated institutional reforms. In some postcommunist societies, international influences sparked the redefinition of legal education and training.

Yet the shortcomings and limits facing those who seek to reshape these core institutions of society are also apparent. Forging efficient, fair, and accessible justice systems takes longer and confronts more complexities than police reform. In all cases, political resistance impeded reforms. In some countries, formal institutions of state and society are weak in comparison with personalized networks and informal institutions. Here efforts to revamp, restructure, professionalize, and hold accountable formal institutions will not go very far (indeed, make little sense) unless security and justice organizations operate minimally as bureaucracies. In societies where local, informal mechanisms have long served to resolve most social disputes, building a Western model of justice makes no sense unless its articulation with local mechanisms is carefully considered.

Most of the chapters in this volume reflect the practical experience of professionals involved in attempts to construct security and justice in war-torn societies. Firsthand tales—of managing a police reform process in postgenocide Rwanda, of UN Civilian Police in East Timor, of OSCE judicial reform efforts in Kosovo, of human rights institution building in Haiti, of designing the government's crime prevention strategy in South Africa—inform and underpin the analysis. Even the contributors not directly holding policy positions have all worked as consultants or advocates in shaping reform processes. The frustration of these experiences is palpable, and the authors direct much of their consternation at international organizations and powerful donors. The manifold limits, even pathologies, are visible in these case studies.[35]

Curiously, a persistence and an optimism prevail beneath the surface of these accounts. The underlying logic of some seems to be, "If only international organizations worked more rationally, if only sufficient resources were available, if only the good-guy reformers had done more to overpower or outwit the bad-guy impediments, then reforms could have worked the way they should have." Unfortunately, these recent experiences and the history of postwar state building suggest that powerful obstacles and organizational pathologies will always exist. Understanding the nature of constructing the infra-structure of justice and security after war requires analyzing and taking into account the power and pathologies of great powers, international organizations, national elites, and community-level dispensers of order and justice. National leaders may have especially propitious opportunities to overcome some of these obstacles, though they themselves often represent the most serious obstacle. This vol-ume, we hope, has shed light on the patterns reflected by recent post-war judicial and security reforms, including the behavioral tendencies of various actors and institutions involved in assisting or subverting those reforms. As the global order increasingly permits the sort of state building examined herein, perhaps these patterns will become more relevant in understanding our world and its many diverse societies.

NOTES

1. Pierre du Toit, "South Africa: In Search of Post-settlement Peace," in *The Management of Peace Processes*, ed. John Darby and Roger MacGinty (New York: Macmillan, 2000), 16–60, cited in John Darby, *The Effects of Violence on Peace Processes* (Washington, D.C.: United States Institute of Peace Press, 2001), 63.

2. See chapter 9, endnote 81, in this volume.

3. On this categorization of violence, see Caroline Moser, "The Gen-dered Continuum of Violence and Conflict: An Operational Framework," in *Victims, Perpetrators or Actors? Gender, Armed Conflict and Political Violence*, ed. Caroline Moser and Fiona C. Clark (New York: Zed Books, 2001).

4. Darby, *The Effects of Violence on Peace Processes*; and Stephen John Stedman, "Spoiler Problems in Peace Processes," *International Security* 22, no. 2 (Fall 1997): 5–50.

5. Moser, "The Gendered Continuum of Violence and Conflict."

6. See the discussion of international efforts at justice and security reforms referenced in the introduction to this volume on pages 6 to 9.

7. John Paul Lederach, *Building Peace: Sustainable Reconciliation in Divided Societies* (Washington, D.C.: United States Institute of Peace Press, 1997); Carlos L. Yorda, "Society Building in Bosnia: A Critique of Post-Dayton Peacebuilding Efforts," *Seton Hall Journal of Diplomacy and International Relations* 4, no. 2 (Summer–Fall 2003): 59–74; Roland Paris, "Peacebuilding and the Limits of Liberal Internationalism," *International Security* 22, no. 2 (1997): 54–89; and Charles T. Call and Susan E. Cook, "On Democratization and Peacebuilding," *Global Governance* 9, no. 2 (April–June 2003).

8. On DDR generally, see Mats R. Berdal, *Disarmament and Demobilisation after Civil Wars*, Adelphi Paper No. 303 (London: IISS and Oxford University Press, 1996); Joanna Spear, "Disarmament and Demobilization," in *Ending Civil Wars*, ed. Stephen John Stedman, Donald Rothchild, and Elizabeth M. Cousens (Boulder, Colo.: Lynne Rienner, 2002), 141–182; Paul Collier, "Demobilization and Insecurity: A Study in the Economics of the Transition from War to Peace," *Journal of International Development* 6, no. 3 (1994); and Nicole Ball, "Demobilization and Reintegrating Soldiers," in *Rebuilding Societies after Civil War*, ed. Krishna Kumar (Boulder, Colo.: Lynne Rienner, 1997).

9. UN High-Level Panel on Threats, Challenges, and Change, *A More Secure World: Our Shared Responsibility* (New York: United Nations, December 2, 2004); and Kofi Annan, *In Larger Freedom: Towards Development, Security and Human Rights*, A/59/2005 (New York: United Nations, March 21, 2005).

10. *Post-conflict Reconstruction: Task Framework*, report of the project on postconflict reconstruction of the Association of the U.S. Army and Center for Strategic and International Studies (Washington, D.C.: Association of the U.S. Army and Center for Strategic and International Studies, April 2002), 7–8.

11. Tracy Wilkinson, "Disparities Steal Thunder of Albright's Balkan Trip," *Los Angeles Times*, June 8, 1997, A1.

12. The exceptions here are formerly socialist countries where police forces already enjoyed genuine separation from the military, as in Bosnia, Kosovo, Iraq, and Nicaragua (after 1990). In such societies, defeat of the military often permits the police to continue providing internal security, even as the external defense forces are restructured, purged, or dismembered.

13. Wherever governments had not been strategically defeated in warfare (Bosnia, Guatemala, South Africa, El Salvador), prior government police leadership tended to continue dominating senior uniformed positions.

14. Kofi Annan, "Report of the Secretary General [to the Security Council] on the U.N. Mission in Bosnia and Herzegovina," June 7, 2001, S/2001/571 (New York: United Nations), par. 16.

15. See Robert Perito, *The American Experience with Police in Peace Operations* (Cornwallis, N.S.: Canadian Peacekeeping Press, 2002); and Renata Dwan, *Executive Policing: Enforcing the Law in Peace Operations*, SIPRI Research Report No. 16 (Oxford: Oxford University Press, 2002).

16. Encouragement for investigative journalism might be one of the "low-hanging fruit" for those who would seek to strengthen transparency and accountability.

17. This section draws extensively on chapter 10 in this volume. See also Moser and Clark, *Victims, Perpetrators or Actors?*; Krishna Kumar, ed., *Women and Civil War: Impact, Organizations, and Action* (Boulder, Colo.: Lynne Rienner, 2001).

18. Ronald West, quoted in draft of chapter 9 presented at authors' meeting at the United States Institute of Peace, Washington, D.C., May 15, 2002.

19. See Robert B. Oakley, Michael J. Dziedzic, and Eliot M. Goldberg, *Policing the New World Disorder: Peace Operations and Public Security* (Washington, D.C.: National Defense University, 1998), 511. Some of these differences appear in my chapter on El Salvador in this volume, but they apply at a more general level.

20. See chapter 8 in this volume and UN Development Programme, "Security Sector Reform: Lessons from Bosnia and Herzegovina and Kosovo" (draft report based on a Joint UNDP/DPKO Mission in August 2001, UN Development Programme Bureau for Conflict Prevention and Recovery, January 2002).

21. UN Development Programme, "Security Sector Reform," 9.

22. See chapter 7 in this volume.

23. One notable exception was a speedy judicial reform process in the internationally administered city-state of Brčko that achieved new laws, new structures, and the replacement of 80 percent of judicial personnel. See chapter 7 in this volume.

24. The laws of war, also known as international humanitarian law, are contained principally in the four Geneva Conventions of 1949 and their additional protocols.

25. General works on transitional justice are cited in the introduction to this volume.

26. Paul Wolfowitz, testimony before the Senate Foreign Relations Committee, "Iraq: Status and Prospects for Reconstruction: Resources," July 29, 2003, 4.

27. See, for example, Niall Ferguson, *Empire: The Rise and Demise of the British World Order and Lessons for Global Power* (New York: Basic Books, 2003).

28. Quoted in chapter 9.

29. Ibid., 336

30. Mahmood Mamdani, *Citizen and Subject: Contemporary Africa and the Legacy of Late Colonialism* (Princeton, N.J.: Princeton University Press, 1996), 168.

31. Rama Mani, *Beyond Retribution: Seeking Justice in the Shadows of War* (New York: Polity Press, 2002), 82.

32. Ibid., 83.

33. Larry Diamond, *Developing Democracy: Toward Consolidation* (Baltimore: Johns Hopkins University Press, 1999); Thomas Carothers, *In the Name of Democracy* (Washington, D.C.: Carnegie Endowment, 1999); John Keane, *Civil Society: Old Images New Visions* (Stanford, Calif.: Stanford University Press, 1998); and Thomas Carothers and Marina Ottaway, eds., *Funding Virtue: Civil Society Aid and Democracy Promotion* (Washington, D.C.: Carnegie Endowment for International Peace, 2000).

34. On the importance of local actors and factors, rather than international ones, in peacebuilding, see Elizabeth M. Cousens, introduction to *Peacebuilding as Politics,* ed. Elizabeth M. Cousens and Chetan Kumar (Boulder, Colo.: Lynne Rienner, 2001), 15.

35. See Michael N. Barnett and Martha Finnemore, "The Power, Politics and Pathologies of International Organizations," *International Organization* 53, no. 4 (August 1999): 699–732.

Index

Academy of the PNC (APNC), 134, 136
Administration of Justice (AOJ), 48
Administration Pénitentiaire Nationale (APENA), 99, 100
AFPC. *See* Agreement for the Strengthening of Civilian Authority and the Role of the Armed Forces in a Democratic Society (AFPC)
African Charter on Human and Peoples Rights, 208
African National Congress (ANC), 159, 162, 163, 171–172
Agreement for the Strengthening of Civilian Authority and the Role of the Armed Forces in a Democratic Society (AFPC), 121
Agreement on the Civilian Implementation of the Peace Settlement, 236
Agreement on the Identity and Rights of Indigenous Peoples, Guatemala, 120

Agreement on the Implementation, Compliance and Verification Timetable for the Peace Agreements, 122
Akayesu, Jean-Paul, 200
Albright, Madeleine, 388
Alkatiri, Mari, 333
American Bar Association's Central and East European Law Initiative (ABA CEELI), 278
Amnesty International, 208, 258–259, 289
Amnesty law
   El Salvador, 50
   Rwanda, 198, 208, 210
   South Africa, 171–174, 184
ANC. *See* African National Congress (ANC)
Anglo-American accusatory system of justice, 52–53
Annan, Kofi, 5
AOJ. *See* Administration of Justice (AOJ)
Apartheid, 159–162
   alienation of police, 161
   counterinsurgency, 160

deregulation of social control, 161–162
escalation of violence, 161–162
military role of police, 160
repression of citizenry, 161
Total Strategy law enforcement, 169
APENA. *See* Administration Pénitentiaire Nationale (APENA)
APNC. *See* Academy of the PNC (APNC)
Applicable laws in Kosovo, 277, 291, 299
The Archive, Guatemala, 117
ARENA. *See* Nationalist Republican Alliance (ARENA), El Salvador
Aristide, Jean-Bertrand, 69, 71–73, 75, 78, 83, 89, 354–355
Arkan, 233
Armed Forces of the Republic (TNI), Timor, 315–317
Artibonite Resistance Front for the Overthrow of Jean-Bertrand Aristide, 75
Arusha Peace Agreement, 194, 216
Arzú, Álvaro, 123, 140
Ashdown, Lord Paddy, 249
Asian Development Bank, 318
Attorney General's Office, El Salvador, 52–55
  Anglo-American accusatory system of justice, 52–53
  civil society, role of, 55
  Continental inquisitive system of justice, 52
  funding and training, 54
  new codes, 53–55
  new criminal laws, 53
  Public Ministry, 53, 54
Australian Federal Police (APF), 325

AVEGA (Association des Veuves du Génocide d'Avril), 202

Bala, Haradin, 306
Balaj, Idriz, 306
Barayagwiza, Jean-Bosco, 202
Barrera, Hugo, 45
Basson, Wouter, 184
Berger, Oscar, 123
Bizimungu, Pasteur, 205
BND. *See* Bureau de Nutrition et de Développement (BND)
Boban, Mate, 234
Bosnia and Herzegovina, 231–270
Bosniak-Croat Federation, 235, 245
Bosnian Serb Army (VRS), 233
Bosnian War, 233–237
Boutros-Ghali, Boutros, 37
Brahimaj, Lahi, 306
Bramshill Academy, United Kingdom, 218
Brčko Law Revision Commission, Bosnia, 252
British Department for International Development (DFID), 7
BUCODEP. *See* Bureau de Contrôle de Détention Préventive (BUCODEP)
Bureau de Contrôle de Détention Préventive (BUCODEP), 94
Bureau de Nutrition et de Développement (BND), 99, 100
Bureau de Poursuites et Suivi, Haiti, 79
Bush, George H. W., 73
Business against Crime, South Africa, 167

Cady, Jean, 320
Carrefour Feuilles trial, Haiti, 95
Carter, Jimmy, 73

Categories of genocide suspects, Rwanda, 197

Catholic Archdiocese of Guatemala, 125–126

CCIU. *See* Central Investigation Unit, CIVPOL (CCIU)

CDRC. *See* Criminal Defense Resource Center (CDRC), Kosovo

CEH. *See* Commission for Historical Clarification (CEH), Guatemala

Center for Social Work, Bosnia, 363

Central American University's Public Opinion Institute (IUDOP), 39

Central Investigation Unit, CIVPOL (CCIU), 291

CFJ. *See* Commission on Strengthening of the Judiciary (CFJ), Guatemala

Chamblain, Louis Jodel, 97

Christians involved in genocide, Rwanda, 210

CICIACS. *See* Commission for the Investigation of Illegal Bodies and Clandestine Security Apparatuses (CICIACS), Guatemala

Civilian Intelligence and Information Analysis Department, Guatemala, 122

Civilianization within Salvadoran police, 38, 45, 58

Civil Registry, Haiti, 93

CIVPOL. *See* UN Civilian Police (CIVPOL)

Clan violence in East Timor, 332–333

Clinton, Bill, 73

CNVJ. *See* National Commission on Truth and Justice (CNVJ), Haiti

Colocation, by International Police Task Force, 242, 302

Colonial administration, East Timor, 314–316

Commission for Follow-up and Support for Strengthening the Legal System (CSA), Guatemala, 128

Commission for Historical Clarification (CEH), Guatemala, 119, 124–125

Commission for Reception, Truth, and Reconciliation (CRTR), East Timor, 328, 338–329

Commission for the Investigation of Illegal Bodies and Clandestine Security Apparatuses (CICIACS), Guatemala, 140

Commission on Gender Equality, South Africa, 163, 176, 365

Commission on Human Rights, 235

Commission on Strengthening of the Judiciary (CFJ), Guatemala, 128

Commission on the Strengthening of the Justice System, Guatemala, 121

Commission on Truth and Friendship, East Timor and Indonesia, 327

Communal Police, Rwanda, 214, 216

Community-Oriented-Policing offices, El Salvador, 45

Community Police Forum (CPF), South Africa, 164

Community Police Intervention Patrols (PIP-COM), El Salvador, 45

Community policing
Balkans, 393
East Timor, 321–322, 329–330, 393

El Salvador, 45–46, 393
Guatemala, 393
Haiti, 82, 86, 393
Rwanda, 218, 220
South Africa, 164–165, 169–170,
    182–183, 393
Comprehensive Agreement on
    Human Rights, Guatemala,
    120
Conference of Directors and
    Commissioners, Bosnia, 248
Conseil Supérieur de la
    Magistrature, Haiti, 95
Conselho Nacional da Resistencia
    Timorense (CNRT), 319
Constant, Emmanuel, 78
Constitutional Court, South
    Africa, 163
Constitutional Framework,
    Kosovo, 285
Continental inquisitive system of
    justice, 52
Coordinating Agency for
    Modernization of the Justice
    Sector, Guatemala, 139
COPAZ. *See* National Commission
    for the Consolidation of
    Peace (COPAZ), El Salvador
CORELESAL. *See* Salvadoran Legal
    Reform Commission
    (CORELESAL)
Corruption in Bosnia, 262–263
Costa e Sousa, José Luis da, 320, 335
Counsel for Human Rights (PDH),
    Guatemala, 118–119, 120,
    147–148
Court restructuring, Bosnia,
    252–253
CPC. *See* Criminal procedure code
    (CPC), El Salvador
CPF. *See* Community Police Forum
    (CPF), South Africa

Crime
    escalation of in El Savador, 44, 58
    escalation of in Haiti, 76
    escalation of in Kosovo, 276–277
    escalation of in South Africa, 164
    Guatemala, 140–145
    by juveniles, El Salvador, 56
    in postapartheid South Africa,
        174–175
    as threat to democracy, 30
Criminal Defense Resource Center
    (CDRC), Kosovo, 287
Criminal Investigations Section
    (SIC), Guatemala, 134, 135
Criminal Investigative Department
    (CID), Rwanda, 205
Criminal law, Bosnia
    European models for, 253
    weakness of, 253
Criminal Procecure Code (CPP),
    Guatemala, 118, 127, 137
Criminal procedure code (CPC),
    El Salvador, 53, 54–55
Cristiani, Alfredo, 31, 35, 36, 50
Croat Defense Council (HVO), 234
Croat Democratic Union (HDZ),
    234, 237
Customary law, 399–401
    central governance, 399–400
    community reconciliation, 401
    compensation, 400
    gacaca, 400–401
    Guatemala, 132
    legal pluralism, 401
    local leaders, 399
    rural societies, 400
    traditional authorities, 399–400

Dakar Declaration, 208
Dayton Peace Accords (DPA), 231,
    234–236, 272
    creation of high representative,
        236

creation of states and cantons, 234–236
intergovernmental organizations, 236
rights to returning refugees, 235–236
state control over institutions, 235
Demilitarization in Haiti, 76–77
Democratic League of Kosovo (LDK), 272
Democratic policing, 30, 83, 162–163, 239
Denizé, Pierre, 85, 88
Department for Safety and Security, South Africa, 163, 165
Department of Anti-narcotics Operations (DOAN), Guatemala, 136
Department of Criminal Investigations (DICRI), Guatemala, 137
Depoliticization of judiciary, El Salvador, 52
DFID. *See* British Department for International Development (DFID)
DICRI. *See* Department of Criminal Investigations (DICRI), Guatemala
Directorate General for Civilian Intelligence, Guatemala, 139–140
Directorate of Special Operations, South Africa, 169
DOAN. *See* Department of Anti-narcotics Operations (DOAN), Guatemala
Domestic war crimes trials, Bosnia, 257–259
Dominique, Jean, 96
DPA. *See* Dayton Peace Accords (DPA)

Drug trafficking, Haiti, 74, 75, 88
Duvalier, François "Papa Doc," 41
Duvalier, Jean-Claude, 72

East African Police Chiefs Committee (EAPCCO), 221
East Timor, 313–350
Indonesian rule, 315–316
international administration, 317–318
national justice system, 319–330, 336–338
Portuguese rule, 314–315
East Timor Defense Force (ETDF), 333
East Timor Police Service Development Plan, 321–322
East Timor Transitional Administration (ETTA), 319
East Timor Trust Fund, 318
École de la Magistrature (EMA), 92–93
El Salvador, 29–67
character of civil war in, 31–32
criminal codes, 53–55
judicial reforms, 48–57
peace agreement in, 32–34
postwar crime wave, 39–44
security reforms implementation, 34–47
Supreme Court, 51–52
UN Truth Commission, 33, 49–51
women and children, 55–56
EMA. *See* École de la Magistrature (EMA)
EMP. *See* Presidential General Staff (EMP), Guatemala
Escobar Galindo, David, 37
ETDF. *See* East Timor Defense Force (ETDF)
Ethnically blind justice, Bosnia, 250

ETTA. *See* East Timor Transitional Administration (ETTA)
EUPM. *See* European Union Police Mission (EUPM)
European Convention for the Protection of Human Rights and Fundamental Freedoms, 235
European Parliament, 364
European Union, 147
European Union Police Mission (EUPM), 240

FAdH. *See* Forces Armées d'Haiti (FAdH)
FALINTIL. *See* Forças Armadas do Libertaçao Nacional do Timor L'Este (FALINTIL)
Farabundo Martí National Liberation Front (FMLN), 31, 35, 38–39
Federal Republic of Yugoslavia (FRY), 273, 274
Fivaz, George, 172
Five-Year Plan for Modernization of the Judiciary, Guatemala, 128
Flores, Francisco, 43
FMLN. *See* Farabundo Martí National Liberation Front (FMLN)
Forças Armadas do Libertaçao Nacional do Timor L'Este (FALINTIL), 315, 316, 335
Forces Armées d'Haiti (FAdH), 71, 77
Forgiveness for abuses
  Rwanda, 210
  South Africa, 172–173
Fort Leonard Wood, Missouri, 83
FRAPH. *See* Revolutionary Front for Advancement and Progress in Haiti (FRAPH)

French Napoleonic Code, 71, 357
Frente Revolucionaria do Timor-Leste Independente (FRETILIN), 315
FRETILIN. *See* Frente Revolucionaria do Timor-Leste Independente (FRETILIN)
FRY. *See* Federal Republic of Yugoslavia (FRY)

Gacaca, traditional ancient council of elders, 203–204
  reintegration of offender, 203–204
Gacaca courts, Rwanda, 203–212
  administrative gacaca, 204–205
  genocide gacaca, 205–212
  jurisdictions of, 206–212
  new gacaca, 204–205
  precolonial ancient gacaca, 203–204
GCE. *See* Spanish Civil Guard (GCE)
Gender Affairs Unit, East Timor, 361
Gender and policing, 351–371, 392–393
  East Timor, 361
  Haiti, 354–357
  increasing violence toward women, 351–354
  institutionalizing gendered justice, 359–366
  Kosovo, 357–359
General Process Code, Guatemala, 128
Genocide case files, Rwanda, 222
Genocide gacaca, 205–212
  amnesty, 208–209
  categories of crimes, 205–206
  criticism of, 207–209
  eyewitness testimony requirement, 207

fairness of, 207–208
judges, 206–207
jurisdictions, 206–212
prison support for, 209–212
process of judging, 207
public satisfaction with, 211, 212
Roman Catholic Church, 210
shortcomings of, 209
social reintegration of suspects,
    210
Gerardi Conadera, Bishop Juan,
    125–126
Governors Island Agreement, 80, 91
Guatemala, 113–155
    conflicts within justice system,
        137–139
    human rights prosecutions,
        124–127
    intelligence reforms, 139–140
    judicial reform, 127–132
    Old Order characteristics,
        115–119
    peace accords, 114–115, 119–124
    police reform, 132–137
    public safety, 140–145
Guatemalan Association for
    Research and Social Studies
    (ASIES), 141–145
Guatemalan Institute for
    Comparative Studies and
    Penal Sciences, 131
Guatemalan National
    Revolutionary Unity
    (URNG), 113
Gun buy-back program, Haiti, 76
Gusmão, Xanana, 319
Gutiérrez Castro, Mauricio, 50–51

Habyarimana, Juvénal, 194, 214
Haiti, 69–112
    drug trafficking, 74, 75
    as failing state, 69–71
    groups of thugs, 75

Haitian National Police (HNP),
    75, 79
    infighting, 74
Lavalas movement, 72
legal apartheid, 71
military rule, history of, 71–73
police reform, 79–82
political environment in 1980s,
    73–74
political polarization, 74–75
as predatory state, 71–76
prison reform, 99–101
repression of civil society, 72–73
women after war, 354–357
Haitian National Police (HNP), 75,
    79, 355–356
    abuse and accountability, 87–88
    brutality in slums, 90
    election security, 89
    human rights violations, 84
    institutional development of,
        85–86
    internal disciplinary system,
        87–88
    morale problems, 89
    physical infrastructure, 84
    police-community relations, 86
    public attitudes toward, 84–85
    rape as political tool, 355
    recruitment of women, 355
    rise in crime, 86
    specialized crowd control, 84
    training about treatment of
        women, 355–356
    value of women as police, 356
HDZ. *See* Croat Democratic Union
    (HDZ)
Helsinki Human Rights Committee
    in Bosnia and Herzegovina,
    260, 261
High-density policing, 165
High Judicial and Prosecutorial
    Councils (HJPC), Bosnia, 252

HJPC. *See* High Judicial and Prosecutorial Councils (HJPC), Bosnia

Holbrooke, Richard, 234

HRFOR. *See* United Nations Human Rights Field Operation for Rwanda (HRFOR)

HSRC. *See* Human Science Research Council (HSRC)

Human Rights Commission, South Africa, 163, 176

Human rights inconsistencies, Kosovo, 278–279

Human Rights Institute of the University of Central America (IDHUCA), 46

Human Rights Office of the Archdiocese (ODHA), Guatemala, 126

Human Rights Ombudsperson's Office, El Salvador, 33, 46

Human rights reform, El Salvador, 46

Human Science Research Council (HSRC), 174

HVO. *See* Croat Defense Council (HVO)

Ibuka (Remember), Rwanda, 198

ICITAP. *See* International Criminal Investigation Training Assistance Program (ICITAP)

ICTR. *See* International Criminal Tribunal for Rwanda (ICTR)

ICTY. *See* International Criminal Tribunal for the Former Yugoslavia (ICTY), The Hague

IDHUCA. *See* Human Rights Institute of the University of Central America (IDHUCA)

IFOR. *See* NATO's Implementation Force (IFOR)

IJC. *See* International Judicial Commission (IJC)

Imposed democracy, 405

Independent Complaints Directorate, South Africa, 163, 176, 177

Independent Investigating Judge, South Africa, 176

Indonesian military special forces (KOPASSUS), 315, 317

Indonesian police (POLRI), 315, 316

Indonesian rule in East Timor, 315–316

Inquisitorial justice system, Guatemala, 118

Institute for Democracy in South Africa, 179

Institute for Security Studies (ISS), 174, 179

Integrated Justice System (IJS), 168

Integrating courts and police, East Timor, 343

Integration of women into police forces, 354

Inter-American Convention on the Prevention, Punishment and Eradication of Violence against Women, 364–365

Inter-American Court for Human Rights, 127

Inter-American Development Bank, 55, 139, 363

INTERFET. *See* International Force in East Timor (INTERFET)

Interim Public Security Force (IPSF), Haiti, 80–81

International Civilian Support Mission in Haiti (MICAH), 82

International Committee of the Red Cross (ICRC), 100

International Covenant of Civil and Political Rights, Rwanda, 207–208
International Criminal Investigation Training Assistance Program (ICITAP), 82, 134, 322, 358
International Criminal Tribunal for Rwanda (ICTR), 200–203
International Criminal Tribunal for the Former Yugoslavia (ICTY), The Hague, 200, 232, 254–257, 282–283, 306
cooperation with, 255–256
domestic war crimes trials, 257–259
fairness of trials in Kosovo, 283
Republika Srpska police, 255–257
Rules of the Road, 257–258
Srebrenica massacre, 256, 257
war crimes arrests, 255–257
weaknesses in police structures, 255–256
International Crisis Group (ICG), 305–306
International donors to police reform, inadequacy of, 12
International Force in East Timor (INTERFET), 317, 319
International humanitarian law, 397–399
alternatives to trials, 398
amnesties, 397–398
redress of past abuses, 398–399
International initiatives in Rwanda, 217–218
International Judicial Commission (IJC), 249, 251
International military leadership, 300, 301
International Monetary Fund, 318

International Office of Migration, Kosovo (IOM), 291
International Police Task Force (IPTF), Bosnia, 237–248
activities of, 237–238
colocation of international officers, 242
democratic policing, 239
participation in ethnic cleansing, 238
IOM. *See* International Office of Migration, Kosovo (IOM)
IPSF. *See* Interim Public Security Force (IPSF), Haiti
IPTF. *See* International Police Task Force (IPTF), Bosnia
ISS. *See* Institute for Security Studies (ISS)
IUDOP. *See* Central American University's Public Opinion Institute (IUDOP)
Izmery, Antoine, 96, 97

JAC/LM. *See* Joint Advisory Council for Legislative Matters (JAC/LM)
JNN. *See* Yugoslav National Army (JNA)
Johannesburg Victimisation Survey, 179
Joint Advisory Council for Legislative Matters (JAC/LM), 278, 279
Joseph, Eucher Luc, 85, 88
JSAP. *See* UN Judicial Assessment Programme (JSAP)
JSSR. *See* Justice and security sector reform (JSSR)
Judicial Career Law, Guatemala, 130
Judicial Reform Law of 1998, Haiti, 96
Judicial reforms in Bosnia, 248–254
changes to trial proceedings, 253

downsizing of courts, 252–253
establishment of state court,
    253–254
ethnic balance of judges, 252
monitoring of court proceedings,
    249
overhaul of criminal law, 253
peer review of judges, 250–251
public confidence lacking, 250
reappointment of judges and
    prosecutors, 251–252
sham trials, 250
Judicial reforms in East Timor,
    319–330
    access to hearings, 338
    applied law of the land, 324
    backlogs in judicial process, 337
    crime trends, 325–326
    customary law, 337, 340
    domestic violence, 326
    formalized legal codes and
        procedures, 324
    judges' competencies, 324
    local level justice, 329–330
    national justice system, 336–338
    organized crime, 325
    overcentralization of judicial
        processes, 334, 337
    prison system, 328–329, 339–341
    public satisfaction, 327
    reconciliation, 330
    recruiting judiciary personnel,
        319–320
    restitution within the
        community, 340
    serious crimes, 326–328
    truth and reconciliation
        hearings, 338–339
    truth commission, 327, 328
Judicial reforms in El Salvador,
    48–57
    Attorney General's Office, 52–55
    deficiency in legal education, 54

image of judiciary, 56–57
judicial independence and
    accountability, 51–52
justice, gender, and youth, 55–56
role of civil society, 55
UN Truth Commission, 49–51
wartime judicial reform, 48–49
Judicial reforms in Guatemala,
    124–132
    access to the justice system,
        128–130
    church-led truth commission,
        125–126
    conflicts within criminal
        procedures, 137–138
    criminal networks within
        intelligence units, 140
    disunity of international donors,
        138–139
    human rights prosecutions,
        124–127
    indigenous customary law, 132
    judges, skill level of, 131
    judicial violations of laws, 138
    legal education, quality of, 128,
        131
    oral traditions of customary law,
        132
    penitentiaries, corruption within,
        132
    professional standards, 128
    prosecution for political violence,
        125–127
    prosecutors, 130–131
    public defenders, 130
    Public Ministry, 130
    reparations, 124–125
    security provisions for judges,
        131–132
    selection of judges, 130
Judicial reforms in Haiti, 90–101
    absortive capacity for reform, 91

emergency training for
personnel, 92, 93
human rights abuses, 95–98
improving court management,
93–94
impunity, assessment of, 95–98
internal accountability, 97
legal aid project, 92
Ombudsman's Office, 97
oversight of personnel, 96
pretrial detention, 93
professionalization of system, 93
sustainable implementation of, 91
violent crime, 97
Judicial reforms in Kosovo, Serbia,
275–289
applicable laws, 277, 291
bar exam, 286
coordination among police,
justice, international,
284–285
courts, judges, prosecutors,
defense, 279–282
cross border hostilities, 288
defense attorneys, 287
discipline of judges, 280–281
extrajudicial detentions, 288–289
fairness of trials, 283
increased international control,
285
increased lawlessness, 276–277
international judges and
prosecutors, 283–284
judicial training, 286
Kosovo Criminal Code, 277
lawfulness of detentions, 283, 289
legal system monitoring, 287–289
limited resources of courts, 282
local involvement, 278–279, 281
multiethnic participation, 280
need for language interpreters,
278
recruitment difficulties, 282

Serb enclaves, 276
trafficking in women, 288
United Nations authority,
281–282
Judicial reforms in South Africa,
175–187
amnesty for security officials, 184
changes in prison population,
176
community participation,
182–183
corruption, 178–179, 182
crime prevention theory, 183
deaths in public demonstrations,
177–178
human rights standards, 176–178,
181–182, 185
institutional reform, 180–182
lustration, 184
new forms of crime, 181–182
overburdened criminal justice
system, 175–176
police brutality, 177
private security, 179–180
professional service delivery, 178
vigilantism, 179–180
xenophobia, 175
Judicial Service Commission, South
Africa, 171
Judicial system, Rwanda, 195–200
alternative conflict resolution,
202–203
classification of genocide
suspects, 197
detention of genocide suspects,
198
gacaca courts, 203–212
genocide prosecutions, 196
genocide trials, 198
infrastructure, 195
international assistance, 196–197
international tribunal, 200–203
justice before reconciliation, 199

negative opinions regarding
    tribunals, 201–202
prison situation, 196
quality of genocide trials,
    199–200
release of detainees from prison,
    198–199
survivors' groups, 198, 202
training for magistrates, 197
Justice
definition of, 8–9
divergent views of in Haiti, 99
Justice and security sector reform
    (JSSR), 7–9, 401–404
assessment of, 15, 17–21, 376–377
contributions by civil society,
    403–404
and history of state-building, 9
mode-of-transition approach to
    security reform, 30
public attitudes and
    expectations, 402–403
roles for citizens, 402

Kambanda, Jean, 200
Karadžic, Radovan, 232, 233, 255,
    256
Kayibanda, Gregoire, 194
KCS. See Kosovo Correctional
    Service (KCS)
KFOR. See Kosovo Force (KFOR)
KJI. See Kosovo Judicial Institute
    (KJI)
KLA. See Kosovo Liberation Army
    (KLA)
Klerk, F. W. de, 161
Koban Strategy for Community
    Policing, East Timor, 321
Kock, Eugene de, 173
KOPASSUS. See Indonesian
    military special forces
    (KOPASSUS)
Kosovo, 271–311

ethnic cleansing by Serbia,
    271–272
international administration,
    273–275
judicial reform, 275–289
resistance by Albanians, 272–273
security reform, 289–298
women after war, 357–359
Kosovo bar exam, 286
Kosovo Correctional Service
    (KCS), 296–298
Kosovo Criminal Code, 277
Kosovo Force (KFOR), 273,
    275–276, 277–278, 287,
    290–292, 304
Kosovo Judicial Institute (KJI), 286
Kosovo Liberation Army (KLA),
    272–273, 292–293
Kosovo Police Service (KPS), 285,
    294–295, 303–304, 357–359
crimes against women and
    children, 359
rape as political tool, 357
recruitment of women, 358–359
training in women's issues, 358
Kosovo Police Service School
    (KPSS), 292–296
basic training, 293
disrespect for police, 295
ethnic and gender cooperation,
    294
field training, 293, 294
human rights principles, 294
international policing styles, 293
organized crime, 295
recruitment, 292–293
Kosovo Protection Corps, 291, 303
Kosovo Standards Implementation
    Plan, 305
Kosovo Verification Mission
    (KVM), 273
KPSS. See Kosovo Police Service
    School (KPSS)

KVM. *See* Kosovo Verification Mission (KVM)

Lavalas movement, 71, 72, 74
LDK. *See* Democratic League of Kosovo (LDK)
Legal apartheid, Haiti, 71
Legal System Monitoring Section (LSMS), Kosovo, 287–289
Legislative weaknesses in Guatemala, 122–124
LeLong, Pierre, 356
León Carpio, Ramiro de, 119, 123
Limaj, Fatmir, 306
Local mechanisms of justice, East Timor, 329–330
López, Carlos, 37
Lustration, 184

Mack, Helen, 126–127
Mack, Myrna, 125, 126
Magistrates Commission, South Africa, 176
Malan, Magnus, 184
Malary, Guy, 80, 96
Mandela, Nelson, 161, 172
Manuel, Robert, 85, 88
Marronage, 102–103
Martins, Paul, 322
Mbeki, Thabo, 168, 177
Memorandum of Understanding, Indonesia, 327
Mendoza, Rodolfo, 133
Metayer, Amiot, 75
MICAH. *See* International Civilian Support Mission in Haiti (MICAH)
MICIVIH. *See* United Nations/OAS Civilian Mission in Haiti (MICIVIH)
Military reform in El Salvador, 34–37
Ad Hoc Commission, 35

National Intelligence School, 35
opposition to, 35
purge of senior commanders, 36–37
State Intelligence Organization, 35
Truth Commission, 35, 36
Miller, Peter, 321, 334, 335
Milošević, Slobodan, 233, 255, 271–272, 275, 277, 286
Ministry of Justice, Haiti, 92, 93, 94
internal disputes, 94
judicial impartiality, 95
lack of continuity, 94, 95, 102
Ministry of Security, Bosnia, 246
Minority recruitment of police, Bosnia, 239, 243–244
MINUGUA. *See* United Nations Verification Mission in Guatemala (MINUGUA)
Mladic, Ratko, 232, 255
Mode-of-transition approach to security reform, 30
Moghalu, K. C., 201, 202
Mouvement Démocratique Républicain (MDR), Rwanda, 215
Mouvement Révolutionnaire National pour le Développement (MRND), Rwanda, 194
MP. *See* Public Ministry (MP), Guatemala
Muis, Noer, 328
Mungwarareba, Father Modeste, 199
Musliu, Isak, 306
Myrna Mack Foundation, 126–127, 131

National Anti-corruption Unit (ACU), South African Police Service, 179

National Civilian Police (PNC),
El Salvador, 33, 37–38,
44–47
National Commission for
Disarmament, Haiti, 77
National Commission for the
Consolidation of Peace
(COPAZ), El Salvador, 34
National Commission on Truth
and Justice (CNVJ), Haiti,
72–73, 77–79, 104
National Consultative Council,
East Timor, 318, 319
National Crime Prevention Strategy
(NCPS), South Africa,
165–167
National Gendarmerie, Rwanda,
214–216
ethnic divisiveness within, 215
Hutu recruits, 215
participation in genocide, 216
Tutsi recruits, 215
Nationalist Republican Alliance
(ARENA), El Salvador, 34
National Judiciary Council,
El Salvador, 51–52
National Justice Reform
Commission, Haiti, 94
National justice system in East
Timor, 319–330, 336–338
National Police College, East Timor,
321, 322
National Police (PN), Guatemala,
117–118
National Prosecuting Authority
(NPA), South Africa, 163,
169
National Public Security
Commission, El Salvador, 43
National Reconciliation Act,
Guatemala, 120

National Security Management
System (NSMS), South
Africa, 160
National Victimisation Survey,
South Africa, 178
NATO's Implementation Force
(IFOR), 236, 238, 273
NATO's Stabilization Force
(SFOR), 236, 239
NCPS. *See* National Crime
Prevention Strategy
(NCPS), South Africa
New criminal laws in El Salvador,
53–54
Nikolic, Momir, 256, 257
Ntampaka, C., 204

Obrenovic, Dragan, 256
Office for the Defense of
Indigenous Women's Rights,
Guatemala, 120
Office of Overseas Prosecutorial
Development, Assistance,
and Training (OPDAT), 93
Office of Professional Responsibility
(ORP), Guatemala, 135–136
Office of the High Representative
(OHR), Bosnia, 232, 236,
247, 252, 253, 262
Office of the Inspector General,
Guatemala, 136
OHR. *See* Office of the High
Representative (OHR),
Bosnia
Old Order, Guatemala
anticommunism, 116
commercial coffee production,
116
guerrilla movements, 117
human rights prosecutions,
118–119
inquisitorial justice system, 118
justice system deficiencies, 116

Liberal elitism, 116
military legal jurisdiction, 117
military repression, 116, 117
National Police (PN), 117–118
Ombudsperson Institution, Kosovo, 289
O'Neill, William, 283
ONUSAL. *See* UN Mission in El Salvador (ONUSAL)
OPDAT. *See* Office of Overseas Prosecutorial Development, Assistance, and Training (OPDAT)
Operation Crackdown, 169, 170
Organic Law No. 08/96, Organization of Prosecutions for Offenses Constituting Genocide or Crimes against Humanity Committed since October 1, 1990, 197, 205
Organization for Security and Cooperation in Europe (OSCE), 7, 236, 273, 274, 286, 358–359
ORP. *See* Office of Professional Responsibility (ORP), Guatemala
OSCE. *See* Organization for Security and Cooperation in Europe (OSCE)

Partnership for Peace Program, Bosnia, 255
Party of Democratic Action (SDA), Serbia, 236, 237
Patten, Christopher, 247
Peace accords, Guatemala, 119–124
constitutional reforms, 123–124
human rights abuses, 119–120
intelligence reforms, 122
judicial reforms, 120–121
police reforms, 121–122
weaknesses of, 122–124

Peace agreement, El Salvador, 33–34
cease-fire provisions, 33
human rights and justice reforms, 33
implementation of, 34
Peacebuilding judicial reforms, 393–397
accountability mechanisms, need for, 395
executive interference, 394
judicial corruption, 395–396
legal and code reforms, 396–397
priorities for reform, 396
transitional powers, need for, 394
Peacebuilding security reforms, 383–393
community policing, 393
composition of police services, 388–389
demobilization, 383–385
disarmament, 383–385
gender and policing, 392–393
human rights ombudspersons, 391–392
intelligence reform, 386–387
investigative journalism, 391–392
military reform, 385–386
minorities in police forces, 388–389
oversight for police forces, 391–392
police reforms, 387–393
police/society relations, 387–388
professionalization of police, 390–391
regulation of private security companies, 385
reintegration, 383–385
shortage of resources, 384
timing within the process, 384
women's security, 392–393

Peace Implementation Council, Bosnia, 236, 251
Peer review of judges, Bosnia, 251
Penal Code, El Salvador, 55
Penal Management Division, Kosovo (PMD), 296–298
Personnel issues in South African Police, 170–174
  amnesty for police officials, 171–174, 184
  politically motivated human rights violations, 172–174
  racial composition, 170–171
  truth and reconciliation process, 172
Petersburg Declaration, 239
Pluralization of courts, El Salvador, 52
PMD. *See* Penal Management Division, Kosovo (PMD)
PNC. *See* National Civilian Police (PNC), El Salvador
Police academy
  Guatemala, 122, 134
  Haiti, 83
Police reform, political nature of, 12
Police Restructuring Commission (PRC), Bosnia, 247
Political influence over police, Bosnia, 244–245
POLRI. *See* Indonesian police (POLRI)
Portillo, Alfonso, 114, 123, 126, 136
Portuguese rule in East Timor, 314–315
Postconflict crime and violence, 377–382
  common crime escalation, 378
  crime waves, 378
  economic violence, 379–380
  ethnic violence, 381–382
  family violence, 381–382
  looting, 380

new forms of insecurity, 377, 379–382
organized crime increases, 380
political violence, 379
public frustration, 377–378
reverse ethnic cleansing, 381
security measures for, 382
youth gang violence, 381
Postconflict societies, reform within, 9–14, 16–21
Postwar crime wave in El Salvador, 39–44
  networks of informants, 43–44
  private security firms, 43
PRC. *See* Police Restructuring Commission (PRC), Bosnia
Preparatory Commission, Haiti, 94
Preparatory Justice and Law Reform Commission. *See* Preparatory Commission
Presidential General Staff (EMP), Guatemala, 117, 122, 126, 139
Préval, René, 85, 94
Prison reform, Haiti, 99–101
  civilian prison administration, 99–100
  ill-treatment by staff, 100
  international support, 100–101
Professional Responsibility Office (ORP), Guatemala, 118
Progress in Kosovo, 302–307
  colocation, 302
  ethnic tensions, 304
  international controls, 302
  Kosovo Police Service, 303–304
  Kosovo Protection Corps, 303–304
  legal profession, 303
  local institutions, 303
  rioting, 304, 305
  stagnant economy, 304
  state-building, 305, 306
  status of territory, 304, 305

transitional justice, 306
war crime indictments, 306
Prosecutor's Office, Bosnia, 254, 258
Public Defender's Office,
    Guatemala, 121, 128, 130
Public Ministry, El Salvador, 53, 54
Public Ministry (MP), Guatemala,
    114, 130, 137
Public Protector, South Africa, 163,
    176
Public security reform in El
    Salvador, 37–39
    civilianization within the police,
        38
    creation of National Civilian
        Police (PNC), 37–38
    former guerrillas incorporated
        within police, 39

Quezada Toruño, Rodolfo, 119

Raboteau case, Haiti, 95, 96
Racial organization of South
    African state, 160
Rambouillet Agreement, 273, 274,
    275
Ramos-Horta, Dr. José, 316, 319
Rape as a political tool, 355, 357
Reappointment of judges and
    prosecutors, Bosnia, 251–252
Reconciliation in East Timor, 330,
    339, 340
Recovery of Historical Memory
    (REMH), Guatemala, 125
Registering of police, Bosnia,
    242–243
Regulation 2000/64, 283–285
REMH. See Recovery of Historical
    Memory (REMH),
    Guatemala
Reparations in Haiti, 79
Republika Srpska (RS), 235, 245, 259

Revolutionary Front for
    Advancement and Progress
    in Haiti (FRAPH), 72, 76
Ríos Montt, Efraín, 148
RNP. See Rwandan National Police
    (RNP)
Rome Agreement, Bosnia. See Rules
    of the Road, Bosnia
RPF. See Rwandan Patriotic Front
    (RPF)
RS. See Republika Srpska (RS)
RS Ministry of the Interior, 245
RS Police Restructuring Agreement,
    239
Rugova, Ibrahim, 272
Rule of law in Bosnia
    absence of, 263
    elections, 263–264
    ethnically motivated violence,
        260–261
    human trafficking, 261
    increased organized crime,
        261–262
    juvenile delinquency, 261
    networks of patronage, 263
    political corruption, 262–263
    public confidence in police,
        259–260
Rule-of-law systems, 64–5
    alternative to, 6–9
    assessment of, 15
    Bosnia, 259–263
    Haiti, 98–99
    maximalist definition, 6–7
    minimalist definition, 6
    modernization theory, 10
    motives behind, 14
Rules of the Road, Bosnia, 257–258
Rwanda, 193–227
    judiciary, 194–212
    police, 213–223
Rwandan National Police (RNP),
    218–219, 224

Rwandan Patriotic Army, 216
Rwandan Patriotic Front (RPF),
    194, 195, 215, 216
Rwandan Police Training Program,
    216
Rwanda Revenue Authority (RRA),
    222

Salvadoran Legal Reform
    Commission
    (CORELESAL), 48, 49
SAPS. *See* South African Police
    Service (SAPS)
SBS. *See* State Border Service
    (SBS), Bosnia
SCIU. *See* Serious Crimes
    Investigation Unit (SCIU),
    East Timor
SDA. *See* Party of Democratic
    Action (SDA), Serbia
SDS. *See* Serb Democratic Party
    (SDS), Bosnia
Secretariat for Administrative and
    Security Affairs (SAAS),
    Guatemala, 139
Secretariat for Safety and Security,
    South Africa, 163
Secretariat for Strategic Analysis,
    Guatemala, 139
Security, definition of, 8
Security reforms in Bosnia, 237–248
    cooperation among police forces,
        245
    democratic policing, 239–240
    ethnic recruitment for police,
        239, 243–244
    EU membership, 248
    fragmented legal framework, 246
    International Police Task Force
        (IPTF), 237–240
    lack of regional experience, 240
    police salaries, 241

    political influence over police,
        244–245
    reduction of police officers, 241
    registration of police, 242–243
    state-level police, 246, 247–248
    training of police, 241–242
    violence against returning
        refugees, 242
Security reforms in East Timor
    abuse of police powers, 334
    accountability of police, 335
    budgeting, 344
    community policing, 321–322,
        331–332
    court/police systems, 343–344
    customary authority, 336
    field training for police, 334
    inexperienced officers, 342–343
    inflormation flow, 334
    intra-clan violence, 332–333
    joint police service, 323
    local leaders/police relationships,
        331–332, 336
    military/police agreements, 333
    mobility of police, 333–334
    police recruitment, 322–323, 335
    prison system, 339–341
    professional prison service, 340
    special police units, 323
    training of police, 322–323, 343
    village level, 320, 331, 333
    witches attacked, 332
Security reforms in El Salvador,
    34–47
    military and intelligence units,
        34–37, 47
    postwar crime wave, 39–44, 47
    public security, 37–39, 47
    role of civil society, 55
    shortcomings of, 44–46
Security reforms in Guatemala,
    121–122
    civilian recruitment, 133–134

civilian security for the president, 122

criminal conduct by police, 136–137

disciplinary code, 135–136

discrimination against Mayans, 133–134

educational weaknesses, 135, 146

National Civil Police (PNC), 121–122

police academy, 122

specialized unit recruitment, 134–135

victimization, 141–145

Security reforms in Haiti, 79–82

community policing, 82

donor assistance for police reform, 82

Governors Island Agreement, 80

implementation of, 83–87

Interim Public Security Force (IPSF), 80–81

International Civilian Support Mission in Haiti (MICAH), 82

new police academy, 81, 83

UN Development Programme (UNDI), 82

United Nations Mission in Haiti (UNMIH), 81

Security reforms in Kosovo, Serbia, 289–298

civilian cooperation, 292

correctional services, 296–297

international civilian police (CIVPOL), 289–292

juvenile offenders, 297–298

mentally ill offenders, 297–298

organized crime, 292

prison funding, 296

recruitment of CIVPOL, 290–291

specialization within CIVPOL, 291

trafficking in women, 291

training of police, 292–296

treatment of prisoners, 297–298

Security reforms in Rwanda, 213–223

community relations, 220

coordination between security forces, 220–221

cross-border cooperation, 220, 221

domestic initiatives, 218–219

drug trafficking, 221

ethnic divisiveness in Gendarmerie, 215–216

gender equality and equity, 219

genocide case files, 222

international initiatives, 217–218

police participation in genocide, 216

police services, 218–219

postgenocide institutions, 216–219

response to crime detection, 221

Rwandan army, 213–214

Security reforms in South Africa, 162–180

community-based corrections, 165, 169–170

community policing, 164–165

crisis of volume, 169

customer-oriented public services, 168

democratic restructuring, 162, 163

efficiency of strategies, 167–168

escalating crime, 164

evidence-based justice, 162

high-density policing, 165

"hotspot" approach, 169

Operation Crackdown, 169, 170

social crime prevention, 165–168

Security sector reform, 7–9

definition of, 7

Serb Democratic Party (SDS),
Bosnia, 233, 237, 256
Serious Crimes Investigation Unit
(SCIU), East Timor, 326, 327
Serrano, Jorge, 123
Service Delivery Improvement
Programmes, South Africa,
178
SFOR. *See* Stabilization Force
(SFOR)
Sham trials, Bosnia, 250
Shortcomings of security reform in
El Salvador, 44–46
coercive apparatus of the state, 45
human rights reform, 46
kidnappings, 44
mentality of police officers, 45–46
National Civilian Police
violations, 46
police-society relations, 45
purge of police force, 44
scandal, importance of, 44
Shortcomings of security reform in
Haiti, 101–105
civil society groups, 103–104
donor insensitivity, 103
electoral cycles of democracy, 104
independent press, 103
lack of continuity, 102
voter apathy, 105
winner-take-all politics, 105
SIC. *See* Criminal Investigations
Section (SIC), Guatemala
SIPA. *See* State Investigation and
Protection Agency (SIPA),
Bosnia
Soares, Abilio, 328
Social crime prevention, 167
Soto, Álvaro de, 37
South Africa, 159–191
apartheid, 159–162
judicial reforms, 180–187
security reforms, 162–180

South African National Defence
Force (SANDF), 163
South African Police Service
(SAPS), 163, 169, 170, 178
South African Truth and
Reconciliation Commission
(TRC), 172–174, 183–187,
328
Spanish Civil Guard (GCE),
133–134, 135
Special representative of the
secretary-general (SRSG),
UN, 274, 278
Srebrenica massacre, Bosnia, 255,
256, 257
SRSG. *See* Special representative of
the secretary-general
(SRSG), UN
State Border Service (SBS), Bosnia,
242, 244, 246
State court, Bosnia, 253–254
State Investigation and Protection
Agency (SIPA), Bosnia, 242,
244, 246, 262
Strategic Analysis Secretariat,
Guatemala, 122
Strategic stalemate, 31–32
Suharto, 316
Supreme Court, El Salvador, 50–52

Ter Horst, Enrique, 96
Timor-Leste Police Service (TLPS),
313, 322–323, 342–343
Timor-Leste Prison Service, 329
TLPS. *See* Timor-Leste Police
Service (TLPS)
TNI. *See* Armed Forces of the
Republic (TNI), Timor
Tobar Prieto, Luís, 37–38
TPIU. *See* Trafficking and
Prostitution Investigative
Unit, Kosovo (TPIU)

Trafficking and Prostitution
Investigative Unit, Kosovo
(TPIU), 291, 358
Transitional justice in South Africa,
183–187
Transitions from war, 353–359
TRC. *See* South African Truth and
Reconciliation Commission
(TRC)
Tshwete, Steve, 169, 176
Tudjman, Franjo, 234

UNAMET. *See* UN Assistance
Mission in East Timor
(UNAMET)
UNAMIR. *See* United Nations
Assistance Mission in
Rwanda (UNAMIR)
UN Assistance Mission in East
Timor (UNAMET), 316–317
UN Civilian Police (CIVPOL), 82,
275, 278, 289–292, 319–330,
342, 353–359
UN Convention on the Rights of
Children, 56
UN Development Programme
(UNDP), 4, 8, 82, 99, 100,
259–260
UNDP. *See* UN Development
Programme (UNDP)
UNHCR. *See* United Nations High
Commissioner for Refugees
(UNHCR)
United Nations Assistance Mission
in Rwanda (UNAMIR),
216–217
United Nations High Commissioner
for Refugees (UNHCR),
236, 273, 274
United Nations Human Rights Field
Operation for Rwanda
(HRFOR), 217
United Nations in Kosovo, 278–279

United Nations Interim
Administration Mission in
Kosovo (UNMIK), 272, 274–
276, 283–285, 290, 358–359
United Nations Mission in Bosnia-
Herzegovina Special
Trafficking Operations
Program, 366
United Nations Mission in Support
of East Timor (UNMISET),
342, 361
United Nations/OAS Civilian
Mission in Haiti
(MICIVIH), 78, 93, 100
United Nations Stabilization
Mission in Haiti
(MINUSTAH), 69
United Nations Verification Mission
in Guatemala (MINUGUA),
114, 119, 130, 131
United States Central Intelligence
Agency, 116
United States Department of Justice
(U.S. DOJ), 278
UN Judicial System Assessment
Programme (JSAP), 249
UNMIBH. *See* UN Mission to
Bosnia and Herzegovina
(UNMIBH)
UNMIH. *See* UN Mission in Haiti
(UNMIH)
UNMIK. *See* United Nations
Interim Administration
Mission in Kosovo
(UNMIK)
UNMISET. *See* United Nations
Mission in Support of East
Timor (UNMISET)
UN Mission in El Salvador
(ONUSAL), 34, 39
UN Mission in Haiti (UNMIH), 354
UN Mission in Kosovo, 299–300,
301

UN Mission to Bosnia and
Herzegovina (UNMIBH),
236, 241
UNODC. *See* UN Office on Drugs
and Crime (UNODC)
UN Office on Drugs and Crime
(UNODC), 175
UN Peacebuilding Commission, 384
Unpeaceful transitions from war, 353
UN Security Council Resolution
940, 81
UNTAET. *See* UN Transitional
Administration in East
Timor (UNTAET)
UN Transitional Administration in
East Timor (UNTAET), 313,
317, 319–330
UN Truth Commission, El
Salvador, weaknesses of, 51
URNG. *See* Guatemalan National
Revolutionary Unity
(URNG)
U.S. Agency for International
Development (USAID), 13,
48, 92, 99, 128–129
U.S. Office of Drug Control Policy,
88
USAID. *See* U.S. Agency for
International Development
(USAID)
USS *Harlan County* incident, Haiti,
83

Valencia Osorio, Juan, 127
Vieira de Mello, Sergio, 318, 361
Violence toward women, 351–354,
359–366
VRS. *See* Bosnian Serb Army
(VRS)
Vulnerable Persons Unit, East
Timor, 361

War Crimes Chamber of the State
Court of Bosnia and
Herzegovina, 258
Washington Agreement, 234
Wolfowitz, Paul, 398
Women after war
Haiti, 355–357
Kosovo, 357–359
Nicaragua, 365
Women in the police and courts,
El Salvador, 55–56
Women police officers, value of,
356–357
Women's police stations, 362, 365
Women's security
accountability of police, 365–366
classify violence as crime, 360
coalitions for security reforms,
361–362
crime statistics, importance of,
363–364
gender entire system, 362
gender police at time of
founding, 360–361
institutionalized violence against
women, 365
numbers of women in policing,
364
training for domestic violence,
363
training for gender crimes, 363
women's police stations, 365
World Bank, 5, 57, 318, 328, 363, 382

Ximenes Belo, Bishop Carlos Filipe,
316, 324

Yugoslav National Army (JNA), 233